T0336476

LEAN AND AGILE VALUE CHAIN MANAGEMENT

A Guide to the
Next Level of Improvement

Ehap H. Sabri, Ph.D.
Salim N. Shaikh

ISBN 978-1-60427-025-9

Printed and bound in the U.S.A. Printed on acid-free paper
10 9 8 7 6 5 4 3 2 1

Library of Congress Cataloging-in-Publication Data

Sabri, Ehap H., 1967-
   Lean and agile value chain management : a guide to the next level of
improvement / by Ehap H. Sabri.
         p. cm.
   Includes index.
   ISBN 978-1-60427-025-9 (hbk. : alk. paper)
   1. Business logistics—Quality control. 2. Business logistics—Cost
effectiveness. 3. Organizational effectiveness. I. Title. II. Title: Lean
and agile value chain management.
   HD38.5.S22 2010
   658.4'01—dc22
                                                              2009045638

Direct all inquiries to J. Ross Publishing, Inc., 5765 N. Andrews Way, Fort Lauderdale, FL
33309.

Phone: (954) 727-9333
Fax: (561) 892-0700
Web: www.jrosspub.com

Dedication

I dedicate this book to my parents Hisham and Alia, my wife Sawsan, and my daughters Jana and Jude. I greatly appreciate their encouragement and support.

—Ehap Sabri

I am thankful to God and grateful to my parents Naeem and Nasreen. My thanks are also due to my brother Omar and his wife Tasneem for their encouragement. This work would not have been possible without the help, patience, and unconditional support of my wife Shafiya and kids Aishah and Abdullah.

—Salim Shaikh

Contents

Preface .... *xvi*
Acknowledgment .... *xxi*
About the Authors ....

Part I Executive Summary **1**

Chapter 1: The Big Picture of the Lean and Agile Value Chain **3**

Wake-Up Call to Market Reality 3
Definitions and LAVC Principles 7
Value Chain Processes' Challenges and Solutions............................21

**Chapter 2: Lean and Agile Value Chain Building Blocks
and Maturity Levels** **39**

Building Blocks and Evolution of the Lean and Agile Value Chain..................39
LAVC Maturity Levels...56
Closing Remarks and Future Trends 61

Part II Best-Practice Processes **69**

**Chapter 3: Supplier Relationship Management
Superprocess** **71**

Introduction..71
North-South and East-West Collaboration.....................................73
SRM Challenges...74
Strategic Sourcing 78
Product Design 93
Procurement 103
SRM Superprocess Workflow Summary..124

Chapter 4: Supply Chain Management Superprocess **131**

Introduction..131
SCM Evolution 132

Goal of SCM..134
SCM Challenges 135
Enablers 137
Strategic Management...139
Sales and Operations Planning 153
Demand Fulfillment 190
SCM Superprocess Workflow Summary...216
SCM Superprocess Workflow for the Fashion Retail Industry 219

**Chapter 5: Customer Relationship Management
Superprocess 231**

Introduction..231
CRM Challenges...231
Evolution of CRM...234
Future of CRM 236
Who Is the Customer? 237
Managing Customer Relationships..239
Customer Lifetime Value...241
Selling Management..256
Customer Service Management 263
CRM Superprocess Workflow Summary..271

**Chapter 6: Lean and Agile Value Chain Technology Applications
and Trends 277**

Introduction..277
New Generation of LAVC Technology Infrastructure 278
SRM-Enabled Software Applications 282
SCM-Enabled Software Applications 292
CRM-Enabled Software Applications..296

**Part III Project and People Management with Lean and Agile
Value Chain Transformation 301**

Chapter 7: Transformation Program Cycle 303

Introduction..303
Aligning the Transformation Program with Corporate Goals............304
Developing Vision, Objectives, and Strategies of the Program...........308
Process Analysis 309
Selecting a Software Provider..310
Calculating ROI 312

Developing Program and Project Plans..314
Project Implementation 315
Updating the Performance Management System............................319

Chapter 8: Change Management Supported Processes 321

Introduction..321
Developing a Winning Transformation Team.................................322
Education and Cultural Support 328
Communication Management...336
Tracking and Controlling..348
Effective Performance Management Systems 350
Closing Remarks 362

Chapter 9: Lean and Agile Value Chain Transformation Case
Study: Office Systems 365

Introduction..365
Office Systems, Inc..365
Aligning the Transformation Program with Corporate Goals.........366
Developing Vision, Objectives, and Strategies of the Program.......370
Process Analysis 371
Selecting a Software Application Provider 379
Return on Investment 380
Developing Program and Project Plans..380
Project Implementation 381
Case Study Questions 383

Chapter 10: Lean and Agile Value Chain Success Stories
and Lessons Learned 385

Supplier Relationship Management-Driven Success Stories............385
Supply Chain Management-Driven Success Stories 388
Customer Relationship Management-Driven Success Stories..........417
Success Story from the Service Industry 428

Index...433

Preface

The way to survive in today's business world is to stay ahead of competitors. Organizations have started to realize that effective value chain management is the key to staying competitive and gaining critical core competence in today's businesses. Current economic challenges have led to a reduction in demand. Many firms are responding by drastic cost-cutting measures, including layoffs, supply reductions, closing production facilities or retail stores, and other traditional measures. This is understandable and expected. But firms should not be too myopic; they need to think beyond merely cost cutting and surviving during the difficult times. They need to think about the future when the environment is capacity-constrained rather than demand-constrained. They need to plan and invest for the future—the day demand comes back, and they have to be competitive when that happens.

Unfortunately, in the last couple of years we have witnessed several firms that have put the brakes on their continuous improvement programs, even though they had initially approved the improvement transformation programs to streamline processes to become leaner and more agile just before the recession. They think that they cannot afford to invest in continuous improvements during recessions. This is shortsighted and a tactical strategy; a recipe for failure in competing in the future.

Firms need to think about this difficult economic time as an opportunity to increase market share by exploring innovative and creative methods to cut waste, thereby reducing prices for their customers and potentially their competitors' customers who are looking for better deals and service. Being lean and agile is the recipe for success to survive in this market and to excel and increase market share once the market is back. For example, during a recession the production rates are lower and fewer inventories are needed. Though this is a challenge, it also poses a great opportunity; an opportunity to revisit the inventory strategy, to explore ideas such as removing excess inventory, and to invest in improving the demand fulfillment process, and so forth. All of these would enable the company to become more lean and agile. Another example is to segment revenue streams and cut supply to customers who undermine profitability. Firms also need to make hard decisions to stop selling at a loss (cost is greater than the selling price).

In addition, firms should streamline and continue improving and enhancing the marketing processes in both good and bad times. Cutting down on marketing campaigns or having significant layoffs to a marketing department during a recession is a shortsighted strategy. On the contrary, being visible through marketing during a time when there is less competitive noise give customers confidence about the health of the firm and its ability to survive the tough times.

The greatest challenge for companies in today's competitive environment is to get products to customers when and where needed, exactly the way they want it, at a competitive price, and in a cost-effective manner. Companies will not be able to address this challenge without collaboration and tight integration with their own supplier-customer bases and efficient value chain operators.

Managing the value chain is becoming more complicated due to globalization, increasing complexity of value chains with outsourcing, the need for shorter time to market, and the urgent need to be flexible and responsive enough to respond to customer changes in a cost-effective manner. Operations managers are faced with a dilemma: look for ways to improve the conventional processes or replace them with new lean and agile processes.

This book addresses that challenge by converting conventional processes into lean and agile value chain (LAVC) processes that will allow enterprises to collaborate with their internal and external suppliers and customers by providing visibility, replacing inventory with information, automating the paper-driven business processes, and interconnecting inventory, logistics, and planning systems.

It also provides answers to many questions raised by value chain managers:

- How can we spend more energy on making improvements rather than on managing transactions?
- How can we move to a proactive mode instead of a reactive mode when dealing with supply problems?
- What is the best way to deal with forecast fluctuation which generates frustration and inability to react to the change in the value chain?

Although most supply chain managers have heard about lean either by taking a course, attending a seminar, reading an article, or buying a book, few firms have implemented and achieved lean successfully. Moreover, it is no longer enough to just have a lean environment. Firms must create an environment that is both lean and agile, one that honors the principles of waste elimination while also enabling the flexibility to deal with the inevitable surprises (human, material, capacity, or demand) that disrupt even the best-designed value chains. Value chain processes must be built so that they can manage unpredictability.

Although the benefits of applying lean concepts or improving the agility of a value chain are clear, decision makers find themselves asking the most fundamental questions: How can we do it? What is the best practice? Are lean and agile contradictory or complementary? How can we be lean and agile at the same time? Does it apply to us? Does technology add value? If so, what's the best way to quantify it and then maximize it? Many have failed in this pursuit of achieving value; how can we make sure that we will not succumb like the others? Are there ways to minimize this risk? What is the recipe of success for successful transformation programs?

Lean and Agile Value Chain Management: A Guide to the Next Level of Improvement addresses those questions and much more in a comprehensive and practical way based on best practices.

This book brings together the field's latest advances, giving business professionals a comprehensive framework for driving out costs, improving efficiency, eliminating nonvalue-added activities, and optimizing the transformation programs to be lean and agile. This framework is applicable for every industry.

This book also offers practical, proven tactics and detailed guidance into every aspect of value chain process redesign: mapping the existing process, intelligently leveraging new technologies, building a strategy for strengthening the relationship with suppliers and customers, identifying comprehensive related metrics, and much more. It includes case studies, industry success stories, and lessons learned.

Although lean and agile concepts are hot topics, there is not a single book that focuses on the recipe of success for a LAVC transformation program. We intend to fill that gap by providing a breakthrough start-to-finish road map for organizations to implement the LAVC transformation programs successfully. The strengths of this unique book are in its management focus and its inclusion of all the elements that are needed during process improvement: best practices, project management, benefits, technology, business justification, and ongoing support strategy for all of the major processes in the value chain.

To summarize, readers will better understand:

- The challenges in the conventional value chain processes and how the conventional approach compares to the best practice
- The benefits of implementing the lean and agile enablers in the value chain processes
- How to build LAVC strategies
- How to leverage leading-edge technologies to support LAVC strategies
- The key performance indicators for the LAVC transformation program
- The framework for organizations to implement LAVC processes efficiently and with lower risk to achieve dramatic cost reductions, lead-time reductions, flexibility improvements, and more importantly, competitive advantage
- Alignment of the LAVC transformation program with corporate goals

In Part I, we will provide an executive review on *how* LAVC principles and enablers can benefit companies to address today's challenges and gain a competitive advantage. We will also explain *why* LAVC can add substantial value to companies and how LAVC principles and enablers apply to any organization in any industry.

In Part II, we will examine the practical use of these enablers on supplier relationship management (SRM), supply chain management (SCM), and customer relationship management (CRM) superprocesses and related processes and sub-processes, and provide best practices to show companies the *way*. Part II also delves into cutting-edge technologies related to the value chain processes and the latest trends.

Part III provides a framework for successful implementation and a systematic step-by-step road map to the LAVC program transformation. It includes several success stories and case studies to provide the reader with real-life scenarios for improvement: best-in-class firms in various industries and their ability to compete successfully. It also highlights the best practices that can be leveraged by other firms.

The concepts in this book are presented in an easy to understand manner that is intended for any reader interested in learning about LAVCs. Since value chain management is involved in several functions within the organizations, this text has been written for the broad audience who is interested in learning the concepts to optimize value chain processes and slash waste.

It's written for both those who deal with value chain processes on a daily basis as well as those who are novices in this field. This book provides strategies for senior managers to be used in planning for transformation programs, and also provides middle managers with the tools to implement and control the best practice effectively.

This book can serve as an excellent resource, training, or educational material for any transformation program team organized to improve a value chain or a process. The following chapters are recommended to be read first by those in the following roles:

- Executive Sponsor: Chapters 1, 2, and 10
- Program Manager: Chapters: 1, 2, 7, 8, 9, and 10
- Functional Consultant: Chapters 1, 2, 3, 4, and 5 (based on the scope of the process that is under consideration)
- Process Consultant: Chapters 1, 2, 7, 8, 9 and 10
- Technical Architect: Chapters 1, 2, and 6
- Change Agent: Chapters 1, 2, 7, and 8

Graduate students can use this book to gain an excellent understanding of how LAVC works and then use this knowledge to either extend research in the field or implement the concepts learned from this book in their chosen industry.

Acknowledgments

The authors have countless people to thank. During the writing of this book, we have received valuable comments and suggestions from clients, colleagues, and students. Although acknowledging the contribution of everyone is impossible, several individuals provided invaluable suggestions and encouragement throughout this project:

Eyas Sabri

Aamer Rehman

Junaid Ali

Dr. Mike Beitler

Beth Elkin

Dr. Said Abublan

ABOUT THE AUTHORS

Ehap Sabri, Ph.D, CFPIM. Dr. Ehap Sabri is a business strategist, keynote speaker, and workshop leader sought after for his expertise in strategy development and supply chain management. Dr. Sabri has held a variety of advisory roles and provided consulting services for several Fortune 100 companies. He has worked with Caterpillar, IBM, Cummins, Toshiba, Vanity Fair, and Sprint to develop and implement best-practice strategies and processess to derive value and significant cost reductions.

Dr. Sabri's book, *Purchase Order Management Best Practices*, is required reading in several MBA programs. Dr. Sabri has also authored numerous book chapters and journal publications that give readers fresh insights into today's business and economic challenges.

Ehap Sabri has a doctorate in Industrial Engineering from the University of Cincinnati in Ohio. He is an adjunct professor at the University of Dallas and the University of Texas–Dallas for the MBA and Ph.D. Programs. Dr. Sabri is a certified Fellow in Production and Inventory Management (CFPIM) by APICS. He also serves as the board president for a nonprofit public charter school.

For questions, or to schedule a workshop or a training session, please contact Dr. Sabri at sabridallas@yahoo.com.

Salim Shaikh, CPIM, CSCP. Salim N. Shaikh has a Master's Degree in Industrial Engineering from Purdue University and a Master's in Business Administration from the University of Texas–Dallas. Salim has had a distinguished academic career and has maintained a constant pursuit of academic excellence by winning several awards and scholarships. He has 12 years of professional experience in management consulting, process improvement, project management, software development, advance planning and scheduling, and e-business solutions across several industries. As a management consultant, Salim has also provided training to several Fortune 500 companies, including Texas Instruments, Daimler Chrysler, Pepsi, Dell, IBM, Toshiba, Dillard's, Sony Entertainment, and Dole Foods, and has a proven record of success in adding value and achieving cost reductions. Currently, he holds the position of Senior Solution Architect at i2 Technologies in Dallas, Texas, which is viewed as a leader in solving supply chain and e-business problems.

Salim is an APICS certified professional in CPIM (Certified in Production and Inventory Management) as well as a CSCP (Certified Supply Chain Professional). He has led training sessions and workshops on supply chain management for the faculty of the Eli Broad School of Business at Michigan State University, Smeal College of Business at Pennsylvania State University, Carey School of Business at Arizona State University, Smurfit School of Business at University College–Dublin, and the National University of Singapore. He is also a guest lecturer at the University of Texas–Dallas and the University of Dallas.

Web
Added
Value™

Free value-added materials available from
*the Download Resource Center at **www.jrosspub.com***

At J. Ross Publishing we are committed to providing today's professional with practical, hands-on tools that enhance the learning experience and give readers an opportunity to apply what they have learned. That is why we offer free ancillary materials available for download on this book and all participating Web Added Value™ publications. These online resources may include interactive versions of material that appears in the book or supplemental templates, worksheets, models, plans, case studies, proposals, spreadsheets and assessment tools, among other things. Whenever you see the WAV™ symbol in any of our publications it means bonus materials accompany the book and are available from the Web Added Value™ Download Resource Center at www.jrosspub.com.

Downloads for *Lean and Agile Value Chain Management* include a transformation program case study, slide presentations illustrating value chain best practices, and a recipe for successful change management.

PART I: EXECUTIVE SUMMARY

Chapter 1: The Big Picture of Lean and Agile Value
    Chains
Chapter 2: Lean and Agile Value Chain Building Blocks
    and Maturity Levels

1

The Big Picture of Lean and Agile Value Chains

WAKE-UP CALL TO MARKET REALITY

When we started writing this chapter on July 1, 2008, Starbucks Corporation announced the closing of 600 U.S. stores due to a substantial downturn in store traffic. On the same day, Home Depot's stock price hit its lowest point in more than five years citing an unprecedented decline in the U.S. housing market. In Q1 of 2009, almost all major retailers reported sales figures declining in the double-digit range. While conducting the final review of this chapter on June 1, 2009, General Motors announced bankruptcy and President Obama addressed the nation to discuss the situation.

It is a well-known fact that a *recession* is a period of tough economic times and a significant reduction of economic activities. Reduced demand for goods and services, bankruptcies, consolidation, and higher rates of layoffs are common traits of a recession. Yet, this is an excellent opportunity to build market share because competitors are struggling to make ends meet.

Prices often fall during a recession as firms try desperately to maintain or stimulate demand, which means lower margins. Several value chain management tactics can keep firms afloat during economic downturns, including:

- Value-based pricing which stresses the value that the customer is getting for their money.
- Bundling or unbundling. Adding features to a bundle (bundling) can give the perception of a good deal and greater value to the customer. Removing a feature (unbundling) to lower the price is another good tactic.

3

- Renegotiating contracts with suppliers.
- Requesting third party logistics (3PL) providers to optimize transportation through better consolidation, routing, and mode selection.
- Continuous improvement for cost reduction.
- Smarter investments in technology to address economic downturn challenges which provide a quick return on investment.
- Reducing supplier base.
- Working with suppliers to make parts simpler and cheaper to manufacture, and contemplating ways activities can be improved as if the company and its suppliers were the same firm.
- Helping customers achieve their objectives and sustain or improve their market share in a business-to-business (B2B) environment.

The way to survive the competition and down economy in today's business world is to stay ahead of competitors by cutting costs intelligently and proving significant value to customers. In a down market, no one can afford wasteful spending at the personal level nor at the value chain level.

Effective value chain management is the key to staying competitive and gaining critical core competency in today's business. This is what organizations have started to realize. In all different businesses—from the relatively slow-moving ones such as utilities and cement industries to the rapidly changing businesses in high technology—effective value chain processes have become critical in achieving competitive advantage by enabling lean and agile value chains (LAVCs). It is believed that we will witness, for the rest of this decade, what is called "a tightly integrated environment" in which supply chain interactions involve tightly integrated databases and applications and processes are significantly redesigned and streamlined to eliminate redundancies and non-value activities.[1]

It is no longer enough to create a lean environment. Firms must create an environment that is both lean and agile, one that honors the principles of waste elimination while also enabling the flexibility to deal with the inevitable surprises (human, material, capacity, or demand) that disrupt even the best-designed value chains. Value chain processes must be built so that they can manage unpredictability.

The *value chain* is commonly called *supply chain*; however, we have selected the *value chain* term instead because it isn't only about "supply," it's more about "demand"; actually, it is "demand driven" that triggers all value-added activities and processes. Another reason for this selection is to indicate the comprehensive scope and the inclusion of all processes that add value, especially since many companies use *supply chain* to refer to the upstream activities to the company and exclude their distribution and customer echelons.

We can't overstate the comprehensive scope of the value chain because, in this business age, the majority of product cost is generated outside the four walls of an enterprise. In addition, most lead time is consumed outside the control of the business. Also, the majority of key activities of manufacturing, assembly, warehousing, inbound logistics, outbound logistics, distribution, and retailing are done outside the enterprise.

Another similar term that is used by lean experts is *value stream*. In 1996, Womack and Jones described a value stream as the set of activities required to bring a good or service through three critical management tasks: (1) the problem-solving task that runs from concept through production launch, (2) the information management task that runs from order taking through delivery, and (3) the physical transformation task that proceeds from raw material to finished products accepted by the end customer or consumer.[2] For the purpose of this book, the terms *value stream* and *value chain* are considered very similar with more emphasis on the end-to-end perspective in the case of a value chain.

People in the supply chain field have different perspectives about lean: (1) a set of tools to reduce waste, (2) it is about lean thinking to reduce or eliminate waste, (3) an initiative to eliminate waste in manufacturing processes, (4) a systematic approach for continuous improvement and eliminating waste, or (5) a philosophy that seeks waste elimination. All these perspectives share the goal to eliminate waste, but differ in the scope. We will consider the last perspective throughout the book, which considers lean as a business philosophy that focuses on eliminating waste in the value chain.

The authors believe strongly that the LAVC concept will grow more in importance for several fundamental reasons:

1. In a recession or flat economy, the only way to be profitable is to manage and reduce costs by reducing waste since increasing or sustaining revenue is typically not an option.
2. Global competition is leading the pressure to reduce costs and is contributing to the growing importance of LAVC. With globalization where the entire world is a potential customer, firms are transitioning from a single-site business serving domestic markets to a truly global business—with multiple locations across the globe, a variety of transportation modes, diverse cost structures, and highly differentiated markets. Decisions about where to source materials, where to produce, and where to sell products are suddenly much more complex. In addition, firms typically arrive in a new international market ready to apply their tools, processes, and strategies that have proven successful in their domestic businesses or value chain. But, they often encounter local value chain partners with technology platforms that are outdated or not used properly, as well as business processes that will not easily mesh with their existing operations because of language and cultural obstacles in addition to the gaps in understanding best practices.
3. Strategic outsourcing creates the need for improved information sharing, inbound supply visibility, and collaboration with suppliers and customers.

4. Making well-informed and timely decisions is a top priority for firms in today's dynamic business environment since it will increase the probability of making the right decisions. It's urgent to ensure not only that firms are making decisions quickly, but also that they are making the correct decisions to support each value chain's success.

5. There is a greater need for increasing responsiveness, building flexibility, and managing and monitoring incoming material and outbound products effectively.

6. Value chains are vulnerable to variability of downstream and upstream activities. A relatively small delay in an upstream process can propagate down the entire value chain, throwing off production scheduling, shutting down assembly lines, and preventing on-time deliveries. Controlling and managing the impact of variability is critical for the success of any firm.

7. There is huge pressure to reduce supply chain risks, especially with the increase of supply chain network complexity. The risk of business disruption or failure increasingly worries global firms. Supply chain risks include violating safety standards, poor quality, supply interruption, delays, and so forth.

8. Many companies, in the last several years, experienced successive waves of mergers and acquisitions that created a proliferation of enterprise resource planning (ERP) systems and other information technology (IT) systems which were complex, stand-alone, and difficult to manage. This has added cost, risk, and waste to the value chain.

9. The Internet's emergence as a retail sales channel has increased competition and price transparency, and leveled the playing field, resulting in significant drops in prices following an initial market launch even on the most exciting, innovative products. This has affected high tech, consumer goods, and retail industries the most. Another related challenge is the rapid commoditization of products today. Even the most innovative designs are quickly copied and even enhanced by competitors that make the product life cycle shorter and shorter. Everyone is looking for the next "killer" product or feature. This has resulted in many companies designing and introducing products so fast that they don't have a good grasp of the real-world risks, payoffs with every new product, and how to maximize profitability over the entire product life cycle.

Add to this the of challenges providing consistently high product quality and generating strong profits while managing increasingly complex supply chains from end to end with outdated supply chain systems, and it's easy to see why so many companies are struggling to keep up.

There is uncertainty and doubt among organizations regarding the new Internet technologies, and although the appeal of best practices and the benefits of implementing these technologies are clear, enterprises struggle in integrating them into supply chain operations because they encounter many challenges such as the following:

1. Drastic improvement needs that must be implemented with aggressive and effective change management
2. New skills to support processes that span across suppliers and partners
3. Lack of comprehensive, global, and agreed-upon metrics
4. Inability to decide when to improve, redesign, or keep as is
5. Need for innovative approach to justify implementation
6. Need to select the right software provider
7. Need for efficient support and maintenance models for post implementation

To date, there have been no studies in the literature directly relating to these important issues, which are the focus of this book. The importance of a structured methodology for tackling these subjects cannot be overemphasized, and is necessary to achieve an effective value chain process in order to reduce operating expenses and obtain and sustain competitive advantage.

DEFINITIONS AND LAVC PRINCIPLES
Lean Versus Agile

Given the current market meltdown and continuous market pressure on margins, lean strategy provides an excellent framework for squeezing costs out of value chains. Lean strategy provides a strong infrastructure to support many innovative manufacturing methods, reduces the lead time of any process, and minimizes cost from activities that don't add value.

However, with today's demand and supply volatility, value chains need to be not only lean but also agile to react quickly when changes occur and even detect changes before they happen. Variability will continue to exist, but agility will help control and even reduce it. The ability to be agile depends on a close relationship with partners (suppliers, customers, carriers, logistics providers, etc.); integrated processes and access to real-time information on the value chain.

Also, the concept of pull is an integral part of lean strategy where no upstream activity can occur before a request by a downstream entity is triggered. The idea in a pull system is that action is taken in direct response to a request (need/demand) rather than an anticipation of prediction of demand that may never occur. In a push system, the action is taken based on an anticipation of demand. The major drawback of the pull system is the focus mainly on operational and execution levels and less emphasis on tactical and strategic levels. It's usually about execution rather than planning. Therefore, agility, which puts significant emphasis on planning and controlling variability, and lean, which strives for excellence in execution, complement rather than conflict with each other and should help companies in today's market.

Managing the value chain is becoming more complicated for many reasons. Value chain managers are starting to move toward a LAVC to address today's challenges. This has put them into unfamiliar situations: manage inventory, personnel, and resources with less waste, while simultaneously giving customers more configuration options, more delivery flexibility, and shorter lead times.

Being lean means working with much less inventory, eliminating waste, and reacting without delay to changing situations. Lean strategy was shaped largely around the 40-year-old Toyota Production System and was originally based on two core assumptions: A low demand fluctuation to ensure smooth production and a network of local suppliers to ensure short lead times and just-in-time deliveries. Neither of these assumptions holds true in today's dynamic and global environment with its fluctuating demand and suppliers scattered all over the world. The leaner the value chain, the greater the impact of disruptions or changes.

On the other hand, being agile alone is a good option no longer. The old concept of building excess capacity, adding inventory, or increasing labor to solve problems is very costly and does not solve the root cause of the problem.

LAVC enables businesses to be flexible in various situations like providing the ability to rapidly determine customer needs, respond to volumes and mixed changes, and respond to crisis. It does not, however, include providing flexibility by maintaining a high inventory of raw material or extra production capacity because that would conflict with the lean strategy. Table 1.1 provides a detailed comparison of the lean value chain versus the LAVC.

While the key lean concepts existed for more than 40 years, the bottom-line savings in environments beyond simple build to stock were not proven widely. Mixed-mode manufacturing, which has elements of build to order, engineer to order, and assemble to order and can be applied to support an ever-increasing product portfolio and fluctuating demand profile, is still a challenge for lean techniques. In addition, the adaptability of lean techniques was not high across all industry sectors.

Lean techniques worked well in high-volume, streamlined production such as the automotive industry. However, it didn't show much success in constraint-sensitive environments, such as the semiconductor industry where raw material is a big constraint, or the steel industry where a wide mix of products is the norm. Therefore, lean didn't work well in low-volume, high-mix environments. In addition, it was not effective in high tech and electronics, where the product mix changed rapidly because of rapid customer demand changes.

Another challenge for lean is the extended enterprise or value chain, where value-added activities are extending beyond a company's four walls. In this case, the material-control techniques using the traditional manual/visual methods to synchronize material flow are outdated.

Table 1.1 Comparison of lean value chain versus LAVC

	Lean value chain	Lean and agile value chain
Primary focus	The factory	Customer and supplier
Strategy	• Reducing waste and excessive materials, inventory, labor, and capital equipment • Suppliers meet material (flow) replenishment requirements via pull triggers and flex limits	• Customer focus, quicker response, greater flex-ibility, quickly adapting to changing customer demands • Lead-time reduction results in waste elimination • Suppliers provide quick response by improving their internal operations and streamlining interac-tions with buyers
Production environment	• Best suited for build-to-stock replenishment strategy • Best suited for repeated or continuous environment • Requires relatively stable or predictable demand	• Suited for all replenishment strategies • Best suited for both continuous and discontinuous environment-like job shop and project job • Can handle both predictable and unpredictable demand products
Complement techniques	• Direct replenishment to the factory with no in-termediate storage • Rapid setup • Just-in-time shipping and receiving	• Postponement • Frequent deliveries of small quantities • Supply chain collaboration with customers and suppliers
Prerequisites	• Strong operational control • Timely visibility about inventory and production • Automated data collections and real-time communications	• Extremely strong operational control • Timely and intelligent visibility about inventory and production • Automated data collections and real-time collaborations • Tight system integration
Critical-to-success metrics	• Inventory turns • Asset utilization	• Response time • Lead time
Pioneers	Toyota	Dell, Wal-Mart

Traditionally, technology used to be considered an obstacle (waste) to lean adoption. However, in recent years, more and more lean practitioners started to consider it as a necessary tool to complement lean.

Benefits of the LAVC Concept

LAVC provides the ability to profitably manage the value chain while addressing effectively the supply and demand variability. With globalization, value chains are becoming more fragile and a small disruption can cause catastrophic implications, so it is essential to detect these disruptions proactively and have the necessary agility to diminish them at the source. LAVC requires constant change of plans and very short lead times. LAVC can't be just about processes; it must be supported by enabling technology to make it broadly relevant and scalable. LAVC-enabling technology should be able to provide visibility to all relevant partners, proactively detect and manage exceptions, and generate alerts when performance approaches set thresholds. It encourages reevaluating conventional or traditional processes and relationships with partners, suppliers, and customers, and collaborating with them in real time.

The LAVC concept provides speed, flexibility, and transparency to the enterprise; value chain managers can use systems and find out what is coming, be proactive, and make the needed adjustments to keep value chain processes aligned with customers' requirements and their own bottom line.

The LAVC concept is a strategic philosophy that is making a lasting and needed impact on the industry and is helping to achieve competitive advantage. Even firms that are not formally adopting this philosophy are practicing some of the lean and agile principles.

The LAVC concept will emerge as perhaps the most compelling enabler for enterprise excellence because of its ability to respond quickly to changing business conditions such as customer demand, resource variability, and its ability to cut waste. LAVC can have a positive impact on the industry by providing important benefits like healthy cost reduction, visibility improvement, lower inventory, streamlined and aligned processes, quicker response time, faster time to market, better asset utilization, higher shareholder value, fulfillment lead-time reduction, flexibility improvement, revenue growth by penetrating new markets, and improvement in customer satisfaction.

LAVC Guiding Principles

Principle 1: Focus on customer success
This principle recognizes the fact that the end customer is the only entity that introduces money into the chain. Being customer oriented is the first LAVC principle.

Under this principle, firms customize product and service offerings based on data gathered through interactions between the customer and the firm. This would organize the firm around the customer, foster customer-satisfying behaviors, and link all processes of a firm from its customers through its suppliers. The Whirlpool Success Story in Chapter 10 is a great example of how this principle can turn a company around.

Principle 2: Create win-win and a trusted environment for all stakeholders

Every member profits from the business. For example, if the relationship between the buyer and supplier is based on a win-lose approach, this supplier will not support the buyer's lean and agile initiatives. This principle encourages firms to look beyond local improvement and start looking to eliminate waste and achieving continuous improvement for the entire value chain for all partners' benefits.

Another example is if the supplier is forced to carry extra inventory to allow the buyer to transition to a lean environment then this will impact the relationship between the supplier and buyer and might affect the quality and cost of the purchase parts. In one of the workshops that a company conducted to educate their suppliers about a new initiative that they are undertaking called *lean*, a supplier raised his hand and asked, "Does this mean that you are going 'lean,' and we are going 'fat' in inventory to satisfy your need?" This type of behavior will not only impact the supplier and buyer relationship negatively, but it will also impact the end customers since they eventually have to pay for this waste directly or indirectly.

One proven method to build trust is through establishing reliability. A tightly aligned firm creates an environment of trust. Internal performance improvements and a trusted environment carry forward across external partners, making the entire value chain more reliable and trustworthy. Another method to build trust is by learning in a collaborative environment with partners on how firms can become better suppliers to their customers, and better customers to their suppliers.

Beyond trust, the next level is creating a sense of loyalty among partners by building on the confidence that promises will be kept and deviations swiftly corrected.

Principle 3: Eliminate waste and reduce nonvalue-added activities

This principle encourages firms to free resources to focus on value-added activities and improve efficiency. Waste is any activity that has no value to the customer and is not required to run the business. Customer, in this context, is not necessarily the end consumer, but is meant to be the customer of the next process. For example, a retailer is the customer of the private-label manufacturer. In case the next process is the consumption, the customer will be the consumer. The traditional seven types of waste are defects, excess inventory, excessive processing, unnecessary motion, waiting, overproduction, and unnecessary transport.

Principle 4: Institutionalize continuous improvement

The fourth principle of LAVC ensures proactive elimination of problems, identification of the root causes, and removal of barriers between functions, departments, processes, and standardization.

The challenge with any value chain problem such as a quality problem is to identify the root cause of the problem (symptom/error), eliminate it, and put a process in place to prevent it from happening again. Striving for excellence is a related lean principle. In a lean environment, there is a little buffer to fall back on when quality errors (defects) occur, therefore striving for excellence and pursuing zero defects are an integral part of lean.

Standardization is not only for common parts and about encouraging the use of standard or previously designed parts that are available instead of extensive use of new or custom designed parts; it goes beyond that. It includes standardizing processes, practices, documents, contracts, performance measures, policies, and procedures across different business units or departments of a firm based on best practice.

Allowing every business unit or operating location to develop its own internal custom processes or procedures, even though these business units or locations share commonality in some of their business processes such as the supplier selection process, is against the continuous improvement principle and standardization. It's often our recommendation for multi-business-unit companies to develop a single process based on the best practice for any common process and share it across the organization.

Principle 5: Close the loop between planning and execution

The fifth principle allows for leveraging optimization, the performance measurement system (PMS), and Internet technologies wherever possible and in conjunction with any of the other principles.

Optimization is one of the methods to eliminate waste, and it's seldom presented in lean books. At the same time, optimization provides agility for the organization. For example, it helps to decide the right number of suppliers, transportation carriers, material flow, and facility locations including distribution, retail, and dealer outlets.

To check if the execution continues to follow the predefined plan, a PMS should be established to provide feedback and an opportunity to adjust the plan. There are several other advantages to measuring the performance of the value chain or a certain value chain process. This starts with motivating people to act in a certain manner that is aligned with corporate goals rather than limited and sometimes conflicting goals, identifying areas of improvement by conducting benchmarking, and conveying what is important to the organization by defining metrics and linking them to corporate strategies and objectives.

Any performance measure should have seven parameters:

1. The category and scope of the measure that it is addressing (e.g., customer satisfaction for the demand fulfillment process).
2. Performance target that represents an external focus (e.g., developed by benchmarking) and internal focus to achieve a certain corporate goal (e.g., developed during internal strategic planning sessions). This target needs to be reviewed and adjusted regularly.
3. Actual performance that requires a system to capture and save it.
4. Time period of the value.
5. Owner of the performance measure who is accountable for success or failure of the measure.
6. Frequency of capturing and communicating. Also the cost of capturing the data should not outweigh their value.
7. Set of action plans in the event the target is not achieved.

The definition of the performance measure, which is part of parameter 1, should reflect correctly the intention and reason behind capturing the performance measure. It's common when we ask a seller about on-time delivery performance to hear a number close to 100 percent, yet when we turn around and ask the customer the same question to hear a number between 60 and 70 percent. My second question to the seller would be, "Can you define on-time delivery for us?" And the answer most of the time is, "If actual ship date equals the latest updated promise ship date, it is on time." As you can see from the definition, there is no mention of customer request date or even original promise ship date. Also, it doesn't take into consideration the receiving date by the customer (ship date + transit time). By checking, you can easily find out that the seller missed the shipping date several times and that the system was updated with a new promised ship date every time. In some companies the system keeps only one field for the promise ship date (latest) and has no place holder for the original ship date. Once an order is shipped the system doesn't compare the actual ship date with the original ship date; rather, it uses the most current promise ship date as a point of comparison.

To make the disconnect even greater between the customer and seller, the customer uses the receiving date and not the ship date, furthermore, sometimes the original request (by customer) date instead of promise (by seller) date is used as the basis for comparison.

In his book *End-to-End Lean Management*, Trent[3] mentions an example from a company that used to measure their distribution center manager on the monthly end-on-hand inventory, which resulted in the wasteful and costly behavior of moving as much stock at the end of the month as possible and working aggressively to replace the inventory at the beginning of the month.

Also, performance measures should promote teamwork and should be comprehensive (cross-functional cooperation across the value chain). It should also stress results instead of activities. Therefore, we should not base the performance of the process on, for example, the number of continuous improvement projects or *kaizens* that are conducted annually because they mean nothing if they are not translated into operational or financial benefits. For example, getting more detailed information about the status of a shop order in a factory is good, but unless this is translated to quantifiable financial or operational benefits like customer satisfaction or inventory reduction, this data may be a form of waste.

Finally, performance measures or metrics should be reliable, lead to action, and address value chain objectives such as inventory reductions, total landed cost reductions, and improving cash-to-cash cycle time.

Parameter 7 (set of action plans in the event the target is not achieved) is crucial to close the loop and get the process back on track. For example, if the target for on-time delivery to customer is 97 percent, but the actual on-time delivery is 90 percent, this indicates a problem and action should be taken.

Another example is during the typical life cycle for a trendy new product, there will be a time when point-of-sale data indicate a drop-off in cash register sales—often in anticipation of a new, competitive product that is about to launch. Instead of holding a series of urgent meetings, and making a not so well-informed decision, a set of predefined actions should be laid down ahead of time for business managers to deal with margin squeeze and extend a specific product's profitability as long as possible. This might also trigger another action, such as expediting the launch of the new product that will replace the current one so that the firm can sustain or boost the market share.

LAVC Enablers

While enablers will address today's challenges, the LAVC principles will guide the firm to implement the enablers the right way. For example, if implementing technology (an enabler) will add more waste and not help in closing the loop between execution and planning, it should not be implemented because it is against LAVC principles 3 and 5. Another example is if adding flexibility (another enabler) can harm the suppliers by asking for additional inventory at their end, it should not be implemented since it violates principle 2.

Enabler 1: Visibility

Real-time visibility reduces the uncertainty and nervousness in the value chain and reduces safety stock that can be translated into cost reduction. It also increases customer satisfaction, which results in increased revenue. Real-time visibility will help mitigate the impact of disruption to the supply chain caused by demand and supply variability by presenting the real picture and providing the ability to solve potential problems ahead of time. We would like to call this type of visibility *intelligent visibility*.

For example, visibility to advanced shipment notices from suppliers eliminates or reduces uncertainty and increases reaction (response) time to late or incomplete shipments.

Additional benefits include improving day-to-day operational performance, logistics costs reductions, controlling supply chain risks, providing data to support well-informed tactical and strategic value chain decisions, and lot-level traceability of products to ensure effective recalls in case of quality or safety problems. It also enables a new level of operation efficiency and profitability for suppliers and partners.

Aberdeen Group[4] mentioned that, with increased visibility, companies can perform necessary *agility actions* like shipment rerouting due to demand changes or infrastructure disruptions, expediting late shipments, cross-docking and distribution center (DC) bypass strategies, and deploying best practice processes such as vendor-managed inventory. In addition, visibility enables firms to warn their customers about potential delivery delays ahead of time, capacity issues, and other value chain disruptions, thus allowing both parties to reach out acceptable issue resolution while sustaining high customer service levels.

An Aberdeen Group survey[4] showed significant differences in the levels of agility between firms with and without visibility into in-transit shipments, order and supplier events, and trade documents. It showed, for example, firms with visibility are 66 percent more likely to reroute in-transit shipments to higher points of demand, like closer to end customer instead of DC, and 11 times more likely to detect disruptions in logistics and distribution.

In addition, the survey showed that firms with visibility had better results in the following performance metrics compared to firms without visibility:

- Percent of orders received from suppliers complete and on time (perfect orders)
- Percent of orders delivered to customers complete and on time (perfect orders)
- Total landed costs
- Frequency of out-of-stocks
- Cash-to-cash cycle
- Average lead time and lead-time variability
- Inventory levels

Enabler 2: Cross-organizational collaboration and simplification

Enabler 2 can cut lead time, improve efficiency, shrink quality risk, and streamline processes.

Cross-organizational collaboration ranges from operational to strategic—between a firm and its suppliers and customers. Collaboration can be as rewarding or as difficult as any other relationship. But in spite of the challenges it entails, it is a must to reach the second level of value chain maturity.

In these challenging economic times, customers expect suppliers to actively help them achieve their objectives and competitive advantage by providing education, expertise, and commitment to measure progress against clearly defined metrics. Firms are taking a closer look at their entire value chains by collaboration upward with suppliers and downward with their customers.

The best way to implement this enabler is by asking customers and suppliers what are the things they would do if we all belonged to the same company.

One application of simplification is to streamline product designs by requiring fewer part numbers, which typically results in fewer suppliers and replenishment signals, lower transportation cost and inventory, and less complexity. This translates to less after sales maintenance issues and cost. In addition, duplication of effort should also be removed.

Simplification is also needed when new products are introduced to make sure that the design and features reflect what the customer wants and would use, and to avoid overdesigning and overloading the products with features that customers are not asking for but marketing is forcing the engineer to introduce, thinking that would give them a market advantage. Hence, there is no point in having a competitive market advantage if it does not materialize into a customer advantage. Finally, as part of simplification, redundant or unnecessary data that are collected should be avoided (imagine the time you spend over hundreds of e-mails asking you for information you receive weekly), and too many performance measures, incorrect measures, and measures not aligned to corporate objectives should be addressed and fixed.

Enabler 3: Technology

Technology is necessary to enable and support best-practice processes and helps in reducing supply chain complexity. Technology, by focusing on supporting best-practice processes, makes a firm more agile and able to manage variability, risks, and exceptions more effectively. In addition, automation to routine activities eliminates errors, improves productivity, and puts more focus on value-added activities.

A flexible technology architecture that overlays existing systems is critical in enabling firms to manage transitions and business changes, facilitate rapid technology deployment and acceptance, integrate many individual processes and applications, and reduce the total cost of IT ownership. Disparate legacy systems and technology platforms can be unified by implementing a service-oriented architecture. Chapter 6 covers technology and its applications in detail.

Enabler 4: Flexibility

Building flexibility into product designs and manufacturing processes is a must in today's market to become more *customer oriented* and to be able to change plans quickly. Having a certain minimal level of flexibility built in the value chain is a must. Flexibility can be measured by the ability to shift production load, change production volumes and product mix, and modify products to meet new market needs. Firms need to manage trade-offs between cost and flexibility effectively because cost reduction initiatives usually inversely affect flexibility.

At a semiconductor company, two types of flexibility are defined: inventory and capacity. These are necessary to buffer against forecast inaccuracies. Capacity flexibility acts as the risk shock absorber between tactical and strategic planning, and inventory flexibility acts as the shock absorber between execution and tactical planning.

The semiconductor company also found a way to control the risk of inaccurate forecasts by developing range forecasts based on the relative risk of the opportunity. Therefore, their sales and marketing teams can communicate their relative confidence in the different long-term opportunities. Using this method, the company can make better decisions on capacity investments by sizing the opportunities more realistically. The lower the confidence level, the less likely the company will be to invest in the risk.

Another example is from the retail industry in which fashion trends change constantly and technologies rapidly become obsolete. Private-label retailers need to delay their most critical decisions about colors, technical capabilities, and other product features as long as possible to ensure the most current and popular assortments. Potential manufacturers are judged on how dramatically they can cut their standard purchase order-to-delivery cycle time. Also, as retailers expand into international markets, they are increasingly looking for suppliers who are local to these new customers for their private-label products. Identifying a source close to the final consumer can dramatically cut transportation costs, as well as foreign taxes and trade tariffs.[5]

Many U.S. retailers may consider dual-sourcing strategies that create local rapid response capabilities for the replenishment of hot-selling products, while still leveraging their Chinese trading partners to meet less time-sensitive production schedules. In addition to speed and agility, retailers must still consider the total landed cost (raw materials, labor, energy, transportation, taxes, currency exchange rates, and government regulations) of their private-label products when making the sourcing decision.

Enabler 5: Risk management

Risk, in the context of this book, can be defined as a potential event or future situation that may adversely affect the value chain. The risk management enabler includes identifying, analyzing, and responding to risk in the value chain. It's a continuous assessment to what can go wrong (risks), deciding which risks are important to deal with and then implementing strategies to address them. Risks must be analyzed on an ongoing basis to deal with changing conditions in the value chain. As new risks are identified, strategies need to be developed to deal with them.

Information sharing and open communication internally and with partners is one strategy to mitigate risks, since it helps all parties to be quickly informed of a potential disruption and respond quickly to minimize the disruption impact. Risk monitoring is another strategy to mitigate risks by predicting the likelihood of occurrence of risky events.

The risk management enabler is the systematic identification, assessment, and mitigation of potential disruptions/risks in value chains with the objective to avoid or reduce their negative impact on the value chain's performance.

Risk identification is the process of coming up with a list of potential events that could negatively affect the value chain.

Risk assessment is the process of finding the greatest risks in the value chain to prioritize resources for risk mitigation. This can be accomplished by understanding how frequently such risky events have happened or can be expected to happen, and their potential impact.

Risk identification and assessment allow an organization to create mitigation risk plans to manage risks before they occur (ideal situation) or reduce their negative impact when they occur. Risk mitigation plans are the output of risk management.

Value chain network configuration or design should consider high risks when determining hub locations, transportation routes, capacity limit, location of facilities, number of suppliers, number of production facilities, supplier priority, customer priority, single source versus multiple source strategy, and so forth.

This enabler addresses the risks related to product quality and service delivery that arise from outsourcing and globalization. It should also include tactical risks such as strikes or natural disasters.

This enabler is crucial because in this era of lightning-fast replenishment and short product life cycles, many firms such as consumer goods manufacturers and retailers cannot afford a single delivery delay or design mistake. For example, suppliers must deliver finished products on time and meet the highest standards for both quality and consumer protection, especially for all pharmaceuticals, food, beverages, electronics, and toys that need to meet stringent safety criteria.

Enabler 6: Process innovation and encouraging employee creativity

Process innovation is crucial when firms want to reengineer their processes to increase speed to market for new products, or conduct process improvements to gain competitive advantage and increase profitability across their total global network. Let us give two examples for process innovation in the area of supply replenishment:

1. One of the supply replenishment techniques is based on fixed replenishment time with variable quantity. It's also called *milk run* replenishment because it uses regular (fixed time) pickup and deliverables across the value chain with return trips carrying the returnable containers. This is similar to the old days when the milkman used to drop off full bottles of milk and bring back empty bottles to the plant. To improve tracking, several companies have started to use "smart" containers, which contain embedded sensors linked to satellites to track the container's location.
2. The challenge in unloading trailers is that goods that are loaded first are unloaded last (last in, first out), which means the order that goods are picked up (based on priority) is not the same order that goods will be unloaded at the receiving facility. One solution is reverse loading the trailer. However, this requires close coordination. Another solution is to use side-loading trucks, which allow goods to be loaded and unloaded from the side instead of the back.

Companies should have a program to track process innovation and reward employees or partners for their innovative ideas once it gets implemented. Ideas or suggestions can be received internally from employees, suppliers, or customers. For example, companies can give employees cash bonuses for their suggestions, price discounts for better service to customers who provide innovative suggestions for improvement, and opportunities for new business for suppliers who are participating effectively in a process innovation program. In *Marketing Management*, Kotler and Keller[6] mention that the 3M Company claims that over 66 percent of its new product improvement ideas come from listening to customers.

In addition, companies should reward suppliers or customers if they agree to be part of the first rollout of a certain process improvement project (being one of the pioneers) to encourage participation and greater involvement. The same thing can be applied for the internal users who volunteer to be the first to use the new system or process effectively. A flat-panel LCD TV can be one example of the reward.

Upper management support is also crucial for process innovation. Putting the right organizational structure and talent (who are convinced of the importance of LAVC) in place is one way to secure and sustain upper management support. One example is to appoint a vice president of the supply chain along with associated staff. This new function should report to the chief financial officer, the chief operating officer, or the head of the business. This will help the supply chain—historically viewed as a cost center—to be seen as a profit center, with clearly defined performance metrics and service-level agreements with other functions.

Enabler 7: Strategy innovation

Strategy innovation is the way to achieve the highest level of maturity for a value chain and sustained competitive advantage.

Adopting a pull-driven replenishment philosophy is a good example for strategy innovation. There are two popular philosophies for replenishment: pull- and push-driven replenishment. The push philosophy is primarily forecast-driven, whereas the pull philosophy is demand-driven. Very few firms use a pull system across its end-to-end supply chain (customers through suppliers). The two philosophies might be applied in the same firm or supply chain. For example, several automotive firms start to use pull with their suppliers, while they would continue to apply push with their dealers. Another firm implemented pull for internal production, but material replenishments with suppliers continued to be based on a push basis and derived forecast. A final example is from a company who succeeded in using pull internally and with Tier 1 suppliers, but Tier 1 is using push with Tier 2 suppliers. In this case, the pull-push decoupling point is between Tier 1 and Tier 2.

In any environment, the further upstream from the end customer (consumer) the pull-push decoupling point, the greater the adherence to LAVC principles because it maximizes the length of the pull part of the supply chain.

This pull-push decoupling point varies across industries and even across various supply chains (products) in the same firm. Most firms produce both high-volume products with stable demand and low-volume products with unpredictable demand. It is appropriate to adopt the push replenishment philosophy when the supply requirements or demand is reasonably well known. It is also appropriate to adopt it when purchasing is the dominant force in determining replenishment quantities in the supply chain.

On the other hand, it is recommended to adopt pull replenishment for fluctuating and unpredictable demand because pull is a supply philosophy in which the supply chain is synchronized to control variability and satisfy customer requirements. Supply variability is addressed by keeping lead times short. Suppliers are usually located near the buyer's site of operations. On the other hand, demand variability can be controlled by more frequent, smaller purchase orders, which in turn increase order cost. Enabling a pull system with suppliers and allowing smaller delivery quantities on a more frequent basis needs close coordination with the buyer's material planning and logistics groups, carrier, and supplier.

The following practices are recommended in a pull-driven philosophy:

- Automate purchase order generation and communication to reduce order-processing costs.
- Counter full truckload (FTL) economies by using 3PL and assorted truckloads.
- Counter volume discount economies by implementing capacity reservations. For example, a buyer can reserve a total fixed quantity (or amount)

for a given period and then get it shipped in smaller increments over that period based on need, as long as the accumulated order quantity is equal to the reserved quantity.

- Counter item shortages by sharing capacity and supply information in real time.
- Counter forecast inaccuracy by improving the forecasting techniques or providing point-of-sale (POS) data as in a VMI program of the retail industry.

VALUE CHAIN PROCESSES' CHALLENGES AND SOLUTIONS

Value Chain Superprocesses

These value chain processes can be grouped into three superprocesses: customer relationship management (CRM), supply chain management (SCM), and supplier relationship management (SRM).

CRM is the superprocess of managing all aspects of customer relationships (attracting, acquiring, retaining, and developing lifetime relationships with customers) supported by effective marketing management, selling management, and customer service management.

SRM is the superprocess of supporting supplier partnership in the value chain, and coordinating processes across product development, sourcing, purchasing, and supply coordination within a company and across companies. SCM is the third superprocess, which is responsible for balancing between supply and demand and optimizing it if possible.

In *The Discipline of Market Leaders*, Treacy and Wieresma describe three distinctive strategies for value creation:[7]

1. Production leadership: to focus invention, innovation, and rapid product development
2. Operational excellence: to streamline operations and optimize cost of production and delivery
3. Customer intimacy: to focus on relationships with customers, rather than transactions, and to be customer centric

It is clear from the definitions that value creation strategy 1 is related to the SRM superprocess, strategy 2 is related to SCM, and strategy 3 is related to CRM. Therefore, the focus of this book will be on three superprocesses (SRM, SCM, and SRM) that have a direct link to value creation. There will be less emphasis in this book on "support" processes such as human resources, finance, and so forth, and their related IT application, such as ERP.

The ongoing advances in advanced planning and scheduling (APS) software development have given SCM an enormous boost and have helped in maximizing enterprise agility. APS is a constraint-based planning logic that emerged in the early 1990s, and considered to be a major breakthrough after material requirements planning (MRP) logic. APICS defines SCM as "the design, planning, execution, control, and monitoring of supply activities with the objective of creating net value, building a competitive infrastructure, leveraging world-wide logistics, synchronizing supply with demand, and measuring performance globally."

SCM is defined in this text as the process of optimizing the flow of goods, services, and information along the supply chain from supplier to customer. It's also the process to strategize, plan, and execute business processes across facilities and business units. It focuses on the internal supply chain, which is under the direct control of the firm.

Information at all points along the supply chain should be captured and presented to enable better decision making in LAVC SCM businesses processes. This includes information regarding maintaining appropriate inventory levels, efficient movement of products to the next production or distribution process, and information pertaining to supporting sales and operations planning. LAVC SCM processes help replace excess inventory with accurate, inexpensive, and real-time information. Also, real-time information about the supply and ability to collaborate with customers on the forecast help producers to balance and match supply with demand.

APICS defines SRM as "a comprehensive approach to managing an enterprise's interactions with the organizations that supply the goods and services the enterprise uses. The goal of SRM is to streamline and make more effective the processes between an enterprise and its suppliers." SRM is often associated with automating procure-to-pay business processes, evaluating supplier performance, and exchanging information with suppliers. An e-procurement system often comes under the umbrella of a supplier relationship management family of applications.

The LAVC SRM superprocess eliminates paperwork, streamlines shipments and payments, reduces the cycle time of finding and acquiring suppliers, helps monitor contract terms, leverages spend consolidation by supplier and part rationalization, increases supplier awareness during design and production phases, and automates the procurement process.

Bob Thompson, CEO of CustomerThink Corporation, defines CRM as "a business strategy to acquire and manage the most valuable customer relationships. CRM requires a customer-centric business philosophy and culture to support effective marketing, sales and service processes." He adds, "CRM applications can enable effective customer relationship management, provided that an enterprise has the right leadership, strategy and culture."[8]

The LAVC CRM superprocess increases customer satisfaction, reduces order-to-delivery cycle time, and minimizes expediting costs.

We will drill down in the next section to detail the SCM, SRM, and CRM business processes and mention the related pain points in the conventional processes.

SRM, SCM, and CRM Business Processes

Each superprocess (SRM, SCM, and CRM) consists of several business processes. In this section each key business process is defined (see Table 1.2) and typical challenges in the current practice (as is process) are highlighted. This chapter shows briefly how the LAVC concept can address these challenges and some typical benefits resulting from adopting the LAVC concept are mentioned. Part II will talk about these processes in details.

Table 1.2 shows the key business processes in each superprocess. Although the name and scope of these processes may differ across different industries, Table 1.2 and the following process definitions give firms a template that would help to map their business to this table and be able to tailor the best practices to their own processes. The criteria used to tie certain business processes to the appropriate superprocess are:

- If a business process has a direct relationship with suppliers based on the best practice, it would belong to the SRM superprocess.
- If a business process has a direct relationship with customers based on the best practice, it would belong to the CRM superprocess.
- If a business process has no direct relationship with either suppliers or customers, and it helps in balancing supply and demand, it would belong to the SCM superprocess.
- If a business process spans across two superprocesses that make it difficult to associate it with a particular superprocess (gray area), its own subprocesses should be evaluated and the business process will be linked to the corresponding superprocess to which the majority of the subprocesses belong. For example, demand fulfillment has several subprocesses such as logistics planning and execution that has a direct link to suppliers and cus-

Table 1.2 Business processes distribution

		Superprocess		
		SRM	**SCM**	**CRM**
	Strategic	Strategic sourcing	Strategic management	Marketing management
Level	**Tactical**	Product design	Sales and operations planning	Selling management
	Operational	Procurement	Demand fulfillment	Customer service management

tomers, but we have chosen to associate demand fulfillment to SCM because the rest of its subprocesses have internal focus and assist in balancing supply and demand such as the scheduling subprocess.

In the second dimension of Table 1.2, the criteria used to decide the level a certain business process belongs to are:

- If a business process is used to generate strategies to run the business, it would belong to the strategic level (long term)
- If a business process is used to generate a plan of execution to convert the strategies defined in the previous level into reality, it would belong to the tactical level (medium term)
- If a business process is used mostly to execute the plans defined in the previous level, it would belong to the operational/execution level (short term)

Execution is included in the third level (operational) instead of dealing with it as a separate level for simplicity. As the processes move up from execution/operational, to tactical, to strategic, the percentage of cost savings goes up and the impact of decisions on the success of the organization increases.

SRM Processes

SRM combines three value chain processes together: strategic sourcing, product design, and procurement as shown in Table 1.3.

Tough economic conditions bring a stronger emphasis on cost reduction and control. Streamlining SRM is a key objective in challenging economic times to achieve cost containment and cash acceleration.

Table 1.3 Business processes distribution for SRM

		Superprocess		
		SRM	SCM	CRM
Level	Strategic	Strategic sourcing	Strategic management	Marketing management
	Tactical	Product design	Sales and operations planning	Selling management
	Operational	Procurement	Demand fulfillment	Customer service management

Strategic Sourcing

Strategic Sourcing is defined as the process of selecting the best sourcing strategy to reduce cost and risk while at the same time maximizing flexibility and strengthening the relationship with suppliers. The main objectives of this process are to reduce the total landed cost while maintaining enough supply capacity to satisfy demand. The pressure to reduce costs is becoming larger and larger, which is forcing firms to become lean and agile when it comes to supplier selection, rationalizing the supplier base, and enabling a pull system with the suppliers. It is also forcing suppliers to be lean and agile to reduce price and control variability. For example, nowadays the ability of suppliers to adjust capacity quickly and efficiently due to changing demand is a crucial requirement for the buying firm.

In a recession, firms need to be concerned about the financial health of their key suppliers because the failure of one key supplier can put them out of business faster than their competitors. For example, if a key supplier goes out of business, the implications might be disastrous, especially if the sourced items from the supplier are custom (e.g., tooling, dies) and not commodity items.

Deciding which functions to outsource without outsourcing a firm's core competency can be a challenging task since exporting a focal or central function of a firm can be catastrophic.

Outsourcing brings its own additional challenges, such as increased transportation cost, dealing with different transportation modes, longer lead times, potential delays, and higher inventory levels.

Introducing flexibility into the sourcing process could mitigate risk; for example, having the flexibility to buy from a foreign supplier or a local one if a faster response time is needed.

Another major challenge in this process is the need to identify and manage the total supplier spend and demand which might be difficult due to disconnected purchasing systems. Another disconnect exists between the engineering and purchasing systems, which causes the lack of visibility to the design engineers of the approved vendor list which typically exists in the purchasing system. Another related challenge is the inability to consider supplier performance during sourcing decisions by design engineers or purchasing analysts, either because it does not exist or exists in a different system for which they do not have access.

Based on the second win-win LAVC principle and leveraging visibility and risk management enablers, companies can afford to reduce the number of suppliers for each purchased part to a single supplier, or two to three at a maximum. This will reduce variability since the buyer will deal with a smaller and reliable set of suppliers, and reduce costs due to volume leverage and inventory level reductions.

An incentive system should be in place for suppliers or carriers who score high on performance measures or metrics. Some incentive options include adding the supplier or carrier to a preferred list, awarding them more business, or signing longer term contracts. Also, mutual goals and performance measures should be established, suppliers' involvement in developing replenishment strategy should be increased, and collaborative problem solving should be encouraged for the relationship to work efficiently and effectively.

A strong relationship between supplier and buyer requires more people from both organizations to collaborate more frequently and not limit the relationship between purchasing (from buyer organization) and sales (from supplier organization) by leveraging LAVC enabler 2 (cross-organizational collaboration and simplification). For example, a buyer's engineering team needs to collaborate with the supplier's operations department during new product introduction and a buyer's operations department needs to collaborate closely with the supplier's fulfillment team on orders and quality issues.

Two-way-communication is essential to ensure an effective relationship and timely performance feedback, fulfilling previous commitments, and protecting each other's sensitive information. Another way to strengthen the relationship is by inviting the supplier to an executive supplier council. All of the above will lead to establishing trust between the two firms, which is the highest level of maturity in the relationship between supplier and buyer that is consistent with LAVC principle 2 (create win-win and a trusted environment for all stakeholders).

Addressing supplier quality issues can be achieved by (1) considering quality as one of the criteria to select a supplier for a certain purchased part in addition to ISO 9000 certification, (2) including a metric for quality in the supplier performance scorecards, (3) sustaining high-quality products as a prerequisite to renew or engage in longer term contracts, and (4) establishing a program for supplier development and corrective action to correct quality issues.

As firms tend to segment their customers, they need to segment their suppliers and purchased parts based on several factors. (This has no contradiction to principle 4, which focuses on continuous improvement and standardization, since the process of dealing with the supplier should be common, but also flexible to accommodate the segmentation.) For example, as a best practice, for low-cost small items like fasteners, small and frequent deliverables are not justified and the savings, if any, would not be significant. In general, the item dollar unit value and item space requirements are the two major factors that determine if a small and frequent deliverables program is applicable to the items.

Other factors in determining the frequency of replenishment are the willingness of the supplier to participate, location proximity of the supplier, relationship/contract between supplier and buyer, and any special characteristic of the item/product, such as hazardous material. Finally, predictable demand is another factor. A small and frequent deliverables program is not a good idea for highly unpredictable items because the supply chain might become fragile. Therefore, LAVC enablers 4 (flexibility) and 7 (strategy innovation) address this challenge by encouraging a hybrid approach depending on the characteristic of the item and nature of the business. For example, if a small and frequent deliverables program is not applicable because demand is not predictable, economic order quantity can be used, which is driven by local parameters such as ordering costs and carrying costs rather than supply chain demand.

A lean and agile strategic sourcing process allows purchasing to quickly strategize, plan, and achieve cost reduction on anything that is purchased. Immediate savings can reach 35 percent in the first few sourcing events.

Product Design

Product design is the process of enabling collaborative design, engineering, and support among companies, partners, and suppliers by sharing product design, schedules, and constraints to arrive at a single bill of material for a finished product. Efficient and effective product design will help bring innovative and profitable products to the market quickly and ensure high product quality standards.

This process is typically triggered either by the need to introduce a new product to the market or by product engineering changes (revisions) due to component cost change, product improvements, process change, quality corrective actions, material shortages, or product obsolescence. Revisions involve engineers, purchasing, suppliers, manufacturing and process managers, contract manufacturers, and service support representatives. The product design process is tightly integrated to several technology applications:

- Computer-aided design, computer-aided manufacturing, as well as 3D visualization.
- Product definition management, which is the database for all designed parts: Stores structured data (e.g., item number, bill of materials, routings, effective dates) and unstructured data (e.g., electronic document formats, drawings). It also provides a powerful search capability to navigate easily in the databases.
- Engineering change management/control workflows: Manages engineering change requests and their approval steps, engineering change order generation to a new revision number, changes to parts, bill of materials and routings, and effective dates.
- Design collaboration: Provides a shared design workbench to collaborate among different members (internal and external), a common, secure, and role-based portal for supplier interactions, exceptions management, visualization, reporting, data analysis and mining, and document control.
- Program/project management: Provides project management capability with cost calculations and is able to evaluate multiple project proposals (i.e., cost, risk, resource needs, launch timing).

One of the main challenges of product design is the urgent need for a quicker new product introduction to the market due to intensified competition. Another challenge is the increasing complexity of the products, which makes optimizing the design more difficult. High prototype cost is a third challenge, which is due to the inability to manage and control frequent design changes, and the inability to identify the right products to launch or fund, the right suppliers to collaborate with early in the design process, and the right standard items to reuse. Also, subcontracting and outsourcing extends the need for real-time collaboration with partners and suppliers, which is a big challenge, especially if the firm has no technology to enable this type of collaboration.

We have found that 20 to 35 percent of a product design cycle can be taken out by sharing information about designs at a much earlier stage. Buyers (purchasing department) can collaborate with engineers or designers, as well as with a key group of suppliers, to choose the most cost-effective materials and manufacturing processes. Instead of being presented with final designs, and then scrambling to line up materials and manufacturing facilities, buyers need to become part of the design process that considers materials and production costs up front. This will add agility and speed to the process.

It is also crucial to involve marketing and sales and to demand that management representatives approve the design early on to give the forecasting team a much greater opportunity to study market trends and create accurate demand projections. By sharing forecast information as early as possible with value chain partners, risk can be minimized and responsiveness can be maximized. This will also allow buyers to gain an earlier understanding of supplier costs and capacity constraints.

Firms that standardize their products and raw material during the product design process gain significant economies of scale in production and procurement and achieve cost reductions.

To summarize, a lean and agile product design process brings products to market faster, and increases profitability and market share.

Procurement

Procurement is the process of planning and executing the sourcing strategies. It includes the request for quote, reverse auction, bid analysis, contract processing, and purchase order processing workflows to select the source of supply, and then managing all daily activities of replenishment with the selected suppliers and transportation with carriers to achieve and execute a synchronized procurement plan. It comprises the following subprocesses: contract management (request for proposal [RFP], request for quote [RFQ], auctions, bid analysis, contract processing and compliance), supply collaboration, and purchase order management. There are several key challenges for this process:

- Inability to capture supplier performance data, which results in the inability to conduct reliable bid analysis since the supplier's previous performance is not well captured and presented.
- Lack of intelligent visibility throughout the life cycle of the purchase order, which results in late detection for inbound material problems.

- The common way of automated communication—electronic data interchange (EDI)—is costly and difficult to maintain because different versions of the software may result in transmission errors, and lack mismatch resolution framework. Although the original business case for EDI was to eliminate manual work (nonvalue-added activities), it often resulted in waste transmission to small suppliers who get the EDI signal from the fax machine and then enter it manually in their order management system.
- The high cost of both expedition and manual mismatch resolution between the purchase order, receipt, and invoice.
- Several non value-added and time-consuming (paper-based) activities like manual RFQ and contracting processes, checking shipment status, and paper invoices.
- The urgent need to reduce supplier selection cycle time, which includes RFP and RFQ lead time since companies are under severe pressure to reduce product development times.

Some solutions to address these challenges and help companies to become lean and agile are:

1. Involve purchasing representatives early on in the product design process (enabler 2: cross-organizational collaboration and simplification).
2. Have an approved vendor list ready and updated in anticipating future supply requirements by continuously prequalifying and requalifying suppliers (enabler 6: process innovation).
3. Leverage technology (enabler 3) to automate and streamline the procurement process whenever possible to allow purchasing to focus on value-added activities such as strengthening the relationship with suppliers and the qualification process. Some examples are sending RFPs and RFQs electronically and also receiving responses electronically, using software to conduct quantitative supplier response evaluation, and keeping ready templates for contracts and electronic forms for communications.
4. Purchase low dollar items (direct or indirect material), by delegating the procurement trigger to internal users instead of purchasing, and allowing them to initiate the requisition online by selecting from a preapproved online catalog (enabler 3: technology and enabler 6: process innovation). This should be accompanied by issuing a blanket purchase order with preapproved suppliers in order for the requisition to be converted automatically to a purchase order and sent directly to the supplier if the internal user is within the budget that is allocated to his/her department or below a certain dollar limit. This best practice reduces transaction costs, frees up purchasing resources to focus on more important activities, and increases satisfaction to internal users since they control the process and lead time.

5. Advance shipment notice and GPS capability tracking provide real-time feasibility about the incoming shipments, allow the receiving crew to be ready for the shipments, and also allow material planners to react if incoming tracking signals indicate a delay. This helps tremendously in achieving agility since it allows downstream processes to plan and stage documents, workers, and receiving equipment in anticipation of the goods' arrival, in addition to being proactive when delays occur for any reason. It also allows the buyer to reroute or expedite shipments that are in transit (enabler 3: technology and enabler 1: visibility).

6. Optimize the trade-offs (cost, service, and risk) between the major types of logistics carriers and select the best for the business—either one type or hybrid (enabler 7: strategy innovation). The three major types of logistics carriers are:

   - Common (public) carriers: All shippers receive very similar services and prices.
   - Contract carriers: These carriers serve only the shippers who have a contract with the carrier. The major advantage of a contract carrier over a public carrier is the ability to provide specialized services. It is also often managed by 3PL providers.
   - Private carriers: These carriers are owned by the shipper of the goods. Therefore, the carrier follows the company's transportation requirements. Private carriers are used primarily for outbound transportation, while common and contract carriers are used more frequently for inbound transportation. The main reason for using private carriers is the perception that the private fleets provide much better service levels and also greater control.

7. Optimize multiple transportation trade-offs to a lean and agile transportation subprocess (enabler 6: process innovation). The trade-offs can be summarized under one high level:

   - Provide total cost vs. customer service: Higher customer service requires higher inventory levels (lower inventory turnover), faster delivery, and wide product variety, resulting in an increase in transportation and inventory costs. This trade-off can be divided into several lower trade-offs based on whether it is related to inbound or outbound transportation. For example, inbound transportation trade-offs are:
     - Transportation cost vs. inventory: Shipment consolidation allows larger shipments (more FTL shipments) and lower transportation cost. However, it leads to higher inventory levels and therefore holding costs at the buyer's locations.

o   Lot size vs. inventory turnover: Larger replenishment lot size from the suppliers leads to higher inventory.
o   Transportation mode cost vs. lead time: Shipping by air is quicker (less lead time) but more costly.
o   Inventory vs. customer service levels: Too much inventory costs money, too little inventory costs customers.

To summarize, achieving a lean and agile procurement process requires strategic steps from a company and their partners:

- Optimize supply chain trade-offs to identify the right replenishment strategy with the suppliers and warehouses.
- Rationalize supplier and carrier base.
- Negotiate a long-term contract with suppliers and carriers based on lean and agile principles.
- Support the lean and agile procurement process with flexible material handling and transportation system.
- Leverage technology to streamline and automate the procurement process.

SCM Processes

SCM combines three value chain processes together: Strategic management, sales and operations planning, and demand fulfillment as shown in Table 1.4.

Strategic Management

The strategic management process supports long-term decision making such as the supply chain strategy and supply chain network design subprocesses. The supply chain strategy subprocess provides the ability for corporations to distinguish themselves from competitors and create value for their customers and investors by selecting and incorporating the right supply chain strategies. Based on

Table 1.4 Business processes distribution for SCM

		Superprocess		
		SRM	SCM	CRM
Level	**Strategic**	Strategic sourcing	Strategic management	Marketing management
	Tactical	Product design	Sales and operations planning	Selling management
	Operational	Procurement	Demand fulfillment	Customer service management

the selected strategies, a question should be answered related to whether a company is operating with the right physical supply chain and is servicing the correct customers with the right products by conducting some analyses and simulations.

The supply chain network design subprocess, on the other hand, deals with determining the optimal number and locations of facilities (plants and distribution centers), flow of goods throughout the supply chain, and best assignment of customers to distribution centers, and should be aligned with the supply chain strategies. This subprocess also helps in deciding whether to keep intermediate distribution channels or cross docks and where to keep them.

The main objectives of the supply chain network design subprocess is to optimize the location of facilities, the allocation of capacity and technology requirements to facilities, the assignment of products to facilities, and the distribution of products between facilities and to customer regions.[9]

The major challenges of this process in today's market are: (1) the lack of flexibility in the supply chain configuration to react fast to the variability in demand, supply, and business needs, (2) the urgent need to introduce new products into the market quickly, and (3) non-repeatable and manual subprocesses.

With globalization, firms transitioned from a single-site business serving domestic markets to a truly global business—with multiple locations around the world. Decisions about where to source materials, where to produce, and where to sell products are suddenly more complex. Although the supply chain network design should put more weight on the largest opportunity in the new market—for example, by building new factories in India or China—the demands of the global marketplace should continue to be tracked to ensure that all market opportunities are leveraged. Understanding the costs and drivers associated with every global supply chain activity is crucial before deciding where to locate manufacturing facilities so as to maximize their contribution to profitability. Whether factories should be located close to raw-material suppliers to take advantage of low-cost labor, or close to the customers they serve, is another decision that should be studied from a cost and benefit standpoint.

Sales and Operations Planning

The APICS dictionary defines sales and operations planning (S&OP) as "a process to develop tactical plans that provide management the ability to strategically direct its business to achieve competitive advantage on a continuous basis by integrating customer-focused marketing plans for new and existing products with the management of the supply chain." The S&OP process forms a vital link between the strategic business planning process and the tactical supply chain planning processes.

The following departments are typically involved in this process to come up with one integrated set of plans: sales, marketing, development, manufacturing, sourcing, and finance. In addition, if a firm has several business units, it is recommended to create and manage the S&OP process at the global or corporate level that aligns and synchronizes regional metrics with corporate goals.

Some of the major pain points or challenges of this process are the lack of a unified demand plan and consensus across multiple departments, demand and supply uncertainty, the lack of historical data related to supply and transportation lead-time variability, and the lack of visibility into unexpected events that could occur downstream or upstream of the supply chain.

Some other problems that we captured from assessing forecast accuracy for several companies are lack of a single owner or group for estimating the monthly demand, and forecast accuracy after human intervention (manual adjustment to system forecast) is lower than the system forecast accuracy (based on historical statistical models). In one company, we also found that marketing or salespeople who override the system forecast have little knowledge and trust in the way that the system is estimating the forecast, and that was the root cause for low forecast accuracy.

The following questions can be used to find the root cause of forecast inaccuracy:

- Are forecasts consistently over or underestimated (look for a pattern)?
- Is there a single owner to the forecast generation?
- Does the company have a process in place for continuous improvement for forecast accuracy?
- Are the forecast errors normally distributed?
- Does the process allow the demand planners, marketing, or sales to override the system forecast? If yes, what are the main reasons for doing so?
- What is the perception about the root cause for the low forecast accuracy?
- Does the company keep evaluating the statistical model used to generate the system forecast?
- Is the frequency of generating the forecast adequate?

One way to control unpredictable demand and low forecast accuracy in a "make to stock" environment is "postponement" (i.e., moving to an "assemble to order" environment). The main advantages of postponement are: (1) it's cost effective since it's much cheaper to hold inventory in a subassembly (semi finished state) rather than a finished state; and (2) it's easier to forecast a base product level rather than a finished product level, which includes all customer configurations. Postponement (the strategy innovation enabler) requires a close coordination with the design team, who needs to design the product in a way that final assembly or production is done after receiving the actual order with the specific requirements from the customer.

Some experts in postponement divide it into two types: form and time. Postponement to the final assembly until demand occurs is *form postponement*, while the postponement for shipping the finished goods in the distribution channel is *time postponement*. An example of form postponement is delaying configuring microcomputer systems until the customer order arrives (e.g., Dell Computer). Filling catalog orders from few warehouse locations is an example of time postponement. Time postponement is about delaying transportation to the distribution center or next operation until the actual order is received.

Experts further divide form postponement into four categories: labeling, packaging, assembly, and manufacturing (e.g., painting).

Build/make to order is the solution when demand is not predictable and postponement is not an option. It also allows the demand fulfillment process to be streamlined because products are produced once the actual order is received and usually sent directly to the customer.

Another challenge for this crucial process is the ability to consider supply constraints during an S&OP meeting in order to make the right adjustments and come up with a feasible consensus plan. Chapter 4 covers this process in detail.

Demand Fulfillment

Demand fulfillment is a process of providing accurate, optimal, and reliable delivery dates for sales orders, and matching supply with demand while respecting supply chain constraints and sales channel allocations. The major pain points for demand fulfillment are: (1) lack of visibility across the supply chain to ensure on-time delivery to the customer; (2) lack of flexibility in meeting customer expectations; (3) lack of flexibility to move to business to consumer by leveraging the Internet; and (4) the need to promise what the company can deliver, and deliver on every promise to gain and sustain competitive advantage.

To address the above challenges, pull systems, uniform loading, and level scheduling methods are used in the demand fulfillment process. Setup time reductions and facility layout changes are needed to achieve effective pull systems and internal flexibility so that operations are not constrained by setups or layouts.

There are several ways to reduce setup times like conducting time-motion studies, purchasing additional equipment, or using operations staff rather than specialized setup staff to perform setups so they do not become the bottleneck if more than one piece of equipment needs changeover. Although adding additional equipment to reduce setup times (while the first equipment is in operation, the second one is being prepared/set up for the next job) might be a difficult sell from a financial perspective, a strong case can be built that this additional equipment can improve the agility of the organization in addition to making it leaner, which will offset the additional cost in several cases.

It is essential to track setup time improvements with a set of performance measures during the effort to reduce the setup time, and also monitor progress and enable corrective actions when expected results are not achieved within a certain timeline to close the loop (principle 5: close the loop between planning and execution).

It is important to note that to continue measuring the setup time after finishing the improvement project might be wasteful since setups are routine (principle 3: eliminate waste and reduce nonvalue-added activities).[3] Research showed improvements to facility physical layout result in production cycle time reduction, less complexity in scheduling and monitoring, less work-in-process inventory levels, and floor space requirement reductions. Certain layouts such as cellular manufacturing also increase ownership among workers for the process since it empowers self-directed teams to manage their work, hire new members, and improve the performance in their work cell.

Another area of improvement is to realign the receiving docks so that incoming trucks can unload closer to the stocking areas because although movement of incoming parts is necessary, excessive movement is non value-added. In addition, realignment is needed for the stocking areas of the finished products to be close to the shipping docks. In the distribution centers or warehouse, fastest moving items also need to be close to shipping docks.

Pull systems require a mind shift and a new culture in the organization, and to come up with a new set of performance measures that replace the traditional push-driven ones (e.g., capacity utilization, throughput, etc.). An integral piece of the pull system is *kanban*, which gives authorization to a downstream center for production or withdrawal of parts from an upstream center. Another important concept is "supermarkets," which hold inventory to ensure a balanced material flow.

Uniform loading is another element of lean and can address some of the challenges in the demand fulfillment process since it strives to link and balance production processes together so a steady state flow of material across the supply chain is accomplished with no shortage or inventory buildup. Uniform loading requires the sharing of the demand picture between work centers or partners. Level scheduling, which is also another element of lean, is about building the same finished product mix every day during a specific period. This works perfectly when there are a limited number of products and demand is more predictable, at least in the short term.

Takt, a German term used in level scheduling, is defined as the rate at which customers demand a product. For example, if the available machine time of a work center is 100 hours a week, and demand is 200 units, then the takt time is 0.5 hour, that is, a completed unit must flow from the work center every half hour to satisfy a demand of 200 units per week. Level scheduling can still be used in an unpredictable demand environment to a certain degree if the operation is flexible enough to shift resources, but it requires cross training for employees.

Technology (enabler 3) is crucial to achieving lean and agile demand fulfillment. Many companies have installed ERP systems to support processes like demand fulfillment. But since ERP systems are good at providing system breadth, but not so good in providing system depth, these ERP systems should be supplemented by advanced supply chain planning and execution systems. Several technology capabilities are required for this process to be effective:

1. Transportation management (transportation planning, vehicle load scheduling, vehicle routing, consolidating orders, carrier communication and payment)
2. Managing timing and replenishment of inventories
3. Allocation of products in short supply
4. Warehouse management: (1) tracking tools, such as bar code readers, RFID, voice recognition, etc.); and (2) optimizing tools for picking and packing

CRM Processes

Consumer behavior is changing and customers are increasingly demanding new and customized products, which has led to shrinkage in the market window for organizations and simultaneous overabundance in options for customers. Companies that cannot keep pace with customer needs in terms of total value (of price, quality, convenience, etc.) by first acquiring and then retaining customers for life run the risk of losing market share and revenue. CRM is the superprocess of managing all aspects of customer relationships (attracting, acquiring, retaining, and lifetime customer relationship) supported by effective marketing, selling, and customer service management (Table 1.5).

Marketing Management

Marketing management is the process of developing and managing effective marketing programs for products and services in order to increase revenue and margin by targeting profitable market segments. It includes identification of markets, market research for opportunities, market analysis, the selection of target markets, developing marketing strategies for the selected markets, developing mar-

Table 1.5 Business processes distribution for CRM

		Superprocess		
		SRM	**SCM**	**CRM**
Level	**Strategic**	Strategic sourcing	Strategic management	Marketing management
	Tactical	Product design	Sales and operations planning	Selling management
	Operational	Procurement	Demand fulfillment	Customer service management

keting plans, and implementing a process to measure the effectiveness of the plan or program.

All marketing strategies begin with market segmentation to identify which markets it can serve effectively. This is followed by selecting one or more target markets to synergize marketing efforts and resources to target the right segment and lastly, positioning, which involves developing a specific marketing mix of the 4Ps (product, price, promotion/communications, and placement/channel) for each targeted marketing segment to match customer perception.

The major challenges for this process are the need to identify appropriate market segments for incentives and promotions, the need to create effective marketing campaigns to achieve revenue and profitability objectives while considering supply chain constraints, and the need for effective new product and new market launches.

Selling Management

Selling management is the process of helping the customer to decide what to buy, and ensuring accurate and reliable information on the product features, price, delivery, and configuration options in order to provide the customer with a consistent and positive buying experience. It also presents the customer with a single, consistent, and positive buying experience no matter which channel is used (contact via the Internet, personal sales contact, telephone call, etc.), and includes capturing the sales order.

The main challenge in the current practice is the urgent need to match offerings to customer needs profitably through intelligent pricing, configuration, and availability checking. Other issues are managing promotions and discounts effectively and the need for markdowns.

Customer Service Management

Customer service management is the process of managing day-to-day customer activities and achieving customer satisfaction. It includes efficiently processsing and fulfilling sales orders from stores, dealers, telephone, electronic, online, and other sources. It also includes shipping, invoicing, returns, and settlement through multiple, complex channels and systems.

This process handles the front end of processing a sales order, while the demand fulfillment process in SCM handles the back end processing of a sales order. The front end includes real-time order promising, allocation management, and rebalancing in addition to credit modeling and order validation and brokering.

The customer service management process also covers all call center activities such as answering calls regarding product complaints or order status, managing recalls, conducting surveys, and so forth.

It is important to talk about a subprocess under customer service management, which is service parts management (valid only for certain industries) since many people overlook this vital subprocess. It consists of service planning and scheduling, service contract management, service order processing, replacement part delivery, and damaged part recycling or return activities.

Service parts management is usually triggered by signing up a service agreement with the customer, which includes several contract items such as discounts on replacement parts, guaranteed response time, technician hourly rate, and support time.[10] Some of the challenges of this subprocess are: (1) the complexity of today's products, which makes managing this process more difficult; (2) customer dissatisfaction due to service parts shortage; (3) inaccurate forecasting for service parts that are considered high dollar value and slow moving items; and (4) managing customer service to become a competitive advantage due to the intensified competition and the need to compensate for revenue losses in a flat economy.[10]

REFERENCES

1. Sabri, E. 2006. Best practice in leveraging e-business technologies to achieve business agility. In *Enterprise Service Computing: From Concept to Deployment*, ed. R. Qiu, 356–387. Hershey, PA: Idea Group Publishing.
2. Womack, J., and D. Jones. 2003. *Lean Thinking, Banish Waste and Create Wealth in Your Corporation*. New York, NY: Simon & Schuster.
3. Trent R. J. 2008. *End-to-end Lean Management: A Guide to Complete Supply Chain Improvement*. Fort Lauderdale, FL: J. Ross Publishing.
4. Aberdeen Group. November 2008. Enabling responsive supply chain execution: The role of visibility. Research Brief, 1–5. Boston: Aberdeen Group.
5. Singh, G. 2008. Private-label sourcing: What's next after China? *Supply Chain Leaders*, no. 6 (October): 4–9.
6. Kotler, P., and K. L. Keller. 2006. *Marketing Management*. 12th ed. Upper Saddle River, NJ: Pearson Prentice-Hall.
7. Treacy, M., and F. Wiersema. 1997. *The Discipline of Market Leaders*. Reading, MA: Addison-Wesley.
8. Greenberg, P. 2002. *CRM at the Speed of Light: Capturing and Keeping Customers in Internet real time*. New York: McGraw-Hill/Osborne.
9. Sabri, E., and B. Beamon. 2000. A Multi-objective approach to simultaneous strategic and operational planning in supply chain design. *OMEGA: The International Journal of Management Science* 28 (5): 581–598.
10. Curran T. A., and A. Ladd. 2000. *SAP R3 Business Blueprint: Understanding Enterprise Supply Chain Management*. 2nd ed. Upper Saddle River, NJ: Prentice-Hall.

2

Lean and Agile Value Chain Building Blocks and Maturity Levels

BUILDING BLOCKS AND EVOLUTION OF THE LEAN AND AGILE VALUE CHAIN

There are four building blocks for lean and agile value chain (LAVC) principles and enablers as shown in Figure 2.1:

1. Strategy and organizational (management) structure
2. Business processes
3. Quality and efficiency
4. Information technology

Figure 2.1 also shows the evolution for every building block from 1980 to the present. In the first part of this chapter, we will cover the main methodologies or technologies that have a major impact on the LAVC concept. However, these are not the only ones.

Strategy and Organizational (Management) Structure Building Block

Upper management support is crucial in any new initiative, especially when it has a potential impact on the future of a company. In this block, we will cover five management methodologies or concepts starting with the 1980s through the 1990s until today, as shown in Figure 2.2.

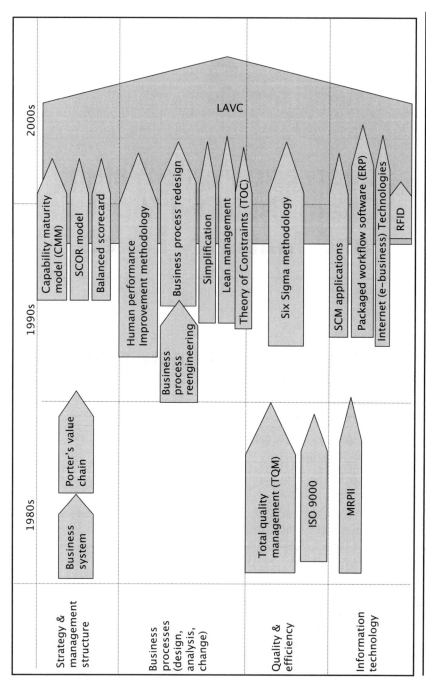

Figure 2.1 Building blocks and evolution of LAVC principles and enablers

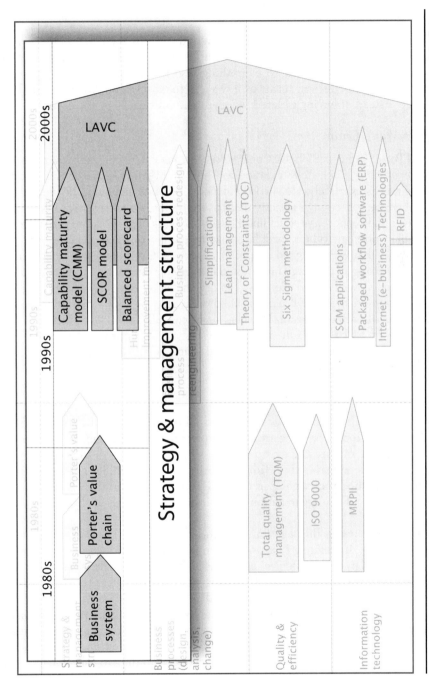

Figure 2.2 Building blocks and evolution of LAVC principles and enablers for the strategy and management block

Business System

Dealing with organizations as systems began in the 1980s and it was derived from operations research and control systems studies. It was based on the assumption that everything is connected to everything else and it's worthwhile to model businesses and processes in terms of flows and feedback loops to close the decision loop instead of having isolated independent entities.

Porter's Value Chain

Michael Porter, in his 1985 book *Competitive Advantage: Creating and Sustaining Superior Performance*,[1] laid the foundation for the current emphasis on comprehensive business processes. He also detailed the concept of value chain and defined it as a comprehensive collection of all activities that are performed to design, produce, market, deliver, and support a product line. Prior to the work of systems and management experts like Porter and others, most firms had focused on dividing processes into specific activities that were assigned to specific departments or functions without much regard for the overall process. This resulted in every department on the organization chart having its own isolated silo. It was an urgent call to move away from a department/function-oriented view to a holistic process view of how activities needed to work together to achieve organizational goals successfully.

In addition, and as a result of Porter's work, a new approach to accounting, called activity-based costing became popular and is still used to determine the actual value of producing specific products.

Capability Maturity Model

Companies launch business process projects all the time with little or no idea of the nature of the process they are trying to improve. In addition, no one comes back to ask how mature the existing process is, and where will the company be once the process improvement effort is complete. The capability maturity model (CMM), which became popular in the mid-1990s, addressed this issue by dividing the maturity of any organization or process into five levels as shown in Figure 2.3.

In the book entitled *Business Process Change: A Manager's Guide to Improving, Redesigning, and Automating Processes*, Harmon[2] explains CMM in a very beautiful way. At level 1, few stable processes exist. There is a "just do it" attitude, "fire fighting" is the way of life, and introducing new technology is too risky at this CMM stage. In addition, data collection and analysis are ad hoc.

At level 2, documented processes are established and problems are recognized and corrected as they occur, while success depends on individuals and management system support. At level 3, strategic processes and operational processes are documented, and training is planned and provided according to roles. Many firms are between levels 2 and 3.

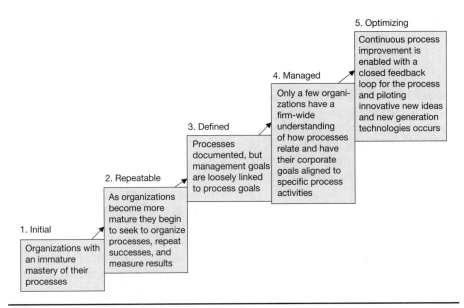

Figure 2.3 Five levels of CMM

At level 4, corporate or upper management goals are aligned to process goals, and a strong sense of teamwork exists. New technologies are evaluated on a quantitative basis. At level 5, continuous improvement is part of the company's culture and everyone's responsibility. Managers and employees work collectively to improve processes in a systemic and efficient way.

Supply Chain Operations Reference Model

The supply chain operations reference (SCOR) model is the product of the Supply Chain Council (SCC). The SCC was established as a nonprofit consortium in 1996. Today, it is a worldwide organization with over 700 members. The Council conducts regular meetings that allow firms to get together to discuss supply chain problems and opportunities. In addition, it has been working on the standard SCOR model to capture the Council's consensus view of supply chain management (SCM).

While much of the underlying content of the SCOR model has been used by practitioners for many years, the SCOR model strives to provide a unique framework that links business process, metrics, best practices, and technology features into a unified structure to support communication among supply chain partners and improve the effectiveness of SCM. It has three broad goals:

1. Help companies to capture the as-is state of a process and derive the to-be future state

2. Quantify the operational performance of similar companies and establish internal performance targets based on "best-in-class" results
3. Characterize the management practices and software solutions that result in "best-in-class" performance

The reference model includes three levels of process detail (top level, configuration level, and process element level). The first level has five top-level process types: plan, source, make, deliver, and return. Process detail (implementation/ activity level) beyond the third level is excluded from the reference model because companies implement specific SCM practices at this level and it is very difficult to generalize it. It also ignores training and corrective actions.

Although SCOR may not cover all the management functions (especially at the strategic level), it does a good job of defining process goals and measuring and defining benchmark information for the process that it defines. This is a good place to talk about an important concept called *benchmarking*.

Benchmarking is a data point that one firm can use to determine how well it is doing in comparison with others in the same industry or others who undertake similar tasks. Benchmarking can help companies decide when to improve, redesign, or keep their processes. It assesses strategies, product, practices, and performance measures of an organization or a value chain process. Benchmarking evaluates the best practices used by competitors or other industries, and helps to understand market dynamics.

This can be done through site visits to different firms in the same industry or a different industry, surveys, third-party consulting and research companies, or benchmarking consortiums. It is important for these consulting or research companies to work with many companies within the same or different area gathering data and publishing benchmarks, because, in most cases, good benchmarks are hard to extract. To summarize, benchmarking can help companies to identify "low-hanging fruit" processes, which can bring the highest and quickest value when improved first.

Balanced Scorecard

The balanced scorecard approach was developed at Harvard in 1996 by Kaplan and Norton.[3] This performance measurement model discouraged the big emphasis on the financial measures and return on investment (ROI) to test the health of a company, and emphasized that a company should monitor several key performance indicators (KPIs) that collectively tell the senior management how the organization is doing. These KPIs are divided into four categories: (1) financial (revenue growth, cash flow, profitability); (2) customers; (3) internal business processes; and (4) innovation and learning (measuring technical infrastructure and providing employees with the required skill and knowledge available). Recently, nonprofit organizations such as schools started to adopt the balanced scorecard approach to improve the performance of their employees and volunteers.

Business Processes

In this block, we will cover six process improvement methodologies or concepts from the 1990s to the present (Figure 2.4). Although lean, theory of constraints (TOC), and Six Sigma are considered to be different process improvement methodologies, the similarities between them are more than their differences since they take from each other. The proponents of each methodology sometimes overlook the similarities and consider the rest of the methodologies as competitors. Our position in this book is that all methodologies (lean, TOC, and Six Sigma) are applicable and complementary to each other and supported by the LAVC concept.

Business Process Reengineering

Business process reengineering (BPR) is a comprehensive view of process transformation to achieve breakthrough improvements. In this methodology, the process is designed from the ground up using best practices, and all assumptions are challenged or questioned. Therefore, it requires major effort and time. BPR theorists insisted in the early 1990s that companies must think in terms of comprehensive processes when it comes to improvement because the company might improve a certain subprocess at the expense of the overall value chain.

Program transformation using this methodology, once it is executed successfully, has the potential to improve the overall process significantly achieving major breakthroughs in productivity and efficiency. The bad news in BPR efforts is that the risk of failure is high because it undertakes a very large scope that typically involves hundreds or even thousands of employees and a significant number of information technology (IT) systems.

Business Process Redesign

By the late 1990s, most BPR theorists had modified their emphasis on total reengineering and began to promote something called *redesign*, which allows for incremental modifications in business processes or subprocesses without the need for redesigning the comprehensive business processes from scratch. It's up to the companies to decide when to redesign, reengineer, or keep the business processes.

Simplification

Simplification was another methodology that gained momentum in the mid-1990s as an alternative to the radical BPR. The focus of this methodology is to

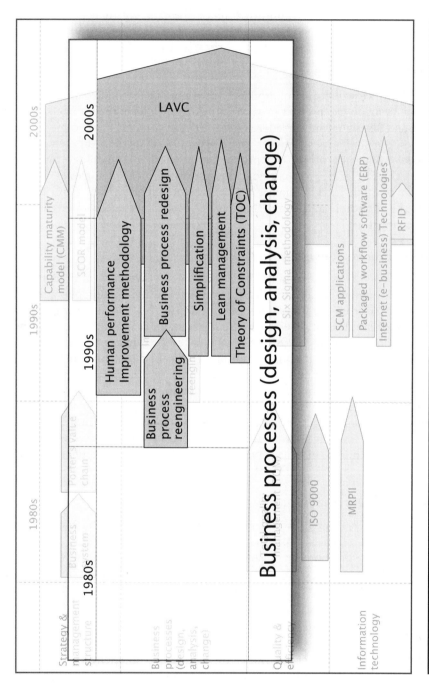

Figure 2.4 Building blocks and evolution of LAVC principles and enablers for the business process block

eliminate redundancies and duplicate efforts in processes to streamline them. The first step in this methodology is to capture the as-is process. The second step is to ask for every activity in the process, is there a need to do it? If yes, can this subprocess or activity be combined with a similar subprocess or activity? If it is decided to keep this activity or subprocess, the next step is to ask if it is a bottleneck. If yes, the next question should be, can things be done in parallel?

This methodology is crucial to streamlining processes and removing unnecessary complexity in the flow or duplication.

Human Performance Improvement Methodology

This methodology focuses on the job design, work environment, employee performance, and employee motivation. It also details how to analyze processes, how to redesign them, and how to sustain processes once they are in place.

Rummler and Brache, in their book *Improving Performance: How to Manage the White Space in the Organization Chart,* mention that many disconnects are often found in the management of processes in addition to the processes themselves.[4] They pointed out many of the major problems in any process result from the failure of communication between departments or functions. Therefore, this methodology has a direct impact on the strategy and management building block in addition to the business process improvement dimension (block).

Theory of Constraints

TOC states that every process contains a bottleneck (primary constraint) that limits the throughput of the entire process. TOC methodology recommends identifying the constraint, analyzing it, and then eliminating it. Once this is done, another constraint moves up to become the bottleneck. The same process is repeated to deal with the new constraint and so on. This methodology is very useful in a complex and job shop environment.

Lean Management

The main driver for lean management, which originated in Japan, is to eliminate nonvalue-adding activities. The first step is to model the as-is process and then ask at each step if this activity will add value from the customer's perspective. The customer here is not necessarily the end customer (consumer); it is simply the receiver of the output of the previous process, that is, it could be an internal customer or the end consumer.

In literature, there are hundreds of tools available and applicable to lean and many books that have already covered this topic. Therefore, in our overview, we will focus on *kaizen*, which is considered to be an integral part of lean implementation methodology.

Kaizen contains two Japanese words: kai, which means continuous, and zen, which means improvement. There are three types of kaizen:

1. Kaizen strike is an unplanned exercise that starts from the very moment a problem is detected, for example, an assembly line shutdown. A kaizen strike may take minutes or hours to resolve the problem. That said, it should be an organized event that follows a certain methodology for problem solving and should be conducted by skilled and trained people.
2. Kaizen blitz is a planned event that usually takes less than a week to complete.
3. Kaizen event is a carefully planned event that might take several weeks or months to complete. In this exercise, the problem and root cause are not clearly defined at the time of initiating this event. Clarity of the problem is obtained by asking the right questions. The kaizen process consists of three steps: (1) documenting the scope of the event and analyzing the event to make sure it's worth pursuing, (2) performing the kaizen event, and (3) ensuring the improvement is permanent.

Quality and Efficiency Building Block

Quality and efficiency is the third building block for LAVC principles and enablers, and in this block (Figure 2.5), we will discuss three methodologies: ISO 9000, total quality management (TQM), and Six Sigma.

ISO 9000

The ISO 9000 standard has became a commodity nowadays and is mandatory for every company to have. It began in the early 1980s when companies were exploring quality and efficiency initiatives such as total quality management (TQM) and just-in-time manufacturing. ISO 9000 efforts focus mainly on simply documenting and managing procedures/processes. It important to highlight that process documentation is a prerequisite for any improvement initiative.

Total Quality Management

Total quality management contributed to the efficiency and quality of organizational processes in the 1980s. The father of TQM, Dr. W. Edwards Deming, introduced the very popular PDCA (plan, do, check, and act) methodology to implement TQM initiatives, based on his discussion with his friend Dr. Walter Shewhart at the Bell Telephone Laboratories of AT&T. This continuous improvement cycle includes four steps: (1) plan a change to a process to improve its performance, (2) execute this change on a small scale, (3) observe the results, and (4) analyze the results and decide what has been learned from the change for the next cycle of improvement.

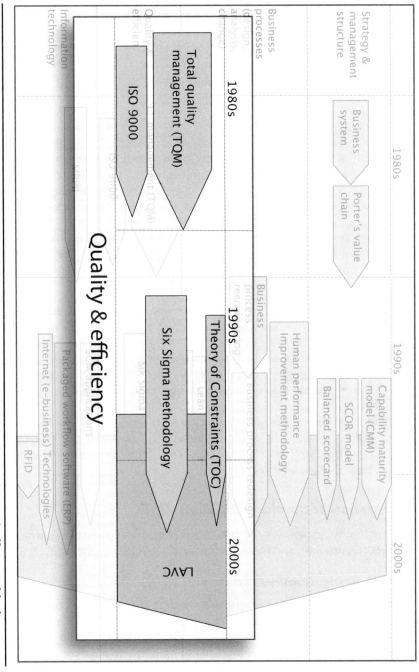

Figure 2.5 Building blocks and evolution of LAVC principles and enablers for the quality and efficiency block

Six Sigma Methodology

In the mid-1990s, Mike Harry and others developed a quality methodology called *Six Sigma* as its statistical approach to measurement at Motorola. It achieved popularity when Jack Welch, then CEO of General Electric, decided to adopt it companywide. Later, this methodology was extended from pure defect measurement to process improvement. Six Sigma has quality and process improvement dimensions.

In the quality dimension, which was how it got started in the first place, it is considered the next version of TQM. In this context, Six Sigma means that the output within a process should conform to its specification target at a defect level of only 3.4 defects per million opportunities. Six Sigma is a data-driven management philosophy and a rigorous statistical technique to measure and eliminate process variation, defects, and waste, and solve quality control problems, which results in an increase in efficiency and productivity.

The process improvement dimension for Six Sigma revolves around a define-measure-analyze-improve-control methodology. It delivers good measures and more consistent processes. Two major threats exist for this powerful and popular methodology in the process improvement dimension:

1. Some argue that it's good only for incremental improvement and short-term projects where the value is clear, and it's not meant for drastic improvement (innovation). They use the fact that most Six Sigma projects are narrowly focused on process improvement rather than on large-scale redesign to prove their point. However, Six Sigma theorists would argue that there are management, redesign, and improvement versions of Six Sigma.

2. Also, there are no standard requirements defined in the industry to become a black belt in Six Sigma, which has led to many certified black belts by simply taking online courses, though they are not really ready to lead Six Sigma projects.

Information Technology Building Block

Information Technology is the fourth building block for LAVC principles and enablers (Figure 2.6), and in this block we discuss five applications.

Manufacturing Resource Planning

In the 1980s, MRPII (manufacturing resource planning) was the predominant methodology to keep the supply chain under control. MRPII is indisputably valuable to firms with a deep bill of materials (BOM) that operate in a make-to-stock environment. MRPII begins with demand requirements and works its way back to supply requirements. It is unidirectional planning, where it starts from a forecast

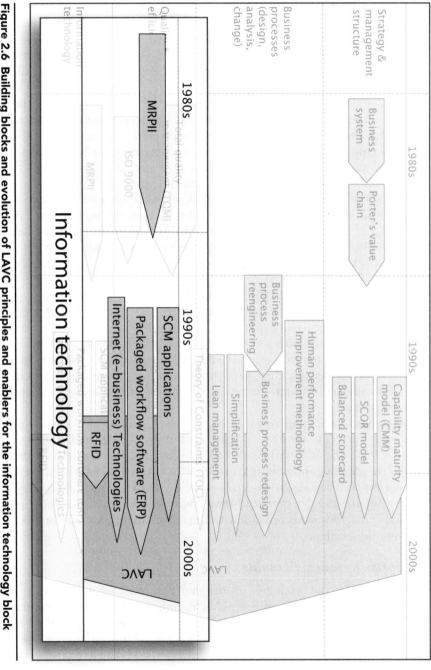

Figure 2.6 Building blocks and evolution of LAVC principles and enablers for the information technology block

and a distribution plan and continues on to develop a master production plan, which enables purchase order generation to suppliers after exploding the BOM. It factors the inventory you have on hand, subtracts it from the demand, and then figures out what you need to produce or purchase, generally on a weekly basis.

The material planning function of MRPII is done by a material requirement planning (MRP) module in enterprise resource planning (ERP). The calculation logic starts with demand (forecast and actual orders) for finished products and the required delivery date. This demand (gross requirements) is distributed among the time buckets (daily or weekly) based on the required date. Then, MRP nets out gross requirements for finished products from on-hand inventory and scheduled shop orders within the specific time period. This generates the "net requirements" for finished products in each time period. The next step involves exploding the BOM down to the components. MRP then nets out components already in stock or on open purchase order to come up with the net requirements. Based on the net requirements, MRP will generate purchase orders for purchase's parts and production (shop) orders for the subassembly parts and finished products considering standard purchase or production lead time. Chapter 4 discusses MRPII in more detail.

The major problem with MRPII is that the constraint calculation is sequential. It calculates first the material needs, and then it calculates the capacity needs. There is limited intelligence to looking at all supply chain constraints simultaneously and coming up with a feasible plan in a timely fashion. MRPII does not have the capability to promise a customer delivery date based on the current supply chain picture because there is no visibility into supply availability or supplier activity; as a result firms have to retain enough inventories on hand to keep their delivery promises.

With today's competitive pressures that are forcing manufacturers to compress lead times, cut inventory, increase asset utilization, and reduce costs, MRPII planning logic (including MRP calculation logic) has became almost outdated except in certain environments. Companies who have relied on MRPII are looking for help and an alternative that can (1) consider finite production capacity, material constraints, and dynamic lead-time constraints simultaneously; (2) perform backward and forward propagation to the requirements; and (3) link customer orders to shop orders.

Enterprise Resource Planning

In the mid 1990s, the vendors of off-the-shelf enterprise resource planning (ERP) software applications such as SAP, Oracle, and others started to organize their application modules so that they can be linked together to represent a business process. ERP is considered to be the backbone of a business information system and system of records for different types of enterprise data like financial records.

An ERP application contains both financial and operational modules like MRPII. Therefore, ERP is the hub to which all other applications logically integrate.

ERP worked best for processes that were well understood and common between companies and industries like accounting, inventory, and human resources processes. The implementation approach of ERP works backward, since you begin with the software application, and then see how the as-is process must be changed to accommodate the new application interfaces (i.e., the process follows technology). This approach is best used in low value-adding processes or support processes, since there is no harm from a competitive advantage standpoint to have these processes very similar to those of the competition. The problem comes when companies try to tailor the ERP applications to better fit the way a company does business, because it's difficult to modify the internal workings of ERP applications once they are installed. Moreover, the maintenance costs will rise in the future, and when new versions of the ERP application are released, a full-blown implementation effort is needed to match the previous modifications a company made or customized. In this case, the value of buying an off-the shelf software application diminishes rapidly.

Customization or configuration is needed only when this functionality will enable a certain subprocess or activity that will add value to the overall process and afford a competitive advantage. In this case, technology has to follow the best-practice process. Also, technology should be used to enable the to-be process and not the as-is process (improve before automate).

Since the Internet emergence in the late 1990s, ERP vendors have experienced major problems integrating ERP applications to Internet (e-business) applications since most ERP applications were designed to be self-contained systems lined to a proprietary database management system. The ERP applications were not prepared to support distributed data management. The good news is that in the past few years most ERP vendors have released a new generation of applications which are designed to communicate via the Internet. The bad news is that integration complexity and effort has surfaced and added a new type of issue that vendors and firms who are implementing need to face and address. Service-oriented architecture (SOA) will be the next silver bullet to solve the integration complexity.

SOA provides flexible technology architecture that cannot only enable current business processes, but also ensures that processes can change as rapidly as the business changes. It also allows a high level of visibility and collaboration across domestic and international partners.

One big lesson learned from the companies who implemented or attempted to implement an ERP application was that ERP is not "the solution;" it is only the enabler to improve business processes. Therefore, business managers and not IT managers must guide the transition. ERP applications must be implemented as part of the overall business transformation effort, not as an independent activity, especially if the transformation is for value-added processes.

Supply Chain Management Applications

Decision support supply chain management (SCM) applications are based on advanced planning and scheduling (APS) logic, which was a major breakthrough after ERP. APS emerged in the early 1990s, and is constraint-based planning. The difference between SCM applications and ERP is that ERP gives you a picture of what has already happened in your value chain, while SCM is a forward-looking system (proactive, not reactive). Hence, traditional ERP notifies of problems after the fact when not many options are available. APS on the other hand notifies of the problem ahead of time so that necessary proactive actions can be taken to resolve it.

Another advantage of APS over ERP (MRPII module) is the speed of calculation. It runs more than 10 times faster than traditional MRPII.

e-Business Applications

E-Business can be defined as the adoption of the Internet to enable real-time value chain collaboration and integration of planning and execution of the front-end and back-end processes and systems. The e-business technologies available through the Internet, combined with ongoing advances in APS software development, have given value chains an enormous boost in visibility and maximizing business agility.

This started with simple workflows between an organization and consumers as business-to-consumer workflows. This was followed by business-to-business workflows that supported connectivity between various internal and external users, and provided the ability to extend workflows beyond an organization into the realm of suppliers and buyers. Therefore, e-business applications are a major enabler for supplier relationship management (SRM) and customer relationship management (CRM) processes.

Radio Frequency Identification

Radio Frequency Identification (RFID) is an automatic identification technology that leverages radio frequency to transmit the identity of an object containing the radio frequency transmitter. Unlike bar codes, where scans have to be done manually, the transmission within an RFID system allows capturing of identification data without a manual scan; what is required is a "reader" that recognizes the radio transmission. Several logistics companies started to leverage RFID with global positioning systems (GPSs) to provide real-time visibility to the package anywhere in the world.

It is very important to note that the identification technologies are enablers of processes and a significant value add for businesses. By themselves, they add no value to the business since they are merely pieces of paper (labels, bar codes) or microchips (RFID). The turning point for RFID came in 1999 when UCC, Gillette, and Proctor & Gamble established an Auto-ID Center (AIC) at the Massachusetts Institute of Technology with the intent of developing low cost (5 U.S. cents) RFID "tags" to be utilized in supply chains. Within the next few years the AIC was supported by over 100 private corporations (including Wal-Mart, Kimberly Clark, Unilever, Tesco), the U.S. Department of Defense, and RFID vendors. Executives in these organizations saw huge potential impact in value chain visibility since RFID technology enabled them to know the exact location of every item in the value chain on demand. AIC developed the electronic product code numbering scheme complementing the universal product code.

To make use of the massive amount of data that RFID captures and transmits effectively, these data should be integrated into e-business applications to filter and extract information from the data. In addition, content (knowledge) management systems should be used to store, manage, and retrieve the massive amount of distributed data.

Summary

If firms are to survive and compete in today's dynamic business environment, they must focus not only on how to produce or sell innovative products but also on LAVC principles and enablers.

LAVC principles and enablers (mentioned in Chapter 1) are being driven by the concepts, methodologies, and applications in the four building blocks (dimensions); best-practice business processes; new technologies; traditional managerial concerns for efficiency and productivity, and the urgent need to maintain a competitive advantage.

In addition, implementing any LAVC process should follow a holistic approach that integrates the impact on strategy, people, management, processes, and enabling technologies. That is the only way to ensure that the transformation is effective.

The first building block, strategy and organizational structure, focuses on the strategy and people aspects (change management). Effective change management is essential in any process transformation since its people will be following the new process and learning how to use the new technology to capture the benefits of the improved process. This change management becomes even more challenging in the context of the entire value chain. For example, buyers are trying to convince the users in the supplier's organization to start using a new process for supply replenishment and leveraging a new web portal for order collaboration instead of a traditional phone call.

In the second building block, business processes, there are several process improvement methodologies. An organization should be open to using any of the methodologies or a hybrid of methodologies, regardless of its name, as long as it helps in the continuous improvement efforts (LAVC principle 4).

The third building block, quality methodologies, addresses the traditional managerial concerns for quality and efficiency, which is the foundation for any value chain.

The information technology building block for LAVC processes should be dynamic, fluid, and easily configurable to support business changes and a continuous improvement principle. The traditional IT rigid thinking of keeping changes to the production system to a minimum (only to fix bugs) to ensure stability will not work in an LAVC environment. A fresh way of thinking and a new mindset are needed. Continuous process improvements that require changes to the enabled technology should be supported. Also, companies should be careful when selecting the software application by not getting into the trap of buying software just because the particular software is considered the "next big thing" or has the "next killer feature." Software should be selected by looking at what the business needs first; otherwise it will only add another layer of waste.

LAVC MATURITY LEVELS

Before discussing how the LAVC concept, principles, and enablers can address the pain points discussed in the Chapter 1, let's first discuss the different maturity levels of lean and agile as shown in Figure 2.7.

There are four levels of lean and agile as shown in Figure 2.7. The higher you go in the pyramid, the more impact these levels have on the success of the or-

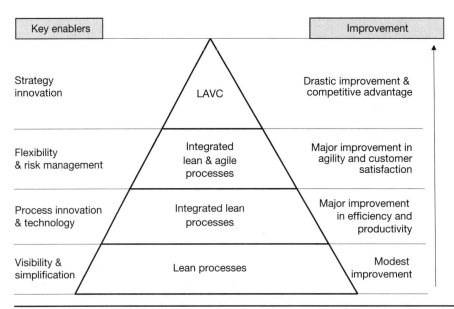

Figure 2.7 Lean and agile maturity levels

ganization and business agility. It's important to mention that achieving higher levels depends on mastering lower levels.

If a firm begins to achieve a series of successes for a certain process or value chain (e.g., by a continuous improvement initiative, etc.), and then suddenly feels like it has run its course, that is, the firm is achieving little success for the amount of time and effort (in some instances, performance even starts to decline again after reaching its peak), this is the time for the firm to try for the next level of LAVC maturity by leveraging the enablers of that level.

Level 1: Lean Processes

In this level, using "visibility" enablers, the following can be established: (1) sharing data across different participants of the supply chain; and (2) presenting the needed information extracted from data to all participants, depending on their roles, online and on a real-time basis. Some examples of data include inventory picture, capacity plans, promotion plans, and delivery schedules. At this level there is elimination of waste in every process, and disconnects between processes are removed using cross-organizational collaboration and simplification (enabler 2 from chapter 1).

It is crucial to start continuous simplification before introducing new technology (which is in level 2) to achieve a significant improvement. Also, automation before process improvement tends to prevent resolving the root cause of the poor performance, and might instead increase the complexity of an already faulty process.

Level 2: Integrated Lean Processes

Integrated lean processes means bridging different groups, functions, and even organizations, either formally or informally, to work jointly and sometimes concurrently on lean objectives; thus enabling technology best-practice processes and leveraging process innovation.

In this level, streamlining and automation of activities between value chain participants is accomplished. For example, streamlining the collaboration on new product specifications between engineers in the buying organization and suppliers to increase productivity and achieve quicker time to market.

This level provides a process-centric view coordinating different business subprocesses while enabling event management. For example, it supports event-triggered planning and replanning. This level blends information gathered from those using collaboration in level 1 and multiple transactions and planning systems to create and communicate synchronized plans and one common view of the value chain. Therefore, in this level, a company can plan based on real-time execution data, and execute based on an up-to-date plan. It also provides feedback on KPIs to executives, managers, and users.

The automation should be done after improving the as-is process by eliminating nonvalue-added activities, simplifying and streamlining processes, and removing barriers (disconnects) between processes, systems, or functions. This means the automation should be done for the redesigned to-be process, and the technology software needs to be configured to follow and support the process to maintain the competitive advantage. No matter how advanced and capable the technology is, without realigning the organization, streamlining processes, and identifying the metrics that are critical to meeting business goals, firms will fail to realize the benefits and capabilities inherent in today's software technology.

On the other hand, automating noncore competency processes can be done using out of the box workflows provided by software companies since there is little value in tailoring or customizing the software to fit the process. In addition, managing noncore competency processes can be outsourced to a third party for cost and service purposes.

Level 3: Integrated Lean and Agile Processes

This level allows companies to respond quickly, uniformly, and effectively to unplanned supply and demand events that may disrupt information and material flow, leveraging flexibility and risk management enablers. In this level, agility is required in every process. For example, lean and agile demand fulfillment should not be pursued independently from other processes. Although a technology enabler is needed in this level and even in the next one, the technology infrastructure should have been implemented in the previous level in a way that can be leveraged in the future.

In an integrated lean and agile process, companies take a global view by aggregating demand across the global business, evaluating total supply needs, and examining the best trade-off opportunities, instead of building a series of regional value chains that serve each of the manufacturing locations of a global firm. This will allow the firm to make intelligent allocation decisions that can maximize the volume of the highest-margin products, meet critical, regional selling season deadlines, and satisfy the needs of key customers. At the same time, when material shortages occur at one facility, they can reassign materials from other locations or reroute inbound material from the source in order to capture the greatest return across the entire value chain.

For many firms, the ability to see and balance the global demand and supply picture requires process and organizational changes. The new global perspective enables firms to more effectively manage demand and supply uncertainty, which will result in agile value chains.

A localized assortment strategy is one example of providing flexibility for local stores, and is also a very effective way to improve sales and margin performance. This is achieved by enabling merchandising decisions that attract and retain local high-value customers, recognizing that these customers come from heterogeneous groups and their preferences could vary by product, place, and time.

One example of "localized assortment" strategy is from Wal-Mart, where a "Store of the Community" initiative was developed in 2006 to meet the shopping needs of local customers, with stores specifically tailored to reflect the demographic makeup and customer preferences of their respective communities. Another example is Kroger (Signature), which was about to open near our home eight years back. My wife received a survey asking us to provide a wish list of grocery store items and she provided that list to the store. To her surprise, most of the items on her list made it to the shelf.

Level 4: LAVC

Typically, each value chain member (buyer, supplier, carrier, third-party logistics, contract manufacturer, etc.) often operates independently and only responds to immediate requirements. But in this level, value chain members (internal and external) share needed information on real-time bases, and react quickly and efficiently to changes in demand, material shortages, transportation delays, and supplier inability to replenish. This organizational culture would permeate multiple tiers of suppliers and not only the buyer with tier 1 (direct) suppliers.

Firms that build collaboration processes with their partners (suppliers, customers, carriers, etc.) have achieved a certain level of maturity (level 2 or 3). Until they take the next step of driving the collaboration into internal business processes to achieve a high degree of efficiency and agility, they will not be able to achieve level 4 of maturity. This is consistent with the fifth LAVC principle, close the loop between planning and execution, that we introduced in chapter 1.

In this level, exceptions are prioritized so that the most important value chain disruptions are dealt with in the quickest and most optimal manner. This provides the value chain partners with the ability to respond to problems in real time to minimize the impact of disruptions on the value chain leading to cost-effective, speedy, reliable, and almost error free value chain activities. The pursuit of LAVCs is a never-ending journey and not an objective by itself.

Once firms master the first three levels, they should start to think of adopting new strategies and models for conducting business and seek not only incremental improvements, but drastic ones that go across partners in the value chain. They might seek to reengineer their processes to leverage the most out of LAVC enablers. Firms might start to define new processes seeking new business opportunities or trying to penetrate new markets and customer segments that were neither apparent nor possible prior to achieving lean and agile processes. Firms can seek the next generation business models to achieve competitive advantage and significant benefits. One example is what Dell Computer did in the last decade when they adopted a build-to-order strategy and provided flexible configuration capability for customers online. Mass customization and online retailing are other examples.

Strategy innovation becomes the next challenge for these companies at level 3 or 4. They look to further differentiate themselves from the competition through significantly improved business processes and technology. Pushing to move toward a better business model becomes a norm and part of the organizational DNA.

For example, by taking a more collaborative view of the value chain between buyers and suppliers, demand and supply uncertainty that plagues the worldwide marketplace can be managed and controlled. This requires a mindset shift where buyers redefine their relationships with suppliers in order to make them true partners.

At this level of maturity, suppliers and buyer create a more open and honest relationship where everyone acknowledges demand variations, and shares risks and rewards among both firms. A buyer has to make demand uncertainty more explicit, and suppliers have to make their actual capacity more explicit. One example is from the automotive industry where a buyer can assign a tiered cost structure to capacity usage at supplier facilities, agree on specific cost terms for the use or nonuse of this capacity, and might even pay in advance to reserve capacity. In return, suppliers can provide additional upside volumes without the usual price premium, or agree to incur penalties if they fail to deliver the promised volumes.

For example, demand can be partitioned into three tiers: 80 percent confidence, 50 percent confidence, and 30 percent confidence. As both organizations progress through the forecasting horizon, uncertainty will shrink and confidence will increase. This creates a buyer-supplier relationship based on informed confidence, where uncertainty is visible, and so are the costs and consequences of missed deadlines. This type of approach is especially valuable when supply capacity elasticity is low and dependency is high—for instance, when a buyer relies upon a second-tier supplier for a critical component required in the late stages of product assembly.[5]

On the other hand, the following behavior cannot be sustained in today's market: Buyers know that their materials forecasts are somewhat inaccurate, they have asked suppliers to commit to them anyway, and then adjust upward or downward as the true demand level reveals itself. In return, suppliers have responded to partially accurate, overestimated buyer's forecast by making unrealistic delivery promises that they could never fulfill.

The change management challenges associated with this level of maturity cannot be underestimated due to the tight integration (data, processes, users, systems, etc.) between the partners. Even after achieving this level of maturity and several improvement initiatives, maintaining and sustaining this level requires a strong change management team, a high-quality training program, and a consistent set of metrics.

The maturity model we presented in Figure 2.7 can be applied to the entire organization or one process in an organization. It's normal to find a process in a certain organization at level 1 of maturity and another process in the same organization at level 4.

Aberdeen Group talks about a new concept similar to level 4 of maturity called *multi-enterprise supply chains.* Nari Viswanathan, principal analyst for Aberdeen's SCM practice, reports that "In today's global economy, businesses are finding an increasing need for multi-enterprise supply chains, or business networks, to be focused on process integration and collaboration. This is due to a variety of business pressures such as rising costs, global competition, and the need for reduced cycle times." Process integration is defined as bi-directional electronic connectivity and data transfer, while process collaboration is an advanced stage of process integration—it's about business processes that span the collaborating enterprises.[6]

Aberdeen's benchmark report applies the multi-enterprise supply chain concept to two processes: (1) order-to-cash (customer collaboration), and (2) purchase-to-pay (supplier collaboration).

Maturity Levels Impact on Value Chain Processes

Tables 2.1, 2.2, and 2.3 summarize how the four LAVC maturity levels can address the challenges of SCM, SRM, and CRM processes and achieve significant benefits.

These tables show the operational and financial gains of climbing from one level to the next among the LAVC maturity levels. The operational benefits can be grouped under inventory reductions, order cycle-time or lead-time reductions, and increases in forecast accuracy, productivity, supplier performance improvements, and customer service levels (percent perfect order or fill rate). The financial benefits are translated from the operational improvements and can be grouped as follows:

- Cost reduction due to cost savings. The tight integration of value chain processes reduces the effort and time needed to exchange transactions and allows efficient procurement, which helps the purchasing staff to focus more on strategic activities, such as strengthening supplier relationships, than managing day-to-day transactions.
- Revenue growth and margin increase due to increased customer satisfaction by delivering on every promise, responding quickly to customer needs, and the ability to penetrate new markets profitably. This would be translated into stronger shareholder value.
- Better asset utilization by replacing inventory with real-time visibility, which would reduce cash-to-cash cycle time.

Table 2.1 The impact of LAVC maturity levels on SRM processes

		SRM business processes		
	Strategic sourcing	**Product design**	**Procurement**	**Benefits**
Lean processes	• Sharing approved vendor list with design and purchasing departments • Consolidation of enterprise spend/demand across separate systems	• Streamlining product design subprocesses • Real-time visibility on engineering change requests	• Sharing supplier and shipment information, real-time visibility, alerts, and tracking	• Reducing part inventory obsoleteness • Improving inventory turns • Reducing safety stock • Reducing expedition cost • Improving quality
Integrated lean processes	• Consider supplier performance during sourcing decisions • Supplier scorecard and KPIs	• Shared design workbench • Tightly integrated to product data management and approved vendor list • Strong control of budget and program	• Automated procurement subprocesses, bid analysis, and resolution workflow • Focusing only on exceptions rather on every transaction	• Reducing design rework • Reducing process cycle time • Improving productivity
Integrated lean and agile processes	• Rationalize supplier base • Ability of suppliers to adjust capacity quickly	• A single user interface for design, sourcing, and procurement with flexible and configurable workflows	• Synchronized replenishment, supporting different replenishment types, and matching execution documents like purchase orders, advanced shipment notices, and invoices • Corrective action playbook • Flexible material handling and transportation system • Optimize multiple transportation trade-offs	• Increasing *reuse* of existing parts in the design • Improving on-time delivery

LAVC maturity levels

LAVC maturity levels	LAVC			
	• Analyzing supplier and value chain performance (slice and dice by site, commodity, time, supplier, and KPIs) • Establishing replenishment strategy • Incentive system for suppliers for collaborative problem solving and improving performance	• Design collaboration with key suppliers early in the design phase	• Optimizing carrier type selection	• Reducing development cost • Improving time to market • Reducing part/raw material cost

Table 2.2 The impact of LAVC maturity levels on SCM processes

		SCM business processes		Benefits
	Supply chain network design	**Sales and operations planning**	**Demand fulfillment**	
Lean processes	• Providing an aggregated view on the supply chain performance and strategic information	• Real-time visibility to unexpected events in the supply chain and audit trail data • Streamlining sales and operations planning process • Balancing supply and cemand	• Real-time supply chain visibility for the order delivery life cycle • Reducing setup time and improving layout pull systems • High inventory record accuracy	• Reducing uncertainty and safety stock • Early issue detection • Accuracy
Integrated lean processes	• Consistent process with friendly user interface	• Unified demand plan across different departments • Improving forecasting process • Accountability system	• Exception workflow resolution for demand changes and fulfillment delays • Transportation, tracking, and warehouse systems	• Increasing efficiency • Fast response • Speed • Improving forecast accuracy
Integrated lean and agile processes	• Adding flexibility and responsiveness in addition to cost to the optimization business function • Integration with strategic sourcing to reduce supplier base	• Synchronized marketing, sales, production, and procurement plans • Playbook scenarios to be ready for fluctuating demand or supply	• Promising what value chain can deliver by considering supply chain constraints and sales channels allocations, and delivering on every promise	• Flexibility • Penetrating new markets
LAVC	• Including suppliers and retail locations for optimal end-to-end value chain network design	• Considering supplier capacity and customer forecast/allocation in the unified plan	• Postponement • Build/deliver to order	• Customer satisfaction

LAVC maturity levels

Table 2.3 The impact of LAVC maturity levels on CRM processes

	CRM business processes			
LAVC maturity levels	**Marketing management**	**Selling management**	**Customer service management**	**Benefits**
Lean processes	• Capturing feedback from customers • Capturing log records every visit of a user in the web servers' log file, including pages visited, duration of visit, and whether there was a purchase	• Visibility to sales history and buying trends • Customer-oriented view • Streamlining quotation processing	• Providing service order status • Service order logging and streamlining billing of services	• Better order tracking • Increasing customer satisfaction • Reducing inventory
Integrated lean processes	• Real-time profiling that tracks the user click stream; allows the analysis of customer behavior and makes instantaneous adjustments to site promotional offers and web pages • Demand collaboration with customers	• Product configuration • Providing up-sell, cross-sell product recommendations and product bundles	• Detecting and highlighting exceptions • Warranty check and service order processing	• Improving response time • Improving productivity • Accurate promise date
Integrated lean and agile processes	• Considering the supply chain constraints while executing the marketing campaigns • Providing customer profiling and segmentation	• Flexible pricing models for markdown/rebates • Online flexible configuration and real-time promise date	• Data mining to service logs to improve service part forecast accuracy	• Increasing revenues and profit • Creating new market/distribution channels • Better prediction of customer demand
LAVC	• Providing a customized mix of products and service offerings to match customer needs effectively	• Supporting different channels for order capturing (web-based, call center, electronic data interchange, phone, e-mail, or personnel meeting)	• Dealing with products and services as one package during selling	• Long-term relationship and trust with the customer • Gaining competitive advantage

CLOSING REMARKS AND FUTURE TRENDS

During these seemingly turbulent economic times, firms cannot afford to adapt old ways of doing business to a world that has been completely transformed. There is no doubt that globalization and this recession represent significant challenges for even the best-managed businesses. A new world requires a new perspective and strategies to achieve excellence.

A sourcing to low-cost countries strategy is proven not to be very effective in a more customer-oriented market. Our expectations are that firms will look for not only the buying price, but they will start to look for the total landed cost and customer service in a balanced way.

It is no longer enough to build a lean environment. Firms must build both a lean and agile environment, one that encourages the principles of waste elimination, while the other enables the flexibility at every level to deal with the unavoidable surprises that disrupt even the most-robust value chains.

LAVC principles and enablers present huge opportunities that are not being tapped yet by many companies. Leveraging them effectively is key to gaining competitive advantage, streamlining processes, slashing waste, and eventually achieving business agility, which is needed in this new age of globalization and intensive competition. It can be thought of in equation form like the following: Lean + Agile = Operational Excellence + Asset Reduction + Cost Savings + Responsiveness + Reliability + Flexibility.

More and more companies have begun to realize that gaining a competitive advantage is no longer feasible only by managing their own firms. They need to get involved in the management of all upstream companies that are responsible for the supply, as well as the downstream network that is responsible for delivery and the after-sales market. The challenge for companies in the next decade is the synchronization across supply chain processes, from product design to customer service management, in order to be more cost effective, responsive, and flexible to customer needs. Customer preferences and product variations will continue to increase exponentially, while customer service levels are getting tighter.

These companies want to become more demand- and value-driven, emphasizing the delivery of value, growth, and profitability in cost-to-serve models. They are moving away from the emphasis on the inside to the emphasis on the outside, and looking at their capabilities across functions and value chains.

Therefore, in the next few years, we will witness the explosion of LAVC principles as firms start redefining their value chain processes to cut cost and waste, reduce lead time significantly, and be agile. The main objective is to ensure that the right amount of the right material and products is available at the right time, at the right place, and at the right cost to meet promises and sustain profitability in today's turbulent economy.

In addition, many fast-growing areas like the Asia Pacific and Middle East have not historically placed an emphasis on end-to-end SCM. Concepts that have been widely embraced in more mature markets like North America—such as being process-oriented across functions and having visibility throughout the end-to-end value chain—have not been broadly introduced in these regions. Also, supply chain technology solutions may exist in some facilities that serve as suppliers to Western businesses, but the majority of firms have not experienced the full promise of these application. Due to globalization, the above trend will change and more and more firms will be adopting core value chain philosophies and using the next generation technologies.

Many companies are struggling with implementing a process and technology upgrade to improve SRM, SCM, and CRM superprocesses. They fall short of achieving the promised value or ROI. In addition, companies are looking for guidelines and strategies for ongoing operational management and support after the go-live, which includes rolling the implementation out to more customers, suppliers, and new business units. A framework in Part III is proposed to address these challenges and provide best-practice guidelines to implement LAVC program transformation successfully.

REFERENCES

1. Porter, M. E. 1985. *Competitive Advantage: Creating and Sustaining Superior Performance*. New York: Simon & Schuster.
2. Harmon, P. 2003. *Business Process Change: A Manager's Guide to Improving, Redesigning, and Automating Processes*. San Francisco: Morgan Kaufmann Publishing.
3. Kaplan, R. S., and D. P. Norton. 1996. *The Balanced Scorecard: Translating Strategy into Action*. USA: Harvard College.
4. Rummler, G. A., and A. P. Brache. 1995. *Improving Performance: How to Manage the White Space in the Organization Chart*. San Francisco: Jossey-Bass.
5. Anson, R. (2008). Overcoming the new demand uncertainty. *Supply Chain Leader*, no. 5 (April): 24–26.
6. Viswanathan, N. (August 2008). Process collaboration in Multi-enterprise supply chains, 1–27. Boston: Aberdeen Group.

Part II: Best-Practice Processes

Chapter 3: Supplier Relationship Management
    Superprocess

Chapter 4: Supply Chain Management Superprocess

Chapter 5: Customer Relationship Management
    Superprocess

Chapter 6: Lean and Agile Value Chain Technology
    Applications and Trends

3

SUPPLIER RELATIONSHIP MANAGEMENT SUPERPROCESS

INTRODUCTION

The APICS Dictionary defines supplier relationship management (SRM) as "A comprehensive approach to managing an enterprise's interactions with the organizations that supply the goods and services the enterprise uses. The goal of SRM is to streamline and make more effective the processes between an enterprise and its suppliers." SRM is the superprocess of supporting supplier partnership in the value chain, and coordinating processes across product development, sourcing, purchasing, and supply coordination within a company and across companies.

SRM combines three value chain processes together: strategic sourcing, product design, and procurement (Figure 3.1). Strategic sourcing involves having a mutually beneficial symbiotic relationship by choosing the right suppliers so as to reduce the total cost and not just the price. Total cost of product means not only the least price supplier, but the least total cost which includes quality, reliability, and inventory, transportation, and customer service costs. To avoid high "supplier switching" costs only the best suppliers must be selected and, once selected, the relationship with the suppliers should be based on partnership rather than exploitation. Forging strategic relationships with suppliers will help leverage global spend and reduce the total cost of product acquisition.

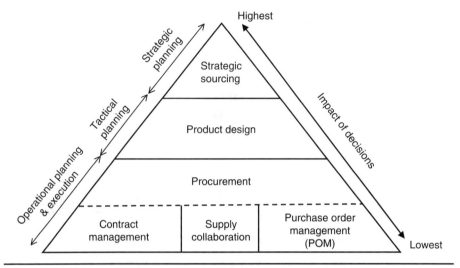

Figure 3.1 SRM pyramid

The next major process in the SRM superprocess is to have collaborative product design, which should use an approved vendor list and approved parts list during the design phase itself and limit the use of new parts. This will help reduce the time to market, ensure product quality, and increase customer satisfaction, which will all lead to ensuring profitable lifetime customers.

The third major process involves procurement. Procurement is the process of planning and executing the sourcing strategies. It includes contract management (request for purchase [RFP], request for quote [RFQ], auctions, bid analysis, contract processing, contract compliance), supply collaboration and purchase order management (POM).

There are interrelationships between the SRM, supply chain management (SCM), and customer relationship management (CRM) superprocesses and a seamless interaction is necessary. CRM's marketing management process drives what customers want as a finished product, which is then translated into component specifications by the product design process in SRM. These component specifications, bill of materials, and routings are then shared between the product design process in SRM and the master planning subprocess in SCM. Similarly, the strategic sourcing process in SRM provides the supply chain network design subprocess in SCM with a visibility into supplier contracts, alternate suppliers, and supplier pricing. The procurement process within SRM provides visibility into the material and capacity constraints of suppliers to the master planning subprocess in SCM. SCM also provides SRM with the purchasing requirements.

NORTH-SOUTH AND EAST-WEST COLLABORATION

Consumer behavior is changing and customers are increasingly demanding new products; which has led to shrinkage in the product life cycle. Internet technology has made it easier for customers to do comparison shopping for the lowest price. Companies that cannot keep pace with the customer's needs by having new product launches and offering customers value for money run the risk of losing market share and revenue. Paper-thin margins, shrinking product life cycles, and mass customization require not only internal collaboration between sourcing, product development, and manufacturing, but also external collaboration with the suppliers and visibility into the material, time, and capacity constraints. When unexpected events occur, actions can be taken to balance supply and demand. Sharing of information between departments and with suppliers is key to increasing visibility and reducing risk and variability. Collaboration is a two-way street, not only should the buyer have visibility into supplier constraints, but the suppliers also need to have visibility into demand changes at the buyers' end. The buyer should also have visibility into any unexpected events at the suppliers' end that might have an impact on the supplier delivery date. Last minute order modifications should be avoided, but when they occur they should be communicated to the supplier as soon as possible to allow for enough time to react.

Merely sharing data is not enough. Collaboration involves sharing the "right information" in both directions on a real-time basis. For example, best-in-class (BIC) companies like Toyota and Honda share only the relevant information in a structured fashion with their suppliers, since they believe that inundating the supplier with too much information will do more harm than good and goes against lean and agile value chain (LAVC) principle 3 (eliminate waste and reduce nonvalue-added activities). (Note: Throughout this chapter, you will see mentions of LAVC principles and enablers which are discussed in detail in chapter 1 and should be considered as you progress through this book.) Even meetings with the suppliers have set agendas, precise times, and stringent formats.[1]

There needs to be collaboration between the buyer and the supplier that is not only north-south collaboration at the strategic long-term (strategic sourcing), tactical medium-term (product design), and operational short-term (procurement) level, but also east-west collaboration between the different cross-functional entities including sourcing, purchasing, design, and production.

For north-south and east-west collaboration to work, it is imperative that the buyer and the supplier speak a common language. By having a supplier who can react quickly to any sudden demand changes, the organization minimizes the risk of not being responsive enough and losing market share. Such a relationship can only be cultivated if every member profits from the business and gains are distributed among the different stakeholders. Firms have been known to reduce their inventory carrying costs by shifting the inventory to suppliers with less leverage, which violates principle 2 (create win-win and a trusted environment for all stakeholders). Also, asking suppliers to build inventory to compensate for a buyer's forecast error does not address the root cause of the problem.

BIC companies try and maximize their profits, but not at the suppliers' expense. As Taiichi Ohno, who created the Toyota Production System, once said, "Achievement of business performance by the parent company through bullying suppliers is totally alien to the spirit of the Toyota Production System."[2]

Supply uncertainty and risk should be tackled not by carrying excess inventories, but with visibility (LAVC enabler 1: visibility), contingency planning, risk-sharing contracts (enabler 5: risk management), supplier certification, and coordination. Visibility should not only be limited to the suppliers, but also the supplier's suppliers since it could impact the potential supply flow.

Texas Instruments (TI) avionics group, facing budget cuts and foreign competition, realized that to be competitive they needed to have a relationship based on collaboration rather than exploitation. TI decided to train their suppliers in statistical process control so that the suppliers could monitor their own products, rather than having TI perform testing and quality assurance. TI also rewarded the suppliers (enabler 6: process innovation of sharing rewards) who participated by giving them a greater share of TI's business. In addition, since suppliers rarely get an opportunity to see their products in action, TI had the suppliers meet with the flight and ground crews who used their gear.[3]

An LAVC SRM superprocess eliminates paperwork, streamlines shipment and payments, reduces the cycle time of finding and acquiring suppliers, easily monitors contract terms, leverages spend consolidation by supplier and part rationalization, increases supplier awareness during design and production phases, and automates the procurement process.

SRM CHALLENGES

1. Move from vertical integration to lateral integration:

In the 21st century, corporations have increasingly turned toward lateral integration instead of pure vertical integration, that is, outsource those aspects of the business which they didn't consider as their core competency. Laterally integrated companies focus on their core competencies and, hence, have to deal with multiple suppliers, contract manufacturers, distributors, and transportation providers. This generates additional communication, coordination, and visibility. As a result, the quality of communication has sharply decreased leading to lack of trust and overprotective behaviors, such as excess inventories, excess buffer capacities, and so forth. A fallout of lateral integration is that a single late delivery (machine breakdown) or a missing part from a supplier can create a snowball effect. For example, the production orders at the manufacturer will need to be rescheduled and pushed out to accommodate for a late delivery from the supplier. All the other raw materials that are already available will be sitting idle and incurring inventory carrying costs. Also, the change in the production schedule will trigger a corresponding change in the distribution plan and hence a change in the delivery promises to the customers, which might eventually result in customer dissatisfaction and even penalty costs.

2. Variability and complexity:

The factors that contribute to variability and complexity include intensified competition, shorter product life cycles, and diversity. SRM is a cross-functional superprocess that requires interaction between people who are diverse in their style of functioning, priorities, and attitudes which defy analytical quantification. This includes not only internal interaction between sourcing, product development, and manufacturing, which in most cases have their own local objectives and metrics, but also external interaction with the suppliers.

Another major factor leading to increasing variability and complexity is the effect of globalization and outsourcing. Globalization has led to "buy anywhere, make anywhere, and sell anywhere." However, outsourcing poses its own challenges; for example, suppliers have their own nomenclature, currency exchange rates, different units of measure, and so forth. Also, one has to take into account trade agreements like NAFTA and GATT before making sourcing decisions. Language barriers make sharing of information a challenge. Outsourcing has led to an increase in supply risk and supply lead times, and therefore an increase in inventory to compensate.

In addition, mass customization has led to an exponential increase in the number of parts, suppliers, and transactions. Because of overwhelming data, planners increasingly have to make decisions based on gut feeling rather than intelligent information.

Mergers and acquisitions have only added to the proliferation and explosion in the number of suppliers and parts. This has led to purchasing departments buying the same items from the same suppliers separately, even after a merger, leading to missed opportunities of negotiating based on cumulative volumes and economies of scale.

3. Lack of complete and consistent data:

SRM is a data-intensive superprocess that requires huge volumes of data pertaining to material masters, supplier masters, purchase order history, etc. Nowadays, it is not uncommon for companies to have terabytes of data pertaining to millions of SKUs and hundreds of suppliers and customers, which, to make things worse, are also constantly changing. Change is the only constant. Managing and maintaining this data can be an enormous challenge, especially if the data are not complete and consistent. For example, the same part could have different internal part numbers or there could be discrepancies regarding units of measure, currencies, supplier codes, and material codes. The same vendor could have different names—one abbreviated and the other complete—and so forth. All of these could lead to multiple contracts for the same part with the same supplier and missed opportunities to leverage economies of scale.

4. Disparate systems:

Organizations might not only have disparate sources of data from their different departments (purchasing, sourcing, engineering, R&D), but sometimes they might even have different systems within a particular department. Most companies don't have an answer to "How much do we spend? And on what?" The reason for this is that purchasing systems of the past didn't follow any specific standards, and each company, and sometimes each department, ended up developing its own home-grown standard. Even though companies implemented ERP systems, the systems were plagued with different releases of the software and different instances that again led to the development of data-silos or islands of information with limited visibility across the departments. This led to local optimal decisions based on local approved vendor lists, material masters, supplier information, and purchasing records, and violates principle 3. Because of disparate legacy and transaction systems for different divisions, companies had a hard time aggregating spend and negotiating contracts to leverage economies of scale. There was also a disconnect between the SRM systems and the SCM systems at a company. This resulted in the SCM systems not having visibility into the contracts, business agreements, and other constraints modeled in the SRM systems.

5. Nonstandard processes in evaluating supplier performance:

Supplier performance data in most companies are scattered across departments and different scorecards are used for different departments. Some evaluate suppliers based on cost, others based on cost and quality, and so forth. There is no common language between different departments and they tend to operate independently of each other to evaluate supplier performance, which leads to a lack of organizational negotiation power with the supplier. SRM initiatives are fragmented and local departmental objectives take precedence over corporate objectives, thus leading to reduced effectiveness. Business processes are not standardized throughout the organization and every department has their own way of getting things done. This leads to redundancy and duplication of effort and goes against principle 4 (institutionalize continuous improvement through standardization). The rewards are given to people with last minute heroics who put out fires, rather than to those who stick to the process.

Purchasing managers are often reluctant to forego the relationship they have built with their long-standing suppliers. From past experience they know that in the event of an unexpected occurrence, they can bank on their "long-standing old suppliers" for responsive delivery, or to go the extra mile—increase production to meet unexpected demand. The company-wide metrics on the other hand might only look at price and quality, might not have responsiveness as a metric, and might decide to do away with that supplier.

6. Lack of trust and conflict resolution:

In many companies, the R&D department is so guarded about new products that, forget the suppliers, even the purchasing department within the company doesn't have a clue until the product is launched. Companies fear that sharing too much information with their suppliers will harm their businesses. This leads to lack of usage of an approved parts list, substitutable parts, functionally similar parts, and volume discounts from existing suppliers. It also increases the time to market because the product development department didn't share the information with the supplier. For example, Sony suffered a serious setback in September 2006 when it announced that it would have to delay the launch of the PlayStation 3 console because of key component shortages (blue laser diodes). Sony said that it would be able to make only two million PS 3 consoles instead of its earlier announcement of four million. This resulted in the disappointment of thousands of children[4] and goes against principle 2, since Sony was so guarded about its much awaited PS 3 console that it didn't give its suppliers enough time to ramp up to the potential demand.

Sometimes organizations have expertise optimizing their own internal process, but little experience in how to extend it to suppliers. There are no clear guidelines for processes on how the supplier and buyer should work together to resolve conflict and manage a mutually beneficial relationship. For example, there is no agreement on how to handle conflict of interest when the buyer needs a product that is available at another competitive supplier, but not yet available with the partnering supplier. The buyers also lack the framework required to share the rewards with the suppliers.

7. Manual processes:

Because the manual RFQ process takes months, most purchasing departments don't even bother renegotiating the contracts, but instead renew them without extensive analysis or looking at supplier performance. Most companies have manual RFP/RFQ processes, manual contract management, and poor documentation on supplier performance, which leads to maverick buying and nonpreferred supplier spending. Most of the time is spent in fire fighting and execution rather than strategic initiatives like leveraging organizational buying volume, monitoring performance of suppliers, contract compliance monitoring, and procurement savings against targets. This violates principle 3.

STRATEGIC SOURCING

Strategic sourcing (Figure 3.2) is defined as the process of selecting the best sourcing strategy to reduce cost and risk, while at the same time maximizing flexibility. Strategic sourcing helps answer questions relating to whether the company should produce in-house or outsource to a supplier. What products should the company buy and from whom? What should be the price, quality, reliability, and so forth? The Aberdeen Group[5] benchmark report of more than 130 procurement and supply chain executives found that, on an average, only 35 percent of companies apply strategic sourcing principles compared to 82 percent for BIC companies who analyze spending and compliance on a quarterly or more frequent basis. As a result, BIC companies are able to achieve a greater percentage of average cost reductions per sourcing project, greater contract compliance, and smaller purchase price variance (%PPV)—the difference in price between the amount paid to the supplier and the standard cost of that item.

Companies such as Lockheed Martin have a Strategic Sourcing Group consisting of 52 employees with cross-functional experience, and their mission is "to be an integrated leading edge team that provides industry recognized supply chain intelligence and innovative sourcing strategies, while fully optimizing customer value." The group was effective in implementing supply base rationalization, increasing the frequency of negotiation, and using reverse auctions wherever possible.[6]

What to Outsource?

The first element of strategic sourcing is to decide what to outsource, that is, which products to make in-house and which to outsource to a supplier. Henry Ford is often considered the pioneer of vertical integration in which Ford owned the supply chain right from the most upstream raw materials (rubber plantations to supply raw material for tires, iron ore mines, and steel mills) to the most downstream dealerships to sell the cars to customers. One company was managing the entire supply chain from raw materials to manufacturing to distribution.

However, when U.S. manufacturers started losing excessive market share in the 1980s to their Japanese counterparts (Honda and Toyota), the Big Three decided to blindly emulate the Japanese *keiretsu* model—a cooperative, close relationship with a few networked suppliers that focuses on continuous improvement, reducing cost, and improving quality. U.S. companies realized the need to outsource those aspects of the business that they didn't consider as their core competency and decided to outsource design, engineering, and manufacturing to their specialized parts suppliers. The Big Three decided to establish strategic, long-term sourcing initiatives for complex subassemblies like steering columns, braking systems, etc., hoping to imitate their Japanese counterparts so as to realize the benefits of increased efficiencies, reduced costs, and waste.[7]

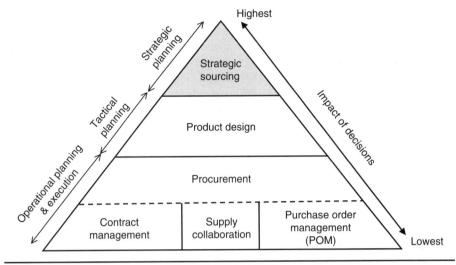

Figure 3.2 SRM pyramid (strategic sourcing)

However, they did not fundamentally alter the nature of their relationship with their suppliers and soon it was back to square one—price haggling over nickels and dimes. They found *keiretsu* to be inflexible because they were locked into buying from only a selected few suppliers, which did not give them enough bargaining power. When the outsourcing revolution began in 2001, The Big Three believed that the short-term benefit of low-cost suppliers in India and China far outweighed forming strategic long-term relationships with innovative suppliers.[1]

On the other hand, when Honda and Toyota started their manufacturing operations in North America, they began by giving the suppliers smaller orders and measuring their performance regarding cost, quality, delivery parameters, and so forth. When the supplier's performance was found to be satisfactory, the suppliers were awarded with larger long-term contracts. Honda and Toyota also believed in creating mutually beneficial partnerships with their suppliers (principle 2: create win-win and trusted environment for all stakeholders) rather than having a superior/subordinate relationship. For example, when Honda was looking into sourcing from Atlantic Tool and Die, Honda sent one of its middle managers to work with his counterparts at Atlantic Tool and Die for 12 months. This led to tremendous improvements on the shop floor at the supplier.[7]

Similarly, when 7-Eleven started to lose money and market share in the beginning of the 1990s, then CEO Jim Keyes realized that 7-Eleven's core competency was merchandising (pricing, promotion, placement). Prior to this, 7-Eleven owned the cows that produced the milk, made its own ice, candy, and distributed the gasoline. Hence, Keyes decided to "outsource everything not mission critical" (enabler 7: strategy innovation) and outsourced product development, packaging, logistics, and distribution without relinquishing control of its competitive differentiators—merchandising. For example, 7-Eleven worked with its supplier, Hershey, to develop an edible straw and in return Hershey gave 7-Eleven exclusive rights to sell the product for the first 90 days (principle 2: create win-win and trusted environment for all stakeholders). Thus, the decision on whether the company should outsource a particular product, process, or function depends on whether the product or process is proprietary, whether the capabilities are competitive differentiators, and whether the capabilities are easily imitable or not, i.e., a product or process which is not proprietary and common across organizations can be outsourced. Deciding on what to outsource to a supplier is only the first step in the strategic sourcing effort. Next comes selecting the right suppliers, negotiating contracts and measuring, monitoring, and rewarding supplier performance.[7]

Supplier Selection

The pressure to reduce costs is growing larger and larger, which is forcing companies to become lean and agile when it comes to supplier selection, rationalizing supplier base, aggregating spend globally across all buying entities, and enabling a pull system with the suppliers. Not just the companies, but their suppliers are also trying to become lean and agile to reduce price and control variability. The days when companies made their sourcing decisions based purely on price and quality alone are gone. The ability of suppliers to adjust capacity quickly (enabler 4: flexibility) and efficiently due to changing demand is increasingly being factored in for the sourcing decision of the buying firm. Also, the ability to consider supplier performance during sourcing decisions by design engineers or purchasing analysts is becoming increasingly important (enabler 6: process innovation).

In this era of short product life cycles and lightning-fast replenishment, many firms, like consumer goods manufacturers and retailers, cannot afford a single delivery delay or design mistake. Hence, when a company looks into strategic outsourcing, it should also look into supply reliability and supply risks (enabler 5: risk management). Suppliers must be able to deliver finished products on time and meet the highest standards for both quality and consumer protection, especially for all pharmaceuticals, food, beverages, electronics, and toys that need to meet stringent safety criteria.

In the retail industry, where fashion trends change constantly and technologies rapidly become obsolete, having supplier flexibility and responsiveness is key. Buyers are increasingly looking for "local" suppliers to cut the order-to-delivery cycle time so that the most current and popular assortments can be brought to market during the fashion season. Identifying a source close to the final consumer can dramatically cut transportation costs, foreign taxes, trade tariffs, and help the company capture the market. Many U.S. retailers are beginning to consider dual-sourcing strategies (enabler 7: strategy innovation) that create local, rapid response capabilities for the replenishment of hot-selling products, while still leveraging their Chinese trading partners to meet less time-sensitive production schedules. In addition to speed and agility, retailers must still consider the total landed cost (raw materials, labor, energy, transportation, taxes, currency exchange rates, and government regulations) of their private-label products when making the decision of sourcing.

When compared with traditional sourcing, strategic sourcing involves using a segmented strategy (enabler 7: strategy innovation) with suppliers rather than a broad-brushed approach, depending upon the product business value, risk, and complexity of the component design. This forges long-term strategic relationships with suppliers who provide products that are high value and high risk while maintaining a more traditional arm's length relationship with others. A simple Pareto analysis on supplier spending can reveal missed opportunities for strategic relationships. A product and service agreement can be established with suppliers who have been designated as critical to the organization's success.

Similarly, for maintenance, repair, operations (MRO) items and office supplies, price might be the criteria for selecting the supplier. MRO items are supplies consumed in the production process, but either they do not become part of the end product or they are not central to the firm's output. On the other hand, for items that are high value and high risk, quality, reliability, and responsiveness of the supplier might be the deciding factor.

To summarize, suppliers should not be selected on least cost alone, but other factors such as financial strength, total cost of ownership (product cost, transportation cost, inventory cost, duty, tax, administration overhead), supplier capabilities, current and future capacity, material and lead-time constraints, responsiveness, delivery lead times, variability of lead times (early, on time, late), delivery reliability (over order quantity, under order quantity), quality (rework, reject, scrap), profitability, current and future technology, and potential risks.

For assessing supplier risk, the company could use commercially available data from sources such as Dun & Bradstreet (D&B). The Supplier Evaluation Report from D&B provides a comprehensive supplier risk analysis based on detailed financial and operational information on a supplier's business. It contains information and analysis on over six million U.S. companies and can help assess the risk of doing business with a supplier.

Also, together with financial information, it is important that the differences in corporate culture, operating process, and business practices are considered, because unless the supplier and buyer entities share a common vision the relationship will not work.

However, care should be taken that there aren't too many unnecessary selection criteria, which can make the supplier selection process a cumbersome, laborious, and lengthy one, which would lead to an increase in nonvalue-added activities.

Managing Supplier Relationships

In her article entitled *Cross-Organizational Collaboration: From Dating to Tying the Knot*, Catherine Boivie presents an interesting analogy. She contends that managing relationships with suppliers is like a spectrum, with a pure transaction-based relationship on one side (dating) and a win-win strategic relationship on the other (marriage) (Figure 3.3). Early on in the dating relationship, organizations are opportunistic and operational focused, that is, the relationship is based purely on cost management (spot buying, reverse auctions). In a pure transactional relationship, cost minimization is the top priority. As time progresses both organizations start sharing information, contractual terms are negotiated based not only on price but also quality, delivery lead times, and so forth. Short- to medium-term contracts are established and the supplier systems and the organizations systems are interfaced and specific joint activities are undertaken (engagement). Even though there is independence, there is an overall commitment to expand the engagement relationship to the next level—the strategic alliance (marriage) where the relationship is more about long-term agreements (greater than a year) than short-term contracts. Finally, in the last stage (marriage) common skills are leveraged and there is a willingness to invest in shared infrastructure to support

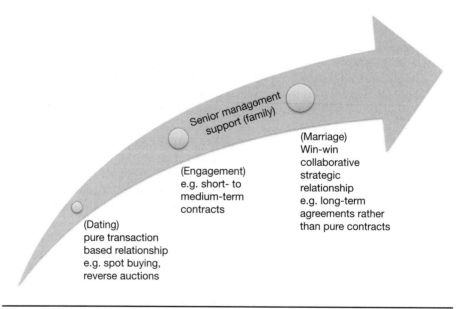

Figure 3.3   Managing supplier relationships

collaborative business processes by sharing business knowledge, people, and processes. There is also joint development of performance metrics. The suppliers are fully aware of the buyer's goals, and strategies are worked together to develop and implement campaigns. Though the independence of each organization is still respected, the cultures are blended and a win-win strategic relationship is established. During the process from engagement to marriage there will be romances, arguments, stresses, and strains, but trade-offs will need to be managed for the common good. It is imperative that the senior management (the family) plays a very important role in this transition from engagement to marriage. Unless there is top management support, it is very difficult to develop organization-wide, supplier base rationalization projects, product design collaboration, and a best-practice procurement process.[8] Even after marriage the supplier performance needs to be monitored and the relationship needs to be enhanced by having constant communication and collaboration (enabler 2: cross-organizational collaboration) in terms of reliability, flexibility, quality, and responsiveness. Also, moving from a transactional relationship to a marriage requires that the purchasing managers develop people skills in addition to bargaining and negotiation skills. The buyer and supplier should agree on the best and most effective and efficient method to communicate on routine and non-routine issues. There needs to be company-wide metrics that give weight not only to cost, but also responsiveness and reliability. Routine performance reviews should be conducted by a cross-functional team and performance against predefined metrics should be measured. Corrective action plans should be suggested with an intention to achieve a win-win situation. Also, since collaboration benefits usually take a long time, they should not be measured in terms of short-term benefits like increase in productivity or cost reduction alone, but long-term in terms of return on investment (ROI), etc. It is important that companies reward their best suppliers and build their trust. There needs to be seamless information sharing, a shared competitive vision, and risk and reward sharing contracts. It is equally important to allow the supplier to rate the buyer and provide feedback on areas of improvement. Every effort should be made to resolve the differences mutually so that the relationship doesn't end in a divorce. One of the primary reasons marriages between buyer and supplier end in divorce is that once the contract is signed the focus fades away.

The supplier-buyer relationship (marriage) will be able to prosper and flourish only when the relationship is based on partnership rather than exploitation. For example, if the relationship between the buyer and supplier is based on a win-lose approach, the supplier will not support the buyer's lean and agile initiatives. This violates principle 2 which encourages firms to look beyond local improvement and start looking toward eliminating waste and achieving continuous improvement for the entire value chain for all partners' benefits. As another example, if the supplier is forced to carry extra inventory to allow the buyer to move to a lean environment, this will impact the relationship between the supplier and buyer, and might affect the quality and cost of purchase parts. In one of the workshops a company conducted to educate their suppliers about a new initiative they are undertaking called "lean," a supplier raised his hand and asked, "Does this mean that you are going 'lean,' and we are going 'fat' in inventory to satisfy your need?" This type of behavior will not only impact the supplier and buyer relationship negatively, but will also impact the end customers since they have to pay for this waste directly or indirectly. The relationships with suppliers should change from transaction management to win-win strategic relationship management. This will lead to lower product development costs, increased reliability, improved quality, increased visibility, reduced risks, and increased manufacturability because of early supplier involvement, lower purchasing costs of goods and services, greater flexibility to manage demand fluctuations, and shrinking the cycle times from product design to production, thus creating more responsiveness to the market.

Best Practices

1. Supplier base rationalization:

In most organizations a simple Pareto analysis will reveal that 80 percent of the suppliers account for 20 percent of the total spend. There is a proliferation of suppliers, especially for the C and D class items since each plant has localized contracts with their own suppliers. It is not uncommon to find different departments within the same company procuring the same part from different suppliers or having multiple contracts with the same suppliers from different plants.

Rationalization strategies aim at producing closer relationships with a smaller number of strategic suppliers. In a recent survey it was found that approximately 86 percent of the companies are actively pursuing a supply base rationalization initiative. The supply base has been reduced in 70 percent of the companies since the rationalization efforts began with 76 percent of respondents expecting to reduce the supply base further in the next 12 to 24 months.[9]

Based on the second LAVC principle (win-win) and leveraging visibility and risk management enablers, companies should reduce the number of suppliers for each purchased part to a single supplier, or two to three at a maximum. This will reduce variability since the buyer will deal with a smaller but more reliable set of suppliers. There would also be a reduction in costs due to volume leverage, inventory level reductions, and reduced waste because of fewer supplier performance reviews, fewer contracts, and fewer transactions. Only the best suppliers should be selected and, once selected, a relationship should be established with the preferred suppliers where rewards are shared. By first rationalizing products and suppliers and then leveraging the existing suppliers for the organization as a whole rather than individual departments, this will help reduce cost of goods sold. Since companies spend more than 50 percent of their sales revenue on purchasing, a small reduction in the purchasing costs can result in a big change in net income. For example, a 5 percent decrease in cost of goods sold will result in a 25 percent increase in net income (Figure 3.4).

Companies like Emerson monitor net material inflation, which it manages to reduce the cost of goods sold. Emerson has developed a proprietary tool to track certain events that influence the material costs. If, for example, there are changes coming in the cost of steel or copper, Emerson gets early warnings and can take appropriate actions to deal with it. (For more details, please refer to Success Story 1: SRM Best Practices at Emerson in Chapter 10.)

Rather than the Big Three's approach of having ten suppliers lock horns with each other and fight for the business, companies like Toyota and Honda restrict the number of suppliers to two or three (enabler 6: process innovation) and reward them with larger contracts based on their performance. For example, Toyota asked several of its suppliers to design tires and evaluated the performance of the tires. The selected suppliers were rewarded with contracts for life. However, if the supplier's performance was found to be unsatisfactory the next contract was given to the next competing supplier.[7]

Decisions pertaining to reduction of the supplier base should be made carefully to minimize the impact of high switching costs. Not only should past supplier performance be considered, but also future market trends, business risks, and company demand. For example, supplier A might be more costly than supplier B, but more responsive. If the company is planning to change its strategy from

Income statement		5% reduction in COGS
Total operating revenues	$100	$100
Cost of goods sold	$50	$47.50
Selling, general and administrative expenses	$20	$20
Operating income	$30	$32.50
Depreciation	$3	$3
Interest expense	$12	$12
Taxes	$5	$5
Net income	$10	$12.50

A 5% decrease in COGS results in a 25% increase in net income

Figure 3.4 Financial impact

minimizing cost to maximizing market share in the future, then supplier A might be selected.

2. Supplier certification:

Supplier certification is an effective way for not only selecting suppliers for a strategic relationship but also a means of monitoring and improving supplier performance. It helps in mitigating risk and ensures that the quality, cost, and delivery performance are maintained. ISO (International Organization for Standardization) certification has become so widespread that it has become a prerequisite for RFPs and RFQs. Most companies however, have more detailed requirements for their specific supplier certification. It is very important that both the buyer and supplier are given the exact requirements for certification, which include ship early/ship late tolerance, number of defects per batch, number of flaws per unit, etc.

It must be clear to the supplier that the information will be used for mutual benefit and not for bargaining with other suppliers. Also, certification measures and procedures should be standardized across the different divisions of the organization, and there should be a process to decertify the supplier if supplier performance has fallen below the agreed standard.

3. Part rationalization:

In most organizations, different departments source the same part from different suppliers because every department has a different internal part number. Product rationalization involves removing duplicate parts, cross referencing the different departmental internal part numbers to the one manufacturer part number, and using functionally equivalent parts rather than designing new parts from scratch (enabler 6: process innovation). There needs to be a global procurement rationalization initiative that will help reduce the number of parts the organization buys from its suppliers. This will assist the purchasing organization in negotiating better deals and leveraging volume discounts with their existing suppliers, thereby reducing administration overhead. Cross referencing the primary part with the alternate part and primary supplier with the alternate supplier will help mitigate risk in the event of an unexpected occurrence in which case the substitute part can be used.

4. Measuring supplier performance and rewarding suppliers:

Strategic sourcing must be integrated with contract monitoring and compliance. This involves measuring organizational spend against contracts to minimize off-contract purchasing and making sure that the supplier is fulfilling its end of the agreement on pricing, delivery lead times, and service levels. Supplier performance needs to be monitored by conducting supplier performance reviews by a cross-functional team of purchasing, marketing, IT, product design, engineering, manufacturing regarding contract performance based on agreed-upon metrics.

The Strategic Performance Measurement for Purchasing and Supply Report of CAPS Research mentioned that on-time delivery is the highest performance measure used regularly to rate supplier performance (94.44 percent), but only 48.27 percent of suppliers are actually measured against it.[10] Also, the supplier performance metrics must be aligned with the other strategic metrics of the firm. For example, if the company is planning to capture market share and the company-wide metrics reflect the same, there should be a supplier metric for responsiveness. In addition, the supplier performance metrics should be consistent across departments. For example, in most companies it is common to find one business unit that defines delivery performance as the percent of orders received on time, while the other business unit defines it as the number of units received on time. This lack of consistency violates principle 4.

BIC firms send supplier performance reports every month to the top management of their core suppliers, some of which are Tier 1 or even Tier 2. The report includes previously agreed metrics on supplier performance, for example, quality, delivery performance, and incidents. Rather than blame the supplier for a problem, both Honda and Toyota encourage senior management involvement from suppliers and work with the suppliers to identify the root cause of the problem and fix it. For example, when Toyota found a problem with its wiring harness, they invited the president from the Yazaki Corporation to observe wiring harness assembly. Only after the president understood the assembly was Yazaki able to identify the root cause and fix the problem.[1]

Process innovation such as an incentive system for suppliers or carriers who score high on performance measures should be in place. Some incentive options could be adding the supplier to a preferred list, awarding them with more business, publicizing it in magazines, going public with their contracts, and signing longer-term deals. Also, goals and performance measures should be established together. Supplier involvement in developing a replenishment strategy should be increased, and collaborative problem solving should be encouraged for the relationship to work smoothly and effectively to create a win-win.

5. Collaboration:

Strong and effective collaboration between supplier and buyer requires more people from both organizations to collaborate more frequently and not limit the relationship between purchasing (from the buyer organization) and sales (from the supplier organization). The relationship should change from a traditional single point of contact between the sales department of the supplier and the purchasing department of the buyer to a relationship that can represent multiple points of interaction between the marketing, sales, operations, finance, customer service, logistics, quality assurance, and purchasing departments of both the buyer and the supplier (see Figure 3.5). This leverages enabler 2. For example, the buyer's engineering team should collaborate with the supplier's operations group during new product introduction. Similarly, the buyer's operations should collaborate closely with the supplier's fulfillment team on orders and quality issues, and so forth. Logistic specialists from both the buyer and the supplier should collaborate on transportation and warehousing. The buyer and the supplier should share a common vision of short-term strategies and have meetings, and web conference sessions on a regular basis which will help them advance toward their long-term goals.

The supplier systems and the organization systems should be interfaced and specific joint activities undertaken. Common skills should be leveraged and there should be a willingness to invest in shared infrastructure to support collaborative business processes. By having a collaborative relationship with a supplier who can react quickly to any sudden demand changes, the organization minimizes the risk of not being responsive enough and losing market share. Such a relationship can only be cultivated if every member profits from the business and gains are distributed among the various stakeholders. One way to strengthen the relationship is to invite the supplier to an executive supplier council. Another way is to increase trust by having open, frequent communication yet ensure sensitive information is protected. All of the above will establish trust between the two firms and strengthen the relationship between supplier and buyer, which is consistent with LAVC principle 2 (create win-win and trusted environment for all stakeholders). For example, Johnson Controls wanted to expand its facility to cater to Toyota's increasing demand for car seats. Toyota advised Johnson Controls against that and worked with them to change the shop floor layout, reduce inventories, and increase productivity by applying Toyota's lean manufacturing techniques. Not only was Johnson Controls able to meet the growing Toyota demand, but this joint venture also made sure that the supplier and manufacturer philosophies were in constant alignment.[1]

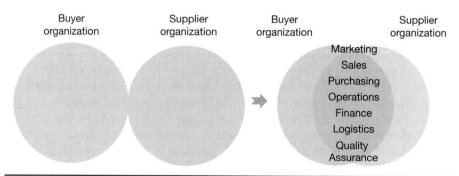

Figure 3.5 Multiple points of interaction between buyer and supplier

6. Sourcing segmentation:

As firms tend to segment their customers, they also need to segment their suppliers and purchased parts based on several factors. This has no contradiction to principle 4, which focuses on continuous improvement and standardization, since the process of dealing with a supplier should be flexible enough to accommodate the segmentation. Figure 3.6 shows one way a company can do its segmentation based on the supply risk on the y-axis and the value to the company on the x-axis. Supply risk includes number of suppliers, supply uncertainty, part substitution, part complexity, supply availability, and so forth. Value to the company includes price, competitive advantage, and profit margin (if it is possible to calculate). Examples of products in the lower left quadrant of Figure 3.6 would include MRO items, standard fasteners, etc., that have a low supply risk (i.e., many suppliers) and are of low value to the company. For these items the company could use business-to-business e-procurement, which harnesses the power of the Internet to get access to a wider supplier base and better deals. In addition, administration overhead can be reduced significantly by automating the process of purchase order issues to suppliers, using blanket purchase orders and online catalogs, buying items in bulk, reducing the number of suppliers, paying via elec-

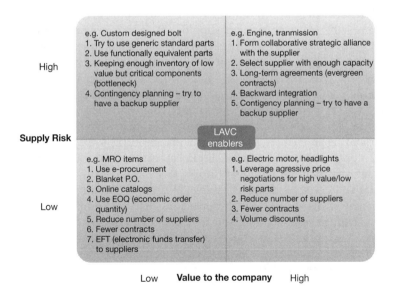

Figure 3.6 Segmentation

tronic funds transfer, and using fewer contracts with suppliers, thereby getting volume discounts since each order would be larger. Economic order quantity can be used, which is driven by local parameters such as ordering and carrying costs rather than supply chain demand.

Examples of products in the upper left quadrant would include unique parts that have a high supply risk (for example a single source supplier) and are of low value to the company. The company should try to explore a part rationalization strategy that aims at using other generic standard parts or functionally equivalent ones instead of the custom design part. Cross referencing the primary part with the alternate part will help mitigate risk in the event of an unexpected occurrence where the substitute part can be used. However, design engineers should use their discretion regarding the use of common parts, as sometimes excessive use of common parts can introduce unnecessary design complexity and limit design flexibility. Also, having another backup supplier will help reduce the supply risk. BIC companies selectively add new parts and new suppliers only when it helps them get a strategic advantage. It is imperative that the number of items in this quadrant is kept to a minimum since they are of low value to the company. This can only happen if there is information sharing between the product development organization and the purchasing organization starting right from the design phase itself. Also keeping enough inventory of this low value but critical component on hand at all times is important to avoid supply shortages.

For items in the bottom right quadrant—low supply risk and high value to the company—the sourcing strategy should aim at supplier base rationalization, i.e. reducing the number of suppliers thereby leveraging volume discounts. Because this is a low supply risk quadrant, the company could leverage aggressive price negotiations with the suppliers. Since typically the high value parts might also be the high priced parts, even a small reduction in price could lead to significant savings for the company. However, the company should be careful not to jeopardize the long-term relationship with the supplier. As we mentioned earlier, if implementing an enabler goes against a principle, it should not be implemented.

The company should pay maximum attention to the items in the top right quadrant, that is, items with high supply risk and high value to the company. The sourcing strategy should aim at having collaborative strategic alliances with these suppliers. It is also important to make sure that the company selects a supplier that has enough capacity and sufficient tolerance to meet the demand, since the chances of a bottleneck are far greater at a supplier operating at 90 percent capacity than one operating at 80 percent capacity. Having another backup supplier will help mitigate risk in the event of an unexpected occurrence, in which case the backup supplier can be used. Companies can reduce risk by establishing long-term agreements, "evergreen contracts," which are rolled over at the end of the year. Companies such as Dow Chemical and Nucor reduce their supply vulnerability through backward integration—by acquiring their suppliers.[11]

BIC companies like Zara segment their product portfolio into functional/innovative products and have an appropriate sourcing strategy for each one (enabler 7: strategy innovation). Zara, the Spanish clothing manufacturer, has a corporate strategy of getting fashions into stores rapidly; hence, it has two sourcing strategies, one for staples and another for fashion clothing. To get a fast response time for fashion clothing, Zara uses European suppliers (speed to market, higher price but more responsive) and also maintains a near vertical integration for their fashion items by outsourcing only the sewing function. Thus, their sourcing strategy is aligned nicely with their corporate strategy. But for predictable demand staple items, it uses Eastern European suppliers, which have poor response time but lower cost. Equipped with more than one sourcing strategy, the firm can move products from one sourcing strategy to another based on product life cycle stage, demand patterns, and so forth.[12] A lean and agile strategic sourcing process will allow purchasing to quickly strategize, plan, and achieve cost reduction on anything that is purchased. Immediate savings can reach 35 percent in the first few sourcing events.

Lean and agile companies continuously monitor their product portfolio as items could move from one quadrant to another depending on the supply and demand. For example, in 2007 and 2008, gasoline moved from a routine purchase item to a strategic one. By continuously monitoring its strategic item (gasoline), Dallas-based Southwest Airlines was able to hedge its expected fuel needs at an average crude price of just $51 per barrel compared to the industry $140 per barrel. Hedging gave Southwest the right to buy fuel at a guaranteed price, thereby protecting the company from rising prices.

7. Total landed cost for supplier selection:

Because of globalization, decisions about where to source, where to produce, and where to sell products are becoming more complex. Understanding the trade-offs between three conflicting objectives—cost, flexibility, and responsiveness—is key before deciding which suppliers to select, where to locate the manufacturing facilities and distribution centers, which products to produce at which facilities, and the distribution of products to customer regions.

Outsourcing to a low-cost supplier should always be taken holistically based on the total cost and the contribution to the total organizational profitability, as outsourcing could also lead to loss of visibility and therefore increased risk. For example, a consumer electronics company that was trying to decide between a China-based supplier and a U.S.-based supplier found that though the per unit cost was considerably lower for the China-based supplier, the company would have to carry a whole lot more safety stock to compensate for the four weeks of transportation lead time between China and the United States, as well as the uncertainty and lack of visibility of the shipment container being held up for weeks in Shanghai. By using linear programming and simulation the company then decided to go with the U.S.-based supplier since it offered a lower total landed cost.

This is what James Geesey, the Director of e-Sourcing at Emerson had to say regarding outsourcing: "These days, anyone can go to Asia and get significant cost reductions, but you also have to consider the additional capital costs required for that decision, or the supply chain risks that enter into the equation. The longer the pipeline, the larger the bullwhip effect—a small variability in end-customer demand expands to successively greater variability to the supplier resulting in both the buyer and the supplier carrying excess inventory to buffer against the increased variability. Of course, we are well established in Asia, but we primarily use Asian sources for supporting domestic production. We also use Asian suppliers to support North American production, but we use a sourcing decision support tool to help us analyze price, working capital, and supply chain risk. It's also a multi-function effort—it's not just procurement sitting in a vacuum. Everyone has a seat at the table and that helps us make the best decisions."

8. Technology:

In most companies a lot of time is spent manually aggregating data from disparate systems, which have different internal product and supplier codes for the same manufactured part and the same supplier. This leaves little time for value added activities such as developing supplier and product sourcing strategies by gaining visibility into supplier spend and performance; measuring and evaluating contract performance and contract compliance; and comparing the expected consumption on the contract versus the actual one. The best-practice approach is to use a master data management technology solution (enabler 3: technology) that will serve to consolidate data across disparate systems into a single, normalized data repository which has all the relevant information pertaining to supplier performance scorecards, supplier surveys, supplier quality reports, and so forth. Also, by automating the processes of data cleansing, consolidation, data validation, audit trail, and enrichment, it will leave more time for analysis and driving globally optimal cost reduction programs across different business units to achieve a repeatable and sustainable process.

Using a multi-dimensional database (Figure 3.7) consisting of product, supplier, buyer, and time will help the company slice and dice the data by number of units and/or dollars and answer questions like: Which suppliers performed poorly for a particular product last year? What was the total spend by business unit? What was the total spend by product group by business unit? This will also expose renegade buys, off-contract and off-approved vendor list spend, and unlev-

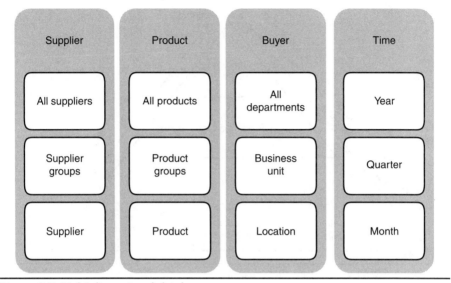

Figure 3.7 Multi-dimensional database

eraged suppliers and products. For more details about strategic sourcing software applications, please refer to Chapter 6.

9. Top management support:

For strategic sourcing to be a true global sourcing initiative and a source of competitive advantage, it is important that strategic sourcing be regarded as an organization-wide philosophy with involvement from all the different cross-functional teams (product design, purchasing, engineering, quality assurance, etc.) and executive support from management.

Top management should also encourage training for the sourcing managers who should think in terms of total cost of ownership (enabler 6: process innovation) rather than transaction-based nickel and dime price haggling.

PRODUCT DESIGN

Product design (Figure 3.8) is the process of enabling collaborative design, engineering, and support among companies, partners, and suppliers by sharing product designs, schedules, and constraints, to arrive at a single bill of material for a finished product efficiently and effectively. This will help bring innovative and profitable products to the market quickly, and ensure high product quality standards.

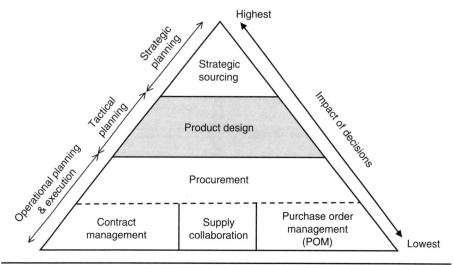

Figure 3.8 SRM pyramid (product design)

The product design process is typically triggered either by the need to introduce a new product to the market or by product engineering changes (product revisions) due to component cost change, product improvements, process change, quality corrective actions, material shortages, or product obsolescence. Product revisions involve engineers, purchasing, suppliers, manufacturing and process managers, contract manufacturers, and service support representatives. The product design process is tightly integrated to several technology applications such as the following:

- Computer-aided design, computer-aided manufacturing, and 3D visualization.
- Product definition management (PDM), which is the database for all designed parts, stores structured data (e.g., item number, bill of materials [BOM], routings, effective dates) and unstructured data (e.g., electronic document formats, drawings). It also provides a powerful search capability to navigate easily in the databases.
- Engineering change management/control workflows: Manage engineering change requests and their approval steps, engineering change order generation to a new revision number, changes to parts, BOM and routings, and effective dates.
- Design collaboration: Provides a shared design workbench to collaborate among different members (internal and external), a common, secure, and role-based portal for supplier interactions, exceptions management, visualization, reporting, data analysis and mining, and document control.

- Program/project management: Provides project management capability (similar to Microsoft Project) with cost calculation, and the ability to evaluate multiple project proposals (cost, risk, resource needs, launch timing).

While product design incurs a relatively small portion of the total new product development cost, it can "lock in" as much as 80 percent of the total product cost.[13] Decisions made early on in the product design phase can have a significant impact on the product quality, cycle time, and cost, as once the product is designed it has implications on sourcing, manufacturing, warehousing, transportation, repairing, and even recycling.

In most companies it is quite common that the design engineer will design the product without looking into sourcing and purchasing constraints, that is, the product design happens sequentially using an "over the wall" approach between the design department, sourcing, purchasing, and then production. Hence, if there is a problem with one of the components in purchasing (supplier not available/part not available/not affordable), then the design engineer has to go back to the drawing board. In addition, once the part has been designed and the prototype manufactured, production might realize that the part requires expensive retooling. Hence, production might not approve the design and send it back to the design department. Thus, the design shuttles back and forth between the design department, purchasing, and production until the final design has been approved by purchasing and production. But wait—logistics might still realize that packaging and transporting the final product might exceed the initial budget. This back and forth shuttling goes against principle 3 and increases organizational waste.

Challenges

Mass customization has led to a change in consumer behavior and customers are increasingly demanding new products, which has led to shrinkage in the product life cycle. Companies that cannot keep pace with customer needs by having new product launches run the risk of losing market share and revenue. Product design has been plagued by several challenges that include:

1. Competition:

Intensified competition has led to more rapid, new product introductions to the market, and complex products, which make optimizing the design more challenging.

2. High prototype cost:

High prototype cost is another challenge. This is because of the lack of ability to manage and control frequent design changes, and to identify the right products to launch or fund, the right suppliers to collaborate with early in the design process, and the right standard items to reuse.

3. Outsourcing:

Subcontracting and outsourcing extends the need for real-time collaboration with partners and suppliers, which is a big challenge especially if the firm has no technology to enable some type of collaboration.

4. Lack of visibility:

There is a disconnect between the engineering and purchasing systems that causes the lack of visibility for the design engineers into the approved vendor list, which typically exists in the purchasing system. Because of the lack of visibility, in some companies, different design departments could be working on designing the same component or designing a component that already exists. This just adds waste to the organization.

5. Disparate systems:

Another related challenge is the inability to consider supplier performance during sourcing decisions by design engineers or purchasing analysts either because it doesn't exist, or exists in different systems with which they don't have access. There are disparate systems for design, purchasing, sourcing, and manufacturing. Different internal part numbers exist in these different systems and there could be discrepancies regarding units of measure, currencies, supplier codes, material codes, and so forth, which add to the complexity.

Key Concepts

Design for Manufacture and Assembly

The traditional sequential approach to product development involved the design engineers to come up with the final blueprint and then "throw it over the wall" to manufacturing to determine the manufacturing process. This led to expensive tooling, reduced quality, and parts that did not assemble correctly, which eventually resulted in a product launch delay. Even if the product was launched, the problems would shift to the customers, resulting in a loss of customer satisfaction. Another fallout of this was that the manufacturing process could end up with too many setups and waste in terms of time and cost.

Design for manufacture and assembly (DFMA) involves the design department and manufacturing working together as one unit since manufacturing has firsthand knowledge about the existing tooling/processes and therefore can suggest design modifications so that a high-quality product can be launched on time. DFMA also includes "design for quality," that is, product design meets the quality, performance, and aesthetic needs of the customer while at the same time making sure that the product cost does not exceed the budget. The APICS Dictionary describes design for manufacture and assembly as "A product development approach that involves the manufacturing function in the initial stages of product design to ensure ease of manufacturing and assembly."

Intel used DFMA methodology for their 45-nm CMOS chip. By using co-optimization across design and manufacturing early in the development cycle, Intel was able to balance all the manufacturing requirements during the design phase itself (enabler 2: cross-organizational collaboration). The DFMA methodology ensured that products were ready for ramp-up to high-volume and high-yield manufacturing without changes.[14]

Design for Logistics

Design for logistics involves a collaborative design process in which logistics works with the design department to make sure that the final blueprint takes packaging, warehousing, and transportation into consideration. IKEA epitomizes the concept of design for logistics by making sure their designs of furniture, lamps, beds, and kitchen equipment minimize the wasted space in product packaging, storage, and transportation. Hence, cross-organizational collaboration helps IKEA reduce waste. The products are broken down into the elements that minimize space, but at the same time don't compromise on the function. Also, it's a lot cheaper to ship and handle components of a flat desk rather than finished furniture. IKEA can then transmit the savings to the end customer (principle 1). Thus, even the truck, shipping container, and warehouse affects the product design of the furniture.[15]

Another example is that Rubbermaid's food-storage containers are not only priced right and look good, but were designed to fit into Wal-Mart's 14-by-14 shelving.[16]

Design for Reverse Logistics

Reverse logistics is starting to get more and more attention nowadays because of the connection between reverse logistics and green supply chain initiatives, which include environmentally responsible manufacturing and distribution. Design for reverse logistics involves the design department using principles of simplification, standardization, fewer and lighter parts, and modular parts (enabler 6: process innovation) so that it is easy to return, repair, and recycle. This can help an organization reduce costs, comply with environmental regulations, increase customer satisfaction, and even be a source of competitive differentiation.

This is what James Brittain Ladd, formerly of Dell and currently the Director of Logistics and Manufacturing at Cognizant Technology Solutions, said regarding green product design: "At Dell we spent a tremendous amount of time and effort to design and sell the most green and energy-efficient products on the market. We also designed products configured specifically to require less packaging—thereby saving money for Dell. Companies also need to be aware of what happens to their products at end of life. This is an area that makes a tremendous impact on the environment. If you can design products with end-of-life considerations inherent in their design, you will recognize tremendous savings when it comes to handling waste, and at the same time be environmentally conscious. At Dell, we understood that all of the efforts we put into product design, supply chain analysis and management, packaging, supplier collaboration, and so on, all increased Dell's competitive advantage. Measurable savings from green initiatives come in the form of reduced transportation, packaging and component costs. In addition, when suppliers and customers recognize the value of collaboration, relationships strengthen and sales grow—making a green supply chain a smart supply chain." (For more details, please refer to Success Story 11: Green Value Chain versus LAVC in Chapter 10.)

Concurrent Engineering

In the traditional hierarchical sequential approach to product design, the design goes back and forth from the design, purchasing, and manufacturing departments leading to product introduction delays. In concurrent engineering, multi-disciplinary teams from purchasing, manufacturing, marketing, sales, service, and quality assurance collaborate, and cooperate with a common objective of getting the right product out as fast as possible. Traditional hierarchical organizations are replaced by flattened interdisciplinary teams. For example, Boeing's Ballistic Systems Division used concurrent engineering to develop a mobile launcher for the MX missile production. The multi-disciplinary team (enabler 2: cross-organizational collaboration) included members from design, manufacturing, materials, finance, and maintenance who shared office space and worked together. The outcome was a 40 percent reduction in the time needed to design and build the launcher prototype, and a 10 percent reduction in cost.[3]

Modular Design

Hewlett-Packard (HP) provides an excellent example of modular design in which the inkjet printer design essentially consists of a generic module and some country-specific modules such as power supply, power cord plugs, and instruction manuals. The generic printer module is shipped to the distribution centers in Europe and Asia and customized with the country-specific modules of power supply, etc. The design engineers at HP created a printer module with a generic power supply port that could then be assembled to the final product, complete with instruction manual, power supply, and the appropriate packaging material at the local distribution center. Benefits of this modular design approach include lower transportation cost, packaging cost, and mass customization (enabler 6: process innovation to reduce costs). Modular design also helps HP in implementing assembly postponement, that is, HP keeps the product in its generic state as long as possible and delays the differentiation into specific end products until better demand information is available. The main advantages of postponement include cost-effectiveness, since it's much cheaper to hold inventory in a subassembly (semifinished state) rather than a finished state, and it's easier to forecast a base product level rather than a finished product level that includes all customer configurations. This also leads to increased flexibility because a wide range of specific end products can be derived from the same generic product.[17]

Design for Value Chain

Design for value chain (DVC) involves designing the product by taking into consideration the entire value chain from supplier to the customer. It involves a holistic approach to product design in which the product is designed by not only internal collaboration between the design department, manufacturing, logistics and purchasing, but also external collaboration with the supplier and the customer. Hence, DVC encompasses DFMA and concurrent engineering, i.e., making sure that design, manufacturing, purchasing, marketing, sales, service, and quality assurance collaborate, cooperate, coordinate and combine forces rather than each department working in a silo. DVC includes design for logistics and design for reverse logistics to make sure the product can be efficiently and effectively packaged, stored, and transported and is easy to return, repair, and recycle. DVC incorporates not only intra-company collaboration but also cross-organizational collaboration with the suppliers and customers to make sure that the product is designed using fewer modular parts and standardized processes with a common objective of getting the design right the first time within the cost and time constraints.

Best Practices

1. Simplification:

Simplifying product designs involves using fewer parts, which typically results in fewer suppliers and replenishment signals, and less transportation cost, inventory, and complexity. This process innovation translates into less maintenance issues and cost. Simplification also involves making sure that when new products are introduced, the design and features reflect what the customer wants and would use, rather than overdesigning and overloading the products with features that marketing is forcing the engineer to introduce, thinking that would give them a market advantage. There is no point in having a competitive advantage if it does not materialize into a customer advantage.

2. Product standardization:

Standardization involves using common parts and encouraging the use of standard or previously designed parts that are available, instead of extensive use of new or custom designed parts. There are several advantages to using previously existing parts, since the jigs, fixtures, and tooling used to make them can be utilized. Existing suppliers also can be used which results in lower purchasing costs since less variety leads to economies of scale and volume discounts with suppliers.

In addition, the use of existing parts will result in reduced administrative costs, reduced design time, less maintenance parts, and no need for prototype testing. Fewer parts will result in fewer suppliers, which will lead to leaner supply chains, lower supply risks, and lower inventory levels because of the "pooling effect."

The use of an approved parts list during the design phase itself should not only be encouraged but enforced through appropriate metrics and rewards. This will result in lower product development costs, increased reliability, improved quality, reduced risks, and reduced product development time. However, design engineers should use their discretion as sometimes excessive use of common parts and functionally equivalent parts can introduce unnecessary design complexity and limit design flexibility. BIC companies selectively add new parts and new suppliers, but only when it helps them get a strategic advantage.

3. Process re-sequencing:

When design and manufacturing work together (DFMA) the sequence of steps to come up with the final product can be rearranged. Process re-sequencing involves changing the process sequence so that the later process steps are done earlier and product differentiation can be postponed until better demand information for individual products would be available.

Benetton, the Italy-based fashion designer and manufacturer, used the concept of process re-sequencing (assembly postponement) in the apparel industry by changing their manufacturing process to knit first and then dye at the distribution centers based on the most updated information about the colors that would be in fashion that holiday season.[18] Benetton used the LAVC enablers of process innovation and flexibility to focus on customers' needs.

4. Collaboration:

Sharing of information internally between departments and externally with suppliers is key to increase visibility and reduce risk and variability. In most companies the R&D department fears that sharing information with suppliers might result in outflow of information to their competitors. This leads to lack of usage of substitutable parts, functionally similar parts, and combining orders to get volume discounts from existing suppliers. It also leads to last minute engineering change order requests resulting in delayed product launches and increases in time to market, all because the product development department didn't share the information with the supplier. Product design should go beyond functional silos and there should be internal collaboration (sourcing, purchasing, manufacturing) as well as external collaboration with the suppliers so that there is visibility into sourcing, manufacturing the components, labor costs, safety regulations, and so forth. Collaboration should be carried out through ongoing communication regarding the test requirements to suppliers, validating test results and reviewing them with the suppliers, involving suppliers in cost monitoring/reduction, as well as in manufacturing/assembly process design and program requirements. The more the different internal functions and partners contribute to design, the better the chances that the product will be designed right the first time with minimum last minute engineering changes.

James Geesey, the director of e-Sourcing at Emerson, talked about the involvement of the procurement function during the design phase itself: "We find it very important to get in front of the product development process by inserting the procurement function into new product design, so that our engineers are working with a design-for-sourcing mentality. This is important because once a bill of materials is fixed for a product, a good purchasing person can only take about 10 to 20 percent of the material cost out of that product by using the best sourcing practices available. When you get engineering and purchasing working together in the conceptual phase, however, you can often take 35 to 45 percent of the material costs out of the product. So that's where the biggest gains are made."

BIC companies like Toyota and Honda, rather than outsource to low-cost suppliers in India and China, focus on innovation capabilities of their suppliers and invest in improving the supplier's ability to design and develop products. Toyota, for example, segments products according to whether they can be designed and manufactured independent of the vehicle dynamics. For items such as mirrors, locks, and so forth, the suppliers can design and manufacture the components without much involvement from their Toyota counterparts, but for parts that interface with the sheet metal and trim, close collaboration with Toyota's design engineers is a must. Toyota asks their Tier 1 suppliers' design engineers to work collaboratively with their own design and manufacturing engineers at Toyota's offices. This helps the suppliers' design engineers better understand Toyota's product development process.[1]

5. Technology:

The best-practice approach is to use a master data management technology solution, which will serve to consolidate data across disparate systems into a single normalized data repository that has all the relevant information pertaining to approved vendor list, approved parts list, scorecards, structured data (e.g., item number, BOM, routings, effective dates), and unstructured data (e.g., electronic document formats, drawings, etc.).

The product design process should be tightly integrated into PDM. The PDM, which is the database for all designed parts, should also have information pertaining to strategic sourcing (supplier rating, performance, alternate parts, single source suppliers) and procurement. Powerful search capability based on product attributes and supplier names will help the design engineers navigate easily in the databases. This will assist them in looking at supplier performance, encourage part reuse during the design phase itself, and help reduce product development cost. Also, a common, secure, and role-based portal should be there for supplier interactions and a shared design workbench to collaborate among different members, both internal and external.

There should be exception management and event notification capability to enable prompt proactive corrective actions for effective problem resolution. For example, the design engineer gets a popup message saying he/she would exceed target cost if a certain expensive part is selected to be part of BOM, or purchasing gets an e-mail informing him that a new version of a design has been introduced.

6. Price minus costing:

The traditional cost plus pricing method involves first calculating the total direct cost of production (labor and materials) and then adding overhead and a margin for profit to give the final price. However, this method completely ignores the demand side and the behavior of customers and competitors.

BIC companies use the price minus method (enabler 6: process innovation) in which top management comes up with the final targeted price based on market conditions and profit margin necessary to satisfy the shareholders. Based on the volume of sales and the margin, the cost price is then calculated. The different departments are now forced to work together to achieve the targeted cost price. This requires the design department to work collaboratively with manufacturing, marketing, finance, sourcing, and purchasing to achieve that goal.

Rather than use the traditional cost plus pricing method used by the Big Three, the Japanese auto manufacturers used the price minus method and worked with their suppliers to figure out the prices they can pay their suppliers for the components and subassemblies. Hence, suppliers like Atlantic Tool and Die knew beforehand that they would make a profit, though small to begin.[1]

7. Total cost visibility:

It is important that the design engineers have visibility into not only the raw material costs, but also the manufacturing, handling, and tooling cost, etc., so that they can make well-informed decisions based on the total cost (enabler 6: process innovation). In addition, design engineers should be able to try out multiple designs and select the best one—the one that minimizes cost and risk and at the same time meets delivery deadlines. By having visibility into the total target cost for each design, the design engineers will be able to make well-informed decisions and justify their actions. Total estimated cost = raw material and subassembly cost + overhead cost + tooling cost + transportation and storage cost + labor cost.

8. Top management support for best practices and continuous improvement:

Implementing efficient and effective product design is not a quick fix tool or short-term departmental initiative, but rather an organizational philosophy that requires top management support, cross-functional endorsement, and inculcating a culture of continuous improvement. This cannot be implemented through co-lossal jumps, but through steps that takes place incrementally. Many companies fail to get the true benefits because they don't have the time or budget. There are inadequate resources or staffing and there is no training given. They continue to maintain the traditional reward systems. For example, in many companies designers are typically rewarded for their creativity and flashy designs rather than for functional designs that reuse existing parts. Appropriate incentive systems need to be in place that reward a change in behavior, such as encouraging part reuse.

PROCUREMENT

Procurement (Figure 3.9) is the process of planning and executing the sourcing strategies. It includes contract management (RFP, RFQ, auctions, bid analysis, contract processing, contract compliance), supply collaboration, and POM subprocesses.

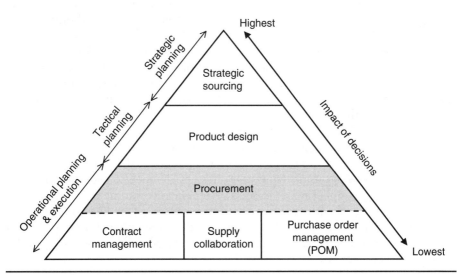

Figure 3.9 SRM pyramid (procurement)

Challenges

There are several key challenges (pain points) for the procurement process, which include:

1. Inability to capture supplier performance data:

Procurement is a cross-functional process that requires interaction between people who are diverse in their style of functioning, priorities, and attitudes. Often, the performance history is not shared between divisions, leading to separate suboptimal negotiations of the disparate divisions with the same supplier resulting in loss of economies of scale. Inability to capture supplier performance data can lead to the inability to conduct reliable bid analysis since supplier previous performance is not well captured and presented.

2. One-size-fits-all approach:

Procurement has to deal with direct items (part of the final product) that could be from the catalog or off catalog, as well as indirect items such as MRO. Many companies do not distinguish between the different items and employ a "one-size-fits-all" approach to procurement without considering the risks or margins for the items.

3. Lack of visibility:

There is a lack of intelligent visibility throughout the life cycle of the procurement subprocesses that include contract management, supply collaboration, and POM because of different systems. The procurement staff has to log into multiple disparate systems to consolidate spend across divisions, which also results in lost buying opportunities. A lack of visibility between the buyer and supplier also results in late detection for inbound material problems. This is one of the primary reasons for expediting, leading to higher transportation costs. Most companies invest a lot of time and effort in contract negotiation but lose the ability to conduct contract monitoring and compliance. This leads to off-contract spending and renegade buying. Also, favorable contract terms experienced by one department are not shared with other departments.

There is also a lack of aggregated visibility for the suppliers. For example, one supplier deals with different business units of the same company, and yet the company can't provide a consolidated demand picture to the supplier. Part of the reason is because each business unit uses different channels to communicate with the supplier. The supplier needs to send several invoices to the company, even if all business units deal with the same accounts payable system, because there is no consolidated demand. The supplier cannot get the complete picture of the buyer forecast or schedule changes, which forces the supplier to carry excess buffer inventory to compensate for the lack of visibility.

4. Lack of communication:

Lack of communication between the buyer and suppliers is another challenge that results in lost productivity. For example, this can result in a partial shipment because a supplier didn't receive the purchase order change request in time, or there was a delay in shipment because the supplier understood the purchase order date as the ship date and not the delivery date. Also, the most common way of automated communication—electronic data interchange (EDI)—is costly and difficult to maintain because different versions of the software may result in transmission errors, and lack mismatch resolution framework. Although the original business case for EDI was to eliminate manual work (nonvalue-added activities), EDI often resulted in waste as small suppliers got the EDI signal from the fax machine and entered it manually in their order management system.

5. Manual processes:

Most companies are plagued by several nonvalue-added, time-consuming administrative and clerical (paper-based) activities such as manual RFQ and contracting processes, checking shipment status, and paper invoices. Manual processes result in too much time being wasted on sending/receiving faxes, phone calls, e-mails, and so forth. This leads to high cost of both expedition and manual mismatch resolution between the purchase order, receipt, and invoice.

Even in companies with EDI, in the event of a change, the new EDI signal overlays the old one and doesn't highlight the change, which makes it difficult for the supplier to figure out what has been changed. The supplier has to compare the new signal with the old one manually and then communicate the change to the system.

Contract Management

Once the suppliers have been qualified and selected to be part of an approved vendor list after the strategic sourcing process, the contract management subprocess (Figure 3.10) involves the following steps:

1. Preparation of RFP, RFQ, auctions
2. Bid analysis
3. Bid award

Preparation of RFP, RFQ, Auctions

Contract management begins with an RFP being sent to an approved supplier or approved vendor list. The APICS Dictionary defines a request for purchase as "A document used to solicit vendor responses when the functional requirements and features are known but no specific product is in mind."

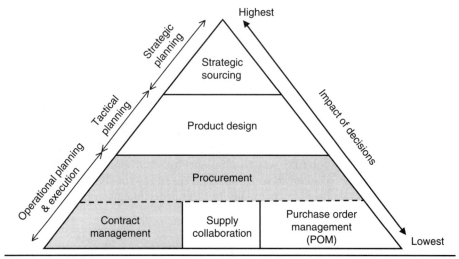

Figure 3.10   SRM pyramid (contract management)

The RFP should contain information regarding the business issue, evaluation criteria for the bids, deadline for proposal submission, estimated quantity to be purchased, terms and conditions, address to which proposals should be delivered, etc. Remember, the RFP is not a contract. Hence, some companies include disclaimers such as "The organization is not obligated to contract for any of the products described in the RFP, the RFPs are the organization's property, and the organization reserves the right to accept or reject any or all proposals, and negotiate with any or all bidders."

Sufficient time and effort should go into making the RFP as detailed as possible to minimize the number of variables for evaluation across bids. This will save a lot of time and effort later in the bid analysis step. Once the supplier has submitted the bid, discussions may be held on the proposals to clarify warranties, insurance, shipping terms, and technical capabilities. A renegotiation can also be held with all or selected bidders to get their best technical and financial proposal, commonly referred to as a *best and final offer*. It is important that timing and type of replenishments, timing and frequency of payments, shipping lot size quantities, transportation methods, ship early/ship late tolerance windows, as well as performance metrics (fill rate, quality, inventory turns, lead times, etc.) be agreed upon.

An RFP should not be used when the sole goal is to get pricing information from the supplier. RFP is typically used when you need a creative and innovative solution to a business issue by having a partnership with the supplier.

A request for quote on the other hand is defined by the APICS Dictionary as "A document used to solicit vendor responses when a product has been selected and price quotations are needed from several vendors." An RFQ is used when the exact requirements are known—usually for standardized and commoditized products or services. An RFQ should include information such as part descriptions, quantities, delivery requirements, terms of contract, and so forth.

Auctions are typically used when price is the main criterion to awarding a contract and the products being awarded are of a nonstrategic, low-risk nature, e.g., MRO items, indirect materials, and office supplies. In a forward auction, the supplier who intends to sell its products sends the documents to the buyers to bid and compete to obtain a good or service. Multiple buyers bid for the product and the highest bid gets the business. In a reverse auction, the role of the buyer and seller are reversed, that is, buyers post the items they wish to purchase and the suppliers bid on them. Reverse auctions, because of competitive bidding, help the buyer get a better price. Typically, the buyers stick to the approved vendor list even if their prices are slightly higher because the switching costs to move work to a new supplier might turn out to be more than the potential savings from the lowest bid.

"We are very fond of online and electronic negotiations—including reverse auctions, Dutch auctions, and multi-variate events—all of which are well-known methods that help us reduce component costs," said Emerson's Geesey. "In those processes, however, we are always very careful to only invite suppliers that we are very comfortable with. We will never invite an unqualified supplier to bid just to drive down costs, as sometimes happens in this business. You introduce a lot of supply chain risk into your operations if you are not careful in that way. When you cut corners, you jeopardize market integrity, and that's something we won't do."

Bid Analysis

Once the RFP/RFQ expiration date has passed and the RFP/RFQ has been received, supplier decisions are made following a comparison and analysis of the responses. Whether it is RFP/RFQ or auctions, requests can be received as sealed or open bid. In a sealed bid response, the buyer and the suppliers have visibility into only the total number of bids received, whereas in an open bid response the buyer and the supplier can see the actual bids that have been received. The supplier however does not see the names of the other suppliers who have bid. In the bid analysis phase, past supplier performance such as the following are considered: percentage of times the supplier participated in bidding; quality of responses; number of times awards were accepted; total cost of ownership (product cost, transportation cost, inventory cost, duty, tax, administration overhead); supplier responsiveness (quantity, timing); delivery lead times; variability of lead times (early, on time, late); delivery reliability (over-order quantity, under-order quantity); and quality (rework, reject, scrap).

Also, it is very important that the negotiation leads to a win-win situation (principle 2). As Woolf[19] points out, "A successful negotiation isn't one where I get everything and you get nothing. You have to give the other people a profit margin and let them live. You want them to thrive and grow." BIC companies like Toyota and Honda try to maximize their profits but not at the suppliers' expense. If suppliers are happy, the company can bank on them in case of an unexpected event in the future. Moreover, the company can use this one-time relationship (dating) to expand into a more strategic long-term relationship (marriage).

Bid Award

Once the bid analysis and negotiation is complete, the winning bidder is selected and a rejection notice is sent to the rest of the suppliers. Next, the purchasing department typically documents the result of the negotiations by creating a contract, blanket purchase order, or a long-term agreement clearly detailing the valid dates, stepped volume discounts, stepped pricing discounts, incentives, rebates, part and cost information, legal terms, conditions, and clauses. If the relationship between the supplier and buyer is in the "dating" phase, a short-term agreement (spot purchase order) is typically sent to the supplier after the selection. However, if the buyer and supplier are already "happily married" then a long-term contract is awarded.

A blanket purchase order (enabler 6: process innovation) is an agreement between the buyer and supplier that details the amount of goods the buyer would purchase over a period of time. When there is a blanket purchase order available, the purchase request is automatically converted to a purchase order and sent directly to the supplier as long as the request is within the budget allocated to his/her department or below a certain dollar limit. When the purchase order is issued to the supplier from a blanket purchase order, the amount and quantities are deducted from the open amounts and quantities on the blanket purchase order. A blanket purchase order is a win-win for both the buyer and supplier. The buyer benefits include economies of scale and therefore quantity discounts. The supplier benefits because future overall purchases from the buyer are known, which facilitates better planning for the supplier. This best practice reduces transaction cost, frees up purchasing resources to focus on more important activities, and increases satisfaction to internal users since they control the process and lead time (principle 3: eliminate waste and reduce nonvalue-added activities).

Companies often do a splendid job at the negotiation stage to come up with the best contract, but lose visibility when it comes to contract monitoring and compliance regarding off-contract spending, price paid versus contract price, purchasing from a noncontract supplier, etc.

Supply Collaboration

Once the contract has been awarded to the supplier, the next step involves collaborating with the supplier over the long-term, medium-term, and short-term horizon (Figure 3.11).

Long-Term Horizon Collaboration

Collaboration at the long-term horizon level involves capacity collaboration and resolution by sharing aggregated forecast at the commodity/product level and capacity picture between the supplier (sales or order fulfillment representative) and buyer (material planner). It allows the buyer to optimize product mix and the supplier to decide on machine or shift trade-offs, that is, if additional demand is expected, the supplier needs to decide if additional equipment is needed, or additional shifts can cover for the demand. Buyers and suppliers need to collaborate on solving the problems by considering alternate assembly line, alternate vendors, alternate supplier assembly sites, overtime, additional shifts, product reallocation, alternate parts, or revisions. Only when the issues have been resolved should the consensus get published to the strategic planning/master planning solutions of the buyer, and to the demand planning solution of the supplier.

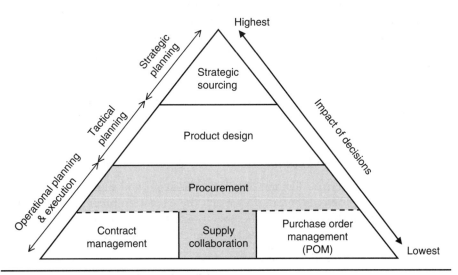

Figure 3.11 SRM pyramid (supply collaboration)

Medium-Term Horizon Collaboration

Forecast collaboration at the medium-term horizon level involves sharing part/raw material forecast and supply commit between the supplier and buyer, and resolving any issues that arise. The mismatches can be divided into three categories:

1. Low severity problems: These are problems within the up and down flexible limit. They can be resolved without any additional cost.
2. Mid severity problems: These are problems outside the up and down flexible limit, but within the supplier capability. They can be resolved but incur additional cost.
3. High severity problems: These are problems outside the supplier's capability.

Too often purchasing executives are aware of the next month's production requirements but lack the bigger picture—demand information over the next three to six months. Forecast collaboration allows the buyer and supplier to be proactive in resolving problems before it reaches the short-term phase. Sharing a material forecast will also help eliminate the "bullwhip effect." Expanded information sharing between the buyer and supplier will also result in early problem detection, more responsiveness to unexpected events, and stronger relationships because of increased trust. Costanza, in his book entitled *Quantum Leap: In Speed to Market*,[20] suggests that a supplier response profile agreement should be established between the buyer and supplier. Rather than share a "one number forecast," in a supplier response profile the buyer shares a range of forecast values. As both organizations progress through the forecasting horizon, uncertainty will shrink, confidence will increase, and the range will constrict itself. Hence, the buyer benefits from increased supplier flexibility to respond to demand variation, and the supplier benefits because of security of production (principle 2). This forms a buyer-supplier relationship based on informed confidence rather than "gut feel."

Only when the issues have been resolved, the consensus gets published out to the master planning solution of the buyer and to the demand planning solution of the supplier.

Short-Term Horizon Collaboration

Operational short-term collaboration allows the buyer and supplier to be proactive in resolving problems before they reach the execution phase. Depending on the type of replenishment trigger, the operational short-term collaboration could be different. Let's examine some available replenishment trigger options:

1. Schedule-driven replenishment:

In schedule-driven replenishment the buyer sends the supplier a schedule (time and quantity) using fax, e-mail, or EDI of when the supplier needs to deliver the ordered materials. The schedule is sent taking into consideration the supplier lead times and response times that have been negotiated during the contract management stage.

Once the schedule is sent, schedule collaboration involves sharing the part/raw material schedule and supply promise between the buyer and supplier, and resolving any mismatches thereof. The buyer and suppliers collaborate on solving the issues by allowing overtime, expediting (considering alternate transportation mode), or a second shift at the supplier site. It is too late for the buyer to consider an alternative supplier at this stage if the primary supplier cannot make it. Depending upon the industry, material planners of BIC companies create an EDC (expedite, defer, cancel) report on a daily or weekly basis, which lists the delivery schedules that need to be expedited or delayed to meet a changed customer request, and communicate the same to the supplier. BIC companies use technology to eliminate the plethora of manual processes involved by enabling automated replenishment triggering and real-time collaboration between the material planner and supplier. This helps eliminate waste and nonvalue-added activities.

Once the issues have been resolved, the consensus gets published out to the POM solution and master planning solution of the buyer, and to the production scheduling subprocess of the supplier. When the ship date on the schedule becomes current, the supplier is expected to ship the product, which will trigger the POM subprocess.

Some of the limitations of schedule-driven replenishment include heavy reliance on forecasts since the buyer needs to communicate the schedule up front before actual orders are received from customers. Also, since the order quantities are typically determined to take advantage of price and quantity discounts it could result in excess inventories.[21]

2. Vendor-managed inventory replenishment:

The APICS Dictionary defines vendor-managed inventory as "A means of optimizing supply chain performance in which the supplier has access to the customer's inventory data and is responsible for maintaining the inventory level required by the customer." The supplier reviews on-site inventory regularly, restocks to predefined levels, and invoices the customer accordingly. Vendor-managed inventory involves inventory collaboration in which the buyer's forecast and inventory position is shared with the supplier. It allows the buyer and supplier to be proactive in resolving problems before they reach the execution phase, and in reducing excess inventory.

In vendor-managed inventory, there is no purchase order sent from the buyer to the supplier, but a reverse replenishment in which the supplier creates a purchase order (can be called *planned shipment*) based on information from the buyer (forecast, point of sale, on-hand inventory, and safety stock). In some vendor-managed inventory cases, the buyer takes ownership of the inventory once it is at the buyer's site. However, in some situations the supplier retains ownership and control until the products are sold to the end customer. This is known as *consignment inventory*.

Vendor-managed inventory is increasingly used across industries, especially in consumer packaged goods which are characterized by high-volume, low-dollar value, and stable demand. For example, in the Wal-Mart and Procter & Gamble (P&G) vendor-managed inventory relationship, P&G would use Wal-Mart sales data and manage the inventory levels of P&G's products at Wal-Mart (enabler 2). In such a symbiotic relationship, P&G and Wal-Mart both benefit. The supplier (P&G) benefits include reduced purchase order discrepancies since the supplier cuts the purchase order, better scheduling and planning because of information sharing, closer collaborative ties with the buyer, and even a preferred status for the supplier. The buyer benefits include lower inventory investment since the supplier continuously reviews the on-hand inventory at the buyers end, leading to lower safety stocks, fewer stock outs with higher turnover, optimal product mixes, and lower administrative replenishment costs.

Similarly, vendor-managed inventory is being used by companies such as ADTRAN that are establishing more vendor-managed-inventory programs with their key suppliers. Better use of vendor-managed inventory helps ADTRAN ensure that many of the standard items are readily available. This process innovation, increased visibility, and cross-organizational collaboration are the main enablers for ADTRAN to achieve success and manage a global value chain. (For more details, please refer to Success Story 5: ADTRAN's Solution for Global Value Chain in Chapter 10.)

Vendor-managed inventory is typically managed using a (s,S) replenishment policy, also known as a *min-max* policy. If the on-hand inventory falls below a minimum order point, "s," an order is placed to get it to a maximum order-level, "S". The min and max safety stock can be entered by the buyer (static safety stock) or be calculated by depending on the days of cover logic (dynamic safety stock). The expected balance-on-hand inventory is compared with max and min safety stock and exceptions are flagged:

- Stock-out alert—if balance-on-hand inventory is less than zero
- Low inventory alert—if balance on hand inventory is greater than zero and less than min safety stock

Once the supplier decides to ship, the POM subprocess is triggered.

However, vendor-managed inventory comes with its own challenges. It shouldn't be a mere shifting of ownership and responsibility of managing inventory from the buyer to the supplier. This could lead to higher inventory costs and expenses for the supplier if the inventory is not properly managed, which would eventually translate into higher expenses for the buyer. Hence, it is imperative that vendor-managed inventory be treated as a joint collaborative approach between the buyer and the supplier where information regarding current on-hand inventory levels, point of sales, and projected consumption is exchanged on a real-time basis so that both parties benefit.[21]

3. Just-in-time replenishment:

Just-in-time replenishment involves the supplier delivering items as and when they are needed based on a "pull" signal from the buyer, that is, the consumption initiates the replenishment. This results in less inventory pileup, less shortages on the shop floor, and less storage space. It also helps avoid the inaccuracy in forecasting and provides a greater level of flexibility by accelerating and streamlining the material flow. An integral piece of pull systems is *kanban* (card signal), which gives "authorization for replenishment" to the supplier. There are two types of pull signals:

- Fixed quantity (bin quantity)-variable time: Once the part bin becomes empty, a pull signal gets sent out to the supplier to replenish a fixed quantity
- Variable quantity-fixed time (min/max): At a fixed time interval, the bin quantity is checked, and if it is below the min level, a pull signal gets sent out to the supplier to replenish enough quantity to reach the max level

The pull signal can be sent out to the supplier as a purchase order, and that triggers the POM subprocess. The bin quantity and min/max levels are studied periodically to accommodate the fluctuation in demand. Deciding the optimal number of *kanbans* and the quantity per kanban is dependent on the demand, demand variability, supply lead time, and supply variability. The higher the variability, the more the number of kanbans in the system, and the more the amount of inventory in the system.

Technology (enabler 3) can be used by the supplier and buyer to have visibility into the inventory (on hand, in process) and to determine the quantity that needs to be delivered (number of kanbans). The supplier can change the status of the kanban from "open" to "in process" over the Internet once an advanced shipping notice has been generated and the items have been shipped. When the buyer receives the items, the buyer can change the status of the kanban from "open" to "in stock." Finally, when the inventory is used by the buyer, the status changes back to "consumed" for the buyer or "open" at the supplier's end.[21]

For just-in-time replenishment to work, it requires a strong win-win partnership and collaboration between the supplier and buyer. Many suppliers are reluctant to join this type of program because of the concern that the buyer might push the inventory cost to them. A recent AMR Research[22] study found that organizations were five times more likely to push inventory cost to their suppliers than they were to co-invest in demand pull. These companies are saving on direct cost, but leaking profits to lost velocity.

When General Motors decided to have just-in-time replenishment with one of its suppliers, they shared its future production schedule with the supplier. The supplier also had to maintain inventory no farther than 300 miles from General Motor's plant. The supplier was in turn rewarded with an increased share of business (principle 2: create win-win and a trusted environment for all stakeholders).[23]

However, having just-in-time replenishment, that is, frequent deliveries based on the pull signal, doesn't make sense for insignificant items like standard bolts and screws because it would only add to the administrative overhead, higher material handling and transportation costs, violating LAVC principle 3.

4. Sequence-driven replenishment:

In a sequence-driven replenishment the suppliers deliver not only just in time, but also in the same sequence as that of the assembly process, which is referenced to the specific end-customer order. Thus, the purchase orders generated to the supplier are pegged to the customer order, which provides much needed traceability in certain industries like pharmaceuticals and chemicals. The consumption pattern on the shop floor is also fed back to the supplier and may act as a settlement trigger for the buyer to trigger payment to the supplier.[21]

Chrysler group implemented sequence-driven replenishment in which the supplier delivered seats in the exact sequence as the vehicle assembly schedule to the shop floor. This eliminated secondary storage and minimized inventory costs.[24]

Purchase Order Management

Purchase order management (Figure 3.12) can be defined as the subprocess of managing the life cycle of the order right from issuing of the purchase order, followed by tracking through its life cycle, until receipt of the order at the buyer's end. It also includes managing all daily activities of replenishment with the selected suppliers and transportation with carriers to achieve and execute a synchronized procurement plan.

POM Workflow

The POM workflow can be broken down into the following steps: (Figure 3.13)

Step 1: Requisitioning starts the POM subprocess. Requisitioning occurs when companies order items from a catalog or through a replenishment signal triggered to the supplier based on the forecast, point of sale, inventory picture, or other information. Most companies will have an approved vendor list with

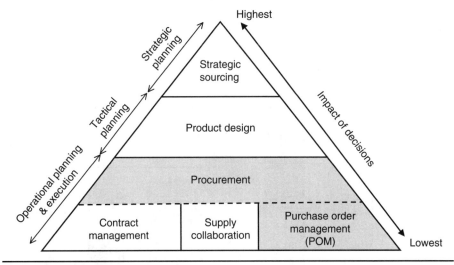

Figure 3.12 SRM pyramid (POM)

negotiated prices based on the strategic sourcing process, which helps companies get economies of scale and at the same time minimizes maverick "off-contract" spending. Once the user selects the items, the user is known to have made an internal purchase request. Requisitioning is followed by an approval workflow—depending on the user's role/approval amount, the requisitioning would require the authorization of one or more approvers. Before the purchase order is cut it is imperative that all the approvers have given the green signal.

Step 2: A purchase order contains supplier information, payment terms, buyer information, item description, quantity ordered, unit cost, unit of measure, ordered amount, request date, and promised date. Buyers from the purchasing department are responsible for converting the internal demand (purchase request) to an external demand signal (purchase order), which will then be communicated to the supplier through the Internet, ERP, EDI, fax, e-mail, etc.

Step 3: Once the suppliers have acknowledged the receipt of the purchase order, they should collaborate with the buyers regarding due dates, quantities and other items that require notice.

Step 4: The supplier would start manufacturing the items listed on the purchase order, depending on the delivery date. Once the supplier is done with manufacturing, it makes the necessary logistic arrangements (picking, packing, storing, and shipping) so that the items can be delivered on time. Depending on

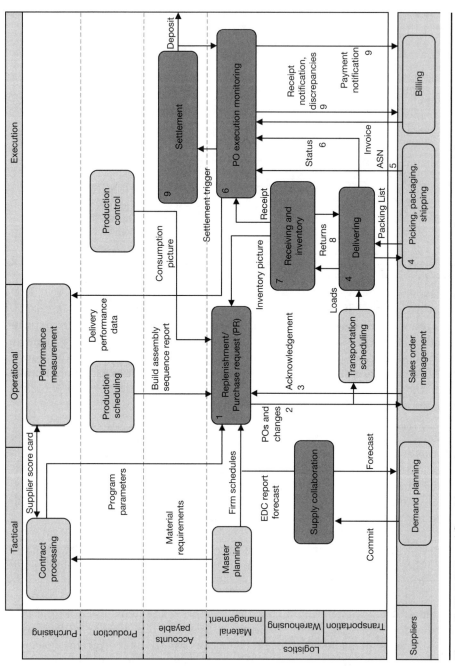

Figure 3.13 POM workflow (the numbers represent the corresponding steps in the POM workflow subprocess)

the contract with the buyer, either the supplier, buyer's private carrier, or a third-party logistics provider is responsible for the delivery to the buyer's site.

Step 5: Once the supplier has shipped the items in the purchase order, the supplier typically sends an advanced shipping notice that contains information pertaining to shipment identification number, bill of lading, gross weight, number and type of containers, transportation method, transport carrier ID, tracking number, estimated departure date, estimated arrival date, line item number, part number, quantity shipped, and so forth. Advanced shipping notices help tremendously in achieving agility since it allows downstream processes to plan and stage documents, workers, and receiving equipment in anticipation of the goods' arrival in addition to being proactive when delays happen for any reason.

Step 6: The shipment status is communicated to the buyer. This allows the buyer to track the shipment location so that the buyer can make the necessary alternative actions such as expediting shipments in the event of an exception, such as a last minute customer order, delay because of traffic problems, and so forth. This step includes all in-transit signals that the carrier typically sends for key stopping points to provide up-to-date status to the buyer.

Step 7: The shipment is received at the buyer's site, the buyer verifies the receipt of the goods, and the items are added to the buyer's inventory.

Step 8: Many times goods get damaged during shipping, may be incorrectly shipped, or rejected during inspection, which necessitates the need for effective returns management to return the defective items back to the supplier for credit and/or disposal.

Step 9: The settlement step involves the supplier billing the invoice and the accounting system issuing the check to the supplier. First, receipt of the goods is matched against the purchase order for the quantity and then the supplier invoices are matched against the purchase order for quantity and price. The match between purchase order and the receipt (two-way match) and the match between the purchase order, the receipt, and the invoice (three-way match) are important since a supplier invoice could have items from multiple purchase orders or the same purchase order could have produced multiple invoices. Also, many times suppliers deliver materials in excess of the purchase order quantity or ahead of schedule to get the inventory off their books, especially during the end of the quarter. The three-way match ensures foolproofing all exceptions. Payments are then made based on approved invoices.[21]

Best Practices

1. Cross-organizational collaboration:

Collaboration is key to overcome the fallout from unexpected events like the customer requesting a change in delivery date/quantities, or the supplier running into production-related problems. Also, the company's forecasts should be shared with suppliers so that they have visibility into the buyer's demand and can therefore help the supplier to respond to any change in demand.

Ace Hardware, a $2.8 billion hardware retailer, was able to use Internet software to come up with a consensus forecast with its supplier Manco (a supplier of tape, glues, and adhesives). Manco's representatives now look at Ace's forecast in real time and collaborate with Ace before coming up with a consensus forecast, which is then sent to Manco's production planning system. This has led to an increase in Manco's forecast accuracy from 80 percent to more than 90 percent.[23]

Cisco uses the concept of e-hubs to connect multiple tiers of suppliers via the web to coordinate supply and demand. This visibility into supply and demand helps Cisco identify potential supply and demand problems early, and provides necessary alerts and notifications so that appropriate corrective action can be taken promptly for effective resolution. Grocery manufacturers like Campbell Soup and Procter & Gamble have also found that synchronized joint replenishment programs have helped improve their inventory turns.[25]

2. Effective returns management:

Another growing area in the POM life cycle is returns management, or how best to handle the returns, including potential disposal of products that make the reverse trip from the buyer to the supplier. For the supplier-buyer relationship to be successful, it is important that the supplier should hear the buyer's feedback regarding the returns, find the root cause of the problem, and eliminate it. The buyer should also have detailed "reason for return" codes and accompany the returned part with the inspection report, which will help the supplier pinpoint the cause of the return. There should also be an effective way of returning the defective items back to the supplier for credit.

On average, almost 20 percent of all goods are returned. BIC companies are not only able to backtrack the defective items to the original purchase order (enabler 1), but their accounts payable department is also integrated into the returns process so that the defective, damaged quantities are excluded when the supplier is paid based on the invoice (enabler 6). BIC companies automate processing of returns upon receipt (including inspection and disposal), speed up the process to reduce risk of obsolescence, and track reverse logistics and net asset recovery to improve effectiveness.[21]

3. Effective settlement process:

BIC companies use an effective settlement process for collecting rebates, conducting spend analysis, and reporting compliance information. Electronic integration, messaging, reconciliation, and reporting solutions (enabler 3: technology) in accounts payable can reduce transaction costs between 63 percent and 67 percent. Yet only 3 percent of accounts payable processes reported having a high level of automation.[26]

Using evaluated receipt settlement (enabler 6: process innovation), the receiving department can scan the bar code or radio frequency identification (RFID) tag of the incoming shipment to electronically verify the purchase order and authorize payment to the supplier without the need for an invoice. This will help eliminate a lot of the nonvalue-added manual processing to resolve price mismatches, quantity discrepancies, and result in faster payment to the supplier thereby strengthening supplier relationships. According to CAPS Research,[27] manual invoice processing has resulted in a mismatch between the paper invoice and the purchase order 20 to 30 percent of the time, which has led to the purchasing professional focusing more time on nonvalue-added activities of discrepancy resolution (quantity and price) and fire fighting rather than undertaking strategic initiatives. These nonvalue-added activities have convinced procurement organizations to consider adopting evaluated receipt settlement in place of the manual process.

4. Push versus pull:

The push replenishment philosophy is primarily forecast-driven, whereas the pull replenishment philosophy is demand-driven. In any environment, the further upstream from the end customer (consumer) the pull-push decoupling point, the greater the adherence to LAVC principles, because it maximizes the length of the pull part of the supply chain. It is recommended to adopt pull replenishment for fluctuating and unpredictable demand, because pull is a supply philosophy in which the supply chain is synchronized to control variability and satisfy customer requirements. Supply variability is addressed by keeping lead times short. On the other hand, demand variability can be controlled by more frequent, smaller purchase orders. The following practices are recommended in a pull-driven philosophy:

- Automate purchase order generation and communication to reduce order processing costs.
- Counter full truckload economies by using third-party logistics and assorted truckloads.
- Counter volume discount economies by implementing capacity reservations. For example, a buyer can reserve a total fixed quantity (or amount) for a given period and then get it shipped in smaller increments over that

period based on need, as long as the accumulated order quantity is equal to the reserved quantity.

- Counter item shortages by sharing capacity and supply information in real time.
- Counter forecast inaccuracy by improving the forecasting techniques or providing point of sale data as in a vendor management inventory program of the retail industry.

However, enabling a pull replenishment system requires close coordination with the buyer's material planning and logistics groups, carrier, and supplier. It is also imperative that the order processing costs are kept low, and a high level of trust and cooperation between partners be developed to adopt this philosophy successfully and achieve the target performance.

BIC companies use an innovative hybrid approach based on the product mix, product life cycle, product characteristics, cost, risk, and so forth. For example, they might use push replenishment for mature products but pull replenishment for the more risky new products. Some examples of hybrid approaches include implementing pull for internal production, but push for external replenishments with suppliers based on a derived forecast. Another example involves a company that succeeded in using pull internally and with Tier 1 suppliers, but Tier 1 was using push with Tier 2 suppliers. In this case, the pull-push decoupling point was between Tier 1 and Tier 2.

5. Rewarding best-practice behavior:

BIC companies stick to an approved vendor list and always update it in anticipation of future supply requirements by continuously prequalifying and requalifying suppliers. Also, having a central purchasing organization to consolidate the purchases across different divisions and buying organizations will help aggregate spend and enable the company to take advantage of volume discounts. The suppliers will also benefit because of larger consolidated orders. Having metrics that reward purchasing agents who stick to an approved vendor list, approved parts list, and contracts will help minimize "off-contract" and maverick buying purchases to minimize procurement spend.

6. Effective contract management:

Sufficient time and effort should be spent in making the RFP as detailed as possible by including detailed information about freight costs, stepped quantity discounts, stepped pricing discounts, lead time or delivery/performance date, payment terms, shipping terms, insurance, duties, taxes, currency, and a warranty with clearly spelled out terms and conditions to minimize the number of variables to evaluate across bids. This will save a lot of time and effort later in the bid analysis step. The more detailed the specifications, the better the chance that the proposal provided will be accurate. Also, it is important that timing and type of replenishments, shipping lot size quantities, transportation methods, and ship early/ship late tolerance windows as well as performance metrics be agreed upon between the buyer and supplier. For example, a shipment with partial quantity, improper quality, or incomplete documentation should not be considered as an on-time delivery shipment. Timing and frequency of payments and payment terms must also be agreed upon during the contract negotiation phase. For example, payment of invoices should be calculated from the date the invoice is in the buyer's accounts payable, or from the date of receipt of goods, whichever is later. There should be clearly stated rules in the contract that a shipment before the delivery request date will not be accepted. For example, "Don't ship if there are more than $50,000 of invoice disputes pending." Having these rules clearly documented will minimize the number of returned shipments, help resolve disputes, inventory discrepancies, and reduce administrative costs (principle 3). Another method of reducing administrative expenses is paying the supplier on a monthly basis by summing up the amount of all invoices due that month.[21]

7. Standardization:

There should be a standardized best-practice process put in place that details the steps from RFP/RFQ preparation to bid analysis through contract management. The response format should also be standardized so that suppliers can provide all the relevant information. Having templates for RFP/RFQ and contracts and reusing them will help reduce variability and drive process consistency across divisions, thereby reducing time, effort, chances of error and waste. There should be a single repository that contains information pertaining to all RFPs/RFQs, existing contracts, contractual terms, business agreements, standard pricing, discounts, legal terms, clauses, and conditions typically used in contracts to prevent wasted time and effort of "reinventing the wheel" for every contract.

8. Leveraging technology:

Technology should be leveraged wherever possible to automate and streamline the procurement process to allow purchasing to focus on value-added activities such as strengthening the relationship with suppliers and the qualification process. Some examples of efficient use of technology include sending RFPs and RFQs electronically and receiving responses electronically, using software to conduct quantitative supplier response evaluation, and keeping ready templates for contracts in electronic format. The requisition approval processing process should also be automated and the requisition creation process should be easy enough to learn, because all the employees in the company including the shop floor people are potentially going to use the solution. Employees should be able to track their requisitions, and check the status and the stage at which they were accepted or rejected and when.

Technology can also be used so that buyers and suppliers are subscribed to exception alerts and notifications on their Blackberrys and computers. For example, the supplier will receive a notification once a purchase order is received, or the buyer can receive a notification once the supplier has sent an advanced shipping notice. Similarly, the buyer would receive an alert if, for some reason, the shipment is delayed from the supplier, or there is some discrepancy with the match between the purchase order, receipt, and invoice (three-way match). Similarly, the supplier should receive related alerts (under-received, over-received, received without advanced shipping notice, etc.).[21]

Service-oriented architecture (SOA) can be used in which traditional legacy systems for POM can expose their functionality as web services, and a custom best-practice workflow can be stitched together in a scalable, flexible, and secure fashion. Using SOA, the company can connect directly to the transportation carrier's website and get the tracking number of the advanced shipping notice, obtain the shipment status information, and display this to the POM application user interface in a seamless fashion. Hence, using SOA results in more time spent on designing the process rather than on nonvalue-added activities of integration and migration.[21]

RFID technology can be used to provide accurate, reliable, and real-time information of the in-transit material from the supplier to the buyer. An advanced shipping notice can automatically be created when an RFID tagged pallet is dispatched from a supplier's site and its status and location can be tracked by the supplier, buyer, and carrier using RFID-enabled trucks. When the buyer receives the shipment, a purchase order receipt can be raised automatically using an RFID-enabled warehouse or plant. This could then trigger a payment workflow to the supplier.[21]

Tracking pallets not only improves real-time visibility, but also reduces the number of claims, claims-processing costs (which could be due to inaccuracies in invoices), receipts, and shipping records, and the resulting time and effort spent reconciling and resolving discrepancies.[21]

Advance shipment notices and GPS capability tracking provide real-time visibility about the incoming shipments and allow the receiving crew to be ready for the shipments. They also give material planners time to react if incoming tracking signals indicate a delay. This helps tremendously in achieving agility, since it allows downstream processes to plan and stage documents, workers, and receiving equipment in anticipation of the goods' arrival in addition to being proactive when delays occur for any reason. It also helps the buyer to reroute or expedite shipments that are in transit.

To summarize, whichever new technology the company decides to implement, the company should always improve the process first; "improve before you automate" rather than the other way around.

9. Procurement segmentation:

Procurement has to deal with direct items that could be from a catalog or off catalog as well as indirect items such as MRO. BIC companies, rather than use a "one-size-fits-all" approach to procurement, employ a segmented procurement strategy (enabler 6) considering the risks, margins, and criticality for the items. For example, when purchasing low-dollar items (direct or indirect material), BIC companies delegate the procurement trigger to internal users using a preapproved online catalog, rather than placing the burden on the purchasing department. In addition, putting business rules in place so the approval process can be bypassed for the MRO items assist in automating the POM process with minimal intervention from the purchasing agents.

The best-practice approach should be to automate the requisition process and have flexible and configurable business rules to address different approval workflows. For example, the approval path should depend on the price of the purchased item (if price of an item exceeds a certain limit, it might need a director or VP's approval in addition to the manager). Similarly, the approval path for hazardous material needs an approval from a certain department in addition to the supervisor's approval. For some parts, no approval path is needed (the employee can order it directly from a catalog).

Segmented rules will allow purchasing to focus on value-added activities like early involvement in the product design, strategic sourcing, strengthening the relationship with suppliers, and qualification process rather than day-to-day fire fighting.

10. Total cost for contracts:

Companies should explore the various trade-offs (transportation, inventory, customer service, and lead time) and then ensure the appropriate contract is in place—the one that minimizes the total cost. For example, transportation costs may rise due to frequent and small deliverables, but storage costs and inventory carrying costs might be reduced. The various trade-offs that need to be considered include:

- Total cost versus customer service trade-off: Higher customer service requires higher inventory levels (lower inventory turnover), faster delivery, and wide product variety, which lead to increase in transportation and inventory costs.

- Inbound transportation cost versus inventory trade-off: Shipment consolidation allows larger shipments (more full truckload shipments) and lower transportation cost. However, it leads to higher inventory levels (holding cost).
- Lot size versus inventory turnover trade-off: Larger replenishment lot size from the suppliers leads to higher inventory.
- Transportation mode cost versus lead time: A slower transportation mode, though less costly in transportation terms, creates a greater in-transit pipeline inventory. As supply lead time and supply uncertainty increases so does the safety stock. Also, as the order lead time increases (time between placing the order and receiving the shipment), more safety stock is needed to guard against the lack of knowledge of demand during that lead time. Having a faster mode of transportation reduces the pipeline inventory and the safety stock but increases the cost of transportation.

To summarize, achieving a lean and agile procurement process requires the following strategic steps from a company and its partners and closely aligns with the LAVC principles and enablers from chapter 1:

- Optimize supply chain trade-offs to identify the right replenishment strategy with the suppliers and warehouses to minimize total landed cost
- Rationalize supplier and carrier base
- Negotiate a long-term contract with suppliers and carriers based on a win-win relationship
- Support a lean and agile procurement process with flexible material handling, and transportation system
- Leverage technology to streamline and automate procurement process

SRM SUPERPROCESS WORKFLOW SUMMARY

Strategic Sourcing

As we have seen, the SRM superprocess (Figure 3.14) is composed of a spectrum of interrelated processes ranging from short- to medium- to long-term activities. Strategic sourcing involves having a mutually beneficial, symbiotic relationship by choosing the right suppliers to reduce the total cost and not just the price. Total cost of product means not only the least price supplier, but the least total cost, which includes quality, reliability, inventory costs, transportation costs, and customer service costs. To avoid high supplier switching costs only the best suppliers must be selected, but once selected, the relationship should be based on partnership rather than exploitation. Forging strategic relationships with suppliers will help leverage global spend and reduce the total cost of product acquisition.

Strategic sourcing requires key inputs from the sales and operations planning (S&OP) process (aggregate demand from demand planning subprocess) of SCM

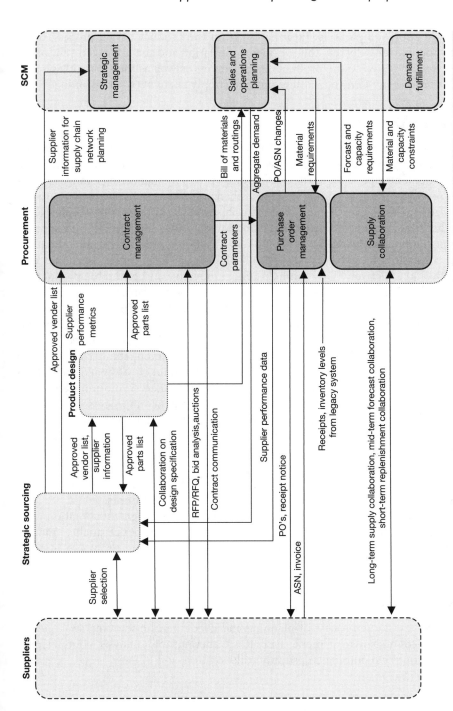

Figure 3.14 SRM superprocess workflow

and the approved parts list information from the product design process. Once the suppliers are selected, the supplier information and the approved vendor list are communicated to the product design process as well as the strategic management process in SCM to facilitate optimal supply chain network planning.

Product Design

The next major process in the SRM superprocess is to have collaborative product design. The product design process is typically triggered either by the need to introduce a new product to the market or by product engineering changes (product revisions) due to component cost change, product improvements, process change, quality corrective actions, material shortages, or product obsolescence. Product design involves enabling collaborative design, engineering, and support among companies, partners, and suppliers by sharing product design, schedules, and constraints to arrive at a single bill of material for a finished product efficiently and effectively. This will help bring innovative and profitable products to the market quickly, and ensure high product quality standards.

During product design, the use of common, standard, or previously designed parts should be encouraged since this will result in lower product development costs, increased reliability, improved quality, reduced risks, and reduced product development time. Only when all efforts to use common, standard parts have been exhausted, then and only then a new part should be designed and added to the approved parts list. The approved parts list is then communicated to the strategic sourcing process and the contract management subprocess. In addition, the resulting output from the product design process, which includes the BOM and routing information, is communicated to the S&OP process (master planning subprocess specifically) of SCM.

Using existing suppliers from the approved vendor list during the product design phase itself should be encouraged, since it will help lower purchasing costs as fewer suppliers lead to economies of scale and volume discounts.

Using an approved vendor and parts list, and having design collaboration with suppliers will help reduce the time to market, ensure product quality, and increase customer satisfaction, which will all lead to ensuring profitable lifetime customers.

Procurement

Procurement is the process of planning and executing the sourcing strategies. It includes contract management (RFP, RFQ, auctions, bid analysis, contract processing, contract compliance), supply collaboration, and POM.

Contract Management

Once the suppliers have been qualified and selected after the strategic sourcing process, the strategic sourcing process communicates the selected supplier as well as the supplier performance metrics to the contract management subprocess. The supplier performance metrics will be used during the bid analysis phase of contract management. The product design process also communicates the approved parts list to the contract management subprocess.

The contract management subprocess then sends the RFP/RFQ to the suppliers on the approved vendor list. This is followed by bid analysis and bid award. Once the winning bidder is selected, the purchasing department typically documents the result of the negotiations by creating a contract, blanket purchase order, or a long-term agreement clearly detailing the supplier details, valid dates, stepped volume and pricing discounts, incentives, rebates, part and cost information, legal terms, conditions, and clauses. This is communicated to the supplier as well as to the POM subprocess.

Supply Collaboration

Once the contract has been awarded to the supplier, the next step involves collaborating with the supplier over the long-term horizon (capacity collaboration), medium-term horizon (forecast collaboration) and short-term horizon (replenishment collaboration). The forecast and the capacity requirements are communicated from the buyer to the supplier through the S&OP process in SCM. The resulting material or capacity constraints at the suppliers end are then communicated to the S&OP process of SCM.

Purchase Order Management

The S&OP process of SCM drives the short-term material requirements to POM. POM can be defined as the process of managing the life cycle of the order right from issuing the purchase order, followed by tracking through its life cycle until receipt of the order at the buyer's end. It also includes managing all daily activities of replenishment with the selected suppliers and transportation with carriers to achieve and execute a synchronized procurement plan.

The POM subprocess involves the buyer sending the purchase order to the supplier, the supplier sending an advanced shipping notice to the buyer, the buyer acknowledging the receipt of the goods, and then the supplier billing the invoice to the buyer. In the event of any changes to the purchase order and/or advanced shipping notices, the changes are communicated back to the master planning subprocess to close the loop.

REFERENCES

1. Liker, J. K., and T. Y. Choi. 2004. "Building Deep Supplier Relationships." *Harvard Business Review* (December): 104–113.
2. Liker, J. K. 2004. *The Toyota Way: 14 Management Principles from the World's Greatest Manufacturer.* New York: McGraw-Hill.
3. Perry, N. J. 1990. The arms makers' next battle. http://money.cnn.com/magazines/fortune/fortune_archive/1990/08/27/73944/index.htm (accessed March 2009).
4. Williams, M. 2006. Sony expects PlayStation 3 shortages. http://www.pcworld.com/article/127048/sony_expects_playstation_3_shortages.htm (accessed December 2008).
5. Aberdeen Group. December 2005. *Strategic Sourcing in the Mid-market Benchmark: The Echo Boom in Supply Management,* 1-26. Boston: Aberdeen Group.
6. Hannon, D. 2004. Lockheed Martin: Negotiators Inc. *Purchasing.* http://www.purchasing.com/article/CA378931.html (accessed May 2009).
7. Gottfredson, M., R. Puryear, and S. Phillips. 2005. "Strategic Sourcing: From Periphery to the Core." *Harvard Business Review* 84 (2): 132–139.
8. Boivie, C. A. 2007. Cross-organizational collaboration: From dating to tying the knot. http://www.backbonemag.com/Magazine/CIO_View_11080701.asp (accessed May 2008).
9. Spend analysis and supply base rationalization survey. December 2005. http://www.ism.ws/files/tools/SpendAnalysisSupplyBase.pdf (accessed May 2008).
10. CAPS Research. (2005). Strategic performance measurement for purchasing and supply. 1-54.Tempe, AZ: CAPS Research
11. Kralgic, P. 1983. "Purchasing Must Become Supply Management." *Harvard Business Review* 61 (5): 110–117.
12. Byrnes, J. 2005. You only have one supply chain? Working Knowledge—Harvard Business Update. http://hbswk.hbs.edu/archive/4929.html (accessed September 2008).
13. Monczka, R. M., R. B. Handfield, T. V. Schannell, G. L. Ragatz, and D. J. Frayer. 2000. New product development: Strategies for supplier integration. Milwaukee, WI: American Society for Quality.
14. Webb, C. 2008. Intel's 45-nm CMOS technology. *Intel Technology Journal* 12, no. 2 (June 17). http://www.intel.com/technology/itj/2008/v12i2/5-design/2-intro.htm (accessed June2009).
15. Malone, R. 2005. Logistics by Ikea. http://www.forbes.com/2005/09/28/logistics-ikea-retail-cx_rm_0929ikea.html (accessed December 2008).
16. Nussbaum, B. 1997. Three designs for living. *Businessweek*, June. http://www.businessweek.com/1997/22/b352918.htm (accessed June 2008).

17. Billington Lee, C., L. Hau, and B. Carter. 1993. "Hewlett-Packard Gains Control of Inventory and Service through Design for Localization." *Harvard Business Review*, July-August, 1–11.
18. Dapiran, P. 1992. Benetton: Global Logistics in Action. *Asia Pacific International Journal of Business Logistics* 4 (3): 7–11.
19. Hopkins, M.S. 1989. How to negotiate practically anything http://www.inc .com/magazine/19890201/5526.html (accessed accessed May 2008).
20. Costanza, J. R. 1996. *Quantum Leap: In Speed to Market*. 3rd ed. Englewood, CO: John Costanza Institute of Technology.
21. Sabri, E., A. Gupta, and M. Beitler. 2006. *Purchase Order Management in B2B Environment: Best Practice & Technologies*. Fort Lauderdale, FL: J. Ross Publishing.
22. AMR Research: June, 2006. The Lean Supply Chain. Boston: AMR Research.
23. Ballou, H. 2004. *Business Logistics/Supply Chain Management*. 5th ed. Upper Saddle River, NJ: Prentice Hall.
24. Mayor, T. 2004. "The Supple Supply Chain." *CIO Magazine*, August. http://www.cio.com/article/119301/The_Supple_Supply_Chain (accessed April 2009).
25. Lee, H., and S. Whang. 2001. *E-business and Supply Chain Integration*, 1–20. Stanford, CA: Stanford Global Supply Chain Management Forum at Stanford University.
26. Pikulik, J. December 2005. *E-invoicing Solution Selection Report: Leading an Accounts Payable Extreme Makeover*, 1–40. Boston: Aberdeen Group.
27. Ruzicka, M. June 2000. "Invoiceless Procurement: Streamlining the Receiving and Billing Processes." *CAPS Research*, 7–10.

4

SUPPLY CHAIN MANAGEMENT SUPERPROCESS

INTRODUCTION

The simplified supply chain consists of a supplier that provides the raw materials, a manufacturer that converts the raw materials into finished products, and a customer who consumes the finished products (Figure 4.1). The APICS Dictionary defines supply chain management as "The design, planning, execution, control, and monitoring of supply activities with the objective of creating net value, building a competitive infrastructure, leveraging worldwide logistics, synchronizing supply with demand, and measuring performance globally."

The supply chain management (SCM) superprocess plays the role of a central nervous system in regulating the product flow, cash flow, and information flow between supplier, manufacturer, and customer and the reverse flow of products returned for repairs, and so forth (reverse logistics). It has very strong linkages with superprocesses such as supplier relationship management (SRM) and customer relationship management (CRM).

SCM provides the procurement process in SRM with the future purchasing requirements that have been derived from the demand and production plans in SCM, and the procurement process in turn provides SCM with the visibility into supplier material and capacity constraints.

CRM provides SCM critical insight about customer priorities, pricing, and promotions, while SCM provides CRM with information on product availability and resulting product allocations by sales channels, etc.

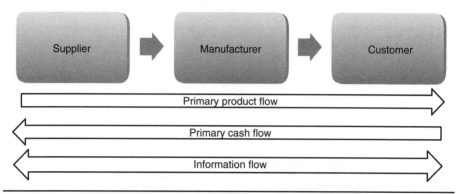

Figure 4.1 Simple supply chain

SCM EVOLUTION

The concept of SCM has really come into the limelight of corporate professionals and academia over the last several decades. However, evidence shows that supply chains were present from the time when mankind understood the need of merchandising and distribution. The evolution of SCM has moved from disparate functions of logistics, transportation, purchasing, and physical distribution to focus on integration, collaboration, visibility, reliability, flexibility, and responsiveness.

Evolution of SCM has been like a spectrum—on one end vertical integration and on the other horizontal integration with various permutations and combinations in between like the different colors of the spectrum. Firms have generally pursued one of three types of SCM integration: vertical integration, lateral integration, and a hybrid of vertical and lateral integration for different businesses. Henry Ford is often considered the pioneer of vertical integration in which Ford owned the supply chain from the most upstream—raw materials (rubber plantations to supply raw material for tires, iron ore mines, steel mills) to the most downstream—dealerships to sell the cars to the customers. One company was managing the entire supply chain from raw materials to manufacturing to distribution. While this structure still persists in some companies, it generally went out of fashion because of globalization, as it became increasingly difficult to excel in all elements of the supply chain. Hence, corporations turned instead to outsourcing those aspects of their business that they didn't consider as their core competency.

As Ford's Director of Material Planning and Logistics Grant Belanger put it, "The days of being 100 percent self-sufficient and capable in today's world of high technology and engineering are gone."[1] Hence, companies started adopting a lateral supply chain in which firms focused on their core competencies and interacted with each other through contracts. For example, General Motors spun off its component supplier—Delphi Corporation. Because the independent company focused entirely on its business it was able to achieve economies of scale, lower pricing, and higher quality. However, this came at a price—loss of control and confidentiality.

Similarly, when 7-Eleven started to lose market share in the early 1990s, the then CEO Jim Keyes realized that 7-Eleven's core competency was merchandising (pricing, promotion, placement). Prior to this, 7-Eleven owned the cows that produced the milk, made its own ice and candy, and distributed the gasoline. Hence, Keyes decided to "outsource everything not mission critical" and outsourced product development, packaging, logistics, and distribution without relinquishing control of its competitive differentiator—merchandising. For example, 7-Eleven also outsourced gasoline distribution to CITGO but maintained proprietary control over the pricing and promotion. Thus, the decision on whether the company should outsource a particular product, process, or function depends on whether the product or process is proprietary and whether the capabilities are common across organizations. In other words, a product or process that is not proprietary and common across organizations should be outsourced.[2] However, even when the organization decides to outsource, the organization should not take its "eye off the ball," i.e., the organization was and always will be primarily responsible in the eyes of the customer.

On the other hand, proprietary processes and unique capabilities should be "insourced," that is, if the company is really good at its competitive differentiators, the company should look at performing that function for other companies. For example, sports vehicle manufacturer Land Rover wanted to improve its after-sales service and was looking for a company to benchmark. After studying Caterpillar's after-sales support operations, Caterpillar was asked by Land Rover, "Why don't you do this for us? We (Mary Bell, chairman and president, Caterpillar Logistics Services) thought that idea made sense. There are opportunities for scale; there are synergies. Service and support are core competencies for us. It was a good business decision to leverage our expertise and provide these services to Land Rover".[3] Today Cat Logistics manages logistics of more than 65 client companies including Ford Motor Company, DaimlerChrysler, Toshiba, Bombardier Aerospace, Eaton, Harley-Davidson, and Irwin Tool, among others.

Companies like Zara have adopted a hybrid of vertical and lateral integration. Zara, the Spanish clothing manufacturer has two supply chains, one for staples and another for fashion clothing. To get fast response time for fashion clothing Zara maintains a near vertical chain for their fashion items. However, for the staples with predictable demand they choose lateral integration by outsourcing most of the functions. By using a hybrid of vertical and lateral integration to serve different demand streams, Zara used lean and agile value chain (LAVC) enablers like strategy innovation (enabler 7) and flexibility (enabler 4) to leverage the first LAVC principle to focus on customer needs.[4] (Note: Throughout this chapter, you will see mentions of LAVC principles and enablers which are discussed in detail in chapter 1 and should be considered as you progress through this book.)

GOAL OF SCM

The goal of SCM is to maximize customer satisfaction in terms of order promising, delivery reliability, flexibility, and responsiveness at the lowest possible cost. This includes not only responding as fast as possible to customer requests, but also being flexible to customer request changes; promising to deliver and then delivering on every promise while minimizing the purchasing, manufacturing, inventory, and distribution costs. If being flexible (enabler 4) and responsive to maximize customer satisfaction demands carrying a lot of excess inventory that could lead to decreased profitability, it should not be implemented since it violates principle 3 (eliminate waste and reduce nonvalue-added activities).

Initial efforts at managing supply chains often focused only on cost reduction, that is, making the supply chain leaner. However, while squeezing excess costs out of a supply chain certainly has the potential to provide value, it has to be done carefully as it might result in spending more elsewhere. For example, too little inventory in the supply chain will result in poor customer service level and lost customers. Shipping full truckloads (FTLs) to cut transportation costs is good (enabler 6: process innovation to reduce costs), but should not be done at the expense of customers who are waiting for their shipments (principle 1: focus on customer success). Lean is good but starvation is not desirable.

For example, Lucent, a communications solutions provider, made a strategic decision to centralize operations in Oklahoma to make its supply chain more cost-effective, efficient, and lean. However, when there was a boom for telephone equipment in Asia, Lucent could not compete with the competitors who had plants spread throughout the world and carried a little excess inventory and capacity for flexibility and agility.[5] Lucent had learned its lesson that it is not sufficient to be lean alone. Lean has to be complemented by agility and focusing on customer satisfaction. Focusing on cost reduction and efficiency at the cost of other desirable qualities such as flexibility and customer service can turn from a market advantage into a serious disadvantage.

To summarize: In order to compete in today's global marketplace of variability and uncertainty, a little buffer (fat/redundancy) in the supply chain in terms of excess capacity and/or inventory can help the supply chain to be more responsive and agile and increase customer satisfaction. The guiding principle always has to be creation of value from the customer's perspective. Since the end customer is the only entity that introduces money into the chain (the rest of supply chain members are merely shuffling the money back and forth), SCM ought to be all about giving the final customer the right product at the right place at the right time.

Also, the gains must be distributed among the different stakeholders of the supply chain. Firms have been known to reduce their inventory carrying costs (enabler 6: process innovation to reduce costs) by shifting the inventory to suppliers with less leverage, which goes against principle 2 (create win-win and a trusted environment for all stakeholders). Also, asking suppliers to build inventory to compensate for buyer forecast error does not address the root cause of the problem. The supply chain will be able to prosper and flourish only when the relationship between the different stakeholders is based on partnership rather than exploitation. To conclude, though maximizing profit might be the ultimate goal of any organization, it is customer value that drives financial value and long-term success.

SCM CHALLENGES

1. Push versus pull:

In a *forecast-driven*, or *push*, or *make-to-stock* supply chain, everything is pushed downstream based on the schedule that has been derived from the forecasts. The supplier pushes the raw materials to the manufacturer and the manufacturer pushes the finished goods to the distributor, that is, make products in advance of demand and hold them in stock to satisfy demand from inventory. The customer order then comes in and consumes (pulls) from the finished goods inventory. On the other hand, in a *demand-driven*, or *pull*, or *make-to-order* supply chain, the finished good is not produced until the customer has placed an order. There is a third intermediate, well-known strategy called *assemble-to-order*, in which products are partially built or the raw materials made available in anticipation of demand, but final assembly is postponed until the order comes in.

Pull or *demand-driven* supply chains offer many advantages including less inventory carrying costs as the raw material inventory is a lot less expensive than finished goods inventory, more flexibility to make different finished goods from the same raw materials, and less inventory obsolescence since the finished good is not produced until the customer has placed an order. The disadvantages of make-to-stock include reduced responsiveness to customers as the cumulative lead time (time from order receipt to order fulfillment) is more in make-to-order as compared to make-to-stock. Also, plants may have to undergo considerable change if they have to produce several different kinds of products under the new circumstances. For example, in make-to-stock, a plant can run a larger volume of each product to send to inventory, but in make-to-order, the plant may have to produce several different types of products in a day. There will be no room for long setup times between runs of different products. Hence, it's a challenge to decide whether the company should choose push versus pull or something in between.

2. Variability and complexity:

The factors that contribute to SCM variability and complexity, among other things, include globalization, intensified competition, shorter product life cycles, mass customization, data, and people.

SCM is a data-intensive superprocess that requires data pertaining to bill of materials (BOM), bill of distributions (BOD), manufacturing routings, item master, location master, yields, setup times and so forth. Nowadays companies have more than a hundred thousand stock keeping units (SKUs) and hundreds of suppliers and customers, which, to make things worse, are also constantly changing. Change is the only constant. Lack of liability or accuracy of planning data ("garbage in garbage out") is often the root cause of failure. You can easily get good data one time, but the bigger challenge is constantly maintaining it and improving it by institutionalizing continuous improvement (principle 4) through Plan → Do → Check → Act.

The second category is related to people who are diverse in their style of functioning, priorities, and attitudes that defy analytical quantification. SCM is a cross-functional superprocess that requires participation from different people with disparate functions (sales, marketing, operations, finance, etc.), which in most cases have their own local objectives and metrics. Having these functions working together seamlessly toward a common goal that is aligned with the organizational goal can be extremely challenging.

In addition to the above-mentioned factors, an increasing shift from a more vertically integrated enterprise to a laterally integrated one has also contributed to increased variability and the complexity of a business. Laterally integrated companies focus on their core competencies and hence have to deal with multiple suppliers, contract manufacturers, distributors, and transportation providers thus generating additional communication needs. As a result, the quality of communication has sharply decreased leading to a lack of trust and overprotective behaviors such as excess inventories and buffer capacities.

3. Supply demand balance:

One of the major challenges of SCM is to achieve an optimal balance between demand and supply and to maintain that balance. Even if you are able to get multiple feasible (achieving the balance between supply and demand) plans, the bigger challenge is to select the most optimal. This requires taking into consideration all different types of costs—purchasing, manufacturing, transportation, and inventory carrying costs, etc. Given so many variables, objective functions, and complex constraints, finding the optimal solution to match supply with demand can be a challenge.

Also, in today's world of demand volatility and supply variability, unexpected events such as order modifications by customers on delivery dates/order quantities happen on a daily basis and can throw the supply chain off balance. The planning processes that were implemented in the past were mostly structured around the material requirements planning (MRP) logic, which could take anywhere from 2 to 10 days, depending on the depth and breadth of the supply chain.

ENABLERS

Some of the enablers to overcome the challenges mentioned include the following:

1. *Business go-live driven rather than IT go-live driven* (Figure 4.2). In most companies, the SCM implementations are extremely IT centric and focus on *IT go-live rather than business go-live*, which means that the effort is mostly focused on implementing an application software and going live with the software within the deadline, rather than improving the process

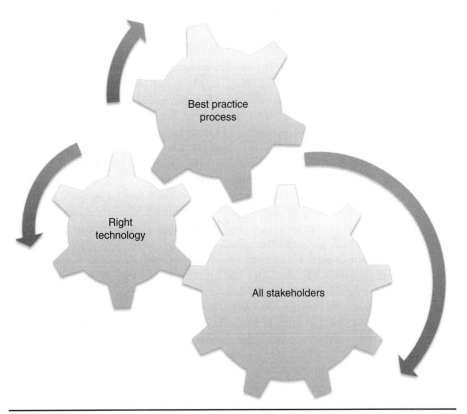

Figure 4.2 People, process, and technology

first before implementing the software. Too often people rush to embrace the latest technology or the quick-fix tool without understanding the root causes of the problem only to find later that it has only exacerbated the problem.

Companies should thoroughly evaluate and pilot test the technology with the help of a cross-functional team to make sure it is in alignment with the organizational goal, adds value to the processes, and increases efficiency rather than creating waste. More than implementing the latest and greatest technology, emphasis should be on improving the process first and then selecting the right technology to increase efficiency of the right processes. This demands a change in the organizational culture from "automate then improve" to "improve before you automate." If implementing technology will add more waste, it should not be implemented.

One semiconductor company switched its employees' roles periodically between the IT department and the business. Also, IT and the business shared the same office space. This led to IT folks realizing the problems business people faced and vice versa. Also, IT was able to understand the SCM concepts a lot better since they had to wear the business hat periodically.

2. SCM concepts: SCM core methodologies and best practices (bottlenecks, frozen periods, inventory pooling, assembly postponement, collaboration) are the result of experiences from many companies over the past decades that can be leveraged by other companies. Senior executives and employees alike need to become more knowledgeable about these key SCM concepts and best practices, and focus on continuous improvement.

3. Global optimization: A supply chain necessitates strong linkages between its chain components and not the parallel functioning of different departments. The chain is only as strong as its weakest link. It is quite common to find different projects going on concurrently without proper coordination or without the project's goal being aligned with the organization's goal. Disjointed, local optimizations never lead to global optimization. For example, the logistics department could be implementing transportation planning projects to select the cheapest mode of transportation, and the inventory planning team could be implementing projects to reduce inventory levels. A slower transportation mode, though less costly in transportation terms, creates a greater in-transit pipeline inventory. On the other hand, having a faster mode of transportation reduces the pipeline inventory and the safety stock, but increases the cost of transportation. These two projects rather than treated as a "my" and "your" project should be treated as an "our" project aligned with the organization's goals. For example, if

the company goal is to maximize market share, it may demand choosing a faster mode of transportation to be more responsive to customer needs and carrying a little bit more finished goods inventory to increase customer service.

STRATEGIC MANAGEMENT

The SCM superprocess is composed of a spectrum of interrelated processes ranging from short- to medium- to long-term activities. The higher you are in the supply chain pyramid the fewer the decisions, but the higher the impact of these decisions on the success of the organization. Also, as you go down from strategic to tactical to operational, the percentage of cost savings goes down. At the top of the supply chain pyramid is the strategic management process, which supports long-term decision-making such as the supply chain strategy and supply chain network design subprocesses and is therefore impervious to different industries, while at the bottom is the operational planning processes like demand fulfillment. (Figure 4.3). The right supply chain strategy will help answer questions relating

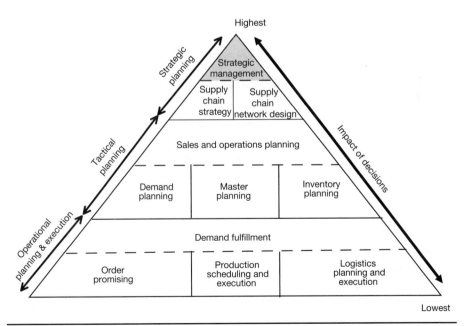

Figure 4.3 Supply chain pyramid (strategic management)

to whether a company is operating with the right physical supply chain and is servicing the right customers with the right products. The supply chain network design on the other hand deals with determining the optimal number and locations of facilities (plants and distribution centers), flow of goods throughout the supply chain, and best assignment of customers to distribution centers. This should be aligned with the supply chain strategy.

Supply Chain Strategy

Building the right supply chain is one of the most powerful ways to get an edge over competition, deliver more value to customers, and be more flexible in the age of uncertainty (Figure 4.4). Hence, supply chain strategy is really a corporate strategy by which firms distinguish themselves from competitors and create value for their customers and investors. Companies need to decide whether the strategy should be primarily forecast-driven or demand-driven and whether the company should use mass production or mass customization.

Forecast-Driven or Demand-Driven

Forecast-driven or demand-driven strategy involves whether the company will adopt a make-to-order model, assemble-to-order model, make-to-stock model, or

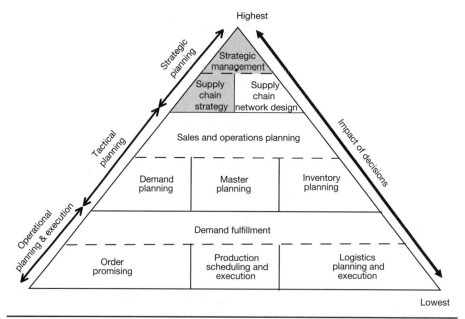

Figure 4.4 Supply chain pyramid (supply chain strategy)

a hybrid model. In any strategy the optimal trade-off between three conflicting objectives has to be considered:

1. Cost: The highest cost is a make-to-stock strategy because all the inventory is stored as finished goods.
2. Flexibility: The highest flexibility is offered by a make-to-order strategy because you don't manufacture a finished product until the customer has placed the order.
3. Responsiveness: The highest responsiveness is offered by a make-to-stock strategy as the finished goods are stored as close as possible to the customer.

The push philosophy is primarily forecast-driven, whereas the pull philosophy is demand-driven. In any environment, the further upstream from the end customer (consumer) the pull-push decoupling point, the greater the adherence to LAVC principles because it maximizes the length of the pull part of the supply chain. This pull-push decoupling point varies across industries and even across various supply chains (products) in the same firm. Most firms produce a mix of high-volume products with stable demand, and low-volume products with unpredictable demand. It is appropriate to adopt a push replenishment philosophy when the supply requirements or demand is stable and reasonably well known. On the other hand, it is recommended to adopt pull replenishment for fluctuating and unpredictable demand, because pull is a supply philosophy in which the supply chain is synchronized to control variability and satisfy customer requirements. Supply variability is addressed by keeping lead times short. Suppliers are usually located near the buyer's site of operations. On the other hand, demand variability can be controlled by more frequent, smaller purchase orders. The two philosophies might be applied in the same firm or supply chain. For example, a firm can implement pull for internal production, but material replenishments with suppliers can continue to be based on a push basis and derived forecast.

It is important to point out that some companies might use a mix of these strategies depending on the characteristics and maturity of the products. For example, they might use a build-to-stock strategy for mature products, while it is very risky to do so for new products. Also, depending on the product mix, which is different across industries, companies might use a build-to-stock strategy for consumer products, assemble-to-order for personal computers, build-to-order for defense projects, and mass customization for sports equipment.

Mass Production or Mass Customization

Mass production was primarily driven by the scientific management techniques of Frederick Taylor and gained popularity in the early 20th century by Henry Ford's assembly line—a conveyor that moved the product from one workman to another, with each individual adding their specialty part. This allowed Ford to produce more cars per worker-hour, leverage economies of scale, and lower the labor cost of the end product which in turn made the "Model T" more affordable. Mass customization on the other hand started to gain popularity in the 1950s when Taiichi Ohno (Toyota's plant manager) was given the responsibility of improving Toyota's manufacturing processes. Ohno liked Ford's idea of continuous production but Japan being a smaller market, Toyota could not leverage the same economies of scale as Ford. Instead, Toyota needed the flexibility to offer their customers what they wanted and when they wanted it at an affordable cost. This led to the development of mass customization. Ohno was also very much influenced by the idea of single-piece flow of the American supermarkets in which products were replaced on the shelves as customers purchased them. He combined the idea of Ford's continuous production and the American supermarkets single-piece flow to pioneer what we know today as the *pull system*. The APICS Dictionary defines mass customization as "the creation of a high-volume product with large variety so that a customer may specify his or her exact model out of a large volume of possible end items while manufacturing cost is low because of the large volume."

While mass production was driven by low cost and job specialization, mass customization was driven by product modularity, product and process flexibility, general purpose equipment, and above all employee empowerment and a collaborative customer relationship. However, mass customization had its disadvantages also, which include longer response times (especially with an increase in outsourcing), increased complexity in forecasting the variety of end products, and decreased resale value as a result of the customized product.[6]

Whether a company should employ a mass production or mass customization strategy should be driven by the customer. It is not uncommon to find that many companies jump onto the latest bandwagon—in this case mass customization (enabler 7: strategy innovation) without studying the key aspects of customer demand and what it would take for the company to move from mass production to mass customization. In other words, if this LAVC enabler of mass customization would violate LAVC principle 1 of focusing on customer success, then it should not be undertaken. For example, some companies spend "an arm and leg" to provide the customer with a gazillion possible car configurations, when in reality what most customers are really interested in would be just the engine, color, and gas mileage. According to Pine (1993),[7] mass production can still be used in industries with low market turbulence, low price, and less product complexity such as the lumber and plywood industry. Mass customization, on the other hand, would make sense for industries with high market turbulence, high product complexity, and high price, such as the electronics industry.

The key point is mass customization should be driven by what the customer values and not what the marketing department wants. Best-in-class (BIC) companies, rather than use a broad-brushed "one size fits all," leverage customer focus by using a blend of mass customization and mass production (enabler 4: flexibility). For example, Dell, who revolutionized the PC business by selling mass customized computers over the web, now also sells the preconfigured, mass produced, low price PC models (Dell Dimension and Dell Inspiron) through retailers like Wal-Mart and Best Buy.

Best Practices

1. Strategies for functional products and innovative products:

Fisher (1997)[8] pointed out that before designing the supply chain one must consider the nature of demand for the products. Broadly, products can be classified as functional products and innovative products. Functional products are characterized by stable demand, long product life cycle, and low profit margins, but at the same time have low cost of obsolescence and less product variety (Table 4.1). Most of the items in grocery stores, basic clothing, and so on, are examples of functional products. Companies with functional products would be successful if they operate their supply chain based on process innovations that eliminate waste, reduce inventories, and maximize production efficiencies. Innovative products on the other hand are characterized by unpredictable demand and high profit margins, but at the same time have high cost of obsolescence and short product life cycles. Examples of innovative products include fashion items.

Companies with innovative products get their competitive advantage from flexibility and responsiveness, that is, where in the supply chain to position inventory and capacity buffers to hedge against risk of uncertain demand (enabler 5: risk management). For firms with these types of products, suppliers should be chosen based on their speed, flexibility, and responsiveness rather than cost. Hence, for innovative products the supply chain strategy should be based on modular design, assembly postponement, and reducing lead times (enabler 6) so that products can be brought to market faster based on the most updated demand information.

Table 4.1 Functional and innovative products

Functional products	Innovative products
e.g., basic clothing like white t-shirts	e.g., fashion items like crocodile boots
Stable demand	Unpredictable demand
Long product lifestyle	Short product lifestyle
Less product variety	More product variety
Lower inventory costs	Higher inventory costs
Low cost of obsolescence	High cost of obselescence
Lower profits margins	Higher profit margins

Postponement involves keeping the product in its generic state as long as possible, and delaying the differentiation into specific end products until better demand information is available. The main advantages of postponement include cost-effectiveness, since it's much cheaper to hold inventory in a subassembly (semifinished state) rather than a finished state, and it's easier to forecast a base product level rather than a finished product level which includes all customer configurations. This also leads to increased flexibility because a wide range of specific end products can be derived from the same generic product.

The problem is that most companies do not do a very good job of classifying their products as functional/innovative and thereby apply the wrong strategy. Also, since innovative products have a higher contribution margin, the benefits received from contributing and investing in supply chain agility and responsiveness far outweigh the benefits received from investing in cost saving initiatives of improving supply chain efficiency. With increased globalization and competition, the demarcation between functional/innovative products may not be crystal clear, as a lot of the functional products like cars, computers, and apparel have gravitated toward innovative products. However, companies still try to apply the same functional measures and metrics of maximizing production efficiencies, reducing inventory, and so forth, which has resulted in unresponsive and fragile supply chains and a loss of customer satisfaction.[8] For example, sticking to our earlier car example, when shopping for a car at a dealer one would find a gazillion configurations (color, interior features, engine, transmission, etc.), and one would think that these exhibit all the characteristics of an innovative product. However, when one asks the dealer for a customized car the dealer's answer likely is, "The customized car would not only cost you $5,000 more, but also would take an additional four weeks. Hence, you are better off picking something from the lot." In other words, the supply chain design is not responsive enough to meet the customer demand and there is a misalignment between the product offering and the supply chain design.

The key here is to segment your product portfolio into functional/innovative products and have an appropriate supply chain strategy for each one. Zara, the Spanish clothing manufacturer, has a corporate strategy of getting fashions into stores rapidly; hence it has two supply chains, one for staples and another for fashion clothing. To get fast response time for fashion clothing, Zara uses European suppliers (increased speed to market, higher price but more responsive) and also maintains a near vertical integration for their fashion items by outsourcing only the sewing function. Thus, the supply chain strategy is aligned nicely with their corporate strategy. However, for predictable demand staple items, Zara uses Eastern European suppliers, which have poor response time but lower cost. Equipped with more than one supply chain, the firm can move products from one supply chain to another based on product life cycle stage, demand patterns, and so forth.[4]

Compaq too decided to produce certain high variety, short life cycle products in-house rather than outsource them to China because local production gave the company increased flexibility and responsiveness.[8]

Zara and Compaq use LAVC enablers like strategy innovation (enabler 7) and flexibility (enabler 4) to meet and exceed customers' needs (principle 1).

2. Strategies to manage supply and demand uncertainty:

Lee[9] included supply uncertainty together with demand uncertainty and suggested strategies to manage supply and demand uncertainty for functional and innovative products. Most functional products are characterized by stable supply processes, and a high degree of automation, and hence have long-term supply contracts. Most innovative products on the other hand are characterized by evolving processes and therefore uncertain yields.

Since it's a lot more challenging and expensive to operate with products of high demand and supply uncertainty rather than those with stable demand and stable supply processes, companies should first try and reduce the level of demand and supply uncertainty as much as possible by using different techniques (mentioned below), and hedge against the remaining by having inventory and capacity buffers at appropriate echelons in the supply chain.

Demand uncertainty can be reduced by having better forecasting techniques in place and using information sharing and collaboration (enabler 2: cross-organizational collaboration). Supply uncertainty (yield and process reliability, lead time, etc.) on the other hand can be reduced through extensive collaboration and exchange of information with suppliers throughout the product life cycle—product development, maturity, and end of life. For example, BIC companies set up supplier hubs in close proximity to the factories, which allow suppliers to have better information about the needs and consumption patterns. This reduces supply uncertainties and creates a win-win situation (principle 2) for both the supplier and manufacturer.

- For stable demand and stable supply processes, supply chain strategies should aim at the lean principles of eliminating nonvalue-added activities, reducing costs, maximizing throughput, minimizing inventories using just in time, total quality management, and automation (Figure 4.5). This will enable them to get costs down and gain a competitive edge.[9]
- For stable demand and evolving supply processes, supply chain strategies should aim at using principles such as multi-sourcing and sharing safety stock (inventory pooling) with other companies.[9]

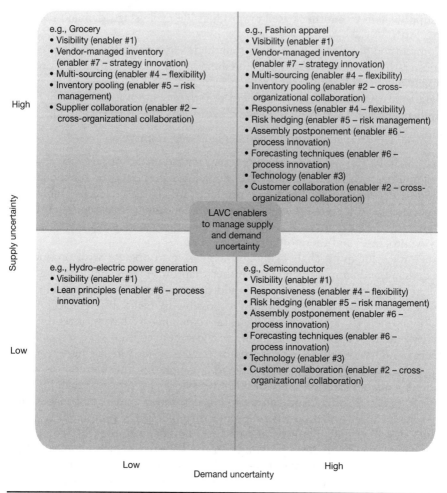

Figure 4.5 Low-hanging fruit (enablers to manage supply and demand uncertainty)

For example, Saturn has adopted a joint inventory management program with its dealers in which they share inventory risks for service parts. This results in not only risk mitigation but also increased inventory turns for the dealer. Also, it has resulted in excellent off-the-shelf parts availability, which ensures higher customer satisfaction.[10] Collaborating with the suppliers and vendor-managed inventory can also help reduce supply side uncertainty.

- For uncertain demand but a stable supply process, supply chain strategies should aim at being responsive and flexible to customer needs by using principles such as assembly postponement and examining the customer ordering pattern so that only the minimum inventory is stored at each echelon of the supply chain.[9]

For example, Benetton used the concept of assembly postponement in the apparel industry by changing their manufacturing process to knit first and then dye at the distribution centers, based on the most updated information about the colors that would be in fashion that holiday season.[11]

Also, traditionally paint manufacturers used to package all the possible different colors in paint cans and ship them to the retail store. This made it not only very difficult to forecast the variety of colors but also created stockpiles of inventory that later had to be discounted if the colors went out of fashion at the end of the season. Sherwin Williams figured out that it could save inventory carrying costs by shipping only the primary colors and mixing the colors on-site at the retail store based on actual demand from the customer. This assembly postponement strategy not only helped reduce costs but also resulted in an increase in customer satisfaction as the colors were always in stock.[12]

Both Benetton and Sherwin Williams used enablers like process innovation, flexibility, and risk management to increase sales and better serve their customers. Using technology to assist in better forecasting and collaborating with the customer can also help reduce demand uncertainty.

- For unpredictable demand and unstable supply, the supply chain strategies should aim at a combination of strategies for managing supply and demand uncertainty.

3. Effective reverse supply chain strategies:

Reverse supply chain as the name suggests involves the handling of customer returns, that is, the reverse material flow from the end consumer to point of disposition, where the decision is made to either reuse or scrap. Once testing and sorting is done at the disposition center, a decision is made based on the product's condition whether to refurbish, remanufacture, remarket, or scrap. Just as we had different supply chain strategies for functional products and innovative products for the forward supply chain, BIC companies use a similar hybrid approach and have different reverse supply chain strategies for different products to optimize value recovery. For short life cycle products like GPSs and PCs, BIC companies realize that the longer the time between the actual customer return and the time they can be re-used, the lower the likelihood of economically feasible reuse options. Hence, they use a more responsive, decentralized reverse supply chain for the short life cycle products.

Blackburn, Guide, Souza, and Wassenhove[13] propose using a differentiated reverse supply chain strategy for the functional products and innovative products. Functional products are characterized by low profit margins, low inventory costs, and long product life cycle. Therefore, for functional products companies should deploy a centralized return center so that all the returns are sent from the different retail stores to one disposition facility for testing and sorting, and then a decision is made on the future course of action based on the products' condition. Having a centralized disposition facility and cheaper mode of transportation will help minimize operating costs because of economies of scale. However, for innovative products like GPSs and consumer electronics with high inventory carrying costs, short product life cycles, and shrinking margins, the sorting and testing must be decentralized, that is, the decision on whether the product might be reused or scrapped should be made at multiple facilities—preferably even at the retailers so that minimal time is wasted from the point of return to the point of disposition. Though more expensive than the centralized strategy, the increase in facility costs can be justified by an increase in revenue as the returned products will be brought back to the market faster, hence faster asset value recovery by being more responsive. Technology can also help by quickly diagnosing the problem at the decentralized facility so that minimal time is wasted. For example, Bosch has equipped some of its power tools with a chip that records the number of hours the tool has been used, the speed, and so forth, so that in the event of a return, a quick diagnosis can be made whether to recycle, remanufacture, or scrap.

The reverse supply chain is starting to get more and more attention nowadays because of the connection between reverse logistics and green supply chain initiatives, which includes environmentally responsible manufacturing and distribution. A well-planned and executed reverse logistics strategy can help an organization reduce costs, comply with environmental regulations, increase customer satisfaction, and be a source of competitive differentiation.

Supply Chain Network Design

Supply chain network design (Figure 4.6) should always be aligned with the supply chain strategy. Supply chain network design deals with determining the optimal number and locations of facilities (plants and distribution centers), flow of goods throughout the supply chain, and best assignment of customers to distribution centers.

The main objectives of the supply chain network design subprocess are to optimize the location of facilities, the allocation of capacity and technology requirements to facilities, the assignment of products to facilities, and the distribution of products between facilities and customer regions. Supply chain network design, being at the top of the supply chain pyramid, has the highest impact on the entire

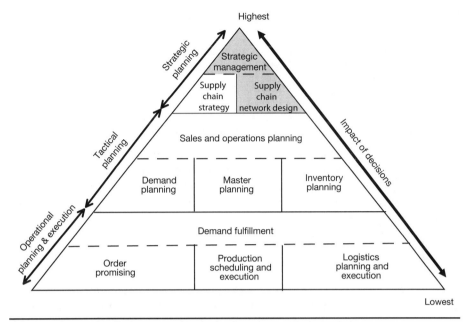

Figure 4.6 Supply chain pyramid (supply chain network design)

supply chain because it provides the framework for the tactical and operational supply chain processes. Though the number of decisions might be less compared to tactical or operational processes, the impact of these decisions on the success of the organization is the greatest. Supply chain network design should provide decision support for many strategic scenarios, such as the following:

- New product introduction: How much should be produced initially, from which facility, and when?
- Supplier base optimization: From where should the raw material and parts be purchased? Should a certain part be purchased from multiple sources? How should the supplier base be reduced without affecting customer service levels?
- Best locations for manufacturing plants: Should the manufacturing plants be closer to customers to reduce delivery time or closer to the suppliers to implement *kanban* with them?
- Customers served from each facility: Which products should move directly from assembly facilities to end customers (to reduce delivery time) and which ones should move to end customer via the distribution centers (indirect channel). How many distribution centers should the company have and where should they be optimally located to minimize the total

costs, which include manufacturing, transportation, and inventory carrying costs.

- Distribution center consolidation or decentralization: Should the company have fewer but larger distribution centers (consolidation) or more but smaller distribution centers (decentralization)? How does the company assign service territories in a consolidated versus decentralized distribution environment? How many transportation hubs (cross-docking facilities) does the company need and where should they be located?

In addition to all these decisions, supply chain network design also has to balance the trade-offs of alternative manufacturing, inventory, distribution, and procurement strategies. For example, marketing's first objective is to increase customer service level by increasing inventory levels, while the inventory strategy (driven by finance) is to get rid of finished product inventory which, in this case, has a conflict with marketing strategy.[14]

Supply Chain Network Design Challenges

Competitive pressures to introduce new products and enter new markets, decreased margins, and a shift from mass production to customized products has forced companies to rethink their physical supply chain network configurations. Companies that used to conduct supply chain network design once every few years now have to do it more frequently, maybe once every quarter to make sure that their network is in sync with their supply chain strategy.

The major challenges of supply chain network design include:

1. Lack of flexibility in the supply chain configuration to react fast to the variability in demand and supply
2. Urgent need to introduce new products into the market quickly
3. The challenge to decide whether to keep a direct distribution model, an intermediate distribution channels, or a hybrid of the two

With globalization, firms have transitioned from a single-site business serving domestic markets to a truly global business with multiple locations around the world. Decisions about where to source materials, where to produce, and where to sell products are suddenly more complex. Also, one would find that though companies want to make decisions based on minimizing cost or maximizing profit, they often lack the relevant strategic planning data at the aggregated level such as variable costs, fixed facility costs, transportation expense, inventory carrying costs, and other financial numbers.

Optimization Techniques

There are several optimization techniques available such as linear programming (LP), mixed integer linear programming (MILP), and so forth. There are other techniques such as heuristics, which use "rules of thumb" to arrive at a good quality solution in a reasonable amount of time. In heuristics the problem-solving is based on certain rules rather than optimization.

Linear programming is defined by the APICS Dictionary as "a mathematical model for solving linear optimization problems through minimization or maximization of a linear function subject to linear constraints." LP and MILP can be used to generate least cost or max profitability network configurations by considering all the constraints such as capacity, material, time, financial, variable costs, fixed facility costs, transportation expense, and inventory carrying costs while at the same time meeting all customer expectations such as delivery quantity, date and place, price, and quality. LP provides an optimal solution within reasonable time and computing power, and is typically used when supply chain configuration is fixed and the main objective is to optimize material flow to reduce cost or maximize profit.

MILP is an extension of the LP approach to include discrete constraints (binary variables) like 0 to close a facility and 1 to keep it open, and is recommended when a small number of discrete choices need to be made such as to optimize supply chain configuration.

Simulation is used to evaluate the model numerically and estimate the true characteristics of the model. Simulation tools can be used for quick evaluation to the scenarios and to validate the results of optimization (LP and/or MILP) because simulation is able to consider demand uncertainty, transportation and supplier lead-time variability, manufacturing variability, seasonality, and inventory policies.

One approach is to use both LP and simulation because though LP is an optimization tool that can provide the globally optimal solution, it does not consider the impact of variability, while simulation can replicate real-world problems like variability, but it doesn't provide an optimal solution. Hence, rather than conflict, LP and simulation complement each other. For example, a consumer electronics company that was trying to decide between a China-based supplier and a U.S.-based one found out that though the per-unit cost was considerably lower for the China-based supplier, the company would have to carry a whole lot more safety stock to compensate for the four weeks of transportation lead time between China and the United States as well as the uncertainty of the shipment container being held up for weeks in Beijing. By using LP and simulation the company then decided to go with the U.S.-based supplier as it offered a lower total landed cost.

Best Practices

1. Total organizational profitability:

Because of globalization, decisions about product sourcing, where to produce, and where to sell products are becoming more complex. Although the supply chain network design should put more weight on the largest opportunity in the new market—for example, by building new factories in India or China, the demands of the global marketplace should be tracked to ensure that all market opportunities will be leveraged. Understanding the trade-offs between three conflicting objectives—cost, flexibility, and responsiveness—is key before deciding which suppliers to select, where to locate the manufacturing facilities and distribution centers, what products to produce at which facilities, and the distribution of products to customer regions. For example, though a consolidated distribution center network design might lead to lower facility costs, lower inventory costs, and greater flexibility because of the "pooling effect," it might also lead to higher transportation costs, lower responsiveness, and increased service costs as the products are farther away from the end customers.

BIC companies also take tax liability into consideration while designing their network. This would involve moving facilities to low tax jurisdictions. Some companies moved their facilities to Canada from the U.S. because the health care costs are borne by the government in Canada instead of the employer. Supply chain network decisions such as being close to raw material suppliers, taking advantage of low-cost labor, or being close to customers should always be taken holistically based on their contribution to total organizational profitability, and always be in alignment with supply chain strategy.

2. Multi-objective optimization:

Technology should not only be able to support multi-objective functions, but also reach the optimal solution in a reasonable amount of time. As we discussed earlier while evaluating the make-to-stock, make-to-order, or assemble-to-order supply chain strategy, one has to deal with three conflicting objectives (cost, flexibility, and responsiveness). Make-to-stock would provide the maximum responsiveness but has the highest cost and is the least flexible. Make-to-order on the other hand is the best strategy if we consider flexibility and cost only. From this example, it's clear that reducing cost, increasing flexibility, and improving responsiveness are three conflicting objectives. To select the optimal trade-off, two methods can be followed:

- Multi-objective function is where each of these dimensions (cost, flexibility, and responsiveness) is assigned a priority percentage. For example, cost is 30 percent, flexibility is 40 percent, and responsiveness is 30 percent. In this case since all objectives have close weights, the optimization solver might select "assemble-to-order" as the best strategy to meet objectives.
- Hierarchical optimization assigns a priority to each of these dimensions. For example, cost is priority 1, flexibility is 2, and responsiveness is 3. In this case, the optimization solver will select "make-to-order" as the best strategy to meet the objectives. It is important to make sure that the hierarchical objectives are in alignment with the company's corporate strategy. For example, if the corporate strategy is to maximize market share then

the responsiveness objective should be higher than the minimize cost objective. However, if the corporate strategy is to minimize cost then the cost objective should be higher up than responsiveness.

3. Scenario management:

The supply chain network design software should be scalable enough to capture all the supply chain constraints and costs and perform what-if scenario analysis to evaluate the impact of certain decisions/assumptions. For example, the initial network model might be based on the assumption that except for U.S. plants, which cannot be shut down because of union issues, any other plant in the world can be shut down if it's not profitable. Now, let's say one wanted to find out the additional cost savings derived by relaxing that assumption. One could run another scenario, the output of which would help in determining the losing opportunity and might be the trigger for union negotiations.

4. Sensitivity analysis:

The supply chain network design software should also be able to provide sensitivity analysis to confirm/reevaluate the assumptions. For example, fixed cost of facilities is an input to the network model to determine the best supply chain configuration. Now, assume the fixed cost that you modeled for facility A is $500,000, and you ran the model and determined the best supply chain network configuration. Later you found out that the estimated fixed cost of facility A is not $500,000 but actually $400,000. If the solution doesn't support sensitivity analysis, you might need to run the model again. However, if the solution provides sensitivity analysis, each input will have a range for which the output will not change if the input stays in a particular range. Assume the sensitivity range for the fixed cost of facility A is from $300,000 to $700,000. In that case you don't need to run the model again, because the new estimate of the fixed cost is within the sensitivity range and it will not change the output.

SALES AND OPERATIONS PLANNING

The sales and operations planning (S&OP) (Figure 4.7) process forms the vital link between the strategic business planning process and the tactical supply chain planning processes. According to one report, "It is the single most important competitive weapon for ensuring that the enterprise is profitably servicing the right customers, through the right channels, with the right products."[15]

The APICS Dictionary defines sales and operations planning as "a process to develop tactical plans that provide management the ability to strategically direct its business to achieve competitive advantage on a continuous basis by integrating customer-focused marketing plans for new and existing products with

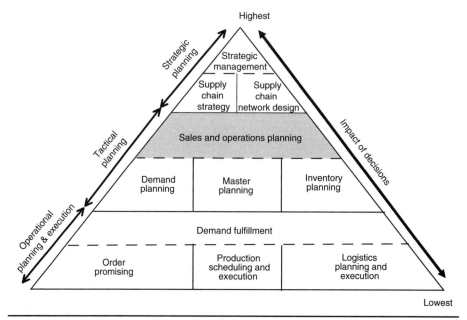

Figure 4.7 Supply chain pyramid (S&OP)

the management of the supply chain." Sales, marketing, development, manufacturing, sourcing, and finance are typically involved in the S&OP process to produce an integrated company game plan that incorporates and reconciles the views of all functional areas at the same time making sure that this plan is in alignment with the strategic business plan. In addition, if a firm has several business units, it is recommended to create and manage the S&OP process at the global or corporate level that aligns and synchronizes regional metrics with corporate goals.

A key goal of S&OP is to achieve a supply demand balance and a volume mix balance. If supply exceeds demand it leads to excess inventories, obsolescence, price cuts, and discounts. On the other hand, if demand exceeds supply it leads to reduced customer service, expediting, overtime, etc. A supply demand balance can be achieved by effective coordination between the different functional areas and active involvement of top management. The other balance is related to volume and mix. Volume deals with how much to make at the product family level and mix is concerned with the detailed decisions about which products to make. Too often companies are myopic and focus on the mix decisions while not putting enough effort on the big-picture volume decisions. BIC companies first plan for the volume and then focus on the mix. The S&OP process provides the key communications link for top management to coordinate the various planning activities in a business. For example, if sales wants higher inventories but top management decides that there isn't enough capital to meet the request, the operations plan will need to be adjusted to reflect top management's decision.

Some of the major pain points or challenges of the S&OP process are the lack of a consensus demand plan across multiple departments, demand and supply uncertainty, the lack of historical data related to supply, transportation lead-time variability, and the lack of visibility into unexpected events.

Evolution of S&OP

According to Gaurang Pandya,[16] the S&OP process has evolved through the following four phases:

1. Local resource optimization: During its infancy, the S&OP process was driven by top management targets. Each functional area had its own plan and hence the focus was on local resource optimization.
2. Performance within functional area: The next level focused on the use of formal processes for each functional area and their measurement with appropriate performance metrics. However, the processes and their measurements were compartmentalized and lacked cross-functional integration.
3. Intra-organization integration: The next level of maturity focused on cross-functional synchronization, where all functional areas have common goals and metrics that are aligned with the organizational goal. However, the synchronization is intra-organization rather than inter-organization, that is, the synchronization does not include the other stakeholders like suppliers, partners, and customers.
4. Customer-driven: The S&OP process in a customer-driven enterprise leverages LAVC principle 1 to focus on customer needs and on coordinating, integrating, and aligning the initiatives of the entire supply chain to meet customer demand, while simultaneously creating a win-win situation for all the internal and external stakeholders (principle 2). The metrics and processes are also geared toward collaboration and partnership and on improving customer and supplier relationships rather than exploitation. Hence, by adopting a holistic approach to the entire supply chain network, companies can achieve an optimal balance between responsiveness, flexibility, cost, and service.

Since a key objective of the S&OP process is to balance supply and demand, one needs to understand the demand planning, inventory planning, and master supply planning subprocesses in detail to achieve a lean and agile best-practice S&OP process. Hence, we shall discuss these in detail because they are a really big part of the overall S&OP workflow that brings these subprocesses together and balances supply and demand for product families.

Demand Planning

Demand planning (Figure 4.8) ensures that the right products will be available at the right place at the right time. Demand planning is the subprocess of anticipating market demand and drives all subsequent supply planning activities. If the demand forecast is higher than the actual demand it will lead to excess inventory across the supply chain and if the forecast is lower than the actual sales, it will result in poor customer service. As competition grows among global supply chains, accurate forecasting and demand management has become even more difficult. Product life cycles are shrinking rapidly and with the Internet, barriers to entry have come down and market share has become dynamic and unpredictable.

To add to this complexity, supply chains also have to deal with the "bullwhip effect." The bullwhip pattern starts with relatively small variability in end-customer demand and expands to successively greater variability up the supply chain. This was first noticed by P&G executives—a relatively uniform demand for diapers in retail outlets was not getting reflected into a stable demand further upstream of the supply chain. Distributor orders to the factory varied more than

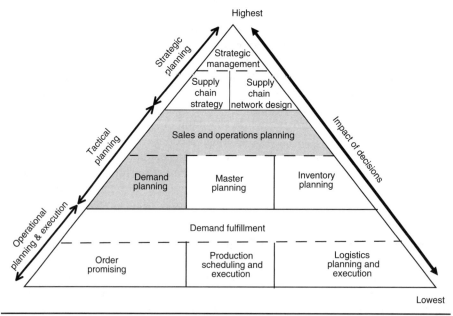

Figure 4.8 Supply chain pyramid (demand planning)

retail demand, and P&G orders to their suppliers fluctuated even more widely.[17] Causes of bullwhip effect include:

- Order batching to take advantage of FTLs
- Forward buying because of promotions
- Cumulative increase in forecast error since everyone in the chain adds a certain percentage to their demand estimates to compensate for the forecast error
- Lack of communication and coordination between the different entities within the extended supply chain

Some ways to tackle the bullwhip effect include reducing high-low promotions with an everyday low price, increased demand visibility, and increasing forecast accuracy using vendor-managed inventory. This creates a win-win situation for not only the manufacturer, but also the retailer. Notice that LAVC enablers 1, 2 and 6 were used to follow principle 2 and create the best scenario for all parties.

Generic Demand Planning Subprocess

The ability to select the right forecasting technique is a major challenge in the demand planning subprocess (Figure 4.9) since there are so many statistical algorithms available (moving average, double exponential smoothing, triple exponential smoothing, etc.) and the identification of the right forecasting technique in a specific situation is not always obvious. The generic demand planning subprocess can be broken down into four steps:

1. Cleaning data: Sufficient time and effort should be spent in this first and critical step to clean up the base historical data regarding one-off events like promotions, outliers like stockouts, and so forth, to avoid the "garbage in garbage out" syndrome.
2. Baseline forecasting: A baseline forecast is an "unconstrained" demand plan. In this step, the initial statistical forecast is created using the different statistical algorithms available and serves as the baseline forecast for the different functions in the organization. Forecasting should always be done only for the independent demand, as once this is done, dependent demand can then be calculated.

| Step 1: Cleaning data | Step 2: Baseline forceasting | Step 3: Exception management | Step 4: Consensus forecasting |

Figure 4.9 Generic demand planning subprocess

3. Exception management: Demand management should be exception-driven. In most organizations there are too many stock keeping units (SKUs) for the demand planner to review and analyze. In these circumstances management by exception is the only effective way of focusing the planner's attention onto the SKUs where the forecast versus actual is outside predetermined tolerances.

4. Consensus forecasting: In this last but critical step, the unconstrained baseline forecast is submitted for evaluation to people from different functions (sales, marketing, finance, etc.). A consensus meeting will then take place to agree on "one number, one forecast." This final unconstrained forecast is then exported for feeding into downstream systems for master supply planning.

Since understanding baseline statistical forecast generation, exception management, and developing a consensus forecast are key to the entire demand planning subprocess, we shall discuss them in more detail.

Baseline Forecast: Forecasting Techniques

Forecasting techniques can be classified broadly as qualitative and quantitative (Figure 4.10).

Qualitative: Qualitative techniques are subjective projections based on judgment, intuition, and so forth. For example, when attempting to forecast the demand for a new product, there is no history on which to base a forecast. Hence, techniques of market research and historical analogy might be used. Qualitative methods consist of:

a. Delphi method—consensus from a panel of experts
b. Analogous data—comparison with a similar product
c. Customer surveys—involves the use of test marketing, focus groups, and panels
d. Jury of executive opinion—group discussion

Quantitative: Quantitative techniques can broadly be classified into extrinsic (causal methods) and intrinsic (time series).

a. Extrinsic forecasting techniques: The theory behind extrinsic forecasting techniques is that the demand for a product (e.g., brick sales) correlates to or is a function of some other factors (e.g., housing starts). The problem is to find an indicator that not only correlates with demand but also preferably leads demand, that is, one that occurs before the demand. For example, the number of construction contracts awarded in one period may determine the bricks sold in the next period. An example of an extrinsic forecasting technique is multiple regression. A drawback of extrinsic methods is that they require information on several variables (the independent

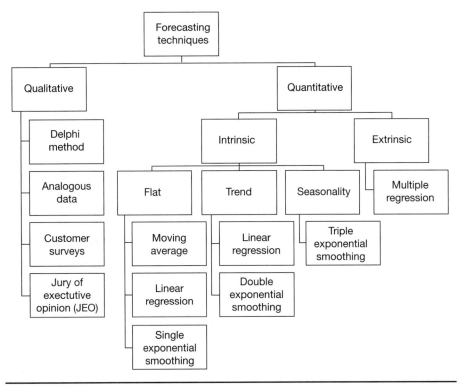

Figure 4.10 Forecasting techniques

variables) in addition to the variable that is being forecast (dependent variable) because the data requirements are large.

b. Intrinsic forecasting techniques: These techniques are based on the assumption that what happened in the past will happen in the future. Identifying and extrapolating that pattern can develop forecasts for subsequent time periods. In time series analysis, the overall pattern can be broken down, or decomposed, into subpatterns such as flat, trend, seasonality, and others (Figure 4.11).

• Forecasting techniques for flat demand: A horizontal flat pattern exists when there is no upward or downward trend in the data. Techniques used for forecasting horizontal patterns include moving averages, linear regression, and single exponential smoothing.

  o Moving averages: The moving averages technique is a smoothing method where randomness is reduced by taking a set of observed values, finding their average, and then using that average as a forecast for the coming period. The term *moving average* is used because as each new observation becomes available, a new average can be computed and used as a forecast. Moving averages can be classified into simple moving average and weighted moving average.

i. Simple moving average: Given a time series 5, 10, 15, a three-period simple moving average forecast is calculated as follows:

Simple moving average forecast for period 4

$$= (5 + 10 + 15)/3 = 10$$

The advantage of the simple moving average method is that it is easy to compute and easy to understand. A possible disadvantage is that all the values in the average are weighted equally.

ii. Weighted moving average: Given a time series of 5, 10, 20, and 15, and weights of .40 for the most recent period, .30 for the next most recent, .20 for the next, and .10 for the next, the weighted moving average forecast is calculated as follows:

Weighted moving average forecast for period 5

$$= .40(15) + .30(20) + .20(10) + .10(5) = 14.5$$

The advantage of a weighted average over a simple moving average is that the weighted average is more reflective of the most recent data. However, the choice of weights is somewhat arbitrary and generally involves trial and error.

○ Linear regression: The linear regression technique uses the least squares method to determine the trend of the time series and finds the best line through some data points. In its simplest form, the familiar straight line equation of $Y = a + b*X$ provides a relationship between Y (dependent series) and X (independent series). The

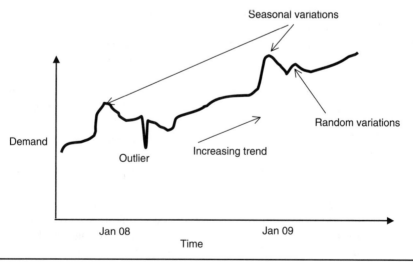

Figure 4.11 Typical demand patterns in data

criterion is that the sum of the squared errors between the actual and the estimated points found through the regression line should be kept as small as possible by appropriately choosing a and b.

○ Single exponential smoothing: The exponential smoothing method uses a weighted average of the data, using weights that decay smoothly (exponentially). More recent points are given more weight. Single exponential smoothing is a technique that applies the most weight to the most recent observed values and decreasing weights to the older values. Each new forecast is equal to the previous forecast plus a percentage of the previous error. Therefore, the equation for single exponential smoothing is:

Next forecast = previous forecast + alpha (actual − previous forecast) For example, if the forecast for May was 200, and the actual demand for May was 150; assuming alpha = 0.2, the June forecast:
$$= (200) + 0.2 (150 − 200) = 190.$$

As can be see from the above example, compared to weighted moving average, exponential smoothing requires little to no record keeping since it requires the actuals and forecast for only one time period earlier. The smoothing constant, alpha, is chosen to be a value between 0 and 1. When alpha is 1, the new forecast will include a substantial adjustment for the error in the previous forecast. Conversely, when alpha is close to 0, the new forecast will include very little adjustment. The higher the value of alpha, the greater the weight placed on more recent observations. Also, the sensitivity of forecast adjustment to error is determined by the choice of the smoothing constant alpha. The closer alpha's value is to zero, the slower the forecast will adjust to forecast errors, that is, the greater the smoothing. Conversely, the closer the value of alpha is to one, the greater the sensitivity and the less the smoothing. Commonly, alpha is between .05 and .50. Double and triple exponential smoothing are more complex versions of the basic model that account for trend and seasonal variation in the time series.

• Forecasting techniques for trend demand: Trend refers to a gradual upward or downward, long-term movement of the data. Typically, in the growth stage soon after the product is launched or the decline stage after full maturity. Forecasting techniques for the trend demand pattern include linear regression and double exponential smoothing. Forecasts based on moving averages and single exponential smoothing works best for data that have no trend, no seasonality, or other underlying patterns. In double exponential smoothing we have another smoothing constant, beta, which serves as the smoothing coefficient of the trend component. Charles Holt, the inventor of double exponential smoothing, extended single exponential smoothing to allow forecasting data with linear trends. He called his method *double exponential smoothing* because it uses two smoothing constants, alpha and beta.

- Forecasting techniques for seasonal demand: Seasonality refers to short-term, fairly regular variations related to factors such as the weather, holidays, etc. This usually occurs within one year and repeats annually. These could include examples such as sales of snow blowers in winter or lawn mowers in summer. Some seasonal patterns in data are artificial such as the "end-of quarter push" or "hockey-stick curve" to meet sales goals. Forecasting techniques for seasonal demand include triple exponential smoothing. To compensate for seasonality, Peter Winters extended Holt's method by adding another smoothing constant, gamma. Triple exponential smoothing has three factors—alpha, beta, and gamma—associated with the three components of the pattern—randomness, trend, and seasonality.

Exception Management

In most organizations there are too many SKUs for a demand planner to review and analyze. In these circumstances management by exception is the only effective way of focusing the planner's attention on the SKUs where the forecast versus actual is outside predetermined tolerances. Since the calculation of safety stocks is dependent on the forecast error, if exceptions are not managed it might have an impact on customer service. Inaccurate forecasts inevitably lead to either not enough inventory, unsatisfactory customer service and reduced revenue, or too much inventory with the associated carrying costs, costs of obsolescence and clearance.

Forecast Error

Forecast error (Table 4.2) is used in supply chain planning to calculate safety stock. Large forecast errors imply low customer service levels, which translate into high inventory. Small forecast errors imply high customer service levels,

Table 4.2 Calculate forecast error

	1	2	3	Mean	
Forecast	100	100	100		
Actuals	80	120	150		
Error	–20	+20	+50	16.67	Mean error
Absolute error	20	20	50	30	Mean absolute error
Percentage error	25%	16.6%	33.3%	25%	Mean absolute percentage error

which translate into low inventory. The mean absolute deviation or standard deviation often provides a measure of spread versus the mean. If the mean absolute deviation or standard deviation is large, it indicates that the data are spread out. Large forecast errors imply large forecast variability.

An approximate relationship between standard deviation and mean absolute percentage error is standard deviation = 1.25 (mean absolute percentage error). The common ways to calculate forecast error include:

- Mean error
- Mean absolute error = mean absolute deviation
- Mean absolute percent error

Biased Forecasts

What is a biased forecast? A forecast consistently higher or lower than the actual demand is called a *biased forecast*. In general, the forecast error should fluctuate around zero. Biased forecasts can be identified by setting a tracking signal. Tracking signal values inside predetermined limits imply that the forecast is performing adequately. When the result exceeds a predetermined value then a 'signal' or an exception is generated. Tracking signal = algebraic sum of forecast errors/ mean absolute deviation.

Causes of biased forecasts could include groups trying to meet their targets. For example, sales could be constantly over-forecasting and finance could be constantly under-forecasting to meet their own local objectives and metrics. Bias, either positive (usually marketing forecast) or negative (usually finance forecast), could cause distrust between the different teams in which every team tries to compensate for the bias by having its own forecast. Educating the players in the process and demonstrating the impact of bias on customer service, safety stock, and inventory levels are key to fixing the root cause of the problem (principle 4: institutionalize continuous improvement). Also, understanding the impact of manual interventions and tracking all the forecasts (sales, marketing, statistical) separately and calculating the bias and forecast error of each is essential, so that there is accountability and responsibility to the forecasting process. Bias could also indicate a "turning point" in the product or business. Maybe the product is having a downward trend because of cannibalization—an end-of-life product life cycle that is not being reflected in the forecast. Maybe the forecasting model or the parameters need to be modified.

Best Practices

1. Cleaning data:

Robust procedures should be put in place to clean up historical data with regard to outliers and causals and ensure that there is no mixing of normal demand with promotional demand. Also, returns and cancellations should be subtracted from the point of sales data since they do not represent true demand. Irregular variations or outliers are onetime events and reflect unusual conditions such as severe weather, plant shutdowns, or one-off orders. These do not reflect typical behavior and therefore should be removed from the data. Also, if the demand is abnormally high or low, it must be filtered out or adjusted to certain minimum and maximum values. In addition, the time series data used to generate the statistical forecast must have sufficient duration to generate reliable extrapolations and trends.

2. Selecting the right forecasting technique:

There are many statistical algorithms available (mean average, double exponential smoothing, triple exponential smoothing, Box-Jenkins, etc.) and the identification of the right forecasting technique for the right set of products can be a challenge. The future of forecasting is towards "rule-based forecasting" (enabler 6) rather than a broad-brushed "one-size-fits-all" approach.

"There is no silver bullet that can plan or forecast across all products and all stores. There are at least 20 very good bullets, and each applies to certain situations that must be factored in," says Randy Fields, CEO of Park City Group and Prescient Applied Intelligence.[18] Rule-based is not a forecasting technique, but a methodology in which the demand is segmented based on several drivers such as variability (high/medium/low), life cycle term (phase-in/mature/end of life), sporadicity (high/medium/low), product type (slow movers/fast movers), time series (short time series/long time series), and then depending on the demand characteristics, the appropriate rule is chosen. For example, at the beginning of its life cycle a product could use rule 1 (high variability and beginning of life), but later as it matures move on automatically to rule 2 (medium variability and mature). Also, specialized techniques like Croston's should be used to tackle sporadic or intermittent demand, that is, when the demand pattern exhibits some zero demand periods, followed by non-zero demand periods, and then again followed by zero demand periods.

Technology can be a significant enabler as can be seen in Success Story 12: Customer-Centric Approach Drives Global Growth for Tata Steel later in this book. Prior to implementing supply chain software (enabler 3), the company had no systematic insight into how to evaluate the accuracy of its forecasts for demand as well as for raw materials. Now, it has the tools to analyze its forecast predictions against actual results, enabling root cause analysis capabilities to identify what has caused the differences. "Improving our ability to forecast allows us to use due-date-based planning, which helps us to meet demand with higher utilization of assets," says Biswajit Roychowdhury, chief of planning for Tata's Flat Steel Division.

However, before implementing technology companies should improve the forecasting process first by asking the right questions such as the following: Are forecasts consistently over- or under-estimated? Is there a single owner to the forecast generation? Does the company have a process in place for continuous improvement for forecast accuracy? Are the forecast errors normally distributed? Does the process allow the demand planners, marketing, or sales to override the system forecast? If yes, what are the main reasons for doing so? What is the perception about the root cause for the low forecast accuracy? Does the company keep evaluating the statistical model used to generate the system forecast? Is the frequency of generating the forecast adequate?

3. Training:

Having people with a strong expertise in forecasting techniques who understand the forecasting algorithms is a must. Forecasting should be a "glass box, not a black box." Since forecasts are almost always wrong they should include an estimate of error. There should be continuous training imparted to people to encourage employee creativity, empowerment, and to teach key demand planning concepts such as demand pooling, that is, forecasts are more accurate for groups than for single items as the low forecasts at the item level balance out the high forecasts. This general principle is called *risk pooling*—taking individual risks and combining them into a pool (enabler 5). The overall risk of the pool is less than the average of all the risks that go into the pool.

4. Accountability and incentives:

Information on promotions, pricing modifications, phase-in and phase-out of products, etc., are typically scattered across the company and belong to many different functional areas (marketing, sales, operations, finance). No matter how sophisticated a statistical forecasting technique you use, if you do not capture all the intelligence the forecast will be wrong. For example, if executive management is providing incentives to the sales group, and the impact of the incentive activity is not being fed into the forecast, the forecast most likely will have a high error.

Also, these functional areas tend to have their own perspective on future demand; hence, it is essential to reconcile all these inputs and arrive at one consensus demand plan. A broad set of metrics and a performance measurement system (PMS) should be set in place (principle 5) so that the different functional areas are not compensated on meeting local objectives alone but broader organizational goals. For example, salespeople may underestimate potential sales to "blow away" their numbers. This can be a major source of forecast inaccuracy. One way to eliminate these shortcomings is to compensate the salespeople not only on whether they meet their quotas, but also on their forecast accuracy. Also, forecasts for the immediate short term should be frozen so that sales and marketing don't change their numbers. This is necessary to avoid the "self-fulfilling prophecy" syndrome of the actual numbers "magically" meeting the forecasted ones.

5. Consensus demand planning:

Consensus demand planning involves not only internal collaboration between the different departments (sales, marketing, finance, operations), but also external collaboration with suppliers and customers. For example, if the marketing department is planning a promotion, the operations department needs to be informed so that they can schedule additional production. Suppliers also need to know about the promotion so that they can acquire the additional raw materials.

While top management sets its goals with a top-down forecast in revenue dollars, sales and marketing might do a bottom-up forecast. In fact, sales might end up forecasting at the product category level and marketing at the brand level in sales dollars. Similarly, operations might focus on what the factory is able to produce based on past experience and hence forecast at plant level by units, whereas finance might forecast at the regional level in sales dollars and margins. This necessitates a multi-dimensional database (enabler 3) to allow disaggregation and aggregation across multiple dimensions (geography, customer, product, time) to provide the planners the ability to integrate/analyze the forecast information with different inputs from different functions.

The consensus forecast should be viewed as "our" forecast and not as "my" or "your" forecast. Past performance of each functional group should be looked at to determine which one was most accurate and consistent. When there is a stalemate, a "tie-breaker" should pick a consensus number. This "tie-breaker" role is usually played by the demand planning group because it has little or no vested interest in the final consensus forecast number. Weights on the different functional (sales, marketing, finance) forecasts should be based on past performance and should change based on the time horizon (enabler 4). For example, sales forecasts tend to be more accurate for the short term because salespeople have up-to date incremental information from their customers as compared to statistical forecasts. Hence, forecasting should be a combination of educated guesstimate, qualitative analysis and quantitative analysis.

Also, the chances of inaccurate forecasts, can be controlled by developing range forecasts based on the relative risk of the opportunity. Sales and marketing teams can communicate their relative confidence in the different long-term opportunities that will help the organization make better decisions on capacity investments by sizing the opportunities more realistically. The lower the confidence level, the less likely the company will be to invest in the risk. In addition, during the consensus demand planning, all manual adjustments should be tracked separately to avoid "stepping on each other's toes" and too many manual adjustments should be avoided as they tend to skew the forecast and make it worse.

6. Minimizing demand variability:

Demand variability is the root cause of forecast error and can be reduced through:

- Information sharing (enabler 2): Develop a process for information sharing between supply chain partners. For example, Dell Computers routes the customers' orders (customized configured computer) directly to the suppliers, which then supply Dell with the necessary raw materials.
- Leverage Internet technologies: For rapid transmission of the demand data to all partners in the supply chain.
- Vendor-managed inventory (enabler 7): Vendor-managed inventory is the practice in which the supplier takes responsibility for maintaining an agreed inventory of the material at the customer/distributor. As mentioned before in the Wal-Mart and Procter & Gamble vendor-managed inventory relationship, P&G would use Wal-Mart sales data and manage the inventory levels of P&G products at Wal-Mart. In such a symbiotic relationship P&G and Wal-Mart both benefit. The manufacturer's (P&G's) benefits include lower inventory investment, better scheduling and planning because of information sharing, closer ties with the retailer, and even a preferred status. The retailer's benefits include fewer stock outs with higher turnover, optimal product mixes, less inventory costs, and lower administrative replenishment costs.
- Reducing lead times: A way to reduce demand variability and thereby safety stocks is through supply lead-time reductions. Lead times can be reduced through supplier collaboration by offering supplier quantity discounts and incentives. Another way to reduce lead times is by using "cross-docking" (enabler 6). Cross-docking involves transferring materials directly from the supplier's vehicles to the vendor's vehicles without storing them at the warehouse.
- Maintaining stable prices: Using an everyday low price can introduce price stability and reduce demand variability. The resulting improvements provide greater forecast accuracy, which will extend to improved customer service, lower safety stocks, and higher inventory turns.

With the current state of the economy, companies will increasingly need to factor in macroeconomic data into the forecasting techniques because the state of the economy affects consumer behavior and pricing among other things. Larry Lapide of the Massachusetts Institute of Technology's Center for Transportation and Logistics had this to say: "All statistical forecasts start out by taking historical data and projecting it forward. Until recently, companies would adjust this forecast by factoring in promotions, seasonality, pricing, competition, and so on." He added, "The state of the economy never really mattered much. Now the impact of a bad economy has to be factored in, but it is just another variable. The techniques remain the same." Commenting on the current state of the economy, Anish Jain, executive director of the Institute of Business Forecasting and Planning, mentioned that current economic conditions have made forecasting much more about minimizing risk than maximizing sales and profits. The focus should be on preserving cash by reducing waste.[18]

Inventory Planning

In today's age of globalization and mass customization, having the right inventory at the right place at the right time to achieve an optimal balance between responsiveness, flexibility, and costs can be a source of competitive advantage. The goal of inventory planning is to calculate and allocate inventory optimally throughout the supply chain to provide a balance between holding costs, ordering costs, and customer service (Figure 4.12).

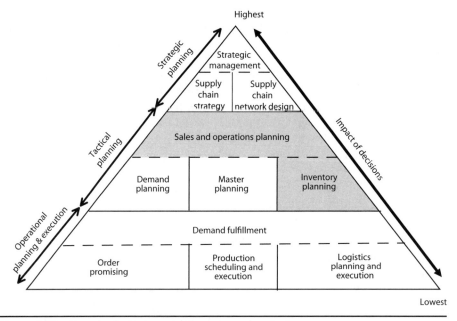

Figure 4.12   Supply chain pyramid (inventory planning)

Why Have Inventory in the Supply Chain?

Inventory is often regarded as a bad thing, but inventory is the lubricant that keeps a supply chain running. Some good reasons to hold inventory include:

- Inventory must be carried in the supply chain pipeline as work in process or in-transit inventory because it takes time to procure, manufacture, and distribute the goods
- Inventories (safety stocks) are also needed to buffer against demand forecast errors and supply and production yield variability
- There are economic incentives for holding inventories including speculative buying, price hedging (hedge on future price increases for commodities like copper, silver, and fuel), quantity discounts, or lower logistics spend by leveraging FTLs versus less than truckloads (LTLs)

Where to Hold Inventory?

In a make-to-stock environment, finished goods are produced based on forecast and the customer buys from the finished goods inventory. In a make-to-order environment, the finished good is not produced until the customer has placed an order. By storing the inventory upstream, the make-to-order supply chain offers many advantages, including less inventory carrying costs as the raw material inventory is a lot less expensive than finished goods inventory, more flexibility to make different finished goods from the same raw materials, less inventory obsolescence, and less inventory because of the inventory pooling effect. The disadvantages of make-to-order include reduced responsiveness to customers as the cumulative lead time is more in a make-to-order versus make-to-stock.

LAVC enablers 4 (flexibility) and 7 (strategy innovation) address this challenge by encouraging a hybrid approach of make-to-stock and make-to-order depending on the customer ordering behavior. Based on these patterns, one can come up with a *customer order profile*, which is the lead time that customers give between placing the order and the time the order is due. For example, if the customer places the order on May 15 and the order is due on June 15, that gives the manufacturer one month advance notice and allows it to stock the inventory at the plant (make-to-order) instead of the distribution center (make-to-stock), presuming it would take less than 30 days to make and move the items between the plant and the distribution center. Rather than use a broad-brushed, "one-size-fits-all" make-to-stock or make-to-order strategy, such a multi-echelon hybrid strategy of a combination of make-to-stock and make-to-order based on customer buying behavior will enable companies to create multiple inventory response buffers throughout manufacturing and distribution networks, and help achieve the optimal balance between responsiveness and flexibility without compromising on customer service.

How Much to Order?

By leveraging the safety stock calculation, it is often possible to reap significant and quick benefits, both in terms of increased customer service and reduced inventory levels. Inventory models tell how to do that by determining how much and how often to order.

The fixed order quantity lot size decision rule specifies a number of units to be ordered each time an order is placed for a particular item. This fixed order quantity may be arbitrary, such as a two-week supply or 100 units, but most companies use the economic order quantity (EOQ) as their fixed order quantity. The EOQ is the order size that gives you the lowest total cost for holding, ordering, and setup. The basic EOQ formula is developed from the total cost equation involving procurement cost and inventory carrying cost. The procurement cost is the cost of placing, processing, and receiving an order, while the inventory carrying cost consists of the costs of space, handling, lost opportunity of the capital tied up in the inventory, cost of capital, inventory risks associated with shrinkage (theft), damage, and obsolescence, and inventory service associated with insurance and taxes. The challenge is that these two costs work against each either. For example, increasing purchase order quantities reduces procurement cost because fewer purchase orders need to be placed, but it increases the inventory carrying cost. The basic EOQ formula, which was originally introduced by Ford Harris in 1913, tries to find a sweet spot, an optimal quantity where the total cost (summation of these two costs) is minimized.

The basic EOQ formula is expressed as

Total cost = procurement cost plus carrying cost

$$TC = S(D/Q) + IC(Q/2)$$

where TC is the total annual relevant inventory cost dollars; Q is the order size to replenish inventory, units; S is the procurement cost, dollars/order; D is the item annual demand occurring at a certain and constant rate over time, units/year; I is the carrying cost as a percent of item value, percent/year; and C is the item value carried in inventory, dollar/unit. If each order has a fixed cost S, and we need to order D/Q times per year, the total ordering cost would be S(D/Q). If Q/2 is the average inventory per-unit time, then total annual holding costs = IC(Q/2).

As shown in Figure 4.13, the EOQ is the point on the total cost curve that lies directly above the intersection of the holding cost and setup/order cost curves.

The EOQ is the quantity where the ordering costs are equal to the carrying costs. Therefore,

the total ordering cost = total holding costs.

$$S(D/Q) = IC(Q/2)$$

$$Q* = \text{optimal order quantity} = \text{sqrt } (2DS/IC)$$

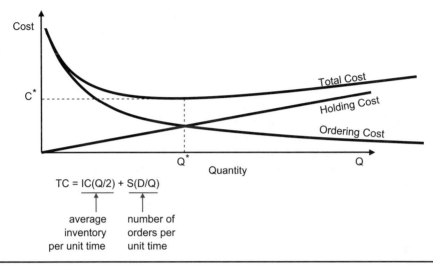

Figure 4.13 Classical EOQ

The minimum total cost occurs where holding and setup costs are equal, that is, at the intersection. After that point of equality, holding costs tend to rise more rapidly than a corresponding decline in order or setup costs. Because of the relationship of the cost curves, you can reduce total costs by reducing setup costs, which is the goal of lean manufacturing. To summarize, the EOQ model is useful to determine the lot size under relatively stable, independent demand and accommodates itself well to reality; even if there are considerable variations in the cost figures, the minimum the order point tends to vary within a fairly small range.

When to Order?

In addition to picking an order quantity, you also have to decide how often to order. Either one could keep inventory and wait for a stockout before replenishment, or not keep any inventory and replenish only when there is a demand. However, these two options will only work when the supply lead times are shorter than the "need" times, which is highly unlikely in today's environment. Nowadays, buyers mostly replenish in advance of the need and use the below-mentioned inventory review systems.[19]

- *Continuous review:* As the name suggests, in continuous review the inventory is counted continuously and the order is placed when the inventory falls below a predefined reorder point (ROP).
- *Periodic review:* Periodic review involves determining the amount of an item in stock at a specified, fixed, time interval and placing an order for a

quantity (either fixed or variable). Since the time period between reviews is fixed, this approach sometimes is called the *fixed review period system*. Typically, the review interval is determined by dividing the EOQ by annual demand.

Compared to continuous review, a periodic review policy has to wait until the next ordering cycle, which leads to a higher order quantity as the quantity on hand plus the quantity ordered must be equal to the demand during the lead time plus the demand during the review period method. This leads to more inventory as compared to the continuous review. However, because you order at predetermined intervals, a periodic order policy can have advantages such as less manual bookkeeping and significant transportation and administration cost savings when a large number of items need to be jointly ordered from the same supplier to get price-quantity breaks.

Inventory Policies

Based on the advantages and disadvantages of continuous and periodic review, companies could choose to use continuous review for some items and periodic review for others. However, within continuous or periodic review, the following inventory policies should be used based on demand characteristics:

- ROP, ROQ (reorder quantity)—If the on hand falls below the ROP, then an order of fixed size ROQ is placed to get the on hand above ROP level. Used for fast movers (Figure 4.14).
- s, S—Also known as min-max policy. If the on hand falls below a minimum order point "s," an order is placed to get it to the maximum "S" level. This policy is assigned to fast-moving parts with lumpy demand. Lumpy demand can be identified when the standard deviation of the demand over a period of time is greater than the average demand.[12]
- S-1, S—If the inventory falls below a set level S, it is replenished up to S. Used for slow movers or expensive parts where you do not want to carry a lot of inventory.

Since the ROP, ROQ policy is more widely used, let's discuss it in more detail: The formula to determine the ROP in (ROP, ROQ) is

$$ROP = \text{lead time demand} + \text{safety stock}$$

Here,

$$\text{Lead time demand (LTD)} = (\text{average lead time*average demand}).$$

LTD is the mean demand during replenishment lead time and is used to guard against demand during replenishment lead time. Safety stock = k*SQRT (average lead time*standard deviation of demand^2 + average demand^2*standard deviation of lead time^2).

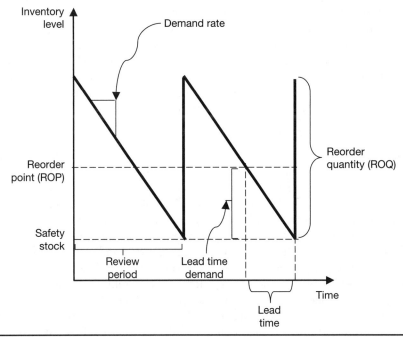

Figure 4.14 ROP, ROQ

Safety stock is used to guard against risk from forecast error and lead-time variability. The k-value is dependent on the service level. For example, if you want a 98 percent service level, you would use 2.05 as the k-value.

As we mentioned earlier, good inventory is the minimum inventory needed to guard against assessed risk (supply and demand risk) and any more is bad inventory. Supply risks could result because of transportation delays between supplier, factory, and distribution centers, process yield variability, machine breakdowns, employee strikes, and so forth. Demand variability could be a result of product discounts, promotion, phase-in/phase-out products, or inherent product characteristics. Safety stock guards against risk from forecast error and lead-time variability. As can be seen the safety stock depends upon several variables. As the mean demand increases the safety stock also increases. The more accurate the forecast or the smaller the demand variability, the smaller the safety stock. Also, the longer the replenishment lead time or supplier uncertainty, the larger the safety stock. Finally, the higher the service level, the more safety stock you have to carry.

Best Practices

1. Clean data on demand and supply variability:

This is the same issue that has already been discussed in the section on demand planning and will come up again in master planning. No matter how sophisticated the inventory optimization algorithm or technology you use, without clean and reliable inputs on supply and transportation lead-time variability, supply lead times, demand and demand variability, the safety stock calculation is bound to give you incorrect results. A sanity check must be completed of the data; otherwise it would result in "garbage in, garbage out." Institutionalized continuous improvement (principle 4) must be leveraged and root causes for poor quality must be systematically analyzed and corrected.

2. "Right sizing of inventory levels":

Rather than use a "rule of thumb" based safety stock logic, a "right sizing of inventory levels" logic must be used. "Rule of thumb" based safety stock logic involves an unscientific broad-brushed "let's use four weeks of cover" approach whereas a "right sizing of inventory levels" involves understanding the safety stock calculation algorithm, and doing more sophisticated analysis to balance demand and supply risk with business priorities. Hence, one must understand the key levers that affect safety stock, namely, mean demand, mean lead time, demand variability, supply variability, and customer service. The higher the supply variability (yields, supply lead times), demand variability (forecast inaccuracy) and customer service level, the higher safety stock level. This approach of "right sizing of inventory levels" (enabler 6) might result in an increase in safety stock for those products that have high demand and supply variability, but at the same time decrease safety stock for other products. But regarding total inventory cost, you would be better off using the "right sizing of inventory levels" than the "rule of thumb" based approach for the same customer service level. According to a December 2004 report by Aberdeen Group, fewer than 5 percent of companies are effectively factoring variability across the supply chain into their inventory policies. However, those that do have typically reported reducing on-hand inventory by 20 percent or more.[15]

3. Alignment with organizational goals:

It is key that the inventory strategies are aligned with business goals. If the organizational goal is to minimize cost it needs to use strategies like production postponement to shift inventories upstream in the supply chain, which leads to reduction in finished goods inventory but an increase in semifinished inventory.

On the other hand, if the organizational goal is to maximize market share, that is, increase the customer service level, then the organization needs to use a segmented strategy based on offering a higher service level based on volume, margin, customer type, and so forth. Also, monitoring customer buying behavior to keep sufficient inventory downstream for more responsiveness will help capture market share. In addition, tracking the customer service level to ensure that it is measured on the "customer request date" and not a self-fulfilling "order promise date" is key if the company has to capture market share.

4. Analysis of variability:

Options should be explored to reduce demand and supply uncertainty rather than just add inventory to compensate for demand and supply risk. Demand uncertainty can be reduced by having better forecasting techniques in place and using principles of assembly postponement, information sharing, and collaboration so that you store only the minimum inventory at each echelon of the supply chain. Supply uncertainty (yield and process reliability, lead time, etc.) on the other hand can be reduced by keeping supply lead times short, and through extensive collaboration, and exchange of information with suppliers. Also, using principles of multi-sourcing and sharing safety stock with other companies will help mitigate the effects of supply uncertainty. Only after a thorough analysis, and when all the options of reducing variability have been exhausted, inventory should be used to guard against the remaining supply and demand risk by placing inventory buffers at appropriate echelons to achieve the optimal balance between flexibility and responsiveness.

5. Using a segmentation strategy:

Segmentation (enabler 6) is the stratification of the product portfolio into groups, which allows the company to have a different level of customer service for the different groups. The groups could be based on revenue, margin, variability, profitability, volume of sales, product life cycle stage, and so forth. For example, a 95 percent customer service level could be set for the A-class group which has high-volume, high-margin products. A 90 percent service level could be set for a group which has medium-volume, medium-margin products, and so forth. As another example, a semiconductor manufacturer found that its vendor-managed inventory customers had lower forecast error. Rather than use a "one-size-fits-all" approach of a single forecast error to compute inventory levels, the company used a segmented strategy by using separate estimates of forecast errors for vendor-managed inventory customers and others. Similarly, a consumer packaged company replaced its traditional inventory policy of classifying products just based on volume to segmenting products by volume and margin.

Also, segmentation can be used in ABC inventory analysis. For example—putting more time, effort, and money into forecasting A items, cultivating relationships with the suppliers of the A items, warehousing the A items in the most secure part of your facilities, and taking more care in transporting the A items etc. As Dirk Petermann, head of the Competence Center of Supply Chain Management for the Continental Corporation's tire unit, said after implementing a best-of-breed inventory optimization solution, "Inventory optimization helps us to define different service levels based on the product and sales channel. This means we are now able to focus our investments in inventory exactly on the products where sales wants to have a high service level. Overall inventory efficiency does not take a hit, and on the other side, we can reduce inventory levels for products with a lower service." As a result, the tire division's distribution network is now extremely responsive and inventory is deployed according to the rules defined by the sales organization. (For more details, please refer to Success Story 9: Continental Tire Speeds Planning Cycles and Inventory Turns in chapter 10.)

6. Using "exchange curves":

Exchange curves demonstrate that the inventory investment increases exponentially as the customer service level gets close to 100 percent. The use of exchange curves facilitates the resolution of the customer service/inventory costs trade-off by providing an integrated view of all possible scenarios. For instance, a 4 percent increase in customer service (from 94 to 98 percent) might necessitate more than double the investment in inventory. Technology can be a significant enabler in this regard if it allows for sensitivity analysis to determine this inflexion point beyond which a small increase in customer service demands a significantly large investment in inventory.

7. Customer ordering patterns:

As we mentioned earlier, storing the inventory further upstream has many advantages including less inventory carrying costs, more flexibility, and less inventory obsolescence, but has its share of disadvantages including less responsiveness. Rather than use a "one-size-fit-all" approach of make-to-stock or make-to-order, BIC companies use LAVC enablers such as strategy innovation and flexibility to come up with a hybrid strategy based on the customer ordering patterns. *Customer order profile* is the lead time that customers give between placing the order and when the order is due. For example, if the customer places the order on May 15 and the order is due on June 15, that gives the manufacturer one month advance notice and allows the manufacturer to stock the inventory at the plant (make-to-order) instead of the distribution center (make-to-stock), presuming it would take less than 30 days to make and move the items between the plant and the distribution center. Rather than use a broad-brushed, make-to-stock or make-to-order strategy, a multi-echelon hybrid strategy of a combination of the two based on customer buying behavior will enable companies to create multiple inventory response buffers throughout the manufacturing and distribution networks. This helps achieve the optimal balance between responsiveness and flexibility without compromising on customer service. Continental's Petermann continued, "After the inventory optimization implementation with i2, we recognized that we often shipped tires much too early into the regional distribution centers. We learned that to increase overall service levels, we have to hold them much longer in the plant warehouses and ship them later. By keeping inventory upstream, we can respond to demand changes with much more agility."

8. Continuous improvement:

BIC organizations leverage institutional continuous improvement and have not only put in place the best-practice processes to calculate and measure inventory targets against their goals, but also to systematically analyze the root causes and take appropriate corrective actions to reduce if not eliminate them. One of the biggest hurdles to overcome is the compartmentalization between the demand or sales side and the operation or supply side. At one semiconductor manufacturer, after having put a closed-loop, root cause analysis in place, it was found that the reason the distribution centers were getting stocked out was not because wrong targets were being set, but because the logistics department used to ship from the plant to the distribution centers only on Wednesday in FTLs. Hence, the distribution centers did not have enough inventory on Monday and Tuesday until the new replenishment arrived. This was remedied, and within months, the company saw measurable improvements in inventory availability to meet customer requested delivery dates.

9. Glass box, not black box:

Having people with strong expertise in inventory planning who can understand the different inputs and outputs of the inventory planning subprocess is a must. The importance of training the employees on the basic concepts of inventory planning cannot be underestimated. Planners should know the right knobs to turn (lead time, lead-time variability, demand, demand variability, customer service level) and the consequences of their actions on safety stock. Technology can play a pivotal role by providing real-time, what-if simulation analysis so that planners have the ability to change the customer service and see the impact on inventory carrying costs. The planners should also have the ability to modify safety stock levels after the inventory planning run and before publishing the results to the master planning subprocess, hence treating inventory planning like a "glass box instead of a black box" where this process is visible across the entire organization.

10. Physical record integrity:

It is crucial to maintain inventory record integrity because if physical on-hand quantity is larger than record on hand, the physical inventory cannot be sold (in the case of a finished product) to the customer or used (in the case of a part) in production to satisfy demand. At the same time, if physical on-hand quantity of an item is less than record on hand, this item might be scheduled for production (in the case of a part) or be sold to a customer while it's not available physically in inventory, which will lead to dissatisfied customers. To maintain high record accuracy, companies need to count their inventory not only annually, but also on a regular basis. Some best practices in this area include:

- The use of a perpetual inventory control system in which a company counts samples of items each day or week. So, a fraction of the items will be counted at a predefined time, with the times for the count staggered throughout the year (cycle counting). The frequency of counting a certain item depends on the criticality of the item.
- Scheduling items for a count when their inventory level is close to zero, which makes it faster to finish the count.

However, to improve inventory record accuracy, the root cause of the problem needs to be identified by asking the right questions: Are the record errors random or do they have a systematic pattern? Is the record error within the tolerance of error? Are receiving, storage, and retrieving policies and procedures defined and enforced? What is the receiving discrepancy percentage for the items that are received from suppliers? Is inventory scrap, obsolescence, and the return process clearly defined and correctly accounted for? Are the employees well trained for inventory management activities?

Master Planning

After demand planning comes up with the forecast, and inventory planning has come up with the safety stock targets, master planning then determines quantity and timing of production, procurement, transportation, and distribution, respecting material, time, and capacity constraints to achieve a feasible (match demand to supply) and optimal (if possible) plan. If the SCM superprocess plays the role of a central nervous system in value chain management, master planning (Figure 4.15) is often considered the heart of the SCM superprocess since it generates the enterprise-wide master plan, which drives the subsequent operational planning process.

Traditional Approach—MRPII/DRPII

In the 1980s, MRPII was the predominant methodology to keep the supply chain under control. MRPII starts with demand requirements and works its way back to supply requirements. It is unidirectional planning, where it starts from a forecast and continues to develop a master production plan, which enables purchase order generation to suppliers after exploding and offsetting the BOM. It factors

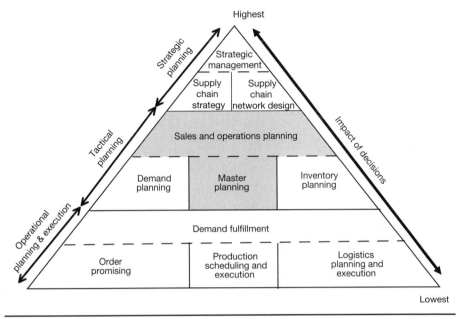

Figure 4.15 Supply chain pyramid (master planning)

the inventory on hand, subtracts it from the demand, and then figures out what you need to produce or purchase, generally on a weekly basis.

The material planning function of MRPII is done by the material requirements planning (MRP) module in enterprise resource planning. The calculation logic starts with independent demand or gross requirements (forecast and actual orders) for finished products, which is distributed among the time buckets (daily or weekly) based on the required date. Then, MRP nets out gross requirements for finished products from projected available on-hand inventory and scheduled shop orders within the specific time period to come up with the "net requirements" for finished products in each time period. The next step is to explode the BOM down to the components. MRP then nets out components already in stock or on open purchase order and comes up with the net requirements. Once MRP is completed, there is a capacity check by capacity requirements planning to compute the labor and machine center capacity required to manufacture all the component parts. Finally, based on the net requirements, MRP will generate purchase orders for purchases parts and production (shop) orders for the subassembly parts and finished products considering standard purchase or production lead time.

On the distribution side, distribution requirements planning (DRP) translates the logic of MRP to the distribution system. The DRP system links the demand information (independent demand sales forecasts) from the receiving points (distribution centers) all the way to the supply points (manufacturing plants). DRP then calculates the net requirements (dependent demand) at all levels of the distribution network by considering on-hand inventories, transportation lead times, bills of distribution, and so forth. DRPII, an extension of DRP, also takes into consideration resource constraints in the distribution system including transportation capacity constraints, warehouse space, and so forth, to support the distribution plan.

Limitations of Traditional MRPII/DRPII

Some of the major limitations of traditional MRPII/DRPII are as follows:

1. Sequential planning: One of the major problems with MRPII was that the calculation was sequential, that is, it calculated first the material needs, and then the capacity needs. MRPII didn't have the capability to promise a customer delivery date based on the current supply chain picture, because there was no visibility into all of the upstream and downstream supply chain constraints concurrently to come up with a feasible plan in a timely fashion. Hence, firms had to keep enough inventory on hand at all times to keep their delivery promises.

2. Lack of demand prioritization: There was no way in MRPII to deal with demand priority. MRPII allocated parts to demands according to date priority and was not able to create a plan that recognized other prioritization logic like satisfying the orders coming from the preferential key customer first.

3. Unidirectional and unconstrained: The information flow during BOM explosion to come up with raw material requirements is top-down only, and could not deal with hard constraints, that is, supplier constraints such as quotas or contracts.

4. Replanning time: In large corporations with thousands of SKUs, BOMs, BODs, and routings, unexpected events (order modifications by customers on quantity or delivery date) occur frequently and can disrupt the supply demand balance. Because of unidirectional sequential planning, the replanning time in MRPII could run into several days, especially since the calculation in MRPII is made by retrieving each planning data separately from a database. This leads to reduced confidence since all new incremental information is not incorporated and planners no longer trust the plans. Hence, people resorted to having their own silo plans which were not in sync with each other and there was no one version of the truth—"one official plan."

Because of the limitations mentioned above, MRPII logic will only work for stable demand where capacity and material constraints are not a big issue and no significant competition exists. Hence, this MRPII logic is not sustainable in today's day and age of increased variability and complexity, which will only cause the supply-demand imbalances to increase. With today's competitive pressures that are forcing manufacturers to compress lead times, cut inventory, increase asset utilization, and reduce costs, MRPII planning logic will not work. Companies who have relied on MRPII are looking for help and alternatives that can consider finite material and production capacity simultaneously together with dynamic lead time, perform backward and forward propagation to the requirements, and link customer orders to shop orders.

Advanced Planning and Scheduling

Advanced planning and scheduling (APS) logic, which emerged in the early 1990s, was a major breakthrough after MRPII planning logic and aimed to circumvent some of the limitations pertaining to MRPII by performing bi-directional concurrent planning taking into consideration material, time, capacity, inventory, and transportation constraints simultaneously. The goal of APS was to be proactive rather than reactive so that planners would get real-time visibility into potential future problems, and they could resolve the same by performing different what-if simulations on the fly using the memory resident engine technology. Another advantage of APS over MRPII was the speed of calculation. APS systems were more than ten times faster than traditional MRPII. Ongoing advances in APS software development have given value chains an enormous boost in maximizing visibility and business agility, which represents a tremendous opportunity to lean and agile companies. According to the January 2008 Aberdeen Group report, BIC companies are 55 percent more likely to use APS software compared to the industry average.[20]

Best Practices

1. Clean Data:

Master planning is perhaps the most data-intensive because it requires data pertaining to BOM, BOD, manufacturing routings, item master, location master, yields, setup times, etc. To make things worse, this data are constantly changing. Being a data intensive process, the importance of having clean data cannot be underestimated. In the past, making adjustments to data required users to go to many sources, and changes were often manual and done by the IT department. The best-practice approach is to use a master data management (MDM) technology solution that will not only serve to consolidate data across disparate systems, but will also be able to perform data cleansing, data validation, audit trail, and data enrichment. It also provides a user interface to easily change data pertaining to safety stocks, calendars, capacities, and so forth. For example, MDM enables Cooper's planners to manipulate criteria to change behavior in DRP based on business needs. "I have difficulty envisioning DRP functioning without MDM," says Rupright (Cooper Tires Inventory Planning Administrator). "We can use MDM to make adjustments to the replenishment system, and the results are visible the next day. It's an iterative process that is pretty amazing." (For details, please refer to Success Story 4: Cooper Tire Rolls Out New System for Better Demand Fulfillment.)

2. Forecast netting:

Best-practice master planning should be scalable enough to capture not only all the static data pertaining to BOM, BOD, manufacturing routings, item master, location master, and so forth, but also dynamic data pertaining to customer orders, customer priorities, forecasts, on-hand inventories. Then it can use all the data inputs concurrently to propagate the demand throughout the supply chain to develop a supply demand match respecting all the constraints. Master planning should also be able to perform forecast netting, which is the ability to subtract the orders from the forecast to prevent double counting. For example, let's assume the current time bucket is April and the forecast for the month of May is 1000. If the company has already received orders for 700 for the month of May, then master planning should be able to subtract the orders (700) from the forecast (1000) and plan the orders of 700 (firm demand) before the netted forecast (300). Hence, forecast netting enables not only the prioritization of orders before the forecast, but also prevents double counting by only planning for the netted, unconsumed forecast. Finally, master planning should communicate and publish the supply plan to other downstream SCM components (production scheduling and logistics planning), and to the suppliers using the SRM superprocess.

3. Optimization:

Master planning requires participation from different people with disparate functions. The only way these conflicting objectives can be resolved is by making trade-offs. One of the options is to use LP since it can help companies make optimal trade-offs between potential product mixes, transportation costs, run rates, inventory costs, and customer service (principle 5). LP is the only way a company can come up with a global optimal plan by determining quantity and timing of production, procurement, transportation, and distribution respecting material, time, and capacity constraints.

However, one has to be careful while using LP because it reduces the entire supply chain to a mathematical equation, and if your global objective is to minimize cost, the optimal solution might short some orders—those that are not profitable or have less profit margin. This might lead to an undesirable situation. Hence, LP optimization should be able to support a hierarchy of objectives to model real-life business practices such as maximize customer service, satisfy demand even if it is late, minimize transshipment between distribution centers and so on, rather than just a single objective of cost minimization. Since LP generates a global optimum plan, which takes more time, planners should have the ability to make minor modifications/overrides to the plan based on actual shop floor dynamics rather than running the LP again. For example, if a machine is down and will no longer be available for the next few weeks.

4. Performance measurement:

It is very important to define key performance indicators and metrics that map to the broader company goal, i.e., global optimization, while also tying individual compensation targets to the same (enabler 6). Master planning is a cross-functional process that requires participation from different people with disparate functions (plant manager, distribution manager), which in most cases have their own local objectives and metrics. Having these functions working together seamlessly toward a common goal that is aligned with the organizational goal can be extremely challenging. For example, a plant manager might be compensated on asset utilization and therefore will tend to have long production runs, which will only increase inventory. The distribution manager might be compensated on the distribution costs and therefore would try and minimize costs by shipping in FTL, which might lead to sacrificing customer service. These myopic metrics only lead to local optimization.

5. Concurrent planning:

One of the limitations of the MRPII logic was the sequential planning of material and capacity constraints. The best-practice approach is the ability to do real-time concurrent planning taking into consideration material, time, and capacity constraints concurrently. This is possible using an APS memory resident engine (enabler 3) that has trimmed the replanning time from a few days down to a few hours. The short replanning times have led to an increase in trust and confidence in the plans and reduced planning nervousness. For example, before implementing APS technology at Continental Tires, the planners had to manually enter in all demand, supply, and production constraints. It took several days to create these production "campaigns," and to support stable production, the production plan was frozen over a period of weeks. Consequently, demand changes within this frozen period had no impact on production. After the APS implementation, Continental's campaign planning functionality was able to create an optimized production plan within hours, cutting the shop-floor stability freeze by half with the potential to reduce it further. Demand changes could now be quickly accommodated on the shop floor, thereby eliminating excess materials, labor, and inventory costs as well as maintaining valuable customer loyalty with superior service. Continental succeeded in making its supply chain significantly more responsive, agile, and reliable. Prior to implementing the technology, planning was done on a monthly basis and, as a result, plans were outdated by the time they went into effect. "Since we implemented Supply Chain Planner, planning is done weekly and replenishment planning is done twice a week. Planning time was reduced by more than 90 percent, and the planning horizon was multiplied by ten. Inventory turns increased substantially," says Petermann.

6. Supply chain visibility:

Best practice includes the ability to do bi-directional (upstream and downstream) propagation so that supply demand imbalances are propagated throughout the supply chain and planners get immediate real-time visibility into potential future problems as related to material, time, and capacity. The highlighted problems should then be divided into different categories: resource overloads, stockouts, safety stock violation, excess inventory, and late/short customer orders. Resource overloads are capacity-related problems. Stockouts, safety stock violation, and excess inventory are all material-related problems. Late/short customer orders are demand-related problems.

Also, planners should be able to filter the problems based on its category and severity, that is, capacity constraints or material shortage for the next day should be ranked as high severity and must be resolved immediately. On the other hand, capacity constraints or issues eight months down the road can be ranked low severity because the facility has the time react to it. Also, tolerances should be set up and linked to severity—a material shortage for 10 units needs to be dealt differently than a material shortage for 100 units. Problem categorization and severity is essential so that in the event of limited time, planners can focus and resolve the problems beginning with the severe ones without losing sight of long-term goals. If the problem still exists, master planning should be able to generate supply allocation to the demand requirements according to order priorities.

7. Scenario analysis:

Planners should be able to use what-if simulation to help visualize whether solving one problem has resulted in creating other problems. For example, if we get a capacity constraint violation then we can either increase capacity, build ahead, build late, or off-load. What-if simulation will help ascertain which of the above approaches gives the best possible solution. Technology, like APS for instance, can be a significant enabler in getting real-time visibility and providing the flexibility through what-if simulations to solve potential problems ahead of time.

8. Flexibility:

Best-practice master planning should be flexible enough to prioritize orders from the forecast and separate hard constraints from soft constraints. In the event of constrained material or capacity, master planning should be able to determine the best product mix based on predefined business rules (e.g., preferred customer, profitable orders) to allocate the limited supply. In addition, master planning should be flexible enough to differentiate between hard and soft constraints. A hard constraint is one that has zero flexibility (like maximum available capacity in the immediate short term). Hence, the propagation of the order from the downstream of the supply chain to the upstream will not proceed unless an alternate source is found, or some workload is moved in or out. A soft constraint, on the other hand, has some flexibility (like safety stock levels in the long term). Hence, in case of a soft constraint the propagation of the order from the downstream of the supply chain to the upstream will continue and a problem will be flagged.

S&OP Workflow

Now that we have understood the demand planning, master planning, and inventory planning subprocesses in detail, it will help us better understand the S&OP workflow (Figure 4.16) which brings these subprocesses together and balances supply and demand for product families. The five steps in the S&OP workflow consist of:

1. Data collection: This step is generally performed at the beginning of the month and involves examining deviations of planned versus actuals as relating to sales, production, inventories, and so forth.

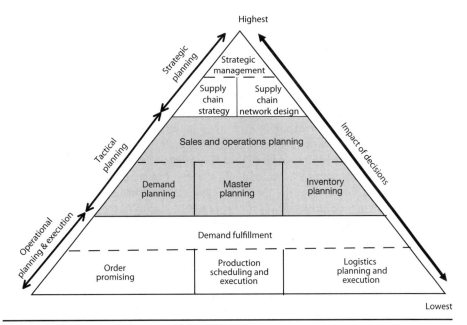

Figure 4.16 Supply chain pyramid (S&OP)

2. Demand planning: Sales and marketing representatives review the statistical forecast from the demand planning subprocess and override the statistical forecast based on new information such as competitive activity, economic conditions, and field sales input, and issue an updated management forecast for the next 12 months for current and new products. Once the forecast has been authorized by sales and marketing, it is applied to last month's operational plan to see how it needs to be changed to incorporate the incremental information. The result is the new unconstrained (supply and material constraints not considered at this time) operational plan for each product family.

3. Supply planning: The supply management team may alter and revise the operations plan after running the master planning and inventory planning subprocess and examining the demand forecasts, capacity, material and time constraints to generate a constrained plan. For example, if demand exceeds supply (capacity) by a small margin, which can be accommodated in the current plant, the supply management team may be empowered to make the necessary changes. However, if there is significant difference between demand and supply it might be necessary to get top management spending authorization, which is typically handled in the Pre-S&OP meeting.

4. Pre-S&OP meeting: Key players from the different functional areas (plant manager, finance, logistics manager, account manager, customer service manager, the scheduler, and the supply chain manager) get together to make decisions regarding the supply demand balance at the product family volume level, resolve differences, suggest alternative courses of action, and set the agenda for the executive S&OP meeting. It's important that the S&OP process is forward looking and not too much time is spent in analyzing past events.

5. Executive S&OP meeting: This is the last step of the S&OP process and the outcome is the final company game plan which should be endorsed by all participants, that is, vice presidents from the different functional areas such as sales, marketing, logistics, operations, and product development need to bless this final plan. Recommendations from the pre-S&OP meeting are discussed and decisions are made on the S&OP for each product family together with its financial implications. These decisions could include authorizing investments in capacity to meet growing demand, postponing a new product introduction, inventory policies versus customer service level trade-offs, and so forth.

Instead of the traditional sequential approach of first developing a sales plan and then giving it to production to implement, S&OP brings together sales, marketing, operations, finance, and other key players (Figure 4.17) to produce an integrated company game plan that incorporates and reconciles the views of all func-

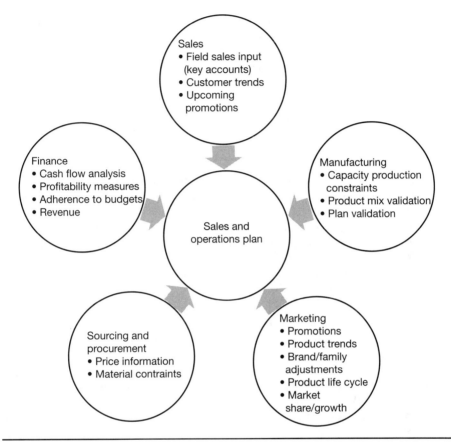

Figure 4.17 S&OP process

tional areas, and at the same time makes sure that this plan is in alignment with the strategic business plan. Apart from the monthly meetings, companies should also take into consideration the annual budgeting process to align the objectives of their different functions at least once a year.

Best Practices

1. Organizational goal:

In the world of mass customization, burgeoning product variety, variability, and complexity the use of only the annual budgeting process to align the objectives with their different functional areas will not work. In BIC companies, the S&OP process does not just balance supply and demand; it also enables the company to continually realign the goals and activities of the different departments to achieve the organizational goal. The S&OP process being in essence cross-functional, senior executives' buy in and arbitration is key to resolve differences between the different functional areas, and organizational culture plays a significant role in this. Whenever there is a constraint in one department, all the functional areas need to modify their plans accordingly. Also, if there is a deviation between the tactical and business plan, it must be resolved by realigning one or the other. For example, because of a quota constraint imposed by a supplier at the tactical level, the business plans might need to be modified.

2. Flexible representation:

In the past many organizations have developed independent data models for strategic, tactical, and operational planning that operate in silos and do not communicate with each other. Thus, there is misalignment between strategic, tactical, and operational decisions. BIC companies have a flexible modeling representation that provides seamless communication between the different planning levels using aggregation/disaggregation logic. For example, having concurrent representation of product families at a strategic and tactical level as well as individual products at an operational level.

Best-of-breed SCM software (enabler 3) helped Cementos Argos establish an organization-wide supply chain model, coordinating weekly with its S&OP team, and conducting daily adherence tracking between the plan and reality (principle 5). The company can define service standards, sales forecasting, production plans, distribution and supply in the long, medium, and short terms. SCM software solutions enable Argos to closely supervise and monitor production plans, and to make quick corrective actions to adjust those plans when necessary. All of these process improvements help Argos to define, ensure, and improve its contribution margins and to better fulfill service offers (principle 1: focus on customer success). (For details, please refer to Success Story 10: Increasing Profits and Service Levels at Cementos Argos.)

3. Risk management:

Some organizations are fixated on the *one number plan*, and since a pessimistic estimate might cause a loss of funding for the subsequent year, the one number plan only has the optimistic estimate. This again has to do with the organization's culture and putting the right performance metrics in place. LAVC best practices include the ability to provide both the pessimistic estimate as well as the optimistic estimate with appropriate confidence levels. Rather than put all the bets on the *one number plan* LAVC best practice recognizes risk as part of life and hedges against uncertainty and variability of supply and demand (enabler 5).

4. Talent and training:

S&OP requires an optimal mix of business acumen and analytical skills. The LAVC concept gives a lot of importance in recruiting the necessary talent required to not only simulate what-if scenarios with the aid of technology, but to also understand the key drivers necessary to hedge against variability of supply and demand. The importance of continuous training to hone this further cannot be underestimated.[21]

5. North-South and East-West integration:

According to Stephen Hochman (2007),[21] best-practice S&OP not only includes North-South integration between the strategic, tactical, and operational planning linking S&OP to annual budgets and daily execution, but also East-West integration between the different stakeholders including suppliers, manufacturers, and customers interwoven harmoniously resulting in a smooth uniform fabric of S&OP. Appropriate metrics should be put in place so that collaborative behaviors are measured and rewarded. An example of east-west integration includes effective coordination between the S&OP and product development teams for faster product launches. BIC companies like Sandisk use North-South integration between executives, middle management, and employees by running a monthly S&OP executive review, quarterly budgeting cycle, and a weekly supply demand balance reconciling product and volume mix plans with aggregate forecasts. At the most granular daily level, even the most lean companies realize the need for buffers at appropriate echelons of their supply chains to compensate for forecast error and supply variability.

6. Performance measurement:

Since S&OP is a cross-functional process, a cross-functional team is required for creating strategic goals and a set of metrics to support them. There should be clearly defined roles and responsibilities and a performance measurement system (PMS) that is aligned with the business plan. A hierarchy of performance metrics should be used, aggregating and disaggregating them between all the levels of the organization. A layered decision-making process should be put in place with employee empowerment to identify the root cause of a problem and use appropriate levers to solve the same. For example, if there is a production line failure, the manufacturing organization should be empowered to solve the problem; provided that the failure does not impact the higher-level sales metric. If it does affect the sales metric, then the manufacturing team should raise an alarm and solve the problem collaboratively with sales. Maybe sales can allocate the constrained supply to priority orders. However, if these actions of the sales team affect the achievement of a financial metric such as revenue for the quarter, then the sales team should also bring finance into the loop.[16]

Timken Steel Group uses a balanced pyramid metrics approach aggregating and disaggregating the metrics between all the levels of the organization, and aligning the tactical and operational metrics with the strategic metrics. William Bryan, the Director of Supply Chain and Supply Chain Economics at Timken Steel Group, suggests that "This approach (pyramid view) helps in understanding the big picture and to figure out easily the root cause for bad performance. These metrics are used in our S&OP process, which my group leads. Every Wednesday afternoon we bring the business representatives to the table to review the metrics, our plan, and where we stand. And, unless it's Christmas Day, we seldom cancel that meeting. It's not unusual for Timken Steel's president to stop by and participate in that meeting—and it is huge for us to have that kind of support. It shows that he views the supply chain as important to the success of the business. In that weekly meeting we balance the needs of the sales team with those of the manufacturing team. These needs are inherently at odds with each other in any organization. Sales folks want every product available in any quantity, at all times, to satisfy customers anywhere in the world. Manufacturing folks want to make batch sizes and sequences of similar items to get production efficiencies. My group is responsible for bringing these teams together and achieving a mutual goal of delivering both customer and shareholder. We're constantly adjusting capacity in response to demand, taking into account the whole picture from raw materials to customer delivery. Our system of checks and balances forces us to think through the overall ramifications of various supply chain decisions. This includes playing the hand you've been dealt as best you can, as well as influencing future scenarios. To me, it's just common sense, although some would argue that common sense is not all that common," (For more details, please refer to Success Story 8: Performance Measurement Best Practices for SCM at Timken.).

To conclude, process and technology innovations with effective communication and collaboration at all levels will lead to reduced planning cycle times, and less information latency. This, in turn, makes the organization responsive, forward looking, and proactive. Coupled with good decision making, it helps such organizations gain a competitive advantage. Success is not a matter of chance, but is the result of maximizing opportunities and minimizing the effect of unexpected untoward events.

DEMAND FULFILLMENT

Operational SCM involves performing detailed validation of tactical plans and incorporating a greater level of granularity. This includes focusing on individual items rather than product families, and considering detail constraints such as setup times, precedence rules, and so forth.

Demand fulfillment is a process of promising the customer what the company can deliver (order promising), and then delivering on that promise (production scheduling and execution, logistics planning and execution) to gain a sustainable competitive advantage. It involves providing accurate, optimal, and reliable delivery dates for sales orders, matching supply with demand, respecting detailed supply chain constraints and sales channel allocations, and then flawless execution to satisfy the customer demand, keeping the promised due dates. Supply chain managers must continue to take a global view by aggregating demand across the global business, evaluating total supply needs, and examining the best trade-off opportunities. This will allow the firm to make intelligent allocation decisions that can maximize the volume of the highest-margin products, meet critical regional selling season deadlines, and satisfy the needs of customers.

The demand fulfillment process can be broken down into order promising, production scheduling and execution, and logistics planning and execution subprocesses.

Order Promising

The goal of the order promising subprocess (Figure 4.18) is to make accurate, optimal, and reliable delivery promises for sales orders by matching supply (on-hand inventory, in-transit inventory, planned) with demand while respecting delivery

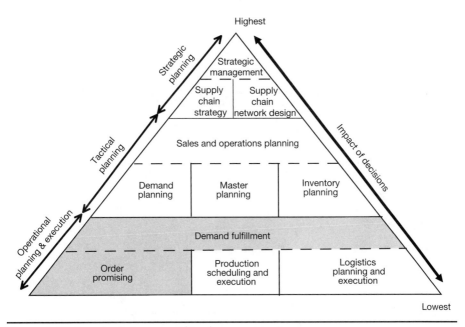

Figure 4.18 Supply chain pyramid (order promising)

transportation constraints, sales channel allocations, and distribution center reservations. Since order promising uses the output from master planning, it is imperative that order promising be tightly integrated with the master planning subprocess.

Traditional Order Promising Approach—MRPII (manufacturing resource planning)

In traditional MRPII, order promising revolves around the available-to-promise (ATP) logic (Table 4.3), which is based on a static predefined supply plan; that is, ATP is equal to the available on-hand inventory plus the expected scheduled receipts minus the customer orders that have already been committed. Hence, it is the uncommitted portion of a company's on-hand inventory and planned production to support customer order promising. In addition, whatever ATP is not consumed in a particular time bucket is carried forward as cumulative ATP. For example, when a customer calls in or sends a fax and requests 40 units in period 3, a company may look at the cumulative ATP and respond saying that it can commit to only 30 units in period 3 and the remaining units in period 4.

Limitations of Traditional Order Promising—MRPII (manufacturing resource planning)

1. Static picture:

If you didn't have in stock what the customer requested, then the customer would have to explore other avenues including going to one of your competi-

Table 4.3 Traditional MRPII order promising logic

Period	1	2	3	4
Beginning on hand	10	10 + 10 − 13 = 7		
Scheduled receipts	10	15	25	10
Customer orders	13	12	5	
ATP	7	3	20	
Cumulative ATP	7	10	30	40

Beginning on hand + scheduled receipts − customer orders = available-to-promise
ATP not consumed in a particular time bucket is carried forward as cumulative ATP

tors. If you didn't have finished goods inventory, the traditional system was not proactive and dynamic enough to take into consideration the transportation and manufacturing lead times and recourse back through the supply chain to get the product from further upstream (a distribution center or plant) to promise the customer.

2. Lack of responsiveness:

In case of an unexpected event like a plant shutdown or supplier material constraint, the traditional MRPII logic took a long time to evaluate the impact on the promised delivery dates. As a result of this the company could not provide the customer with the immediate visibility and, in most cases, the customer would come to know of the problem only after the promised date had passed. Hence, it lacked the responsiveness and visibility that is necessary in today's make-to-order and assemble-to-order environments.

Before Tata Steel engaged in a business process reengineering initiative, customer satisfaction was a real issue. When orders were placed, customers were promised a due date that was not based on hard data, plant capacity, or raw material availability. Orders were delivered when promised only about 50 percent of the time. To make matters worse, customers would generally not receive advance notice if their order would not be ready as promised, and this lack of communication burdened customer resources down the line, in the finishing and distribution channels. The plant would often scramble to address the needs of high-priority customers, further alienating customers whose orders may have been just as important but less urgent. Without a method to analyze forecast versus actual performance, it was impossible to design improvements in the overall delivery system.

3. First-come-first-served:

Another shortcoming that plagued the traditional MRPII logic was that everybody was treated the same, that is, the ATP logic operated on a "first-come-first-served" basis. There was no way to give preferential treatment to your top customers or sales channels.

4. Lack of visibility:

In the traditional system, there was lack of visibility as can be seen in Success Story 4: Cooper Tire Rolls Out New System for Better Demand Fulfillment in Chapter 10. Bob Sager, Cooper's Manager of Supply Chain Research and Design, says, "If we received a customer order on Monday, and the customer service representative did not come over to the replenishment area to inform our planners of the order, they were unaware of it until the next week."

Hence, the traditional order promising logic based on MRPII was plagued by several limitations such as inability to promise a realistic delivery date to the customer while respecting the supply chain constraints, inability to provide flexibility in meeting customer's expectations, and inability to provide visibility across the supply chain to ensure on-time delivery to the customer.

Best Practices

1. Allocated ATP:

The traditional ATP logic was based on "first-come-first-served," that is, every customer order consumed the finished goods inventory from a single, big pool and there was no way to reserve or guard inventory for specific customers or sales channels. The best-practice approach to overcome this shortcoming is using allocated ATP logic (enabler 6) in which multiple local ATPs are created for the different sales channels or customers using different rules. Hence, when the customer places the order, the promise is not offered looking at the globally pooled ATP, but rather the allocated local channel ATP. Also, the workflow should be flexible enough to accommodate custom rules so that when the local allocated ATP is not enough, the order can still be fulfilled by stealing ATP from other customers/distribution centers/sales channels. If this also results in an unsuccessful order promise, then the workflow should be able to search into the future and promise the customer a late but realistic delivery date.

2. Segmented workflows:

The optimal balance between stability and responsiveness can be reached by developing differentiated, segmented workflows for promising high-priority and low-priority orders (enabler 4). For example, if finished goods inventory is not available to promise a high-priority order from an important customer, then the workflow should search back through the supply chain into the manufacturing operations and see if there is material and capacity in the plants to build the product and promise the customer. This is known as the *capable-to-promise* (CTP) logic, which involves performing additional searches throughout the manufacturing and distribution network to determine optimal ways to meet the customer order by the due date.

Segmentation need not be for only high-and low-priority customers, but can also be done for sales channels, margins, etc. The higher the margin, the higher the responsiveness. In this dynamic and flexible CTP order promising workflow, a real-time comparison is made of the additional margin provided by a specific customer order with the additional cost, and then a decision is made on the responsiveness. However, the CTP, being dynamic in nature, must be handled with care because it might lead to lack of stability in the plans, which might increase nervousness in the supply chain. This is why this CTP order promising workflow should be offered only for the most important customers or the most profitable products, to benefit from the higher responsiveness without disrupting the stability of supply chain operations.

3. Concurrent order promising for make-to-stock, make-to-order, and assemble-to-order:

BIC companies use concurrent order promising that can be used for make-to-stock, assemble-to-order, configure-to-order, or make-to-order environments (enabler 4). For assemble-to-order products, the concurrent order promising performs a concurrent dynamic ATP check on the components as well as on the resources. If all the components for assembly are not available, then workflow should check for alternative sources of components, and then finally perform a CTP search on missing components. For configure-to-order products, the order promising workflow concurrently checks the technical feasibility and the availability of the components. Such a concurrent order promising workflow will lead to an increase in customer satisfaction by reducing due-date quote cycle time and increasing due-date quote accuracy.

While doing root-cause analysis, Mary Wilson, the Director for Global Supply Chain Management, Planning Systems at Fairchild Semiconductor, had this to say: "We found that our order promising system was not adequately accounting for a number of secondary constraints. Despite some products being nearly interchangeable in our system from a capacity perspective, we were not fully allowing for these when promising orders. Consequently, we factored more detail for significant secondary constraints into our process models, and the problem was resolved." (For more details, please refer to Success Story 7: Global Supply Chain Management System at Fairchild.)

4. Dynamic order promising:

BIC companies use dynamic order promising and fulfillment in which customer orders are sent electronically (using Internet-enabled technologies) not only to the company's promising system, but also to the company's planning system. This allows for seamless flow of information between the customer and the manufacturer (enabler 2) that can enable maximum responsiveness and visibility for both the manufacturer and customer throughout the extended supply chain.

However, this should be handled with caution since it could cause a lack of stability and more nervousness if the capacity and materials have already been committed to other "firm" orders. Hence, it is necessary to establish time fences for the frozen, slushy, liquid zone so that the customer update received in the short-term frozen zone is not automatically propagated throughout the company's supply chain and does not require manual intervention.

5. Customer collaboration:

To guarantee effective order promising, companies must separate the normal demand from the abnormal (outliers). For the abnormal demand, they must compare the potential margin versus the potential additional cost. Also, eliminate demand spikes by smoothing customer orders to reduce unnecessary planning nervousness. To reduce this, it is necessary to identify the customers who generate the highest level of disruptions through large and erratic ordering and work with these customers to convince them to move from ad-hoc ordering to a more scheduled ordering, say weekly. This low-demand fluctuation will also help to ensure smooth production schedules, and so forth.

Production Scheduling and Execution

The production scheduling and execution subprocess (Figure 4.19) is one level below master planning and differs from it in a sense that the objective of production scheduling is to generate a detailed sequence of jobs at each resource considering detailed constraints like actual setups, sequence conditions, production incompatibilities, critical raw material availability, detailed resources capacity, etc. The objective of production scheduling includes the ability to minimize

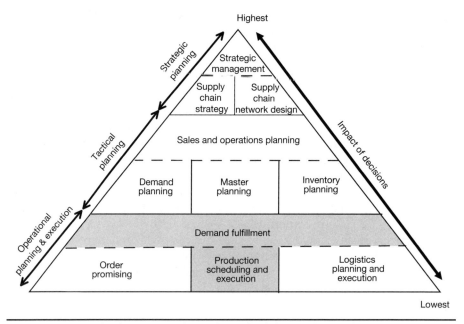

Figure 4.19 Supply chain pyramid (product scheduling and execution)

changeovers, late orders, work in process, and production costs while at the same time maximizing customer service. The production scheduling subprocess should also be in tight integration with master planning so that the plans are in constant alignment.

The criticality of production scheduling has increased because of customer movement from mass production to mass customization, which demands frequent changeovers. The criticality of production scheduling also depends on the frequency of changeovers and the cost and complexity of changeovers. For commodities, the frequency and number of setups are less; hence, master planning might be sufficient and production scheduling is least important. However, in process industries such as metals, paper, chemical, and so forth, the cost and time of a setup is very significant, which makes production scheduling even more critical.

Types of Production Scheduling

The common types of scheduling include forward scheduling and backward scheduling. In forward scheduling the material procurement and manufacturing scheduling start when the order is received irrespective of the due date. However, this could lead to a proliferation of changeovers and the order could end up being late. In contrast, backward scheduling does take into consideration the due date. The last operation in the routing is scheduled first, then the previous operation, and so on. However, this could also lead to excessive changeovers and might even generate an infeasible solution, as some plan start dates will end up being before the current date.

Thus, most of the traditional techniques share the same limitation in that they focus on only one objective and cannot consider multiple objectives concurrently. Genetic algorithms (enabler 6), which can consider multiple objectives concurrently (minimize changeovers, minimize number of late orders, etc.) can overcome this limitation. A genetic algorithm uses evolutionary computation to find the best possible solution. Several feasible sequences (known as generations) are developed and then compared with one another to find the best possible one, that is, the one with the least penalties depending upon the multiple objectives. This best solution then replaces the earlier original solution. This process is repeated in an iterative manner thus moving toward an optimal solution. The schedule generated by the genetic algorithm is more "optimal" than the traditional scheduling approaches as it balances the different objectives of the scheduling function.

Companies like Deere were facing numerous variations from its planters. Some farmers wanted 4-row planters, others 24-row planters, or something in between. A farmer could order a planter from Deere according to more than a million permutations. That's when Deere decided to use a genetic algorithm to juggle the planter assembly schedule until it arrived at the best sequence of options across the assembly line.[22]

Best Practices

1. Modeling all the constraints:

It is critical that all the production characteristics such as setup times or changeover times, precedence rules between operations, production incompatibilities between products, etc., are all taken into consideration. Also, the production schedule and the master plan should be in sync, that is, whenever the production schedule is changed there should be bi-directional propagation with the master plan, and changes should be immediately reflected in the master plan.

2. Understand and reduce process variability:

The higher the process variability, the higher the inventory to buffer against the variability. Hence, using techniques such as TQM (statistical process control, fishbone diagram, etc.), effort should be made to understand the root causes of process, yield, and manufacturing lead-time variability, and how to eliminate them. Uncertainty can also be reduced through intercompany collaboration and exchange of information between the different departments.

3. Reduce changeover time:

Reduction in the total manufacturing cycle time (queue time + setup time + run time + wait time + move time) will enable companies to react faster to customer requests thereby moving from a make-to-stock to make-to-order environment. As we mentioned earlier, storing the inventory further upstream (make-to-order) has many advantages including less inventory carrying costs as the raw material inventory is a lot less expensive than finished goods inventory, more flexibility to make different finished goods from the same raw materials, and less inventory because of the inventory pooling effect. One of the key enablers to maximizing manufacturing flexibility is to reduce the setup time, which will not only reduce the manufacturing cycle time but also allow more changeovers in the schedules, hence smaller batch sizes and higher inventory turns. At the same time, with more flexibility to define the schedules, reducing setup time allows increased responsiveness toward customers. Toyota was able to reduce the setup times using a setup time reduction program, such as the "Single Minutes Exchange of Dies" (SMED). SMED consists of separating internal setup that can be performed only when the machine is stopped (mounting, calibrating, or removing dies) from external setup (checking up all required materials, transporting the old die to the stores, and getting new dies to the machine), and converting as much of the internal setup to external setup, thereby reducing the total setup time. Using standardized and simplified equipment and tooling, cross-training the machine operators to perform the setup rather than having to wait for the setup specialist will also help reduce the changeover time (enabler 6). There are several other ways to reduce setup times: conducting time-motion studies, purchasing flexible machining centers, agile machining centers, and so forth. Although purchasing additional equipment to reduce setup times might be a difficult sell from a financial perspective, a strong case can be built that this additional equipment can improve the agility of the organization in addition to making it leaner, which will offset the additional cost in several cases. For example, using agile machining centers will not only eliminate the setup between families, but also the setup for parts within a family. This would provide the necessary flexibility for multifamily batches.

4. Cellular manufacturing:

Product flow layouts are useful when volumes are large enough to justify a dedicated assembly line. The advantages of product flow layouts include less work in process, smaller cycle times, and higher throughput. However, the lack of flexibility and high capital investment makes pure product flow layouts difficult in this day and age of mass customization and increasing product variety. The other type of layout is the job-shop/process layout, which provides a great deal of flexibility (enabler 4), but violates principle 3 to eliminate waste and reduce nonvalue-added activities since the products incur a lot of wasteful travel. Also, since machine utilization is often the metric in a job-shop/process layout, it leads to large batch sizes to minimize setup time and therefore higher inventory.

Cellular manufacturing combines the efficiency of product flow layouts with the flexibility of process layouts. In cellular manufacturing, products with similar process requirements are grouped together into families and manufactured in a cell. By grouping similar products into families, the volume increases as compared to a pure process layout and, by having dissimilar machines in the cell, the flexibility increases as compared to a pure product flow layout. Setup times decrease because of common tools and collaboration of cell workers during setups, hence the batch size can be reduced. These smaller batches travel less as compared to a job shop/process layout, and offer less material handling, less work in process, shorter lead times, higher throughput, and much less complex scheduling. But most importantly, by being responsible and accountable for the cell, cellular layout increases employee morale and empowers self-directed teams to improve the performance in their work cell. Therefore, by implementing cellular layouts BIC companies use cross-organizational collaboration (enabler 2), flexibility (enabler 4), and employee creativity and empowerment (enabler 6) to eliminate waste and reduce nonvalue-added activities (principle 3) and institutionalize continuous improvement (principle 4).

5. Push versus pull:

Frequent changes in the demand and supply make the schedules generated from the push production process (MRP) outdated as soon as they are created. Also push production systems are usually evaluated based on efficiency and machine utilization, which tends to increase inventory and waste. On the other hand, in a pull system the production and movement of material is only authorized purely as a reaction to the utilization of material downstream, that is, initiated by the downstream consumers. An integral part of the pull system is kanban, which gives authorization for a downstream center for production or withdrawal of parts from an upstream center. Another important concept is "supermarkets," which hold inventory areas to ensure a balanced material flow. This leads to less inventory pileup and a greater level of flexibility by accelerating and streamlining the material flow. This pull logic can be extended to the entire supply chain where downstream entities pull material from upstream entities all the way back to the suppliers.

BIC companies use a hybrid approach in which they might choose a combination of push and pull depending upon product characteristics, product life cycle, and so forth. In any environment, the further upstream from the end customer (consumer) the pull-push decoupling point, the greater the adherence to LAVC principles because it maximizes the length of the pull part of the supply chain. This pull-push decoupling point varies across industries and even across various supply chains (products) in the same firm. However, the implementation of pull systems requires a mind shift and a new culture in the organization, and to come up with a new set of performance measures that replaces the traditional push-driven ones (e.g., capacity utilization, throughput, etc.).

6. Uniform loading and scheduling:

In a pure pull based system, you don't produce until the customer has placed an order. Hence, if on a particular day the customer requests 500 units, you produce 500 units, and some days when the customer requests 200 units, you make 200 units. Though this pure pull based system looks great at first sight and might be very responsive with little to no on-hand inventory, in reality this demand variability creates a lot of waste. Scheduling 500 units one day and 200 units the next day means unnecessary complexity and volatility in the production system and contributes toward *mura* (lumpiness in productivity and quality), and *muri* (excessive stress and strain on the machines and labor). Mura and muri together create *muda* (waste because of nonvalue-added tasks).[23] Therefore, though being flexible and responsive is great, it actually increases waste so a pure pull based system would not be recommended.

BIC companies like Toyota use uniform loading and scheduling *heijunka*, which aims to level out the production schedules so that a steady smooth demand is imposed from the most downstream operations (finished goods) all the way to the most upstream operations (raw materials from the supplier). Hence, rather than make 500 units on a given day and 200 units on another day, heijunka involves calculating the total volume of orders within a period and running the production process smoothly with a uniform schedule of say 350 units per day, thereby leading to a balanced load on labor and machines and smooth demand on upstream processes. Hence, for MTS items, one could produce the finished goods at the rate of 350 units per day and for make-to-order or assemble-to-order, one could keep the inventory of raw materials or subassemblies before the point of consumption to be able to produce 350 units per day. Again, the amount of inventory you keep depends on the stability of the production process and the customer demand variability. The important thing to remember is that the customer should not suffer since satisfying the customer request is paramount. If, for example, there is a strong chance that the customer might order 500 units continuously for a few days, one might have to carry more inventory (make say 400 units every day) to compensate for the same. This inventory acts as a shock absorber and buffer between the actual volatile customer orders and the smooth rhythmic manufacturing process. Hence, a steady state flow of material across the supply chain is accomplished.

7. Mixed model production:

Mixed model production is about building the same finished product mix every day during a specific period. This results in a smooth demand for upstream components rather than the traditional approach of mass producing—striving to achieve economies of scale by minimizing changeovers between products. For example, in mixed model production you would schedule production of the four products A, B, C, D as ABDACDABDACD rather than in the traditional approach to minimize changeovers as AAAABBCCDDDD. The idea behind mixed model production is that a steady mix production schedule would translate into a smooth demand being imposed from the most downstream operations (finished goods) all the way to upstream work centers, manufacturing cells, and finally to the suppliers. Mixed model production schedules would also increase responsiveness toward customers while at the same time providing more flexibility to define the schedules. However, for mixed model production to work, changeover times should be reduced, which would translate into smaller batch sizes and lower inventory levels.

As Masaharu Yamaki, Mazda's senior managing executive officer in charge of production and business logistics, said recently, "Achieving mixed model production for the V6 and in-line four cylinder gasoline engines at the Ujina plant is the first step toward volume and model mix flexible production, which lies at the heart of Mazda's concept of manufacturing innovation."[24]

8. Process agility:

Process agility is key in this environment of high demand variability and burgeoning product variety. Process agility can be achieved by using process standardization and process re-sequencing, both of which are postponement strategies to help improve agility (reliability, flexibility, responsiveness). Process standardization involves combining common process steps of different products; typically, the initial steps in the manufacturing process, so that the product differentiation can be postponed until later when better demand information of individual products would be available.[25]

For example, Zara, in order to offer customers larger product variety and quick response, uses process standardization to combine the initial process steps and create "vanilla boxes," which they use as base modules until more demand information becomes available.[26]

Process re-sequencing, as the name suggests, involves re-sequencing the process so that the later process steps are done earlier to achieve similarity between the first few steps so that product differentiation can be postponed until later when better demand information of individual products is available.

For example, sticking to the apparel industry, Benetton changed their manufacturing process from dyeing, then knitting, to knit first, and then dye based on the most updated information about the colors that would be in fashion that holiday season.[11]

9. Technology:

The assumption that lean initiatives like kanban, heijunka, and cellular manufacturing can be implemented purely based on visual signals and that IT has no role is no longer valid. In today's day and age of high demand variability and burgeoning product mix, technology is not an enemy of lean but rather an enabler of it.

For example, technology can be used in complex, high product mix environments to calculate kanban sizes on a more frequent basis rather than manually calculating them once a year. Hence, technology could relieve the planners to focus on more value-added tasks like *kaizen* initiatives to do continuous improvement. Robust software scheduling algorithms (multi-objective genetic algorithms) can be used to come up with a heijunka level schedule for the "pacemaker," which is typically the final assembly process that controls the pace of production of all the upstream processes. Without technology, this would be impossible to do manually because of increasing product variety, complex routings, precedence sequencing constraints, setup constraints, and so forth. Visual signals such as kanban can then be used once the "pacemaker" creates the necessary pull signal.[27]

As the CIO of Toyota, Yoshikazu Amano, said in 2006, "Despite what those in the business will tell you, information technology is not the solution to problems of how products sell or how we move materials from place to place. IT is a tool and an enabler to world class operating systems." He adds, "When information made visible is used to do kaizen according to the proper thinking (TPS philosophy) you can achieve results that traditional thinking could not."[28]

Logistics Planning and Execution

The Council of Supply Chain Management Professionals (CSCMP), formerly known as the Council of Logistics Management (CLM), defines the management of business logistics (Figure 4.20) as "the process of planning, implementing, and controlling the efficient and effective flow and storage of goods, services, and related information from the point of origin to the point of consumption for the purpose of conforming to customer requirements."

Key takeaways from this definition include *efficient* and *effective flow* from the *customers'* perspective. Effectiveness in demand fulfillment involves not only promising to deliver but also delivering on your promise. Some companies like Toys-R-Us learned this the hard way when they failed to deliver on their promised delivery during the Christmas of 1999. Thousands of U.S. customers did

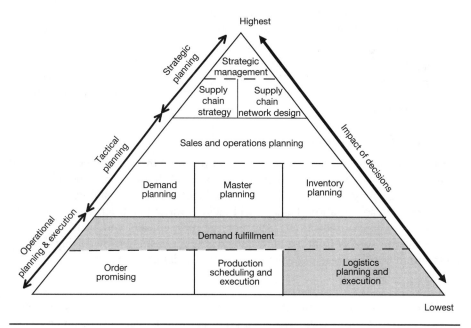

Figure 4.20 Supply chain pyramid (logistics planning and execution)

not receive their orders in time, and the Federal Trade Commission fined the company $350,000. Toys-R-Us suffered from a lack of customer satisfaction and posted a 75 percent slump in profits. Efficiency in logistics involves utilizing resources in the optimal way—both for inbound flows from suppliers (point of origin) to manufacturers, as well as outbound flows from manufacturers to distributors and customers (point of consumption), to serve the customer the right product at the right place at the right time. Outbound logistics includes two major components: warehousing (including inventory control), and transportation.

Traditionally transporting, warehousing, and inventory control were thought of as disparate functions in which the transportation was handled by a traffic manager, warehousing by a warehouse manager, and so forth. However, in the 1980s, companies realized that these functions were closely interrelated and cross-functional, and that logistics could dramatically improve customer service and be a source of competitive advantage. While efficient and cost-effective logistics could improve a company's performance, not all companies had the in-house logistics expertise and systems that are needed. This led to the emergence of third-party logistics (3PL) in which the company could contract out the warehousing, inventory control, and transportation to a 3PL provider, who would receive all the product from the suppliers and ship it out to the individual stores so that companies could concentrate on their "core" business function. Profits are made by 3PL providers due to economies of scale. In transportation, the provider can consolidate shipments from different clients and ship at a truckload rate. For warehousing, one large space utilized by a number of clients will be less expensive than individual small warehouses.

Another growing area of SCM is reverse logistics, or how best to handle the returns and possible disposal of products that make the reverse trip from the customer to the supplier. This business can be handled at a loss, or it can actually become a profit center.

Modes of Transportation

Since transportation and warehousing account for more than 95 percent of the total logistics cost, we shall examine them in greater detail. Transportation usually represents the single most important element in the logistics cost of most firms. The different modes of transportation (Figure 4.21) include water, rail, truck, air, pipeline, intermodal, and specialized carriers. Selecting the most efficient combination of these modes can measurably improve the value created for customers by cutting delivery costs, improving the speed of delivery, and reducing damage to products.

1. Water:

Water is perhaps the oldest mode of transportation. Large ships are typically used for carrying high-density cargo of low value over long distances using containers that typically measure 8 feet in height by 8 feet in width by 20 feet in

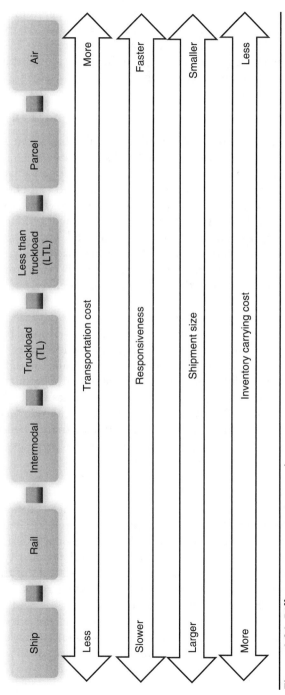

Figure 4.21 Different transportation modes

length. These containers are a convenient, safe, and economical way to ship product. Large container ships can hold about 5200 containers. Like trucks and unlike rail, water carriers have low fixed costs, that is, the waterways are maintained by the taxpayers. The primary value driver for using water transport is its low cost at less than a penny per ton mile. Two of the primary disadvantages include limited accessibility and slow speed.

2. Rail:

Rail has been used for more than 150 years in all parts of the world. The largest portion of freight transported within the United States is on rail. Railroads are characterized by high fixed and low variable costs. After deregulation a lot of the smaller companies went out of business or consolidated and only a few companies such as Union Pacific and Burlington Northern survived. To overcome the limitation of lack of flexibility and accessibility to new locations, railroads have begun entering into agreements to provide intermodal transportation together with trucks, ships, and so forth. Though still cheaper than truck, rail is still limited by slow speed, damage to fragile products, and it simply can't provide the kind of service required for lean production and just-in-time deliveries.

3. Truck:

In the 1950s, the importance of rail as a means of transport began to decline for the reasons just mentioned. After the Second World War, as populations became more affluent, more consumer goods were manufactured. Fuel was cheap, roads were more accessible, and consumers wanted new products. This led to a steady growth in the trucking industry, and today it has the highest dollar revenue of freight moved in North America. Trucks are referred to as *tractor trailers* and can range in length from 26 to 53 feet. Tractor trailers benefit from faster speed, low fixed costs, high degree of reliability and accessibility, but have high variable costs including wages for drivers and repairs.

4. Air:

Airfreight serves a niche market for product that needs to move quickly including high value products, perishable items, fragile products, and time-sensitive documents. Some airlines carry only cargo, but the majority of airfreight is carried on planes that transport both passengers and freight. The majority of airfreight is carried in containers that are designed to fit the curved walls of the airplane and maximize the usable space. The largest of these containers is 8 feet by 8 feet by 20 feet and looks like a rail/water/truck container. Smaller containers are igloo-shaped and can have their bottom corners tapered to fit the sidewalls of a plane. Like truck, air is also characterized by low fixed costs (airports are maintained by taxpayers), but high variable costs, and low degree of accessibility.

5. Pipeline:

Pipelines transport much of the world's natural gas, oil, liquid natural gas, and coal slurry. In the other modes we have already discussed, the cargo remains stationary while in a pipeline the cargo moves and the pipeline remains stationary. It is a low cost, low maintenance, and low labor method for moving suitable products.

6. Intermodal:

To take advantage of the benefits of the different modes of transportation, intermodal, as the name suggests, moves containerized freight using more than one mode. One of the earliest forms of intermodal transport was the rail-truck integrated intermodal transport, also known as *piggyback*. Relatively new intermodal includes *fishyback*, which uses truck and ship and *birdyback*, which uses truck and air. Nowadays it is not uncommon to find a shipment put in a container in Shanghai, and travel by ocean to Long Beach, California; the container can then be put on a rail car and moved to Dallas, Texas, where it can be loaded onto a truck and delivered to a warehouse in Lubbock, Texas, when it will finally be opened. The container would have traveled as a single shipment, with one price for freight. Also, being in a sealed container, there is less possibility of damage or pilferage since only the container is handled, not the actual freight itself. The intermodal concept is the fastest-growing method of shipping product because the "containerization" concept offers logistics managers flexibility, efficiency, and reduced costs.

After deregulation the legal barriers to mixed mode and specialized carrier services have come down and new types of specialized carrier services such as UPS, Federal Express, and DHL are growing in importance. This type of transportation is limited to shipments of a certain size and weight, often 150 pounds or less. The freight cost is high but the transit time is short. However, in order to compete in this era of globalization, deregulation, lean production, and just-in-time deliveries, speed has become a competitive necessity. By combining deliveries from many customers (online, catalog, and small- to medium- sized companies), express services benefit from economies of scale.

Warehousing

When inventory isn't on the move between locations, it may have to spend some time in storage. Warehousing can be in a traditional warehouse building, or in a temporary space such as a truck trailer or cross-dock. Storing the finished goods close to the final customer is the ideal situation to prevent running out of stock (responsiveness). However, warehouses cost money to set up and operate, so a trade-off has to be made in locating the warehouse further away from the customer, that is, close to the source of raw material, and spending more money on transportation to get the product to and from the warehouse versus storing the finished goods close to the final customer.

Common Transportation and Warehousing Terms

Some of the commonly used terms in transportation and warehousing include:

- *Carrier:* Carrier is the entity that provides the required equipment and moves freight via road, rail, and ocean. Carriers sometimes deadhead; that is, after they have dropped their last shipment, there is nothing to be picked up, they are miles from home, and they have to travel back to their destination terminal empty, which is not a desirable situation (e.g., companies like Ryder, etc.).
- *Equipment type*: An identifier used to represent a unique type of equipment such as a tractor or a trailer. Equipment types include reefers (refrigerated), ocean containers (20 feet by 40 feet), and trailers (40 feet, 53 feet).
- *Shipment:* A shipment is the physical collection of containers with common characteristics that move from an origin to a destination. Example: 100 boxes of PCs from Seattle to San Diego. A shipment can potentially be broken into several "legs." Each leg of the shipment will define specific beginning and ending locations of each portion of the shipment's journey. For example Seattle to Memphis and then Memphis to San Diego are two shipment legs.
- *Bill of lading*: A document given to a carrier to accompany a shipment and provides a list of shipment contents including quantity, product, weight, pickup, and delivery locations.
- *Truckload:* The entire truck or trailer has been "bought" by the shipper and can be filled as the shipper sees fit. Sometimes it can turn out be less expensive to buy the entire truck (truckload) rather than LTL even if the shipment might not fill the entire truck. For example, a shipment going from New York to Dallas, weighing 13,000 pounds and taking up 35 feet of space in a 48 foot trailer, may cost $1,500 to ship when rated on its weight. A truckload rate may work out to be $1,100 between these points, making it less expensive to send the shipment as a truckload. The shipper can then attempt to fill the leftover space with other freight, since this will not affect the cost. Truckload service may be deliberately chosen for reasons other than cost such as security or shorter time, since a truckload shipment might not have to stop at hubs for consolidation and/or deconsolidation.
- *Less than truckload (LTL):* Shipments that are picked up from the shipper and consolidated with other shipments. The shipper pays LTL rates, but the carrier will realize a profit because the carrier combines several LTL shipments from different shippers and fills an entire truck. Third-party

providers, who may be handling the transportation for a number of shippers, can consolidate shipments from several shippers into one truckload.

- *Hub:* Shipments can be consolidated, deconsolidated, or rerouted at the hub. If the hub is a hub-and-spoke facility, such as Federal Express in Memphis, Tennessee, all shipments will go into it and be rerouted out of it. For example, a FedEx shipment from Seattle going to San Diego will be picked up in Seattle and flown to Memphis, where it will be re-sorted and flown out to San Diego for delivery the following day. Looking at a map, it would seem more efficient to ship it directly from Seattle to San Diego, but because of the large volumes it is actually more efficient and cost-effective to have a centralized sorting facility in Memphis and to route all shipments through it.
- *Cross-docking:* In a traditional distribution center, the inbound receiving process is disjointed from the outbound shipping process and storage acts as an intermediary between the two processes. At a cross-dock the freight is moved from the incoming vehicle docking point to the outgoing vehicle docking point for delivery without going through warehouse storage. Cross-docks could be used as the interface between local and line haul carriers, or even to transfer freight between different trucks owned by the same carrier. In its simplest form cross-docks can also be a parking lot where trucks will exchange inbound and outbound freight. Three common types of cross-docking are:

  1. Trans-shipment—no sorting or consolidation at the distribution center
  2. Flow-through—some sorting or bulk breaking at the distribution center
  3. Merge-in-transit—involves merging items from different sources (supplier, plant, distribution centers) as well as existing inventory in storage at the distribution center into a single customer shipment without compromising on order integrity and delivery reliability

Best Practices

1. Transportation decisions:

Lean and agile transportation should be about aligning the transportation method with the corporate goal rather than simply choosing the carrier with the lowest transportation cost. The various trade-offs should be explored and an appropriate transportation method should be selected that aligns with the corporate strategy and achieves the lowest total cost. For example, transportation cost may rise due to frequent and small deliverables but might reduce the storage costs and the inventory carrying costs. The various trade-offs that need to be considered include:

- Total cost versus customer service: Higher customer service requires higher inventory levels (lower inventory turnover), faster delivery, and wide product variety, which leads to increases in transportation and inventory costs.
- Transportation cost versus inventory: Shipment consolidation allows larger shipments (more FTL shipments) and lower transportation cost. However, it leads to higher inventory levels (holding cost).
- Transportation mode cost versus lead time: A slower transportation mode, though less costly in transportation terms, creates a greater in-transit pipeline inventory. As supply lead time and supply uncertainty increase so does the safety stock. Also, as the order lead time increases (time between placing the order and receiving the shipment), more safety stock is needed to guard against the lack of knowledge of demand during that lead time. Having a faster mode of transportation reduces the pipeline inventory and the safety stock, but increases the cost of transportation.

2. Freight consolidation:

Freight consolidation (Figure 4.22) is a process innovation that involves consolidating smaller shipments into larger ones to achieve a lower transportation cost per unit. It can be achieved through multi-stop vehicle routing, pooling, and efficient vehicle scheduling.

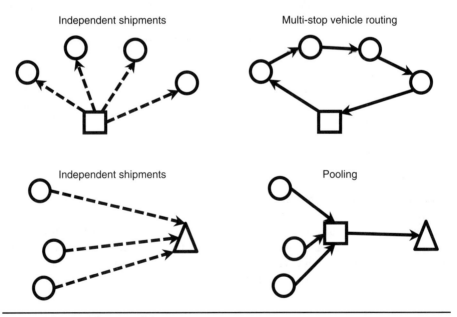

Figure 4.22 Freight consolidation

- In multi-stop vehicle routing, rather than have separate independent shipments from the central distribution center to the regional distribution center, the individual shipments are combined and share common transportation equipment (tractor or trailer) that does the pickup and delivery at different facilities.
- Pooling involves using large shipment sizes over large distances and small shipment sizes over small distances. Hence, getting LTL shipments from different manufacturing facilities to a central distribution center, consolidating the same to get economies of scale, and then shipping FTL to the downstream facilities. It could also involve getting an FTL shipment from a central distribution center to a warehouse, breaking bulk, and then shipping LTL shipments from a central distribution center to a number of regional distribution centers.
- Vehicle scheduling involves adjusting schedules forward or backward to combine with other shipments and get FTLs. Though multi-stop vehicle routing, pooling, merge-in-transit, and efficient vehicle scheduling process innovations are great, care should be taken that these process innovations are implemented without compromising on customer service, order integrity, and delivery reliability.

Brittain Ladd, formerly of Dell and currently the Director of Logistics and Manufacturing at Cognizant Technology Solutions, suggests in Success Story 11: Green Value Chain versus LAVC, that companies can find efficiencies combined with environmental friendliness in a number of areas, starting with transportation. One of the best investments a company can make is to have its entire supply chain analyzed to identify the optimal transportation network. Optimal transportation networks identify opportunities to consolidate parcel shipments into LTL, LTL shipments into truckload shipments, and to convert air shipments to more efficient ground shipments where feasible. Many companies are achieving significant reductions in logistics-related costs by ensuring that they have a network in place that eliminates unnecessary transportation and uses the optimal mode of transportation for all shipping. With Dell, supply chain analysis and transportation management software (enabler 3) has made reduced logistics costs a reality. This analysis not only ensures cost savings and efficiencies for companies, but renders their supply chain greener.

3. Inbound and outbound consolidation:

Traditionally, most companies have had separate inbound and outbound transportation planning (Figure 4.23). BIC companies coordinate pickup and delivery routes, that is, consolidate inbound and outbound shipment planning, routing, and scheduling to achieve higher utilization of resources and economies of scale.

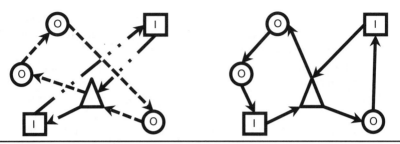

Figure 4.23 Inbound (I) and outbound (O) consolidation

Also, using continuous move routes where drivers are kept highly utilized by co-coordinating the drop-off with a pickup will help reduce deadhead costs.

General Mills reduced its empty truck time from 15 to 6 percent and saved 7 percent on its shipping costs by combining one-way shipping routes into a cross-country loop.[29]

4. Effective carrier agreements:

Having carrier agreements specifying service levels, payment terms, and so forth, can lead to reduced lead times, increased on-time deliveries, lower raw material and finished goods inventory, and improved customer service. However, carrier agreements should be based on a win-win partnership rather than exploitation. Only then will the carriers make additional capacity available to partners when there is a sudden surge in demand and responsiveness is required.

In Success Story 6: Managing Sprint's Value Chain, Michael Hahn, the vice president of Product Operations, highlights the importance of consolidating and centralizing logistics needs by going from 19 warehouses (after the merger) to 2 central warehouse facilities. He also stresses the importance of technology and having a close partnership with a 3PL company, in this case UPS, to enable best-practice processes. The partnership between UPS and Sprint is excellent and involves executives at the most senior level of each company's management team. UPS provides the "brick and mortar" as the 3PL partner, but Sprint manages the processes and requirements. By consolidating and centralizing the logistics needs, Sprint can leverage tremendous savings and maximize efficiencies.

5. Visibility and dynamic routing:

Regular routes that use historical data have always been easier to plan and manage as the drivers are familiar with the territories and the customers. However, BIC companies use technology to do dynamic routing in which the routes are adjusted based on the most updated demand information in the form of customer orders. At the same time, when material shortages occur at one facility, materials can be reassigned from other locations or rerouted from the source in order to capture the greatest return across the entire value chain. Advance shipment notice and GPS tracking capabilities provide real-time visibility about the incoming shipments, and also allow material planners to react if incoming tracking signals indicate a delay. This helps tremendously in achieving agility since it allows downstream processes to plan and stage documents, workers, and receiving equipment in anticipation of the goods' arrival in addition to being proactive when delays occur for any reason. It also allows the planners to reroute or expedite shipments that are in transit.

Aberdeen Group (November 2008)[28] mentioned that with increased visibility companies can perform necessary "agility actions" such as shipment rerouting due to demand changes or infrastructure disruptions, expediting late shipments, cross-docking and distribution center bypass strategies, and deploying best-practice processes such as vendor-managed inventory.

In addition, visibility enables firms to warn their customers about potential delivery delays, capacity issues and other value chain disruptions ahead of time. This allows both parties to reach acceptable issue resolution while sustaining high customer service levels.

6. Process excellence:

Companies should have a program to track process excellence and reward employees for their innovative ideas when they are implemented. Some examples of process excellence are:

- The challenge in unloading trailers is that goods that are loaded first are unloaded last (last in, first out), which means the order that goods are picked up (based on priority) is not the same order that goods will be unloaded at the receiving facility. One solution is reverse loading the trailer, which requires close coordination. Another solution is to use side-loading trucks, which allow goods to be loaded and unloaded from the side instead of the back.
- Another area of improvement is to realign the receiving docks so incoming trucks can unload closer to the stocking areas because, although movement of incoming parts is necessary, excessive movement is nonvalue-added. In addition, realignment is needed for the stocking areas of the finished products to be close to the shipping docks.
- In the distribution centers or warehouse, fastest moving items need to be close to shipping docks.
- The best-practice process of wave picking in the distribution center, which leads to an increase in labor productivity and order fulfillment reliability, and reduces wasteful material handling movements. In wave picking,

rather than pick each order when it is received, orders are consolidated into waves where orders with similar characteristics are picked at the same time. For example, if there are ten orders each with one unit of Item A, rather than make ten trips to the location of the A items, wave picking involves making one trip and picking up ten units.

7. Effective reverse logistics:

Reverse logistics is starting to get more and more attention nowadays because of the connection between reverse logistics and green supply chain initiatives, which includes environmentally responsible manufacturing and distribution. A well-planned and executed reverse logistics strategy can help an organization reduce costs, comply with environmental regulations, increase customer satisfaction, and be a source of competitive differentiation. However, for reverse logistics to be a source of competitive advantage the reverse logistics initiative must be supported by senior management and all the cross-functional teams (sales, customer support, environmental and regulatory, logistics, manufacturing, packaging, distribution). The customer feedback should be captured, heard, and communicated by having detailed codes that can be used to track the reason for each individual return. This can provide invaluable information that can help drive new product and process design.

BIC companies like McKesson make the customer choose from approximately nine reason codes, which are then tracked and reported to the appropriate process owners so as to eliminate the underlying root causes. Also, disposition strategies should be put in place so that the material handling and inventory carrying costs for the returned items are minimal. Similarly, by having collaborative relationships with retailers, wholesalers, and liquidators, GENCO sells its returned items through bulk liquidation, refurbish liquidation, and value-added liquidation. In addition, the importance of having targeted and visible reverse logistics measures that institutionalize continuous improvement cannot be underestimated.[30]

Reverse logistics not only involves having a reverse supply chain to handle repairs, but also designing the product keeping returns in mind, that is, having a cross-functional product design between the different departments so that while designing the product itself, research and development can make sure the product uses a modular design with fewer parts so that it is easy to repair.

8. Effective cross-docking:

Cross-docking has changed from a strategy innovation into a competitive necessity. In a recent survey conducted by the Saddle Creek Corporation, of the 547 respondents 52 percent currently cross-dock, 13 percent plan to cross-dock, and 31 percent have no plans to do so.[31]

As cross-docking involves moving the freight from the incoming vehicle dock-ing point to the outgoing vehicle without storing the freight, it leads to less mate-rial handling and less storage space while improving inventory turnover.

By implementing cross-docking, companies can extend the just-in-time sys-tem from the shop floor to encompass the entire supply chain. Instead of restrict-ing the kanbans only to the shop floor, cross-docking would allow manufacturing facilities to pull small lot sizes from their suppliers using standardized containers, which would lead to a reduction in material handling and inventory. Milk runs, which involve picking up materials from different suppliers and then delivering the mixed loads of materials to the production facilities using regular pickup and drop off routes, can be implemented successfully using cross-docking. This would again lead to not only transportation consolidation efficiencies but also a uniform, smooth rhythmic flow of materials and level workload (heijunka) at the suppli-ers, manufacturers, and eventually throughout the entire supply chain.[32]

However, to implement cross-docking successfully requires that the dock doors are labeled correctly with the loading/unloading times, designated docks on one side for incoming shipments and on the other side for outgoing shipments to ensure foolproof operation, use of kanban tickets to track shipments inside the cross-dock, and above all, a change in corporate culture that enables collaboration with suppliers and employee empowerment. Before Eastman Kodak implemented cross-docking, each plant was managing its own material movement and did not take advantage of transportation consolidation efficiencies. Since the suppliers de-veloped the delivery schedules, unscheduled deliveries from Eastman Kodak's per-spective were common, which led to poor material handling and labor utilization. Also, since suppliers waited until they had an FTL to minimize on the transporta-tion costs, it led to higher inventory carrying and storage costs. To implement cross-docking efficiently and effectively, the project team at Kodak took control of the transportation from the suppliers, designed routes to implement milk runs using cross-docks, redesigned the cross-dock layout to have designated areas for incom-ing shipments from suppliers and outgoing kanbans for deliveries to the plant, and used kanban cards for tracking shipments at the cross-dock. These efforts resulted in a reduction in the inbound material order cycle time from seven to two days, reduced inventory levels at the plant because of smaller frequent deliveries, and a more level workload at the suppliers and manufacturers because of predefined regular schedules and milk runs.[32]

SCM SUPERPROCESS WORKFLOW SUMMARY

Strategic Management

As we have seen, the SCM superprocess (Figure 4.24) is composed of a spectrum of interrelated processes ranging from short-term, to medium-term, to long-term activities. The strategic management process supports long-term decision making, such as supply chain strategy and supply chain network design. Once the company has formulated the right supply chain strategy, the supply chain network design, which should be aligned with the supply chain strategy, will help determine the optimal number and locations of facilities (plants and distribution centers), flow of goods throughout the supply chain, and best assignment of customers to distribution centers. For the supply chain network design subprocess to truly come up with a global optimal network, it requires not only internal aggregated strategic planning data such as variable costs, fixed facility costs, transportation expense, and inventory carrying costs, but also external data pertaining to supplier contracts, alternate suppliers, and supplier pricing from the strategic sourcing process in SRM. Also, understanding the trade-offs between three conflicting objectives—cost, flexibility, and responsiveness—is key before deciding which suppliers to select, where to locate the manufacturing facilities and distribution centers, which products to produce at which facilities, and the distribution of products to customer regions.

Sales and Operations Planning

Next comes the S&OP process, which forms the vital link between the strategic business planning and the tactical supply chain planning. A key goal of S&OP is to achieve a supply demand balance and a volume mix balance. If supply exceeds demand it leads to excess inventories, obsolescence, price cuts, and discounts. When demand exceeds supply it leads to reduced customer service, expediting, overtime, and so forth. A supply demand balance can be achieved by effective coordination between the different functional areas and active involvement of top management. Since a key objective of the S&OP process is to balance supply and demand for product families, it consists of demand planning, inventory planning, and master supply planning processes.

The demand planning subprocess consists of anticipating market demand using internal inputs from statistical forecasts, sales, marketing, finance, etc., as well as external demand collaboration from the customers through the marketing management process in CRM. Once a consensus has been reached, the "one number forecast" is then exported into downstream systems such as inventory planning and master supply planning. It is key that the consensus forecast should be viewed as "our" forecast and not as "my" or "your" forecast, and past performance of each functional group should be looked at to determine which functional group was most accurate and consistent.

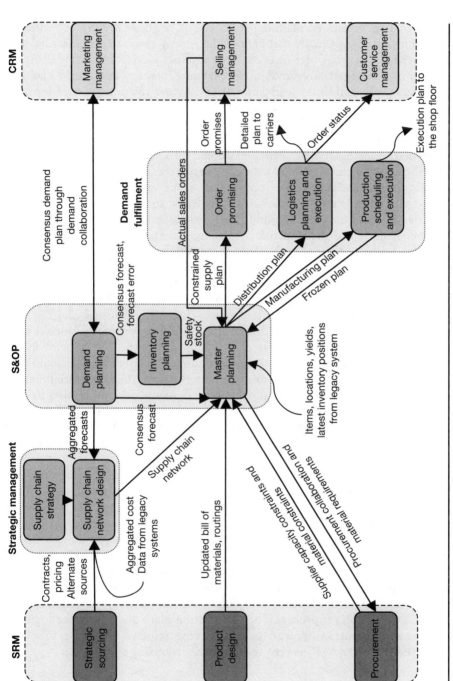

Figure 4.24 SCM superprocess workflow

The goal of inventory planning is to calculate (how much) and allocate (where) inventory optimally throughout the supply chain to provide a balance between holding costs, ordering costs, and customer service. Inventory planning typically uses information from demand planning forecasts and their variability, as well as supply lead times, lead time variability, and customer service levels to come up with safety stock targets to be fed into master supply planning. Supply risks could result because of transportation delays between supplier, factory, and distribution centers, process yield variability, machine breakdowns, employee strikes, and so forth. Demand variability could be a result of product discounts, promotion, phase in/phase out products, or inherent product characteristics. Safety stock guards against risk from forecast error and lead-time variability. It is important that a thorough analysis be done first to reduce demand and supply variability, and only then should safety stocks be used to guard against the remaining supply and demand risk by placing inventory buffers at appropriate echelons to achieve the optimal balance between flexibility and responsiveness.

After demand planning comes up with the forecast, and inventory planning has come up with the safety stock targets, master planning then determines quantity and timing of production, procurement, and distribution, respecting material, time and capacity constraints to achieve the optimal plan. Master planning is often considered the heart of the SCM superprocess since it generates the enterprise-wide master plan, which drives the subsequent operational planning process. Master planning requires not only the static data pertaining to BOM, bill of distributions, manufacturing routings, material master, location master, and yields. But, it also needs dynamic data pertaining to customer orders, customer priorities, forecasts, on-hand inventories, and so forth. Additional inputs into master planning include visibility into the material and capacity constraints at the suppliers as well as procurement collaboration using the procurement process in SRM.

Master planning uses the forecast information from demand planning and the actual orders from the selling management process in CRM to do forecast netting, which is the ability to subtract the orders from the forecast to prioritize orders over forecasts and also prevent double counting of orders. Master planning then uses the orders and netted forecast information to come up with procurement, manufacturing, and distribution plans, which drive the subsequent operational planning process. The procurement plans are sent to the procurement process in SRM for collaboration with the supplier on availability of components. Manufacturing plans are sent to the production scheduling and execution subprocess. The distribution plans are sent to the logistics planning and execution subprocess, and the constrained supply plan to satisfy the netted forecast (ATP) is sent to the order promising subprocess.

Demand Fulfillment

Operational SCM performs a detailed validation of tactical plans by incorporating a greater level of granularity and considering detailed constraints such as setup times, precedence rules, and so forth. Demand fulfillment is a process of promising the customer what the company can deliver (order promising), and then delivering on that promise (production scheduling and execution, logistics planning and execution) to gain and sustain a competitive advantage.

The goal of the order promising subprocess is to make accurate, optimal, and reliable delivery promises for sales orders by matching supply (on-hand inventory, in-transit inventory, planned) with demand while respecting delivery transportation constraints, sales channels allocations, and distribution center reservations. Order promising is tightly integrated with master planning since it uses the constrained supply plan from master planning (ATP) as its input to generate the allocated available to promise (AATP) as its output. AATP involves disaggregating the global ATP into multiple local ATPs (AATP) for the different sales channels or customers using different rules. Therefore, when the customer places the order through the selling management process in CRM, the promise is not offered looking at the globally pooled ATP, but rather the AATP.

The production scheduling subprocess generates a detailed sequence of jobs at each resource and considers detailed constraints such as actual setups, sequence conditions, production incompatibilities, critical raw material availability, and detailed resources capacity. The objective of production scheduling includes the ability to minimize changeovers, late orders, work in process, and production costs while at the same time maximizing customer service. Production scheduling also has tight integration with master planning because it uses the manufacturing plans' output from master planning to generate the detailed plan, which drives the execution on the shop floor. Also, the frozen plans (capacity and materials committed to specific orders) from production scheduling are sent back to master planning to ensure that master planning doesn't change these plans, since any changes in the frozen plans would result in excessive costs and planning nervousness.

The distribution plans from master planning are sent to the logistics planning and execution subprocess, which then generates a detailed transportation schedule by combining shipments into loads and loads into trips. These detailed transportation schedules are then sent to the carriers for execution. Hence, logistics planning and execution makes sure that the organization not only promises the customer but also delivers on that promise.

SCM SUPERPROCESS WORKFLOW
FOR FASHION RETAIL INDUSTRY

This section will show the reader how to map the generic SCM blueprint mentioned in this chapter to a specific industry. We have selected a fashion (seasonal) retail company as an example to show that the blueprint that we discussed in this chapter can be applied to the retail industry as it can to the manufacturing industry.

Fashion retailers always look for a differentiator either by achieving superior customer intimacy or cost leadership. They typically look into their own internal processes to provide this differentiator. Figure 4.25 illustrates the SCM superprocess workflow for the fashion retail industry and related processes.

Strategic Management

The strategic management process consists of two long-term, decision-making subprocesses: (1) defining supply chain strategy and (2) optimizing supply chain network to support the strategy.

Supply chain strategy should be aligned to corporate strategies for the retail firm and should consider and incorporate new store openings, brand positioning, competition changes, brand equity, advertising budget, and so forth. Also, the supply chain strategy should be aligned to business key performance indicators (KPIs) such as customer service and business profit objectives.

Once the company has formulated the right supply chain strategy, the supply chain network design should be aligned with the supply chain strategy by optimizing the: number of stores, location of cross-docks and distribution centers, storage and handling capacity at each cross-dock and distribution center, modes and routes that should be used to move inventory throughout the demand chain, and products to be sourced from which suppliers. Also, this alignment should include which products should be located within each distribution center and which channel/store should be serviced from which distribution center.

Sales and Operations Planning

A key goal of S&OP is to achieve a supply demand and volume mix balance. This process is called (mapped to) *merchandise planning* in the retail industry. Merchandise planning breaks down broad level strategic plans into more detailed tactical plans at a category level. It is typically a financial-driven process in which merchandise financial goals are set based on past, present, and future demand. It is also the process of developing optimal merchandise plans down to the store level. It includes forecasting, performance and trend analysis, and identifying gaps and opportunities by analyzing data at different levels of the location, time, or merchandise hierarchy. The best-practice process uses standard KPIs to maintain consistent measurement between departments, categories, and locations.

Increased pressure on profit margins is forcing fashion retailers to focus on better understanding the demand for merchandise throughout the product life cycle. There is an urgent need to address the profit pressure and learn how to maximize

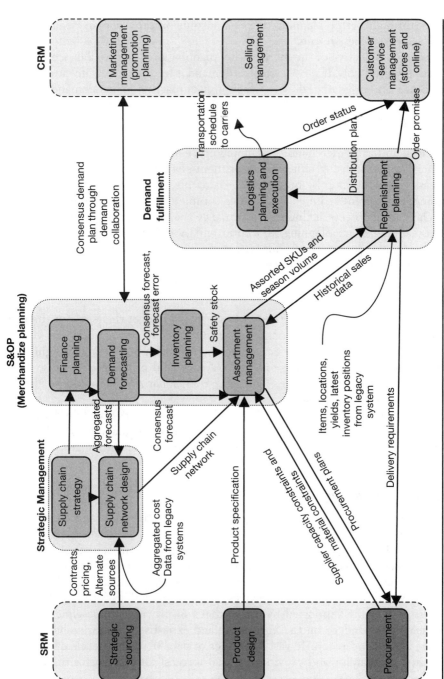

Figure 4.25 SCM superprocess workflow for the fashion retail industry

profits through better planning, fewer stockouts, improved margins, and more solid overall business results.

The main objective of the merchandise planning process is to balance demand and supply profitably. If supply exceeds demand it leads to excess inventories, obsolescence, and price markdowns, which impact margins. When demand exceeds supply it leads to lost sales, which impacts revenue. A supply demand balance can be achieved by effective coordination between the different functional areas and active involvement of top management.

A lean and agile merchandise planning process integrates and then reconciles financial, merchandising, store, and assortment plans. Once plans are created, this process closes the loop by monitoring, evaluating, and adjusting the plan to accommodate current realities. It provides complete planning capabilities for the merchandising process, including performance analysis, financial planning, assortment planning, space planning, allocation, and more. This process can be divided into four major subprocesses: financial planning, demand forecasting, inventory planning, and assortment management.

Financial Planning

Retailers start their planning cycle with a financial budget that sets out the plan to secure target revenue and margins. The budget is based on a previous year or season. The chief financial officer is the owner of this subprocess with significant participation from merchandise planners. At the end of the merchandise planning process, the expected sales (forecast) after dollarizing it should be aligned with the budget.

Demand forecasts along with financial targets serve as the foundation for all subprocesses of merchandise planning. Merchandise planners should build merchandise, financial, and assortment plans that better anticipate consumer demand.

Demand Forecasting

The demand forecasting subprocess provides an effective means to create a demand forecast for both fast- and slow-moving SKUs at all locations. It consists of anticipating market demand using internal inputs from statistical forecasts, sales, marketing, finance, etc,, as well as external demand collaboration from the customers and suppliers to form an integrated view of demand coupled to the budgetary and merchandising objectives of the organization. Although this subprocess is typically supported by a tool that can provide the baseline forecast, it is heavily dependent on the knowledge and expertise of the merchandiser to review, adjust, and reconcile vast quantities of data at various levels of the item or location hierarchy, and provide the final forecast after intensive market and merchandise analysis.

Many factors influence the quality of a forecast, such as seasonality, trends, sales velocity, dependency, internal and external causal factors, and promotions. Therefore, one single forecasting technique cannot be used for every situation. For example, a periodicity forecasting technique is recommended for items with repetitive selling patterns unrelated to seasonality, while multiple regression is recommended for items that have selling patterns strongly impacted by other items.

The selected forecasting tool should provide a library of techniques that have been proven to be successful in the retail environment. It should have the ability to generate forecasts based on underlying trend, seasonality promotions, inventory effects, and other known causal factors in addition to having "best pick" functionality.

The demand forecasting subprocess should be integrated with the marketing process (which is responsible for promotion planning)—for causal (event-based) forecasting, to accurately predict and segregate the impact of promotions, product transitions, pricing changes, markdowns, and other events.

It is crucial for any fashion retailer to be able to conduct detailed analysis of point-of-sale data and promotional history to analyze various promotional event scenarios for building traffic and driving profits through effective advertising. The integration of promotion planning to replenishment is also crucial to efficient execution of promotions.

Fashion retailers today must strive to satisfy the demand of their individual customer segments. Long gone are the days of the mass market where a single assortment, standard pricing, and a single "average location" forecast would satisfy consumer demand in all stores. To be lean and agile, forecasts today must account for demand differences across all stores, geographies, and product lines. Better forecast accuracy in this environment requires sophisticated capabilities delivered via a highly automated and scalable solution. This solution should also help in reconciling the forecast, including seasonal and regional variations, product introductions, and retirements (end-of-life) to be aligned with budget goals. Providing analytical and collaboration capabilities to determine the best prices for products across different stores and through their life cycle goes a long way in helping the retailer achieve their targets.

It is important to mention that the demand forecasting subprocess is less tactical in the fashion retail industry. This is because the majority of SKUs are new in the fashion industry. Statistical forecasting then helps within the season once initial allocations to stores have been made. Therefore, assortment management has to receive "guesses" (subjective forecast) before any statistical forecast can be created in the fashion retail industry.

Inventory Planning

The objective of the inventory planning subprocess is to balance the retailer's investment in inventory against a target customer service level. It defines the time-phased inventory stocking policies based on key parameters like average demand, average variations in demand and supply, actual or predefined distributions of variations, lead times, replenishment intervals, order sizes, and holding costs. Inventory planning calculates dynamic safety stock levels for stores and associated distribution centers, while balancing required service levels with inventory investments. The output is the safety stock levels for each inventory carrying SKU-location combination.

Assortment Management

Assortment management is a complex, time-intensive undertaking for many retailers. Improving the situation usually requires the ability to account for space constraints and local demand—insights that many assortment professionals don't have. For merchandise managers and store operations managers alike, poor assortment management results in missed financial targets and profitability goals. The objective of this critical subprocess is to ensure that the most attractive assortment of items are in the right stores at the right time, quantities, and price, and to optimize the "real estate", whether in the physical store or online.

Assortment management determines which items should be planned and made available where and in what quantities. During this subprocess, product mix is synchronized with financial objectives, and breadth and depth of product is built based on customers' real interests, location, demographics, and buying trends—not rough estimations.

Included in assortment management are store allocation and space planning. Effective store allocation provides retailers the ability to fulfill demand by facilitating distribution of the right merchandise to the right stores and channels based on fashion and seasonal trends, customer demand; and store, channel, and location attributes.

The objective of space planning is to align store space allocations and shelf assortments with consumer demand. Effective space planning is a key part of the planning life cycle. A well-designed shopping environment attracts customers, prevents stockouts, drives inventory productivity, reduces operating costs and, most importantly, improves the financial performance of the store. It helps planning with financial performance reports that incorporate calculations of capacity, allocated space, and used space.

Assortment management is often considered the heart of the retail SCM superprocess since it drives the subsequent operational planning process. It determines which merchandise products will sell in which stores week by week to meet the targets set in the budget. In addition, it plans pricing over the life cycle of the assorted products, and determines the allocation of inventory to stores and the space allotted to each item in each store's display.

As soon as the merchandise plans are finalized, the purchasing department starts the procurement subprocess. It negotiates contracts with suppliers, specifies the merchandise to be provided, and gives an expected schedule for delivery (procurement plans), as shown in Figure 4.25.

Lean and agile assortment management enables analysts to identify gaps and opportunities. It maximizes effects of special promotions and clearance sales, enables retailers to optimize allocations using accurate insights into customer demand and ensures that the right merchandise goes to the right stores. This is crucial for the proper flow of goods, managing inventory efficiently, increasing turns through optimal product mix, and freeing up time and resources moving and storing unsold goods. It also frees up merchants' time for more strategic tasks, such as product life cycle planning for the next season.

Demand Fulfillment

Fashion retail demand fulfillment is the process of fulfilling the demand effectively and efficiently while respecting delivery transportation constraints, sales channels allocations and distribution centers reservations. The lean and agile process can increase sales, reduce labor costs, and reduce order cycle time by keeping the stores and distribution centers appropriately and efficiently stocked.

It consists of two major subprocesses: replenishment planning and logistics planning and execution. Replenishment planning is considered to be the soul of this process and it is equivalent to order promising and production scheduling combined for the manufacturing industry.

Replenishment Planning

Replenishment planning is the subprocess of examining SKU-location combinations in order to determine the replenishments that would be needed to maintain high service levels with efficient, profitable investments in inventory.

Replenishment planning should look at the entire supply chain for the item when creating replenishment plans and understand the average lead times and lead-time variations, forecasts and forecast variations, and the current inventory position at each location. It also must consider all on-order and in-transit inventory to generate an optimized replenishment plan to meet service level goals while minimizing inventory investment. The algorithm that is used for the optimization can range from simple min-max order point comparisons to time-of-supply calculations. This depends on the buying strategies that are chosen and the characteristics of the product, such as movement, packaging, customer service level goals, and nature of the item (slow or fast moving, or a basic or seasonal item). Therefore, this process should be highly automated.

For online and catalog orders, this subprocess should be able to provide order promise dates based on the inventory picture and in-transit shipments coming from suppliers.

It should also generate forecasts in addition to replenishment plans based on the needs for the current planning period, as well as multiple future periods in anticipation of future sales, and provide visibility and early detection into anticipated supply constraints so appropriate action can be taken while multiple options are still available.

A lean and agile replenishment planning subprocess can result in increased sales, reduced labor costs, and reduced order cycle time by keeping the stores and distribution centers appropriately and efficiently stocked.

Logistics Planning and Execution

The main objective of logistics planning and execution is to enable firms to accurately move and deliver products to ensure efficient physical fulfillment and increased profitability.

The replenishment plans from the replenishment planning subprocess are sent to the logistics planning and execution subprocess, which then generates a detailed transportation schedule by combining shipments into loads and loads into trips. These detailed transportation schedules are then sent to the carriers for execution. This subprocess includes the following:

- Scheduling inbound shipments based on real-time evaluation of all constraints (financial, sourcing, logistics) in addition to the need date.
- Picking, packing, shipping, and delivering the final products.
- Selecting the transportation mode (air, ocean, truck, etc.) based on the need date, origin and destination, and cost.
- Monitoring and providing status across the entire fulfillment route, detecting shipment or delivery exceptions in real-time, and managing their resolution.

Some of the replenishment requirements cannot be fulfilled fully from the distribution centers or warehouse. In this case, these requirements are converted into purchase orders and get sent to suppliers through the purchase order management subprocess, which is part of the SRM superprocess.

In closing, fashion retail firms who achieved lean and agile SCM have witnessed significant benefits such as the following:

- Reduction in inventory due to connected store-distribution center replenishment (inventory turn improvements of 10 to 30 percent.
- Reduction in stockout occurrences for fast-moving items.
- Achieving competitive advantage by providing intelligent order promising and fulfillment for Internet/catalog customers, and the ability to anticipate and react to changing customer dynamics and demand. This has led to sales increases of 1 to 5 percent.

- Transportation cost savings resulting from lowest-cost carrier selection and load consolidation (logistics cost reductions of 5 to 20 percent).
- Markdown and obsolescence reductions of 10 to 30 percent.

REFERENCES

1. Shister, N. 2005. "Manufacturer of the Year for Global Supply Chain Excellence: Ford Motor Company." *World Trade Magazine*, May 1. http://www. worldtrade mag.com/Articles/Cover_Story/de9907fc6aaf7010VgnVCM100000f 932a8c0 (accessed January 2009).
2. Gottfredson, M., R. Puryear, and S. Phillips. 2005. "Strategic Sourcing: From Periphery to the Core. *Harvard Business Review* 84 (2): 132–139.
3. Harrington, L. July 2006. Building a 3PL: Cat Logistics Services.http://logis tics.cat.com/cda/components/fullArticle?m=115228&x=7&id=379991 (accessed May 2008).
4. Byrnes, J. 2005. "You Only Have One Supply Chain? *Harvard Business School-Working Knowledge*, August 1. http://hbswk.hbs.edu/archive/4929. html (accessed September 2008).
5. Lee, H., and D. W. Hoyt. 2001. "Lucent Technologies: Global Supply Chain Management." *Harvard Business Review*, January 26, 1–18.
6. Albright, T., and M. Lam. 2006. "Managerial Accounting and Continuous Improvement Initiatives: A Retrospective and Framework." *Journal of Managerial Issues* 18 (2): 157.
7. Pine, B. J. II. 1993. *Mass Customization: The New Frontier of Business Competition*. Cambridge, MA: Harvard University Press.
8. Fisher, M. L. 1997. "What is the Right Supply Chain for Your Product?" *Harvard Business Review*, March-April, 105–116.
9. Lee, H. L. 2002. "Aligning Supply Chain Strategies with Product Uncertainties." *California Management Review* 44 (3): 105–112.
10. Cohen, M. A., C. Cull, H. L. Lee, and D. Willen. 2000. "Saturn's Supply-Chain Innovation: High Value in After-Sales Service." *Sloan Management Review* 41 (4): 93–101.
11. Dapiran, P. 1992. "Benetton—Global Logistics in Action." *Asia Pacific International Journal of Business Logistics* 4 (3): 7–11.
12. Ballou, H. 2004. *Business Logistics/Supply Chain Management*. 5th ed. Upper Saddle River, NJ: Prentice Hall.
13. Blackburn, J. D., V. D. R. Guide, Jr., G. C. Souza, and L. N. Van Wassenhove. 2004. "Reverse Supply Chains for Commercial Returns." *California Management Review* 46 (2): 6–22.
14. Sabri, E., and B. Beamon. 2000. "A Multi-objective Approach to Simultaneous Strategic and Operational Planning in Supply Chain Design. *OMEGA: The International Journal of Management Science* 28 (5): 581–598.

15. Aberdeen Group. December 2004. *Supply Chain Inventory Strategies Cenchmark Report: How Inventory Misconceptions and Inertia are Damaging Companies' Service Levels and Financial Results*, 1–22. Boston: Aberdeen Group.

16. Pandya, G. 2006. "S&OP best practices enable consistent profitability." *Supply Chain Leader*, no. 6 (October): 27–31.

17. Lee, H., V. Padmanabhan, and S. Whang. 1997. "The bullwhip effect in supply chains." *Sloan Management Review* 38 (3): 93–102.

18. Foster, T. A. 2008. "Forecasting, Demand Planning in a Difficult Economy." http://www.supplychainbrain.com/content/headline-news/single-article/article/forecasting-demand-planning-in-a-difficult-economy/ (accessed date February 2009).

19. Sabri, E., A. Gupta, and M. Beitler. 2006. *Purchase Order Management in B2B Environment: Best Practice & Technologies*. Fort Lauderdale, FL: J. Ross Publishing.

20. Aberdeen Group. January 2008. *The Next Generation of Manufacturing Systems: Manufacturing and Operations Management*, 1–16. Boston: Aberdeen Group.

21. AMR Research. July 2007. "Next-generation S&OP: The Path to Bottom-line Value." 1–32. Boston: AMR Research

22. Petzinger Jr., T. 1995. At Deere They Know a Mad Scientist May Be a Firm's Biggest Asset. *Wall Street Journal*, July 14.

23. Jones, D. T. 2006. "Heijunka: Leveling production." *Manufacturing Engineering*137 (2). http://www.sme.org/cgi-bin/find-articles.pl?&ME06ART49&ME&20060809&&SME&article (accessed May 2009).

24. Mazda Press Release. 2007. Industry-first Production Line Capabilities Increase Volume and Flexibility. http://www.mazdausamedia.com/content/mazda-begins-mixed-model-production-v6-and-i-4-engines(accessed April 2009).

25. S. C. Graves, A. G. De Kok. December (2003). *Handbooks in Operations Research and Management Science: Supply Chain Management: Design, Coordination and Operation*. Amsterdam, The Netherlands: Elsevier Publishing Company.

26. See URL http://www.solvay.edu/FR/Programmes/documents/MSZara_Case-final.pdf accessed February 2009) Harle, N., M. Pich, and L. Van der Hayden. 2002. Marks and Spencer and Zara: Process competition in the textile apparel industry. *INSEAD* case.

27. Supply Chain Digest Newsletter. (December 2008). Lean and Technology. 11–15. Springboro, OH: Supply Chain Digest

28. Miller, J. 2006. How Toyota Uses Information Technology (IT) for Kaizen. Gemba Research, June 21.http://www.gembapantarei.com/2006/06/how_toyota_uses_information_technology_it_for_kaizen.html (accessed January 2009).

29. Cross, K. 2001. "Fill It to the Brim." *Business 2.0*, March 6, 36–38.

30. Subject Matter Experts Dr. James R. Stock. Cheryl Harrity. 2007. "Reverse Logistics: Backward Practices that Matter,"ed. K. Campos and L. Trees, 17-27. Houston, TX: *APQC Publications*. (Research sponsored by Warehousing Education and Research Council.)

31. *2008 Cross-Docking Trends Report*. August 2008.http://outsourced-logistics .com/field_reports/cross_docking_trends_report_0808/ (accessed May 2009).

32. Cook, R. L., B. Gibson, and D. MacCurdy. 2005. "A Lean Approach to Cross Docking." *Supply Chain Management Review*, March, 55–59.

5

Customer Relationship Management Superprocess

INTRODUCTION

If you google the term *customer relationship management* (CRM), you will get a number of definitions. Anderson and Kerr[1] define CRM as "a comprehensive approach to creating, maintaining, and expanding customer relationships."

Bob Thompson,[2] CEO of CustomerThink Corporation, defines CRM as "a business strategy to acquire and manage the most valuable customer relationships. CRM requires a customer-centric business philosophy and culture to support effective marketing, sales, and service processes."

CRM is the superprocess of managing all aspects of the customer relationships (attracting customers → acquiring customers → retaining customers → life-time customers) supported by effective marketing management, selling management, and customer service management (Figure 5.1).

Consumer behavior is changing and customers are increasingly demanding new and customized products. This has led to shrinkage in the market window for organizations and simultaneous overabundance in options for customers. Companies that cannot keep pace with the customer's needs in terms of total value (price, quality, convenience, etc.) by first acquiring and then retaining customers for life run the risk of losing market share and revenue.

CRM CHALLENGES

CRM is changing rapidly because of technology, globalization, and mass customization. Customers have, by far, become the dominant player in the seller-customer

Figure 5.1 CRM pyramid

relationship. Firms are increasingly having to manage inventory, personnel, and resources with less waste, while simultaneously giving customers more configuration options, more delivery flexibility, and shorter lead times. Some of the CRM challenges faced by organizations are mentioned below.

1. Privacy and security:

Though the Internet and data mining technology have led to customer empowerment and informed consumers, where the customer has a wealth of information for comparison shopping and companies can monitor customer buying behavior to give personalized shopping recommendations, this situation has created numerous challenges. The plethora of information out there also endangers one's privacy and security. For example, I once received a call from my credit card company and the customer service representative told me that since I had been paying all my monthly balances on time I had been selected to upgrade to the platinum card with a minimal annual fee of $50. I responded politely by saying that I was very much happy with my present card. What happened after that really threw me off. The customer service representative gave me information from my credit history that even I didn't know. He mentioned that I had several credit cards with different interest rates and I could actually consolidate them by transferring balances from the others into one low rate card. I was astonished and frankly scared at the level of information he had. The customer service representative was using my information to lure me into upgrading to a new credit card. He was very insistent, persistent, and pushy to the point that it got annoying. That was the end of my relationship with the credit card company.

2. Lack of a single face to the customer:

With the astronomical rise of the Internet, it has become increasingly difficult for companies to have the traditional one-to-one personal relationship with customers. It has become a big challenge for the same person to manage a growing customer base, let alone making sure that his/her actions are in congruence with the overall corporate strategy. Also, it has become nearly impossible to ensure a seamless, consistent, and delightful experience to the customer, especially since the departments (sales, marketing, customer support) are diverse in their functioning, priorities, attitudes, and often have little or no knowledge about the customer's past experiences with the company.

Once when I visited one of the big toy stores, I wanted to find out the balance on my gift card. I was shocked when the teller told me that she would not be able to help me since she didn't have visibility into the gift card balance information, and I would have to call the 1-800 number and speak to the customer service representative to find out the balance. I had to actually call the 1-800 number, wait for ten minutes to talk to the service representative, get my balance, and then give my cell phone to the sales representative to make sure the customer service representative and the sales representative were on the same page. Talk about having a single face to the customer and offering a seamless shopping experience. That was the last time I visited that store.

3. Globalization:

Globalization has allowed the smallest of companies scattered around the globe to compete with the largest. With the entire world as a potential customer, firms are finding it a challenge to transition from a single-site business serving domestic markets to a truly global business with multiple locations around the world, a variety of transportation modes, diverse cost structures, and highly differentiated markets. Decisions about where to source materials, and where to produce and sell products are suddenly much more complex. In addition, firms typically arrive in a new international market and try to apply the same tools, processes, and strategies that have proven successful in their domestic businesses or value chain. Or, they often encounter local value chain partners with business processes that will not easily mesh with their existing operations because of language and cultural obstacles in addition to the gaps in understanding best practices.

4. Top management support:

CRM is not a software tool but an organizational philosophy. Many companies implementing CRM don't have a clue as to what CRM is. How long will it take? How much will it cost? Companies try and match their corporate strategy to the CRM technology they have purchased. Technology should be selected to match the company's strategy and not the other way around. Rather than improving business processes like customer service and order fulfillment first, they look for quick fix tools and the next silver bullet. Rather than change the performance metrics and incentive systems, they think technology is the panacea for all their problems. Even when technology is implemented and is in congruence with the corporate strategy, organizations don't give enough attention to change management issues. The implementation is often treated as a stand-alone information technology (IT) project rather than a business improvement decision, and lacks the total organizational buy-in, which is necessary for the project to be successful. (Note: Throughout this chapter, you will see mentions of lean and agile value chain (LAVC) principles and enablers which are discussed in detail in chapter 1 and should be considered as you progress through this book.)

According to a survey by CRM Forum, managers said that 87 percent of the CRM projects fail because of a lack of change management. Best-in-class (BIC) companies like General Electric (GE), rather than jump on the CRM technology bandwagon, first understand the business processes and then implement technology (enabler 3) to overcome employee and customer problems (principle 1) and eliminate nonvalue-added activities (principle 3). For example, when GE capital examined their existing processes, they realized that the customer order forms shuttled back and forth between the customer and the salespeople because the customers left some fields blank. GE implemented an internal Six Sigma initiative to first simplify the customer interface and improve the old process and only then implemented the software to overcome the problem. Improve before you automate. To make sure that sales folks actually used the new software, their performance metrics and incentives were modified (principle 5: close the loop between planning and execution by tying metrics to adoption of software).[3]

Another case involved BMC software, a business service management company that failed to implement a CRM solution two times. The reason: top management thought CRM was an IT solution and handed it off to the IT managers without any executive support. Finally, the third time around they realized their mistake. This time they put the VP of sales and the manager of marketing in charge of heading the CRM initiative. The CRM implementation was broken into phases rather than a big bang implementation with direct sales function automation first. This was followed by sales-lead management and then business-partner channel managers. Employees were involved in coming up with the user configurations (enabler 6: process innovation by encouraging employee empowerment). This ensured their early adoption rather than apprehension. Also, the potential benefits were communicated to all the employees to get organizational buy-in. Six months later, 80 percent of the sales and marketing staff were using the new system.[3]

EVOLUTION OF CRM

Brent Frei,[4] president and CEO of Onyx Software, suggests that the CRM typically evolves within a company in four stages.

Stage 1: Collaboration, cooperation, and coordination within a particular team (either sales or marketing or customer service) is a challenge and between teams practically absent. Every department is closely guarded about the information they get about the customer and doesn't share it across departments. Even if someone tries to develop a cross-functional workflow, it is met with stiff resistance. Initiatives are implemented to target specific business processes within the department. For example, automated e-mail response, surveys, and so forth. Hence, the benefits are localized and limited to specific business processes within the department.

Stage 2: Collaboration, cooperation, and coordination excel within a particular department (either sales or marketing or customer service) and initiatives are implemented at the departmental level, which help the entire department become more efficient and effective. In stage 2, CRM is about stand-alone initiatives or islands of automation being implemented within a particular department; for example, sales force automation for tracking leads and managing prospective opportunities. Though the individual department performs well and gets the recognition, seldom does this materialize into recognition of the entire company. The return on investment (ROI) in stage 2 is typically two to five times the initial and ongoing investment.

Stage 3: Collaboration, cooperation, and coordination start to take place between the different departments and is the beginning of cross-functional synchronization. For example, sales and marketing share the same customer database. The ROI in stage 3 is typically four to seven times the initial and ongoing investment.

Stage 4: Finally, in Stage 4, all the departments work together (enabler 2: cross-organizational collaboration) and the departmental initiatives are in congruence with a corporate business strategy—maximize revenue, maximize market share, and so forth. The company's goals are aligned with the customer's goals. Traditional top-down hierarchical decision making is replaced by bottom-up decision making by cross-functional teams (enabler 7: strategy innovation). Managers move from micromanagement to being process owners and mentors. In stage 4, the cross-functional synchronization is seamless to the customer. For example, a single master customer database is used by the entire organization (sales, marketing, customer service, etc.) for market segmentation, targeting promotions, personalizing websites, and so forth. Even the departmental incentives are aligned with the corporate strategy. The traditional and online processes are stitched together to offer a single face to the consumer. Companies in stage 4 appoint a chief customer officer (CCO) who is responsible for making sure that all the customer touch points (sales, marketing, customer services, etc.) are identified and standardized to deliver an enriching seamless experience to the customer. The CCO also makes sure that all the customer information is captured and leveraged throughout the organization. ROI in stage 4 is typically five to ten times the initial and ongoing investment.

It is quite possible that different divisions/business units within the same company could be at different stages. In that event, the organization should first try and get all the divisions to the same higher stage, rather than one division at stage 4 and another at stage 2, since in that event the division at stage 2 will act as the bottleneck and prevent the overall system from achieving a higher level of performance.

FUTURE OF CRM

Traditionally, CRM was about stand-alone initiatives or islands of automation being implemented within a particular department. However, the future of CRM is more than just implementing stand-alone sales force automation, call center management, business intelligence, or marketing automation; it's about forging a long-term, mutually beneficial symbiotic relationship with customers and knowing consumer buying behaviors and preferences. It involves marketing, sales, and customer service working seamlessly together as one fabric, having real-time access to relevant information, and delivering a single face to the customer; having one comprehensive system that supports the total customer experience and works across multiple departments. For example, when you go to Amazon.com you can see a record of all your transactions, your preferred as well as alternate credit cards, your shipping and billing addresses, and the status of all your orders. When you e-mail or talk to anyone from Amazon at any time, they can swiftly deal with your problems because all the employees have customer focus imbibed in their organizational DNA. Amazon uses visibility (enabler 1) and technology (enabler 3) to focus on customer success (principle 1), and eliminate nonvalue-added activities (principle 3) of navigating to multiple customer service screens.

Similarly, companies such as Dell have established corporate agreements that include hardware and software configurations, pricing schedules, etc., with the different companies' purchasing departments. This allows the employees of the company to order a PC via snail mail, over the web, or by phone. When the employees have a technical problem they can contact their own IT department, or the Dell technician can directly access diagnostic information over the web. This results in a seamless experience for the employee whether its sales or service (enabler 6: process innovation by offering single face to the customer).

The customer service representative, salesperson, and telemarketer all need to have knowledge about the customer and deliver a delightful customer experience consistently. Only when the customers feel cared for will they become loyal and give the company more business. For CRM to be truly effective it must integrate not only to the front office functions of sales, marketing, and customer service, but also the back office processes of accounting, purchasing, operations, and logistics. How many times have you had to wait for ten minutes on the phone only to get the answer from the customer service representative, "Please wait, I shall transfer you to the billing department," and you have had to repeat your name, order number, and issue all over again to the accounting person.

CRM involves examining a customer's online and offline habits and being proactive to give the customer relevant recommendations. It involves getting customers' inputs and getting them involved during the product development phase itself so that the business creates a sense of partnership (enabler 2: cross-organizational collaboration) between the customer and the organization. Even after the launch, each customer interaction is used to gain knowledge about the customer so that the level of service can be enhanced and the interaction used to build a relationship. It involves segmenting the customers and having differentiated service treatment to the top-tier customer and then delivering exceptional service to the most profitable ones. For example, if a top-tier customer calls to change the destination of the order that has already been shipped, logistics needs to work hand in hand in a seamless fashion to make sure that the customer's request is met.

By doing customer segmentation the Royal Bank of Scotland (RBS) was able to create and focus on the more profit-generating segments (enabler 6) such as first mortgages and estate settlements, which led to an increase in revenue of more than $1 billion over three years.[5]

Similarly, my credit card company waived my annual fees since I had been using my credit card for eight years. Another example involved my cable company. When I wanted to cancel my Internet connection after two years because of slow speed, the customer service representative immediately upgraded me to a high-speed Internet connection at no extra cost.

Effective CRM involves finding out the root cause of why some customers are not profitable and taking measures to make them profitable to the company. It's about engaging the customer with a personalized and compelling experience. It's about pulling the customer rather than pushing irrelevant information or being intrusive.

WHO IS THE CUSTOMER?

When I used to work in the design department of an automotive company and was given a short-term assignment in the production department, I got a little confused when my manager first told me, "Don't forget to charge your time to the production department." When I asked him the reason, he politely explained that this helps the design department get the necessary internal cost transfers. In this manner the production department is the customer of the design department. Before that, I always used to think that there was only one customer, that is, the end consumer. This was the first time I realized that there are both internal and external customers and that customer is not necessarily the end user but the customer of the next process. For example, the manufacturer is the external customer of the supplier, the retailer is the customer of the private-label manufacturer, and if the next process is consumption then the customer is the end consumer.

Companies such as Honeywell ask each department to not only rate its strengths and weaknesses, but also strengths and weaknesses of the departments (internal customers) it interacts with.[6] If all the stakeholders have a "customer focus" on their immediate downstream customer, then the value chain will be completely aligned in its focus on the end customer (consumer).

To instill customer focus, companies like Xerox make sure that the job description of the employees includes an explanation of how the job affects the customer.[6] This instills customer focus in Xerox employees (principle 1: focus on customer success).

The guiding principle always has to be creation of value from the customer's perspective. Rather than overdesigning and overloading the products with surplus features that are based on marketing's gut feel, the organization should focus on what the customer wants (e.g., price, quality, product features). Similarly, there is no point having the fastest delivery time in the industry when what the customer truly values is price. Hence, there is *no point in having a competitive advantage if it does not materialize into a customer advantage.*

Since the end customer is the only entity that introduces money into the value chain and the rest of value chain members (manufacturers and suppliers) are merely shuffling the money back and forth, CRM should be about disseminating and communicating the right information about the right customers to the right people (sales, marketing, customer service), and then empowering them so that they can ensure an enriching customer experience by offering and delivering the final customer the right product at the right price, with the right features and service from the customer's perspective.

Each manager must understand his or her role in making the value chain profitable, and employees must be rewarded, motivated, and trained in alignment with the needs of the end customers, that is, aligning the organizational goals with the customers' goal and not the other way around. Too often companies say that they are customer focused, but when you peel the onion and examine the employees' bonus and incentive structure, seldom will you find a metric that includes some measure of customer relationship satisfaction. To conclude, though maximizing profit might be the ultimate goal of any organization, it is customer value that drives financial value and long-term success.

MANAGING CUSTOMER RELATIONSHIPS

CRM should not be about one-time (dating) single transactions, but about long-term, mutually beneficial sustained relationships (marriage) (Figure 5.2). It's the responsibility of the organization and not the customer to do whatever it takes to keep the relationship (marriage) intact. Too often, companies place all their focus on making the sale rather than caring for the customer and building a relationship. Also, it is important that the company does not invest in building a long-term relationship (marriage) with all customers. Companies need to stratify their customers into different groups based on volume and margin (enabler 6: process innovation through segmentation), and then build the right relationship with the right customers.

For example, Dell developed strong relationships with its corporate customers, which comprise about 70 percent of Dell's business. Dell has a top-notch sales team to manage the corporate customers, installs software for them, has customized web pages, and has a 24/7 order entry system. Similarly, Amazon.com offers free rapid shipping to its preferred customers.

In the dating phase (acquiring new customers), the cost of attracting new customers is more than revenue obtained from a single one-time transaction, i.e., the company might spend more in advertisement, sales, and marketing efforts compared to the revenue obtained. In this phase the customer will most likely do

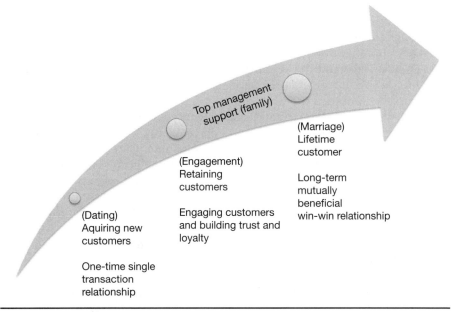

Figure 5.2 Managing customer relationships

comparison shopping, frequently for price before buying the product. Since the cost of attracting and acquiring new customers is exponentially greater than targeting and selling to existing ones, it is imperative that the organization expand this dating relationship into an engagement and eventually marriage because unless the customers come back and make repeat purchases, profits will continue to elude the company. Also, a lot of times companies lose focus by having great websites with an overabundance of features, functionality, and information, but that just serves to make the website slow and complicated. In some cases, so much so that the first-time buyer is confused to the point that he/she might never return. These websites are good for dating but not for marriage. Thus, if implementing sophisticated technology to add excess feature and functionality (enabler 3) will actually create more waste, it should not be implemented because it adds nonvalue-added activities (principle 3) and removes focus on customer success and satisfaction (principle 1).

A recent survey revealed that because of the initial fixed cost to acquire customers, it is important that customers keep coming back for at least the next two to three years for the company to recover its initial investment. The survey also found that as much as 50 percent of the customers defected before the end of the three-year period.[7]

The relationship will not go to the next engagement phase (retention) if the customer has an unpleasant experience and the minimum expectations are not met. The customer might switch to your competitor instead. On the other hand, a pleasant experience that exceeded the customer's expectations such as faster delivery, better prices, faster service and support, good returns policy, and so forth, might increase customer loyalty and therefore the desire to purchase again. As the relationship develops in the engagement phase, loyal customers will return automatically and the revenues obtained will exceed the expenses. Loyal customers also indirectly act as salespeople by referring new customers using viral marketing (word of mouth).

A survey found that increasing the customer retention rate by 5 percent could increase profits by as much as 25 to 95 percent.[7] BIC companies like Deere & Company boast of a 98 percent annual retention rate. They use retired employees to interview with the 2 percent of the defectors.[8] In the engagement phase the organization gets to know more about the customer's buying behaviors and preferences since they spend more time together. The more time spent together, the better the organization will know the customer and the greater the chances of the customer's desires being met.

As the relationship matures into a marriage (long-term relationship-lifetime customer), the revenue and profits margins soar as these types of customers tend to value trust, service, convenience, and quality more than just price. American Airlines frequent flier programs, Marriott's reward program, Hilton's Honors program are all geared toward building trust and customer loyalty. After marriage, it develops into a long-term intimate relationship based on this trust and loyalty. Also, this offers companies increased opportunities to cross-sell—selling more and more goods to an existing customer, and up-sell—selling something that is more profitable or preferable for the seller instead of what was in the original sale. Customers are more inclined to go with companies they already have a relationship with rather than do comparison shopping every time, since that is a lot more risky and time consuming. This is the same reason that companies create an approved vendor list, which is a list of suppliers that have been prequalified based on customers requirements (total cost of ownership, delivery reliability, quality), so that they don't have to go through the process of supplier selection every time they want to procure a part.

This relationship (marriage) gets to a point that the company and the customer become dependent on one another, leading to a win-win situation for both. For example, Dell has become a "technology trusted advisor" to its corporate customers, which has led to an increase in Dell's sales. Also, the corporations are dependent on Dell's advice regarding hardware stacks and software usage (principle 2: create win-win and a trusted environment for all stakeholders).

Loyal customers also indirectly act as salespeople by referring new customers using viral marketing (word of mouth). Even after the honeymoon, it is key that the customer experience is monitored and a delightful customer experience is delivered consistently to make sure that the marriage doesn't end in a divorce, since the cost of acquiring new customers could be as high as five times the cost of retaining existing ones.[9] Also, customers who have had a bad relationship (divorce) can turn into vocal critics and bad mouth the company through websites, web logs, chat rooms and social networking sites.

Dallas Morning News discovered that the telemarketing program was irritating customers rather than attracting them. Hence, rather than use its resources for telemarketing it started using them to call up existing customers to make sure they were happy with their service. Dallas Morning News also used a direct mail program instead for 12 of their customer segments. This led to an increase in its retention rate.[3]

CUSTOMER LIFETIME VALUE

Customer lifetime value (CLV) is used to estimate the cost of acquiring a customer and the net present value (NPV) of all the future cash flows expected over the entire life cycle of customer purchases. Thus, if:

N is the number of customers,
NP is the number of times the average customer makes a purchase each year,
CL is the average number of loyal customer life (in years), and
PS is the average profit per sale (total sales revenue-costs)/number of sales,
then, CLV = N × NP × CL × PS.

To increase the lifetime value of their customers, organizations can:

- Increase the size of the customer base
- Increase the number of times the customer makes a purchase each year
- Increase the average loyal customer life
- Increase profits per sale

Thus, a higher CLV translates to greater financial growth and long-term success. Even though a Crunchy Taco might cost only 89 cents, companies like Taco Bell have estimated that the total CLV of one customer can be as high as $11,000. Taco Bell uses this number to help its employees focus on customer success.[10] Similarly, a customer entering a car dealership for the first time represents a potential customer lifetime value of close to $300,000.[11]

It is clear from the above formula that no matter how big your customer base and how long your loyal customer life, if the company is not making a profit, that is, the costs are greater than the revenue, the company will be burning cash and heading for bankruptcy. Before trying to manage the loyalty of a customer or customer base, it is important that the company do a thorough analysis whether the particular customer/customer segment is even worth pursuing by calculating potential profits per sale.

It is also very important that enough time is spent on calculating the costs and sales revenue and that all the departments have visibility into the same. Costs should not only include the cost of attracting (marketing) new customers, but also costs over the entire customer life cycle, which includes acquisition (sales) and cost of service to the customers (customer service staff costs, training, etc.).

BIC companies like Dell measure the customer lifetime ownership cost (enabler 6: process innovation), which includes customer order cost, operating cost, installation cost, servicing cost, and cost of disposing hardware.[7]

MARKETING MANAGEMENT

The American Marketing Association defines marketing as "the activity, set of institutions, and processes for creating, communicating, delivering, and exchanging offerings that have value for customers, clients, partners, and society at large."[12] (Figure 5.3).

Often, people get confused regarding the scope of marketing. People argue that "In my company the marketing department is responsible for only advertising and the finance department is responsible for coming up with the break-even price." So is pricing within the realm of marketing management?

The term *marketing management* encompasses all marketing activities, even those marketing activities that are not actually performed by a company's marketing department and might actually be performed by other departments, such as sales, finance, or operations. For example, if the finance department comes up with the break-even price for the new product, the finance department is per-

Figure 5.3 CRM pyramid (marketing management)

forming a marketing management activity (pricing).[13] In other words, when we mention marketing management, we mean the process and not the department or function.

Operations, finance, accounting, and purchasing will only be in business if there is sufficient demand for the products. Marketing management is about creating demand and then communicating the forecast to demand planning subprocess in supply chain management (SCM). Marketing is charged with generating the demand for the products and services sold by the company. The amount of revenue generated from the sales, as well as the achievement of other corporate objectives, such as growing market share or providing a high level of customer service, can be dramatically impacted by how well marketing management performs. The marketing management process must be able to accurately predict and control the demand that is generated by their efforts. Failure to do so can cause major disruptions in the customer relationship and quickly erode any margins. It can also have a long-term effect on customer relationships that take time and money to repair.

Marketing management also involves creating and maintaining the right kind of relationship with the right groups. Effective marketing management involves not only internal cross-functional relationships (enabler 2: cross-organizational collaboration), but also an effective network of relationships with key stakeholders. For example, if marketing is planning to sell one million units in the next year, the production department must have the essential tooling and capacity to produce the necessary units, finance must have the required funding from the top management, sourcing should have the required supply from the suppliers, and human resources should have the necessary trained staff.

The marketing management process is changing rapidly because of the following:

1. The Internet has allowed for more segmented, precise, and targeted marketing campaigns. New technologies such as data mining and data warehousing are providing a much more cost-effective and targeted alternative of marketing to individual customers.

For example, using the Teradata Warehouse Miner, Pizza Hut was able to slice and dice the data of more than 40 million households to figure out the best coupon offers for each household and also predict the success rate of these targeted marketing campaigns.[14]

2. Globalization has resulted in "buy anywhere and sell anywhere." Improvements in logistics and transportation have not only made it easier for companies to market and sell their products anywhere, but also for consumers to buy products from anywhere in the world.

Customers have become less brand-loyal, more price-sensitive, and expect better quality and service at a lower price. They are looking more and more for a marketing experience rather than just a simple product.

3. Companies can only be successful if they can change to accommodate the changing customer expectations (principle 1: focus on customer success). For example, BMW now offers its customers 90 exterior colors, 170 trims, and 500 options, and claims that 80 percent of the cars bought in Europe are make-to-order.[15] (Note: We use the terms *make-to-order* and *build-to-order* interchangeably in this book.)

Market Strategy

The very first subprocess in marketing management is to come up with a market strategy (Figure 5.4) that needs to be creative and disciplined, and at the same time agile enough to incorporate changing market dynamics.

Most organizations can be broken down into the corporate level, strategic business unit (SBU), and product lines within the SBU. The classification of an SBU is based on whether the business unit is responsible for its own strategic planning, has its own competitors, and manages its own resources. GE, for example, has 49 SBUs. Though each SBU is responsible for its own strategy, they are usually coordinated by the parent organization. Each business unit then decides the best product lines to focus on and then each product line develops a marketing plan to accomplish its own objectives. The delineation between corporate, SBU, and product line tends to vary from company to company. For example, in certain mid- to small-size companies there might only be one SBU (corporate) and the SBU level are one and the same. In a startup company that is planning to launch a new product the corporate level, SBU and product line are all the same.

Figure 5.4 CRM pyramid (market strategy)

The corporate level is responsible for developing the corporate strategy, which governs what resources (funding, labor, etc.) to assign to which SBU based on industry attractiveness, current and future business strengths, industry growth rate, relative market share, and so forth, to maintain a balanced business portfolio. Different tools such as the Boston Consulting Group (BCG) Portfolio Matrix and GE's Strategic Business Planning Grid could be used for allocating resources among SBUs.

The BCG matrix consists of a figure with market growth rate on the y-axis and relative market share on the x-axis. Rather than have a broad-brushed, one-size-fits-all approach of say a 10 percent growth rate across all SBUs, companies need to make sure that they have a well-diversified and balanced portfolio of high-growth SBUs which need cash and low growth ones that generate cash. We have filled in a sample BCG Portfolio Matrix for Time Warner Inc. in Figure 5.5. The bottom left quadrant consists of the cash cows which have a low growth rate in a mature market, require low investment, and command high market share. The company should harvest the cash cows, that is, use the profits generated from the cash cows to finance the question marks that will hopefully be the stars of the future. The company should decide on which question marks to finance because, as the name suggests, they could either turn out to be stars or dogs in the future.

The stars will eventually move to a cash cow as they mature from a high growth rate to a low growth rate. The company should divest and liquidate the dogs since there is little chance that the dog will come back.

GE's Strategic Business Planning Grid was developed as a tool for examining GE's large portfolio of SBUs. It consists of a matrix with industry attractiveness

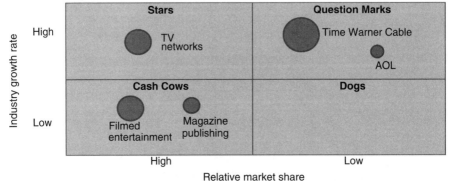

- AOL: consisting principally of interactive consumer and advertising services
- Time Warner Cable: consisting principally of cable systems that provide video, high-speed data and voice services
- Filmed Entertainment: consisting principally of feature film, television and home video production and distribution
- TV Networks: consisting principally of cable television networks that provide programming
- Magazine Publishing: consisting principally of magazine publishing

Figure 5.5 Sample Boston Consulting Group (BCG) portfolio matrix for Time Warner Inc.

on the y-axis and SBU strength on the *x*-axis. The company should try to invest in the SBUs that have: (1) a strong to average competitive position and high industry attractiveness; and (2) a strong competitive position but medium industry attractiveness. It should hold its funding for: (1) an average strength business with average industry attractiveness; (2) a strong business in an unattractive industry; and (3) a weak business in an attractive industry. Similarly, it should try to harvest an average business in an unattractive industry and divest itself out of a weak business in an unattractive industry. A sample GE Strategic Business Planning Grid for Time Warner Inc. is shown in Figure 5.6.

After careful analysis the corporate level might decide to enter into new businesses (SBUs), and harvest, trim, or divest older businesses. This involves comparing the growth sought by corporate management with the projected expected growth of the SBUs, and then trying and fill the gap in between using one or more of the following strategies:

1. Existing market and existing product strategy (expand and gain market share in existing markets with existing products)
2. New markets strategy (expand into new markets with existing products)
3. New products strategy (develop new products for existing markets)
4. New market and new products strategy (expand into new markets with new products)

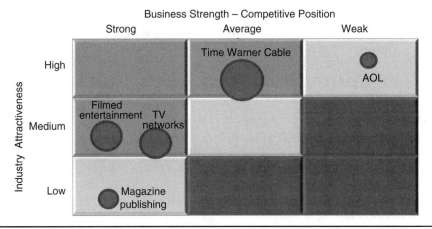

Figure 5.6 Sample GE strategic business planning grid for Time Warner Inc.

5. Alliance strategy: alliances could be done to access new products or new markets
6. Acquisitions strategy: acquire companies using forward, backward, or lateral integration
7. Divesting strategy: divest loss or stagnant businesses to focus on core businesses

For example, Starbucks expanded into the niche market segment of serving gourmet coffee to consumers in Seattle (existing market and existing product strategy). After its success in Seattle, Starbucks expanded into new markets in North America and eventually throughout the world (new markets strategy). Starbucks soon expanded its product portfolio to include music and hi-speed Internet (new products strategy). After its success in the new products, it diversified into retail and grocery stores with Starbucks-branded ice cream and Frappuccino bottled drinks (new market and new products strategy). Starbucks later entered into a geographical alliance with Shinsegne in Korea and Sazaby in Japan to access the markets there. They also entered into a product alliance with Dreyer's ice cream to offer premium coffee ice cream.[16] Finally, Starbucks pursued an acquisition strategy by acquiring tea retailer Tazo Tea.

Porter[17] has suggested three generic strategies that could be used as a starting point to come up with the market strategy:

1. Overall cost leadership strategy: This strategy focuses on being lean and efficient by reducing costs and competing on price to gain market share. For the overall cost leadership strategy the business unit should have strong skills in purchasing, manufacturing, and distribution as compared to marketing.

2. Differentiation strategy: This strategy focuses on a particular customer satisfaction area (quality, flexibility, etc.) where a firm can differentiate itself in this area from its competitors and win consumers.
3. Focus strategy: This strategy targets a niche market segment and then pursues an overall cost leadership or differentiation strategy for that market segment.

Priceline.com, as the name suggests, tries to compete on price by allowing customers to name their own price. Expedia, on the other hand, competes on providing a range of services (flexibility) and hence pursues a differentiation strategy. Lastminutetravel.com focuses on a niche market segment for last-minute travelers.

Steps in Developing a Market Strategy

All market strategies start first with market segmentation to identify which markets it can serve effectively. This is followed by selecting one or more target markets to synergize the marketing effort, and resources to target the right segment. Lastly, positioning, which involves developing a specific marketing mix (product, price, communications mix, and placement/channel) for each targeted marketing segment to match the customer's perception.

The marketing mix can be defined as the set of tools a firm uses to pursue its marketing objectives.[18] Product includes quality, design, features, and so forth. Price includes list price and discounts. Communications mix includes the combination of advertising, public relations, and direct marketing. Placement includes which distribution channels to use.

Market segmentation: Market segmentation involves stratifying a market into groups that share similar characteristics. Evolution of marketing has been like a spectrum: On one end of market segmentation is "one-size-fits-all" (the mass marketing approach that involved mass production and mass distribution—Ford's Model T) and on the other a customized micromarketing approach that aims at individual customers. Various permutations and combinations are in between (cluster marketing, niche marketing, etc.) like different colors of the spectrum.

An excellent example of niche marketing involved Enterprise Rent-A-Car. Enterprise Rent-A-Car targeted the niche marketing segment of insurance replacement vehicles by renting to consumers whose cars have broken down or have been in an accident.[6] Market segmentation can also be done by geographic, demographic, behavioral, business type, etc. Geographical segmentation involves segmenting the markets by regions, territories, and neighborhoods; demographic segmentation involves dividing the market into groups based on gender, age, income, family size, and so forth; and business-type segmentation involves stratifying groups by what customers value in a transaction or business relationship.

Examples of geographical segmentation include companies like Wal-Mart, Sears, Roebuck & Company, and Bed Bath and Beyond, who give their local store managers the authority to stock products according to local customer tastes (enabler 6). Bed Bath and Beyond managers get to pick up to 70 percent of their merchandise.[19]

Examples of demographic segmentation include Home Depot which realized that about 80 percent of home improvement projects are initiated by women and hence, Home Depot introduced "Ladies Night at the Depot" to specifically target women.[20] Similarly, Toyota introduced the $15,000 stylish, fashionable, and trendy Toyota Scion to specifically target the Gen Ys (18- to 25-year olds).

Rackham and DeVincentis[21] proposed a segmentation scheme that classifies business customers into three groups:

1. Price-oriented customers (transactional selling)—customers who want the lowest price
2. Solution-oriented customers (consultative selling)—customers who want a trusted advisor
3. Strategic-value customers (enterprise selling)—customers who want co-investment from the manufacturer in the customers' business

Market targeting: Once the market segmentation is done, the company needs to evaluate the attractiveness of the different segments based on size, risk, profitability, growth, and alignment with the company's objective and resources. They must decide which markets to target and how many to target based on which market segments the company can serve effectively. Market targeting is a very important step as evidenced in Kotler's[6] definition for marketing management. "Marketing management is the art and science of choosing *target* markets and getting, keeping, and growing customers through creating, delivering, and communicating superior customer value."

In deciding which target markets to go for, the company has to balance the classic risk reward paradox; that is, while targeting only one particular segment (putting all the eggs in one basket) will help the company synergize all its resources on that segment and reap rich rewards if successful, it also has the associated risk of dire consequences if it does not succeed.

For example, when the digital camera market took off, Polaroid which had focused all its resources on the camera film market, fell from the cliff and its earnings declined sharply. A multi-segment targeted strategy on the other hand, though not as lucrative in terms of ROI, mitigates the risk (enabler 5) and provides the necessary flexibility. For example, Sony (from "sonus," the Latin word for sound), which started in 1957 with the world's first pocket radio, has now diversified into everything in consumer electronics under the sun, including cameras, TVs, Blu-ray players, video game consoles (PlayStation 3), etc.[6] A company could also decide to first target a particular segment and then gradually expand into other target markets. For example, Toyota first focused on the small car segment (Toyota Tercel) and once it got a foothold in the United States, it gradually expanded into midsize cars (Toyota Camry), luxury cars (Lexus) and eventually into small size (Toyota RAV4), midsize (Toyota 4Runner), and large SUVs (Toyota Sequoia).

Some credit card companies might target multiple segments with the same card. This "killing multiple birds with the same stone" approach is done by having different incentive programs (frequent flier, low balance transfer, credit card points, home equity line of credit, etc.) on the same card to target different customer segments.

Market positioning: The positioning step involves developing a specific marketing mix (product, price, communications mix and placement/channel) and highlighting the differentiated benefits to customers for each targeted marketing segment by examining the competitive landscape and customer's perception. A very important aspect of positioning is developing the perceptual map, which consists of mapping the location of other products in customers' minds and then positioning your product on the map based on strengths and weaknesses so as not to conflict with the existing products. Examples of different positioning strategies include:

- Product: When BMW entered the U.S. market in the 1980s, it positioned and differentiated itself as a car that had luxury and performance. American cars in the 1980s were known to have luxury or performance but not both. Hence, the BMW slogan "the ultimate driving machine."[6] Similarly, Dodge RAM emphasizes ruggedness and power, Jaguar—speed and agility, and the Honda Civic—civic sense for city driving.
- Price: Southwest Airlines has positioned itself at the "low-cost fun airline" with not only cheap fares but also humorous in-flight commentary.
- Placement/channel: Apollo Group targeted the market of working adults by launching University of Phoenix online which is positioned to deliver classes through a different channel (online) while at the same time charges lower fees.[22]
- Communications mix: Rather than use the traditional cookie cutter approach, rapper Eminem's marketing team used social networking websites like Facebook, myspace, and micro-blogging websites like twitter to create a buzz for his new album *The Relapse*.

It's very important to balance the communications mix between advertising, public relations, direct marketing, etc. (enabler 4), since each medium has its pros and cons. The effectiveness of the medium used also varies based on the product life cycle stage and whether the company is planning to target the consumer markets or corporate businesses.

Advertising (TV, radio, newspaper) is good for the long-term brand awareness of the product. Though advertising can be used to inform consumers of a new product or remind them of an existing one, it's proven to be most effective in the introductory stage of the product life cycle. Advertising also allows the company to target a much wider and geographically dispersed consumer base.

The direct marketing (mail, Internet, telemarketing) form of communication is increasingly rising in popularity since it offers several advantages compared to the other media, since the communication can be customized to a particular individual and being interactive, the message can be customized based on the consumer's response. Hence, direct marketing could be used across the entire product life cycle, whether to encourage brand awareness in the introductory stage or get a short-term spike in sales in the mature or decline stage. The Internet has become the most effective form of direct marketing showing double-digit growth rates. By using cookies, it allows individualization and customization of the marketing message since the marketers can track the customer's clicks and can personalize the message and website specifically for that individual.

Whatever communications mix is used, it is imperative to have a synergistic, consistent, clear, compelling, and seamlessly integrated message across the entire communications mix. The American Association of Advertising Agencies defines integrated marketing communications[6] as "a concept of marketing communications planning that recognizes the value of a comprehensive plan that evaluates the strategic roles of a variety of communication disciplines—advertising, public relations, personal selling, and sales promotion and combines them to provide clarity, consistency, and maximum communication impact." For example, as opposed to using only a direct mail campaign, Citibank used a combination of direct mail, 1-800 number, telemarketing, and print advertising to market its home equity loans. Though more expensive, the combination approach contributed to a 15 percent increase in the number of new accounts.[23]

Market Strategies Based on Product Life Cycle

The market strategies need to change based on the stage of the product life cycle. Being the first to launch the new product can be rewarding but at the same time risky. The introductory stage is marked by high advertising expenses and high product costs, but it can also capture the market and the customer for life if the product is aligned with the customer's requirements. Examples of such first movers include Coca-Cola, Amazon.com, and eBay.

The growth stage is evidenced by rapid sales growth with sales rising at a much faster rate relative to the costs (fixed, variable) since the costs are spread over a larger volume. This leads to an increase in profits. It is critical that the different departments work together (enabler 2) to make sure that there are no stockouts or delays which could result in customers switching brands. During the growth stage the company can use several strategies focused on the marketing mix by adding new product features, lowering the price to attract price-sensitive customers, and exploring new distribution channels/entering new markets. During the growth stage the trade-off is between capturing market share by investing in growth versus capturing profit. For example, though Amazon.com went online in 1995, it continued to focus and invest in growth, technological innovation, and capturing market share. It achieved profitability only in the fourth quarter of 2001. If Amazon had focused only on profits and refrained from investing in growth and technology innovation, it would have suffered the same fate as many other dotcoms.

The maturity stage is evidenced by a gradual leveling in sales growth (rate of increase in sales decreases), intensified competition, increase in profits, and a reduction in price. The maturity stage poses a big challenge to marketing managers. However, BIC companies thrive in this competitive atmosphere through process and product innovation.

For example, Wolverine World Wide, the manufacturers of Hush Puppies, enhanced the fashion appeal of its shoes in the mid-1990s in the mature market of shoes to include offbeat colors like powder blue and lime green. It also expanded into new markets of sandals and walking shoes. This resulted in an all-time sales high in 2002.[24] Listerine Pocket Pack, Neosporin Neo To Go, and Tide To Go Pen instant stain remover are all aimed at adding new product features to already mature products.

The decline stage is marked by sales, price, and profit reductions. If the company has done a good job in creating brand loyalty, profitability will last longer. The marketing strategies at the decline stage should be aimed at exploring a reduction in costs (R&D, production, distribution) while maintaining sales, exploring divestiture, or revitalizing itself in the declining market. This also leads to a minimal advertising strategy. For example, facing cutthroat competition and shrinking margins of the mature and slowly declining PC market, IBM divested out of the PC business so that it could focus on the high-margin services industry.

A life cycle portfolio matrix is an effective tool that can be used to make sure that the company has a well-diversified portfolio which consists of SBUs/product lines that are at different stages of the life cycle. A sample life cycle portfolio matrix for Time Warner Inc. is shown in Figure 5.7.

Marketing Plan

According to Wood,[25] "A marketing plan is a written document that summarizes what the marketer has learned about the marketplace and indicates how the firm plans to reach its marketing objectives." A marketing plan is one of the most important outputs of the entire market strategy subprocess. It is a written document that acts as a guide to marketing activities for the marketing manager as well as serves as an input to the selling management process, which we shall discuss later. The contents of the marketing plan include:

1. Executive summary:

This contains a brief summary of the market dynamics and the target market the company is planning to go after. It also contains specific marketing, sales,

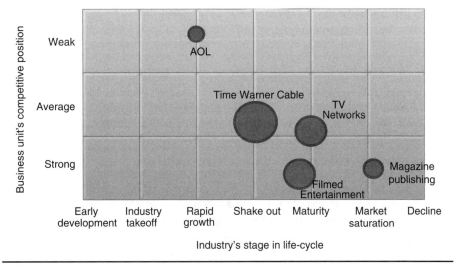

Figure 5.7 Sample product life cycle portfolio matrix for Time Warner Inc.

and financial objectives like how much market share the company is planning to capture, what the expected sales revenue will be, and when the company plans to break-even.

2. Situation analysis:

Situation analysis involves performing SWOT (strengths, weaknesses, opportunities, threats) analysis, examining market trends, and a thorough competitive analysis. SWOT involves analyzing the external environment, including customer demographics, competitors, technology, political environment, and cultural environment to come up with the future market opportunities and threats. It also involves analyzing the businesses own internal strengths and weaknesses so as to decide whether it should focus on only those opportunities where it possesses strength, or diversify into opportunities where it thinks it can develop the necessary strength.

For example, a dilemma for Texas Instruments was whether it should focus on its core competency in industrial electronics or diversify into other businesses like consumer electronics.[6]

3. Marketing strategy:

Marketing strategy involves market segmentation to identify which groups the business can serve effectively. This is followed by selecting one or more target markets and, lastly, determining market positioning.

It is important to decide the marketing mix with inputs from all the different departments, namely, purchasing, operations, sales, finance, and human resources to make sure that there is total cross-departmental buy-in and support.

4. Financials:

Financials include coming up with expected sales revenues looking at the demand forecast and performing analysis using fixed and variable costs to find out the break-even volume and break-even price. Financials also include an expected time frame of achieving profitability.

5. Feedback and controls:

The last section of the marketing plan involves having a process in place to continuously monitor and obtain feedback from the implementation of the marketing plan. This includes measuring progress in terms of time, scope, and cost. It also involves having contingency plans in place if the market dynamics change because of competitive action, price wars, demand exceeding supply or vice versa, and other possible events.

For example, as a result of component shortages for the PlayStation 2 (PS2) and demand exceeding supply in Japan, Sony was forced to revise its marketing plan by reducing the number of PS2s to be shipped to Europe and the United States.[25] This also highlights the importance of developing a marketing plan that includes not only internal collaboration between the different departments, but also external collaboration with the other stakeholders like suppliers and customers (enabler 2: cross-organizational collaboration).

Market Research

Market research (Figure 5.8) and analysis involves the systematic design, collection, analysis, and reporting of data and findings relevant to a specific marketing situation facing the company.[6] Market research is used throughout the cycle of developing effective market strategies, implementing the strategies, and obtaining feedback from the implementation of the marketing plan.

During the strategy development phase, market research is used to perform internal company analysis (strengths, weaknesses), external competitor analysis (opportunities, threats) and customer analysis (market size, trends, demographics, customer needs, customer perceptions) to formulate effective segmentation, targeting, and positioning strategies.

Even the process of developing a marketing plan requires extensive market research and analyzing the consumer demographics, cultures, economics, and current and future technological landscape. Market research also helps in coming up with the marketing mix as to what product features should be included, price points, distribution strategy, and what marketing communication channels should be used?

Figure 5.8 CRM pyramid (market research)

Finally, as the strategies are being implemented, market research helps gauge the market response and provides appropriate feedback so that necessary actions/contingency plans can be implemented. For example, when gas prices rose sharply in 2007-2008, we saw all the automobile manufacturers scramble to increase the gas mileage of their cars, develop hybrids, and emphasize the same in advertising campaigns.

Developing a market research plan involves decisions regarding the research approaches (focus groups, surveys, mail questionnaires, telephone interview, on-line questionnaire, etc.) to be used as well as deciding how many people should be surveyed. The trend moving forward is toward online surveys that are comparatively less expensive and a lot faster than traditional surveys. However, online surveys tend to be skewed toward only those who use the Internet.

Companies like Fuji not only conduct their own market research, but also rely on a syndicate service research firm to study the market for digital cameras and other products. As Fuji's director of category management and trade marketing puts it, "If you don't have market research to help figure out what is changing and what the future will be, you will be left behind."[26]

While performing market research, it is very important that the organization has visibility into the macro- and micro trends regarding consumer demographics, cultures, economics, and the current and future technological landscape.

For example, in 2003, Hispanics became the fastest growing ethnic group in the United States to become the largest minority in the United States. In an effort to tap the Hispanic market, Procter & Gamble Company (P&G) added a scent to its Gain detergent called *white-water fresh* after finding that 57 percent of Hispanics liked to smell their purchases. This eventually led to Gain's double-digit sales growth in the Hispanic market, outpacing general U.S. sales. "Hispanics are a cornerstone of our growth in North America," says Graciela Eleta, vice president of P&G's multi-cultural team in Puerto Rico.[27] Similarly, scanning the economic environment helped Gap Inc. to offer a segmented market strategy to the different economic segments—the upscale Banana Republic, mid-market Gap, and budget-priced Old Navy.[28]

Voice of the Customer

Apart from the traditional market research, BIC companies are increasingly looking toward capturing the voice of the customer (VOC). According to Jim Barnes,[29] "Voice of the Customer initiatives should give voice to things that the firm would not normally hear. It should allow a firm to hear, straight from its customers, insightful things that do not surface through conventional marketing research." VOC involves a less structured approach as compared to the traditional approach of focus groups, surveys, mail questionnaires, telephone interview, and so forth. VOC involves having an informal conversation with customers to find out what customers really want and value as opposed to targeted questionnaires and interviews that are based on what companies think customers want. "Giving voice to customers suggests that a company is interested in hearing from them, in giving them their say, so that improvements can be made and creative initiatives launched," Barns notes.[29]

SELLING MANAGEMENT

Selling management involves helping the customer decide what to purchase, by providing accurate and reliable information on product features, price, delivery, and configuration options. At the same time, it presents the customer with a single, consistent, and positive buying experience no matter which channel is used (contact over the Internet, personal sales contact, telephone call, etc.) (Figure 5.9).

Once marketing management has decided on the marketing mix, selling management involves the tactics that will be used to accomplish the marketing strategies. Activities involved in selling management include coming up with a sales forecast (communicated to the sales and operations planning [S&OP] process in SCM), deciding on the allocations for the different sales channels (communicated to the demand fulfillment process in SCM), customer quotation processing, product configuration and bundling, providing cross-sell and up-sell recommendations, pricing and revenue optimization, and promotion planning. The selling management process handles the front end of promising a delivery date for a sales order or quote, while the demand fulfillment process in SCM handles the

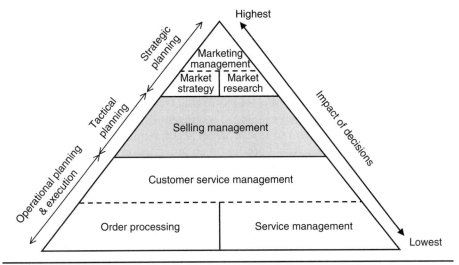

Figure 5.9 CRM pyramid (selling management)

back end of order promising. (For more detail, please refer to the order promising subprocess in SCM in chapter 4.) Since the selling management process typically involves the first touch point the customers have with the organization, it is important the experience be a delightful one so that this one-time (dating) single transaction relationship develops into a long-term mutually beneficial sustained relationship (marriage).

The main pain point or challenge in selling management is the urgent need to match offerings to customer needs profitably through intelligent pricing, configuration, and availability checking. There are several challenges that the retail industry faces in the area of selling management including:[30]

1. Managing the complicated pricing process
2. Managing the growing product catalog with the challenge of limited space
3. The need for speed in the complex supply network of short-life products
4. Managing promotions and discounts effectively, and the need for markdown optimization

Sales Mix

We group the tactical activities involved in selling management as the sales mix that consists of product, price, promotion, and channel. Let's examine each of the sales mix components in more detail. The first component of the sales mix consists of product configuration and bundling.

Product configuration

Consumer behavior is changing and customers are increasingly demanding new and customized products, which has led to a shrinkage in the market window for organizations and simultaneous overabundance in options for customers. Mass customization, burgeoning product variety, and product complexity have led to an explosion in the number of possible product configurations. Effective selling management involves determining the customer's needs and then configuring the products in real time to match those needs. Also, it means providing the customer with alternate possible product recommendations, pricing the offering, and generating a quote or proposal for the offering. Companies need to be able to make cross-sell recommendations and suggest alternative products for out-of-stock items at the same time the customer is placing the order.

Whether the customer is using the web or any other medium (telephone, face-to-face, etc.), the selling management process should be able to guide the customer through the selection process and finally recommend the product configuration that best matches the customer's requirements. Also, as the customer is choosing possible configurations, the customer should be alerted of possible conflicts automatically (availability, feasibility), thus ensuring not only a feasible configuration, but also an available one. This is done by verifying component level availability and leveraging the available-to-promise (ATP) logic in the demand fulfillment process of SCM. It is imperative that the back-end demand fulfillment process is synchronized in real time with the front-end sales configuration environment. Lack of such synchronization could lead to excess inventories of items that customers are not interested in, or a shortage of components that customers are really buying. This could lead to increased obsolescence and/or expediting costs. When certain product options are not available, substitute and alternative options should be suggested. If the customer is flexible, then sales should suggest alternate products and configurations so that the buyer can be guided to a more profitable substitute.

Also, pricing should be integrated into the sales configurations so that customers have visibility into the component level pricing, and don't have to go through the entire buying experience all over again if the final price exceeds the price the customers are willing to pay.

All of the above will help ensure that the salespeople know exactly all feasible, profitable, and available configurations. This will help reduce error rates and increase customer service levels.

Product bundling

Product bundling involves selling a "bundle" of goods together as one unit rather than selling them individually. Pure bundling occurs when a consumer can only purchase the entire bundle and cannot purchase the individual items separately. For example, try asking your cable TV provider for only the Disney channel or only ESPN. Cable TV providers never sell basic individual channels separately but instead bundle them into a package.

Mixed bundling on the other hand occurs when the consumer has the option between purchasing the entire bundle or its individual items. Examples of mixed bundles include combo meals at fast food restaurants; buying a Big Mac as part of a value meal with fries and a drink or just the Big Mac by itself.

Product bundling leads to a win-win situation for both the seller and the customer (principle 2). The customer benefits since the price of the bundle is typically cheaper than buying the individual items. The seller gets an increase in sales volume by promoting sales of additional products. Additionally through bundling, firms can cross-sell a slow-moving item with a fast mover to increase customer awareness or get rid of excess inventory. Similarly, companies can sell a new product part of a bundle with an established mature product to encourage greater customer acceptance of the new product.

However, sales needs to effectively manage product bundles by analyzing the consumer's buying behaviors and then coming up with the most popular and profitable standard configuration bundles. Then sales needs to provide the option to the customer to either go for the discounted standard bundle pricing or the more expensive "customize it your way" pricing.

Dell truly epitomizes the concept of product configuration and bundling (enabler 6). For example, when you want to buy a computer from Dell.com or by telephone, Dell offers the most popular standard configurations up front at a discount. If you visit Dell.com, you will find the standard most popular configurations of desktops and laptops on the first page. You also have a "Build Yours" button at the bottom of the page, which will walk you through the entire process of customizing your desktop or laptop based on all the possible permutations and combinations (system color, processor, operating system, office software, warranty and service, memory, hard drive, optical drive, monitor, video card, sound card, speaker, TV tuner, keyboard, media reader, modem, wireless card, customer service plan). Dell.com also shows you the add-on price for each customization. As it walks you through all the product configuration bundles, it also tries to cross-sell and up-sell additional popular software and accessories. For example, it asks you if you would like to install third-party software like Intuit Quickbooks, Norton 360, Sony Imagination Studio Suite, Corel Paint Shop Pro, or hardware accessories like power protection (Belkin Surge Protector, APC Back-UPS), storage backup (Seagate Freeagent 1.5 TB, Sandisk Cruzer), wireless routers (Linksys, Netgear), just to name a few.

In addition to hardware accessories and software, you could also pre-load your laptop/desktop with the hottest movies (*Spiderman, Godfather,* etc.) digitally in Windows Media format for enjoyment on your PC or TV anytime. For the environmentally conscious customer and as part of Dell's "Green Earth" initiative, Dell will plant a tree with every order (for an additional $6.00). Once you have configured your selection, Dell also provides you with additional recommendations based on the most popular requested configurations. For example, upgrade to a 20-inch wide-screen, digital flat monitor for an additional $200 or Bose companion multi-media system for $110. Hence, Dell is able to help the customer by presenting alternate popular product recommendations, price the offering, and generate a quote or proposal for the offering immediately.

Throughout this process of product configuration and product bundling, Dell makes sure that the configurations are not only feasible, but also available by checking component and accessory availability. To sum it up, Dell offers its customers the flexibility to choose standard, popular bundled configurations at a discount or completely customize their computers at a price premium. Hence, Dell is able to achieve maximum revenue per order by selling all the related products and services in addition to the original item.

Price

In today's dynamic business environment customers have become less brand loyal, more price sensitive, and expect better quality and service at this lower price. Shortened product life cycles and cut-throat competition are forcing companies to change their prices every month, if not every week or every day. According to Marn and Rosiello,[31] "the fastest and most effective way for a company to realize its maximum profit is to get its pricing right." A 1 percent increase in price (with volume remaining the same) can increase operating profit by 11.1 percent. Compare that with a 1 percent increase in volume, which will increase operating profit by only 3.3 percent.[31]

The most important goal of sales pricing is to maximize profit margin and revenue. Because companies are selling the same product to different customers through different channels at different prices, sales needs to be able to come up with a dynamic flexible pricing logic and calculate the final price on the fly in real-time based on the specific customer, volume of sales, dollar amount of sales, volume-based discounts, time-based discounts, customer specific discounts, ongoing promotion discount, and so forth. An example of a tiered, segmented discount could be a discount of 10 percent if sales are greater than $1,000 and a 25 percent discount if sales are greater than $10,000. Hence, the final customer price = base price × specific customer discount × dollar sales discount × ongoing promotional discount × rebates (if applicable).

Price can be an effective lever to increase or decrease sales and maintain the supply demand balance. For example, when the demand is more than the supply, price can be increased so that the demand drops just enough to balance supply. At the same time when demand is less than supply, price can be lowered to stimulate sales and get the necessary lift to increase resource utilization.

Also, sales needs to be cognizant of the product life cycle since the price curve is usually inverse of the product life cycle curve. During the growth stage the price might be higher because of lower volumes. As the product matures, the price drops because of economies of scale. Finally, during the decline stage the price might go up because there are few competitors left and the products are difficult to find, or the price might go down to get rid of remaining inventory by offering optimal discounts for the end-of-life products. Discounting too early in the life cycle might cause stockouts and insufficient inventory, whereas discounting too late will end up with excess inventory on the shelf and obsolescence, clearances, and fire sales. Hence, the goal is to maximize the margins by providing optimal discounts at the right time.

It is important that sales decide the pricing by taking into consideration competitors pricing, price elasticity of demand, current inventory levels, sales forecast, and how much customers value the product, since pricing can be an effective lever in steering the demand in a particular direction. By having visibility into the item-level price elasticity of demand, current inventory levels, and sales forecast, companies can plan effective price breaks to get the desired lift in sales.

It's also important that the company have visibility into the "pocket price" and not just the list price. As Castle Battery Company found, salespeople were giving special discounts to their preferred customers as well the flexibility of an additional 30-60 days for them to make their payments. These undocumented discounts were costing the company millions of dollars. Hence, it is critical that the metrics and incentives (principle 5) for sales should include an improvement in "pocket price" and not just list price, because after all it's the "pocket price" which governs the bottom line revenue that goes into the organization's pockets.[31]

To conclude, effective selling management involves determining optimal price points for each product by customer or by market segment, and rewarding salespeople based on "pocket price" improvements. All this will lead to maximizing profitability, capturing market share, increased revenue, and reduced inventories.

Promotion

Whereas marketing advertising is geared toward long-term brand awareness and building brand loyalty, sales promotions are geared toward more tactical short-term incentives (coupons, price-offs, rebates, free trials, etc.) to promote/stimulate a spike in sales. Also, sales promotions can be leveraged to maintain the short-term supply demand balance. For example, if the demand is less than supply, sales promotions can be used to stimulate sales and get the necessary increase.

Twenty years ago the marketing advertising to sales promotion budget ratio was 60:40. However, nowadays, sales promotions typically account for approximately 75 percent of the total budget expenditure in many consumer packaged industries and that number is only increasing. Sales promotions help entice customers to try new products instead of only sticking to their usual ones, or attract on-the-fence switchers away from competitor's brands. They can also be used to stimulate off-season sales and sales of excess inventory items. Sales promotions can be used to increase turnover of slow movers by bundling them with fast movers and putting the bundle on promotion.[6]

It's very important that companies evaluate the effectiveness of a sales promotion campaign by not only comparing the sales with and without promotions, but also capturing information on whether the promotion was strong enough to lure new customers to switch brands. By analyzing the sales lift with and without promotions, companies will be able to better plan for them in the future.

Firms also need to calculate the total cost of running a sales promotion campaign, which includes the cost of the extra sales effort, increased production runs, printing and mailing, and incentive costs to make sure the benefits from increased sales outweigh the costs. The timing, length and incentive should be planned carefully since too deep discounts might erode profit margins, while too small price breaks will result in an utter failure of the promotional campaign.

Companies also need to be careful not to offer sales promotions too often, since it might devalue/liquidate the brand to the point that customers only buy the product when it is on promotion.

For example, customers got so used to the zero percent financing and additional incentives during the economic downturn at the turn of the century, that more than 66 percent of Americans indicated they were willing to wait for the next sales incentive to purchase their next vehicle. Thirty-three percent also indicated that they would not buy their next vehicle without an incentive.[32]

Channel

The last component of the sales mix deals with presenting the customer with a single, consistent, and positive buying experience no matter which channel is used.

The order capturing should be seamless and comprehensive enough to capture the orders from web storefronts, telesales/call center order entry, electronic data interchange (EDI), and other standard order capture mechanisms. Order capturing serves as the entry point into the order-processing step, which we shall discuss in greater detail in the customer service management process.

It is important that the selling management process capture all the relevant information (who are the customers, their past purchase history, their preferred purchasing channel, likes, dislikes, account history, etc.) of all customer interactions across all channels. This data must be made centrally available (enabler 3) for other business processes like marketing and customer service management so that a seamless, delightful experience is delivered to the customer.

Effective selling management involves promising only what the company can deliver by having visibility into the ATP and capable-to-promise (CTP) supply picture across multiple enterprises from the demand fulfillment process in SCM. Selling management needs to provide the customer with the delivery date by having visibility (enabler 1) into whether the item is available in stock, not in stock but the raw materials are available (can be assembled to order), or not in stock and the raw materials are not available (needs to be built to order). This visibility of supply across multiple enterprises will ensure that the marketing and sales efforts are coordinated with actual availability of inventory and production capacity. It's important that customers be given realistic, truthful, and feasible delivery estimates taking into account all the constraints (sourcing, manufacturing capacity, logistics, etc.), while at the same time making sure that the order can be met profitably and on time. Failure to do so will result in loss of customer satisfaction, brand switching, and will destroy the company's long-term relationship with the customer.

Companies like Dell have a top-notch sales team to manage corporate customers, and they can order the computer via snail mail, by phone, or over the web. Dell has developed customized web pages for their corporate customers giving them access to a 24/7 order entry system. Dell's personalized web storefront makes it easy for the customer to buy products from Dell. Before the computer is ordered, Dell checks for component and accessory availability, which helps it provide a realistic delivery estimate, as well as a single, reliable, and positive buying experience.

CUSTOMER SERVICE MANAGEMENT

After the selling management process captures the order, customer service becomes the front line in customer interaction. Customer service management consists of two subprocesses: order processing and service management (Figure 5.10).

Order processing involves efficiently and effectively managing the sales order throughout its entire life cycle. This includes processing and fulfilling sales orders from stores, dealers, and through the telephone, EDI, web, and other sources; brokering of the order to multiple business divisions (sellers); and coordinating delivery, order tracking, customer invoice generation, order return (if necessary), and financial settlement.

Figure 5.10 CRM pyramid (customer service management)

Service management consists of service contract management, service planning (parts and labor) and scheduling, service order processing, replacement part delivery, and damaged part recycling or returns activities.

Effective customer service management is about delivering a consistent and seamless customer experience no matter what channel is used by the customer. Also, there should be the same pleasant experience to the customer not only during the marketing and sales processes, but also during the customer service management process. For example, when the customer calls in to report a problem or a discrepancy in the billing.

The customer service personnel or customer service representatives (CSRs) need to be trained on how to handle returns, repairs, and refunds. There should be a detailed process map in place that walks the CSRs through a flowchart with decision points. For example, if a customer wants to cancel a service/order, there should be series of questions with corresponding standardized responses. All efforts should be made to retain the customer by providing alternatives/incentives since the cost of acquiring new customers is a lot more than retaining existing ones.

In addition, the right people need to have the right information available to respond to the customer's needs. CSRs must have all the relevant information at their fingertips when a customer calls in, and handle customer issues by accessing the relevant information. If the customer experiences a problem with the product, then the CSRs should have visibility into all the possible solutions to resolve the issue. If the customer has a question about the order, then the CSRs should have visibility into the order status and returns processing.

Effective customer service management makes sure that the communication with the customer doesn't end once the order is promised and the sale is made. It's about having a long-term continuous bi-directional communication channel between the customer and the organization, a two-way street in which customer feedback is captured through different channels. Different channels and avenues should be available to the customers to provide their feedback and the channels should be easily accessible (toll-free numbers), convenient (minimum handoffs to the appropriate person who can actually solve the problem), and flexible (not just web chat but also toll-free numbers for customers who don't have immediate access to the Internet). Hence, the customers should have multiple access methods to provide feedback and acquire information. Whatever access method is chosen, the information should be the same so that a consistent experience is delivered. This feedback then needs to be communicated to the marketing management process so that it can be incorporated. As an example, companies such as 3M claim that over 66 percent of its product improvement ideas come from listening to customer complaints.[6]

The customer service activities should be in congruence with the overall corporate strategy while at the same time make sure that customer service costs are kept in line with the financial goals so that it results in a win-win situation for all stakeholders (organization and customers). Also, appropriate metrics need to be in place to monitor and measure customer satisfaction and service.

Relying on customer complaints alone is not a good metric to measure customer satisfaction since in this day and age of cut-throat competition most customers don't complain, but rather just stop buying from the company. Dell has set up a customer experience council (enabler 6) that includes senior executives from the companies' major business lines. The council reports directly to the corporate vice chairman and is responsible for tracking and measuring customer experience and loyalty. As senior vice president and council member Paul Bell said, "Every public company tells shareholders how it's doing every quarter, but few companies have a set of metrics that measure the customer experience from month to month (as we do)." The metrics that the council tracks include order fulfillment (percentage of orders delivered to the customers on time with complete accuracy), product performance (frequency of product problems encountered by customers), and post-sale service and support (percentage of problems fixed on the first visit by the customer service technician who arrives at the time promised). Just measuring and tracking a metric doesn't add value, but instead contributes to waste unless it is tied to the compensation and incentive target for the employees. Hence, Dell management bonuses are tied to the improvement targets that have been set on each of the measured metrics.[7]

Effective customer service management is about finding out the root cause (principle 4) of why some customers are not happy and then going out of your way to satisfy them. BIC companies like Dell learned from its mistakes. For example, when customers complained about the poor customer service (strong accent, poor phone connections, etc.) from the India-based call centers, Dell immediately set up a U.S. based customer service center to address the issue.[33]

Order Processing

Order Processing (Figure 5.11) involves managing the sales order throughout its entire life cycle including brokering of the order to multiple business divisions (sellers), and coordinating delivery, order tracking, order visibility, customer invoice generation, order return (if necessary), and financial settlement.

Steps in Order Processing

The steps involved in order processing include:

1. The selling management process, which captures the order (web storefronts, telesales/call center order entry, EDI, and other standard order capture mechanisms) serves as the entry point into the order processing process. In CRM, the order is known as a *sales order* because we are looking at the order from the

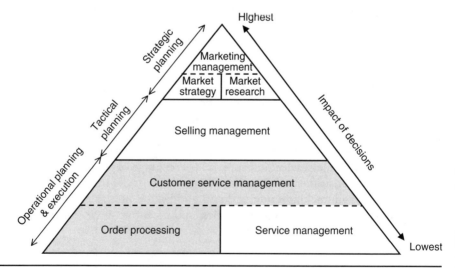

Figure 5.11 CRM pyramid (order processing)

seller's (supplier) perspective, while in supplier relationship management it is called a *purchase order* because we are looking at the order from the buyer's (customer's) perspective.

2. Once a sales order is created, there is a credit limit check on the customer incorporated in the credit modeling feature of order processing.

3. When a customer places an order with an enterprise, which has, for example, five different line items for five different divisions, the customer is only concerned with whether the order will be delivered on time, and at the agreed upon terms and conditions. Hence, order processing should be able to broker the order to the appropriate business division, while at the same time hide the back-end complexity by providing a single face to the customer (enabler 6). Once the order is brokered to multiple business divisions, order processing needs to be tightly integrated with the master planning subprocess (assigns demand to appropriate plants and distribution centers within a business division) and the logistics planning and execution subprocess (warehousing and transportation) in SCM, so that the order can be planned and fulfilled according to the promise. All the above would result in the CSRs having a consolidated view of multi-line item sales orders that are brokered out optimally, considering all the constraints.

4. Lastly, order processing should be able to provide real-time order status visibility to the customer across all channels.

Benefits of Effective Order Processing

Order processing should be able to provide scalable, secure, online transaction processing, order tracking, order visibility, and billing. It should be reliable at the same time since the order is considered the heart of the enterprise, and losing the orders means losing the business. Some of the benefits of efficient and effective order processing include:

1. Greater customer satisfaction by delivering product at the right price, at the right place, and at the promised delivery time
2. Lower operating and order fulfillment costs because of fewer order error rates
3. Faster processing of order transactions
4. Greater order visibility to the organization and the end customer, and better tracking of item defects and returns

SERVICE MANAGEMENT

Service management (Figure 5.12) consists of service contract management, service planning (parts and labor) and scheduling, replacement part delivery, and damaged part recycling or returns activities.

Some of the challenges of the service management subprocess include:[34]

- The complexity of today's products, which makes managing this process more difficult
- Inaccurate forecasting for service parts that are characterized by sporadic intermittent demand
- High customer dissatisfaction in the event of service parts shortage

On the positive side, if managed efficiently, service management offers high profit margins and can be a source of competitive differentiation. Aftermarket sales can help grow revenues in a flat economy as aftermarket sales are less cyclical and unaffected by the seasons compared to new equipment sales. Companies need to stop thinking about service management as a cost center and start thinking about it as a competitive differentiator and a profit center.

The different components of service management include:

- Service contract management
- Service planning and scheduling
- Returns management

Figure 5.12   CRM pyramid (service management)

Service Contract Management

Service contract management is usually triggered by the customer signing up for a service agreement. This includes several contract items like discounts on replacement parts, guaranteed response time, technician hourly rate, and support time.[35] In the past, organizations employed a "one-size-fits-all" approach and offered the same level of customer service to everyone. However, BIC companies have product service agreements that offer differentiated customer service for different customers based on volume, profit margin, price, key account, products being purchased, purchase frequency, and so forth. Long-term, mutually profitable service contracts do not just provide added revenue to the service provider, but they also provide stability to customer relations. For example, Dell offers differentiated service contracts for corporate customers who buy storage units and servers, which account for 80 percent of Dell's business compared to its retail customers.

Similarly, having these customer service contracts can lure first-time buyers offering peace of mind for the customer while at the same time being lucrative for the company. For example, Korea manufacturers Hyundai and KIA gained a foothold in the U.S. market by offering munificent extended warranty terms of 10 years, 100,000 miles on their line of cars and SUVs. Such agreements are helpful in acquiring first-time buyers because they increase buyer confidence and likelihood of initial purchase.

According to Jim Ilaria,[36] leading original equipment manufacturers use their aftermarkets to drive 40 to 60 percent of total revenue and 50 to 90 percent of gross margin. Companies such as such as Caterpillar, GE Power, and Otis Elevator understand the importance of the aftermarket business to total revenue and make the necessary investments to make the aftermarket service a source of competitive differentiation. For example, when GE Power was experiencing flat growth, Robert Nardelli, former head of GE Power, was able to grow revenues from $6.5 billion in 1995 to $15 billion in 2000. This was mainly due to the aftermarket business—long-term maintenance contracts, inspection and monitoring services, and consulting services. Nardelli later joined Home Depot and launched the "do it for you" home services market—a classic retail aftermarket.

Service Planning and Scheduling

Once the appropriate service agreement is in place, service planning and scheduling controls the deployment of service resources (parts, skilled labor) to ensure that the customer problem/service issue is resolved within the defined service level agreement at the lowest possible total cost. Effective service planning and scheduling should make sure that the customer's expectations are exceeded and the problem is fixed properly the very first time and within the time tolerance specified in the service contract. This requires maintenance of adequate levels of spare parts inventory and service personnel to meet customer demands as they occur. Also, firms can reduce service costs by better scheduling and coordination so that overtime and last minute expediting costs are avoided. Reduce repair cycle time by making the service parts available on time and providing all necessary information to the service personnel before and during the service execution.

Once the repair service is completed, the technician needs to record the root causes and the actions taken to repair the damage (principle 4). This should be logged into a database and accessible to all the service personnel so that they don't have to "reinvent the wheel" every time they go out on a call. The feedback should be documented and passed onto appropriate departments (enabler 1) so that it can be incorporated in future product enhancements/designs.

In addition, this technical and financial information would help the organization perform analysis and assist in the development of an early warning system. Examples of technical information include number of breakdowns per customer, breakdown by equipment style, and breakdowns per time period. Examples of financial information include average cost per order, total cost and revenue generation for the service center, and average profit per order.[35]

Having service parts available on time requires good spares forecasting, inventory planning, and replenishment planning capabilities. All these capabilities together will help the organization have the right quantities of the right parts at the right store. Companies need to make sure that the service interactions are positive and consistent. This will lead to superior customer satisfaction and establish a lifetime relationship and trust with the customer, as well as repeat business.

Returns Management

An important part of customer service management is the ability to effectively handle returns. Returns management is starting to get more and more attention nowadays because of its connection with green supply chain initiatives and minimizing the carbon footprint. A well-planned and executed returns management system can help an organization reduce costs, comply with environmental regulations, increase customer satisfaction, and be a source of competitive differentiation. However, for returns management to be a source of competitive advantage, it must be supported by senior management and all the cross-functional teams (sales, customer support, environmental and regulatory, logistics, manufacturing, packaging, distribution).

Also, customer feedback should be captured, heard, and communicated by having detailed codes that can be used to track the reason for each individual return. This provides invaluable information that can help drive new product and process design.

BIC companies like McKesson make the customer choose from approximately nine reason codes, which are then tracked and reported to the appropriate process owners so as to eliminate the underlying root causes. Disposition strategies should be put in place so that material handling and inventory carrying costs for the returned items are minimum. Similarly, by having strong, collaborative relationships with retailers, wholesalers, and liquidators, GENCO sells its returned items through bulk, refurbish, and value-added liquidation.[37]

CRM SUPERPROCESS WORKFLOW SUMMARY

The CRM superprocess (Figure 5.13) is composed of a spectrum of interrelated processes ranging from long-term (marketing management) to medium-term (selling management) to short-term (customer service management) activities.

Marketing Management

Marketing management is about creating demand for the products and then communicating this (aggregate level demand) to the demand planning subprocess (S&OP process in SCM). Marketing management consists of the market strategy and market research subprocesses.

Market Strategy

Market strategies start first with market segmentation to identify which markets the organization can serve effectively. This is followed by selecting one or more target markets to synergize the marketing efforts and resources to hit the right segment. Lastly, market positioning involves developing a specific marketing mix for each targeted marketing segment to match customer's perception. The market strategy subprocess in CRM and the strategic management subprocess in SCM need to be in alignment with the corporate strategy. A marketing plan is one of the most important outputs of the entire market strategy subprocess, and is a written document that acts as a guide of marketing activities for the marketing manager, as well as an input to the selling management process.

Market Research

Market research and analysis involves the systematic design, collection, analysis, and reporting of data and findings relevant to a specific marketing situation facing the company.[6] Market research is conducted throughout the cycle of developing effective market strategies, implementing the strategies, and obtaining feedback from the implementation of the marketing plan. It involves getting customer feedback through various approaches—focus groups, surveys, mail and

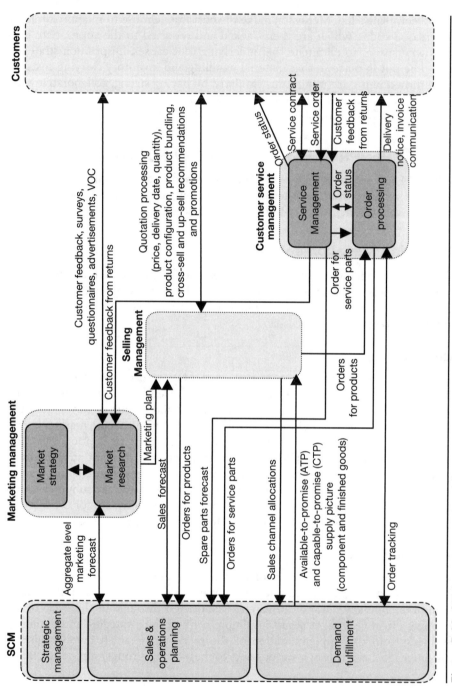

Figure 5.13 CRM superprocess workflow

online questionnaires, interviews, etc. Apart from the traditional market research, leading companies are increasingly looking toward capturing the VOC, which involves having an informal conversation with customers to find out what customers really want and value as opposed to targeted questionnaires and interviews that are based on what companies think customers want.

Selling Management

Once marketing management has decided on the marketing mix, selling management involves the tactics that will be used to accomplish the marketing strategies. Activities involved in selling management include coming up with a sales forecast (communicated to the demand planning subprocess in the S&OP process in SCM), deciding on the allocations for the different sales channels (communicated to the order promising subprocess in the demand fulfillment process in SCM), customer quotation processing, product configuration and bundling, providing cross-sell and up-sell recommendations, pricing and revenue optimization, and promotion planning.

The selling management process handles the front end of promising a delivery date for a sales order or quote, while the order promising subprocess in the demand fulfillment process in SCM handles the back end of order promising. The selling management process needs to be tightly integrated with the order promising subprocess so that selling management has visibility into not only feasible configurations, but also available configurations. This is accomplished by verifying component level availability—leveraging the ATP logic in the order promising subprocess of SCM. It is imperative that the back-end order promising subprocess is synchronized in real time with the front-end sales configuration environment. Effective selling management involves promising only what the company can deliver by having real-time visibility into the ATP and CTP supply picture across multiple enterprises from the order promising subprocess. The selling management process is also responsible for communicating the orders for products to the master planning subprocess (S&OP process in SCM).

Customer Service Management

Customer service management consists of two subprocesses: order processing and service management.

Order Processing

Order processing involves efficiently and effectively managing the sales order throughout its entire life cycle. It involves brokering the sales order to the appropriate business divisions of the organization. Once the order is sent to the correct business division, order processing needs to be tightly integrated with the master planning subprocess and the logistics planning and execution subprocess in SCM so that the order can be planned and fulfilled according to the specifications. This integration with the master planning subprocess and the logistics planning and execution subprocess will help order processing provide real-time order tracking visibility to the service management subprocess, which in turn will provide the customer the order status visibility across all channels.

Service Management

Service management consists of service contract management, service planning and scheduling, replacement part delivery, and damaged part recycling or returns activities.

Service contract management is usually triggered by the customer signing up for a service agreement. This includes several contract items like discounts on replacement parts, guaranteed response time, technician hourly rate, and support time. When the customer reports a service issue, service planning and scheduling controls the deployment of service resources (parts, skilled labor) to ensure that the customer problem/service issue is resolved within the defined service level agreements at the lowest possible total cost.

To make sure the right spare parts inventory is available at the right store at the right time, the service management subprocess needs to integrate with the demand planning subprocess (spare parts forecast) and the inventory planning subprocess.

The service management subprocess is also responsible for capturing customer feedback on returns and communicating it to the market research subprocess so that it can be incorporated into enhancements and/or new products.

REFERENCES

1. Anderson, K., and C. Kerr. 2001. *Customer Relationship Management*, 2 New York: McGraw-Hill Professional.
2. Thompson, B. 2002. What is CRM? http://crmguru.custhelp.com/cgi-bin/crmguru.cfg/php/enduser/std_adp.php?p_faqid=416 (accessed April 2009).
3. Rigby, D. K., F. F. Reichheld, and P. Schefter. 2002. "Avoid the Four Perils of CRM." *Harvard Business Review*, February, 101–113.
4. Greenberg, P. 2002. *CRM at the Speed of Light: Capturing and Keeping Customers in Internet Real Time*. New York: McGraw-Hill/Osborne.
5. Selden, L., and G. Colvin. 2003. *Angel Customers and Demon Customers, Portfolio*. New York: Penguin Group.
6. Kotler, P., and K. Lane Keller. 2006. *Marketing Management*. 12th ed. Englewood Cliffs, NJ: Prentice Hall.
7. Reichheld, F. F., and P. Schefter. (2000. "E-loyalty: Your Secret Weapon on the Web." *Harvard Business Review*, August, 105–112.

8. Reichheld, F. F. 1996. Learning from Customer Defections. *Harvard Business Review*, March-April, 56–69.

9. Reichheld, F. F. 1996. *The Loyalty Effect.* Cambridge, MA: Harvard Business School Press.

10. Butscher, S. A. 1996. "Welcome to the Club: Building Customer Loyalty." *Marketing News*, September 9, 9.

11. Sewell, C., and P. B. Brown. 1990. *Customers for Life: How to Turn That One Time Buyer into a Lifelong Customer,* 162. New York: Pocket Books.

12. American Marketing Association (December 2007). AMA Definition of Marketing, Chicago,Illinois. <http://www.marketingpower.com/Community/ARC/Pages/Additional/Definition/default.aspx> accessed April 2009.

13. Kotler, P. 1977. "From Sales Obsession to Marketing Effectiveness." *Harvard Business Review*, November, 67–75.

14. Brown, J. 2003. Pizza Hut Delivers Hot Results Using Data Warehouse." *Computing Canada*, October 17, 24.

15. Mazur, L. 2003. "Personal Touch is Now Crucial to Growing Profits." *Marketing*, November 27, 18.

16. Serwer,A.2004."HotStarbuckstoGo."*Fortune*.http://money.cnn.com/magazines/fortune/fortune_archive/2004/01/26/358850/index.htm (accessed December 2008).

17. Porter, M. E. 1980. *Competitive Strategy: Techniques for Analyzing Industries and Competitors.* New York: Free Press.

18. Borden, N. H. 2003. "The Concept of Marketing Mix." *Journal of Advertising Research*, Volume II, September 1984, 7–12.

19. Byrnes, N. 2004. "What's Beyond for Bed Bath & Beyond?" *Business Week.* http://www.businessweek.com/magazine/content/04_03/b3866059.htm (accessed February 2009).

20. Ridge, P. S. 2002. "Tool Sellers Tap Their Feminine Side." *Wall Street Journal,* June 16, B1.

21. Rackham, N., and J. DeVincentis. 1999. "The new selling: From communicating value to creating value." Chapter 1 in *Rethinking the Sales Force: Redefining Selling to Create and Capture Customer Value.* New York: McGraw Hill.

22. Symonds, W. 2003. "Working for Working Adults." *Businessweek.* http://www.businessweek.com/magazine/content/03_23/b3836719.htm. (accessed June 2008).

23. Roman, E. 1995. *Integrated Direct Marketing: The Cutting Edge Strategy for Synchronizing Advertising, Direct Mail, Telemarketing, and Field Sales.* Lincolnwood, IL: NTC Business Books.

24. Gellene, D. 1997. "An Old Dog's New Tricks: Hush Puppies Return in the '90s is No Small Feet." *Los Angeles Times*, August 30. http://articles.latimes.com/1997/aug/30/business/fi-27351 (accessed April 2009).

25. Burk Wood, M. 2003. *The Marketing Plan: A Handbook.* Upper Saddle River, NJ: Prentice Hall.

26. Maddox, K. 2004. The ROI of research. *B to B*, April 5, 25, 28.

27. Grow, B. 2004. "Hispanic Nation." *BusinessWeek*. http://www.businessweek .com/magazine/content/04_11/b3874001_mz001.htm (accessed June 2009).

28. Lee, L. 2004. "The GAP Has Reason to Dance Again. *BusinessWeek*. http://www .businessweek.com/magazine/content/04_16/b3879059.htm (accessed May 2008).

29. Barnes, J. 2005. "To Hear the Voice of the Customer, Listen Outside the Box." http://crmguru.custhelp.com/cgi-bin/crmguru.cfg/php/enduser/std_adp .php?p_faqid;eq1542 (accessed December 2008).

30. Sabri, E. June 2005. Value chain management to achieve competitive advantage in retail industry. In *Proceedings of Middle East Retail Conference*. United Kingdom: MEED.

31. Marn, M. V., and R. L. Rosiello 1992. "Managing Price, Gaining Profit." *Harvard Business Review*, September-October, 84–93.

32. Lundegaard, K., and S. Freeman. 2004. "Detroit's challenge: Weaning Buyers from Years of Deals." *Wall Street Journal*, January 6, A1, A2.

33. Johnson, M. 2003. "User Complaints Push Dell to Return PC Support to U.S." *Computerworld*, December, 6.

34. Sabri, E. 2006. *Best Practice in Leveraging E-business Technologies to Achieve Business Agility. In Enterprise Service Computing: From Concept to Deployment*, ed. R. Qiu, 356–387. Hershey, PA: Idea Group Publishing.

35. Curran, T. A., and Ladd, A. 2000. *SAP R/3 Business Blueprint*. 2nd ed. Englewood Cliffs, NJ: Prentice Hall PTR.

36. Ilaria, J. 2006. "Avoid Turning Your Aftermarket into an afterthought." http:// www.industryweek.com/articles/avoid_turning_your_aftermarket_into_an_ afterthought_11509.aspx (accessed April 2009).

37. Subject Matter Experts–Dr. James R. Stock. Cheryl Harrity. 2007. *Reverse Logistics: Backward Practices That Matter*, ed. K. Campos and L. Trees, 17-27. Houston, TX: APQC Publications. (Research sponsored by Warehousing Education and Research Council.)

6

LEAN AND AGILE VALUE CHAIN TECHNOLOGY APPLICATIONS AND TRENDS

INTRODUCTION

This chapter, in its first section, will focus on the technology infrastructure or foundation that has enabled the value chain management (VCM) software vendors to provide us with lean and agile value chain (LAVC) technology applications across supplier relationship management/supply chain management/customer relationship management (SRM/SCM/CRM) superprocesses. The second section will give an overview on these LAVC applications and market trends based on articles from leading information technology (IT) research and advisory companies like Gartner, AMR Research, Forrester, Aberdeen Group, and others. We will focus in this chapter mainly on the latest applications. We will not talk about the mature applications that have been in the market for a long time since a lot of literature on them is already available.

IT spending continued to fall in 2009, despite the fact that existing IT systems are aging and new capabilities to support new business environments are urgently needed. Therefore, new supply chain implementations should be simpler and faster to integrate and should deliver value sooner to justify the investment. This puts more pressure on supply chain software applications to be more easily integrated into existing IT applications.

In several situations, the cost of integrating a large supply chain application into an existing IT system is more expensive than the actual supply chain application package. More and more firms are therefore basing their supply or value chain investments on the presence of common platforms or integration ease rather than functional capability differences.[1]

Forrester expects an increase in software investment in 2010, after the 2008–2009 slump, on the back of strong demand by early adopters for new service-oriented architecture (SOA) application suites from the following: (1) enterprise resource planning (ERP) vendors, (2) SOA infrastructure from infrastructure vendors such as IBM and Microsoft, and (3) smaller software vendors who provide specialized products for improving business results in vertical industries. This will trigger a comeback for IT consulting and systems integration services.[2]

NEW GENERATION OF LAVC TECHNOLOGY INFRASTRUCTURE

Service-Oriented Architecture

SOA brought significant opportunities for firms to extend and improve their existing VCM solutions without large-scale upgrades and re-implementations. So far, SOA implementations are intended for large firms rather than mid- or small-size firms due to the initial needed investment to enable SOA solutions.[3].

Whenever we discuss SOA, we should talk about web services. The simplest definition of web services is accessing software services over the web. Web services have gained a lot of visibility in software circles. The software industry considers standards, technology, and architecture as components of them. They offer the means to connect the service provider to the service requestor, and, finally, provide the service over the web (hence web service). This enables applications to connect to other applications to form a meaningful workflow. Web services are considered to be an integral part of enabling business-to-business (B2B) models.[4]

SOA is an architectural framework for developing software-based business solutions. It is made up of components and interconnections that stress interoperability and location transparency. It is similar to building with Lego blocks. Web services and SOAs provide the components necessary to design and build systems using heterogeneous software components.[4]

A common misconception is that web services are required to achieve SOA. However, SOA can be achieved through multiple technologies with web services being the most common one. Other technologies like Java RMI (remote method invocation) can also be used to achieve SOA.[4]

SOA presents a different paradigm to use IT in business processes (event-driven) instead of the traditional processes (control flow-driven). The event-driven paradigm is necessary to respond to business activities such as triggering a replenishment request when inventory *projected on hand* falls below a certain level. It prevents ad hoc and proliferated integration, a common contributor to integration issues of today. This results in accelerating application deployment, thereby reducing deployment costs. It is important to mention that SOA models can leverage IT investment by being able to utilize existing applications, which allows an organization to extend the life of its applications.[4]

In addition, SOA allows for a heterogeneous portfolio in which *best-of-breed* solutions can be implemented. Earlier, due to integration and technology constraints, use of best-of-breed solutions resulted in a suboptimized solution. Finally, SOA allows an organization to become more lean and agile and respond to changes faster than before. SOA promotes assembly of applications from reusable components instead of redeveloping them.[4]

Business Process Platforms

A business process platform (BPP) framework leverages SOA to drive commoditization of business processes that can be standardized and deployed widely. It enables differentiated and innovative business processes that cannot be enabled by a packaged application, but as a custom-assembled set of application and data services. BPPs are more easily replicated than packaged applications, thus driving up commoditization of innovation. They will be more easily revised to reduce the cost of developing new innovative process forms for many more firms. The basis for how IT supports business requirements will change; it will no longer be serviced by application vendors but from innovative business processes delivered by a range of vendors as "interoperable services" in the form of business process templates and industry-specific data models.[5]

BPPs will reduce the reliance on packaged applications. In time it will be a set of reconfigurable application and data services. Also, the direct provider will no longer be the application vendor, but the integrator who understands how to assemble a useful composite application for the company's business. Sample BPP vendors are i2, Manhattan Associates, Steelwedge, and TCS (Tata).[5]

Business Process Hubs

A business process hub (BPH), historically known as an *e-marketplace*, is a process-specific instance of multi-enterprise applications between two or more firms. It is delivered by a range of IT vendors and private communities who arrange the design, orchestration, and execution of a specific business process, such as order to cash, design, and sourcing between trading partners. The scope of a BPH can be "one to many" or "many to many." One to many is historically known a as *private marketplace*, while "many to many" is historically known as a *public e-marketplace*.[5]

BPHs never created their promised value because many focused on business processes that were not relevant to how firms behaved or were willing to behave. Those that have survived have shifted their focus to catalog and item data content synchronization, hosting of traditional applications, web-based collaboration, supply chain visibility, and performance analytics. The BPH can offer significant value to its customers by providing industry-specific hosted applications, or multi-enterprise applications that are often procurement-related and supply chain-related. Sample vendors are Agentrics, Ariba, cc-Hubwoo, E2open, Elemica, Enporion, Exostar, Liaison Technologies, Mitrix, Quadrem, and Wesupply. com.[5]

Radio Frequency Identification

Radio frequency identification (RFID) is an automatic identification technology that leverages radio frequency to transmit the identity of an object containing the RF transmitter. It allows capturing of identification data without a manual scan; what is required is a *reader/interrogator* that recognizes the radio transmission. These readers can be combined with cellular or GPS devices for in-transit updates.

The value assessment of using RFID has returned to the first principle in assessing a technology: what business problem can it solve and how much value can it add? RFID has shed its hype. Manufacturers are increasingly moving away from compliance-driven initiatives to specific-use cases where RFID is the best technology choice and tangible return on investment (ROI) exists.[1]

Wal-Mart is the most prominent user of this technology, and Wal-Mart's delays and difficulties with passive RFID-enabled inventory management indicate to many observers a broader dissatisfaction with RFID. However, Gartner maintains that Wal-Mart's success doesn't depend on technological success or maturity. Rather, it is tied to the business case and the ability of the firm to construct business processes that leverage additional information about the inventory and products provided by RFID[5] (i.e., process maturity).

It is true that there are more and richer data available to the value chain, but firms are struggling to identify what data is useful, how to analyze it, and where the resulting information can be used in short-, medium-, and long-term supply chain operations.[6]

Master Data Management

The guiding principle of master data management (MDM) is that the core business data (about customers, products, vendors, etc.) is an enterprise-wide data that must be managed from an enterprise perspective, and leveraged by many applications. MDM ensures the consistency, accuracy, and accountability of the core data of the organization, which enables greater enterprise agility and simplifies integration activities.

MDM enables firms to collect master data from different existing systems, validate it against common business rules, store it in a central database, and use it across the enterprise. For example, one can collect core customer information (such as name, address, etc.) in a central location, remove duplicates, fix incorrect names and addresses, and use it across the enterprise as the system of truth.

MDM can be used to enable data to be synchronized across multiple systems while ensuring data integrity. This would remove the need for traditional point-to-point integrations since there is a common view of the company's master data.

It is recommended to make MDM part of your overall enterprise architecture strategy, and determine when, not whether, the firm should adopt MDM. IT should decide the right timing for introducing a single master data, rather than the traditional piecemeal approach on managing master data.

In building the business case for MDM, IT should focus on key business problems, analyze the potential scenarios in which the enterprise wants to use an MDM system in the short and long term, highlight potential benefits, review the organization's readiness from an education standpoint, and be aware of the political willingness to use a single view for master data.[5]

Event Management

Event management is software that detects exceptions to planned and unplanned events, and then facilitates the response to get the value chain or process back under control. An integral part of event management is supply chain visibility, which links every stage of the value chain and tracks the movement of goods in real time.

Based on certain business rules and a set of parameters, notifications are triggered to appropriate organizations or departments when certain events occur in the value chain, or when exceptions to those events happen. So, event management is the enabler for the exception-driven concept. This concept is all about improving efficiency and effectiveness by focusing only on the transactions or events that have potential negative impact on the value chain. It eliminates the need for the users to sift through every transaction or event.

Event Management can also facilitate the resolution of an exception, either manually, by suggesting certain alternatives for users, or automatically, based on predefined business rules. It not only detects the exceptions/problems (which mitigates business risk), but also resolves them (which improves agility). Other capabilities for event management that can help any value chain process are:

- Ability to link events to key performance indicators (KPIs) to improve the decision-making process.

- Supporting "priority" for exception notification. For example, high priority events like stockout for a key component, which can shut down the assembly line, should be escalated to a manager or plant manager by sending an urgent message to a cell phone instead of a simple alert on a computer.
- Ability to simulate and determine the impact of actual or projected events happening in the value chain. For example, a one-week delay to an ocean shipment from a supplier (due to custom issues) would generate a safety stock violation at the receiving warehouse, after adding the in-transit time, one month down the road.
- Providing root-cause analysis (telling why an exception occurred, not just that it occurred). For example, the delivery performance of a certain supplier is very low this week due to changing the purchase orders within the firm period three weeks back. So, the root cause of the problem is that the supplier couldn't recover from changing the schedule during the firm period.

SRM-ENABLED SOFTWARE APPLICATIONS

SRM applications enable buyers to negotiate and manage prices, terms, and conditions for strategic contracts (for direct and indirect materials), as well as tactical services through online "requests for information" (a technology enabler for the product design process), electronic sealed bids, and reverse auctions. These applications could help the buyer compare and rank the resulting bids and optimize source selection against constraints, such as "award no single vendor more than 60 percent of the total supply requirement" to enforce flexibility.[7] In addition, these applications enable the operational and execution levels of the procurement process as shown in Table 6.1.

Emphasizing the "one-stop-shopping" model by ERP vendors has been an attraction and has been appealing to the C-level executives for the past few years. This marketing strategy works very well with the CFO who is getting more involved in value chain application buying decisions due to the finance and supply management integrated touch points that ERP provides. Supporting the financial backbone of the organization, the ERP vendors are in a better position to connect the dots between SRM and finance for all types of spend.[8]

The best-of-breed software vendors are expanding their functionality across buyer organizational functions to enhance their value to C-level executives. The SRM vendors, in general, will focus more on the following capabilities:[8]

- Collaborative exchange and visibility across all spend types, functions, and supply partners
- Global sourcing capabilities, like total landed cost equation and management of the global trade areas (such as lines of credit and export documentation)
- Track-and-trace capabilities
- Product life cycle management (PLM) functionality

Table 6.1 Technology applications distribution under business processes

		Applications under superprocesses and processes		
		SRM • SaaS SRM applications	SCM	CRM
Level	Strategic	Strategic sourcing • Strategic sourcing suites • Supplier performance management • Spend analysis	Strategic management • SND	Marketing management • Marketing analysis • MDM for product data–sell side
	Tactical	Product design • MDM for product data– buy side	S&OP • S&OP • SCP suites • Demand planning • Inventory planning • Supply planning	Selling management • Campaign management • Configuration and pricing • Direct POS analytics • Multitier supply chain collaboration
	Operational	Procurement • Procurement suites • Contract management • Online supplier directories • Supplier portals • POM • TMS • E-procurement	Demand fulfillment • SCIV • Mobile (wireless) SCM • CTP • Supply chain analytics	Customer service management • Customer service • SPP

SRM applications span various delivery methods: hosted, software-as-a-service (SaaS), and on-premise. *Hosted* refers to any software application offered and managed by a third-party provider. *SaaS* is subscription software that is delivered on demand and not behind a firewall. *On-premise* refers to a traditional delivery method of placing a software application on-site, typically behind the firewall, and is usually licensed.

Although the traditional license model still retains the largest share of the overall market, SaaS is gaining traction. Strategic sourcing has been the primary source for SaaS adoption in SRM, followed by indirect procurement (e-procurement) and contract management. In contrast, invoice settlement represents the lowest SaaS deployment share in SRM.[8]

SaaS SRM Applications

The outward-facing nature of SRM applications has made them a natural candidate for SaaS. A variety of SRM applications, including strategic sourcing applications, e-procurement, and contract management solutions, are available and deployed via SaaS.

SaaS applications have steadily gained traction in SRM since their introduction in the early 2000s. Early entrants into the SaaS market (including Ketera Technologies and Procuri) positioned their subscription-based solutions as easy-to-implement, user-friendly alternatives to the more cumbersome ERP-based, on-premises offerings. Web technology helped them in their marketing strategy since it is more practical to provide external access to the suppliers rather than arranging supplier access to an internal application. Furthermore, the subscription pricing model that typically accompanies the SaaS solution is appealing to companies since it is a good vehicle to spread out the fees for these services over time. SaaS offerings also promise to minimize or even eliminate IT involvement in selection and implementation, as long as there is minimal need for integration with other existing applications. In addition, the SaaS model enables users to quickly and routinely access new functionality rather than waiting for the upgrade process to happen, which typically takes several years.[8]

The key to the success of the SaaS delivery model in procurement is the degree to which a solution can be implemented stand-alone or with standardized connections, such as strategic sourcing applications, since the SaaS model doesn't support any major customization. Several SaaS providers such as BravoSolution, Global eProcure, Quadrem, and Ariba have successfully penetrated this market with applications that delivered mainly or even exclusively in SaaS. Until 2006, SaaS-delivered SRM applications were viewed by many as novel and risky due to worries around the security of the data, the reliable availability to the hosted system, and the user interface performance. These worries have proved to be largely unfounded. Ariba's transformation from an on-premises provider to an SaaS promoter has helped in terms of bringing SaaS into the mainstream.[8]

Strategic Sourcing-Enabled Software Applications

Strategic Sourcing Suites

The most successful strategic sourcing applications provide event management services, optimization modeling services, spend analysis, supplier performance management, and market opportunity analysis. Most ERP vendors do not provide all of these services, which puts them at a disadvantage in the strategic sourcing market.

Recessionary pressures in 2008 increased interest in strategic sourcing applications because firms, during tight economic times, tend to focus on bottom-line cost savings. There are also noticeable trends in this area: (1) the movement of several application vendors into the public sector, (2) the rise of aggressive, low-cost point solution providers, and (3) the growing popularity of SaaS as the preferred implementation mode for supporting strategic activities. Since strategic sourcing applications work well as stand-alones, they are naturally great candidates for delivery via SaaS. Therefore, most strategic sourcing implementations are SaaS or hosted.[9]

Investing in strategic sourcing applications should be a top priority for any firm with more than $1 billion in revenue. Firms with less than $1 billion in revenue may not have sufficient volume to justify an investment, but should evaluate the potential (ROI) for the strategic sourcing application.[7]

Supplier Performance Management

These applications collect and publish a set of quantitative (transactional-based) and qualitative (survey-based) supplier performance data spanning price, delivery, lead time, responsiveness, quality, flexibility, and technology.[7]

The business objectives are to rate and monitor the suppliers' ability to provide products/services in accordance with the specifications, use it as a tool to help in the supplier selection process for future purchases, and use it as a baseline for improvements.

For decades, firms have successfully compiled transaction-related metrics (KPIs) to track and rate the performance of suppliers. ERP and supply chain applications routinely provide data on delivery, quality, and purchase price, which proved useful for buyers and suppliers if it was used effectively. However, many firms are challenged to create usable supplier performance data because it requires painstaking attention to the accuracy of data (such as the delivery date), and because the definition of the metric often varies across business units and/or across types of replenishments. Furthermore, a good evaluation for supplier performance extends beyond the scope of quantitative metrics into qualitative data collected via a survey or poll.

Recognizing the opportunity to develop a more comprehensive set of data that augments transactional metrics with qualitative assessments, many strategic sourcing vendors have entered the supplier performance management solution. Corporate performance management and business intelligence software vendors are also expressing interest in the area, especially since their focus is on performance analytics of any type of market.[7]

These applications offer a reporting capability (dashboard) in addition to extracting and consolidating data from heterogeneous, transaction-oriented systems and survey tools. They provide an intelligent dashboard and a set of supplier-facing web pages to post results; however, this constitutes the easy part of supplier performance management implementation. The more difficult is process and change management, which include building a consensus on defining measurable and appropriate KPIs of success, determining how many metrics to track and their targets, and ensuring that the data used to compile the ratings are clean and credible. Supplier performance management is an important discipline, but it will take years for procurement to mature from a process standpoint to the point of being able to effectively manage all strategic vendors in a holistic manner considering not only delivery and quality, but also other factors. Eventually, the procurement function will evolve to the point where this application will be useful and can be broadly deployed. Firms that implement a supplier performance system successfully and achieve a best-in-class supply base will significantly outperform organizations that do not in terms of profitability and agility.[7]

Spending Analysis

The focus of spending analysis applications is on preparing data for analysis by extracting, de-duplicating, classifying, cleansing, and aggregating procurement transaction data. They also offer reporting and analytical capabilities and provide procurement with a single view of enterprise-wide spending by spanning multiple, heterogeneous transaction systems. Unlike pure data warehouses or business intelligence tools, spending analysis applications deliver value through content and by providing reporting and analytical capabilities. Standard functionality includes:[7]

- Creating a single database of information by extracting data from multiple systems
- Combining duplicate suppliers spending by leveraging matching and a database of common iterations of supplier names
- Classifying each item into a logical category leveraging public/industry classification codes such as the United Nations Standard Products and Services Code
- Reporting and drill-down capabilities (slicing and dicing)
- Ability for the users to correct classification errors at the point of discovery
- Multilingual support

The spending analysis applications evolved significantly since they hit the market in the mid-1990s due to web enablement, maturity in the extraction tools, and a more granular classification. Spending analysis applications will continue to help firms identify opportunities for cost savings and monitor contract compliance. It is a must have for large firms with $1 billion or more in spending, and with multiple ERPs. Sample software vendors are Ariba, BIQ, BravoSolution, Emptoris, Global eProcure, SAP, and Zycus.[7]

Product Design-Enabled Software Applications

The PLM suite is the main enabler for the product design process. The PLM suite includes the following applications:

- Product data management (see next section for details)
- Program management
- Collaborative design/engineering leveraging RFI workflow
- Computer-aided design/Computer-aided manufacturing
- Event management

MDM *for Product Data—Buy Side*

MDM for product data applications is used to achieve a "single version of the truth" for product data across the enterprise by cleansing, identifying, linking, harmonizing, and publishing common product information. These applications can be used to help the product design process by managing product and purchase parts effectively which, in return, would lower costs and increase agility through more effective operations, more leverage over suppliers, and faster product introduction.[5]

MDM for product data applications (buy side) typically encompasses product, supplier, location, financial master data, item master, vendor master, bill of material, bill of distribution, routings, location master, resources, and other planning parameters.

These applications have the potential to fully address the challenge of inconsistency and the fragmentation of product data across many systems. This challenge makes it very difficult for firms to streamline business processes and develop lean and agile business processes. For example, without a single view of the products and items, gaining benefits on the buy side from the ability to conduct spending data analysis efficiently, or achieving a competitive new-product introduction process would be difficult. It is important to note that successful implementation of this application requires architectural vision and business commitment to the MDM strategy.[5]

Procurement-Enabled Software Applications

Procurement Suites

The procurement process spans a rich and diverse range of subprocesses and activities, and the variety of software applications available to enable the procurement process is expanding and maturing.

Procurement software suites that are marketed as a complete solution set include inventory replenishment ordering, e-invoicing, request for quotation, request for proposal (RFP), supplier enablement and connectivity, reverse auction, contract management, catalog management, online collaboration, and order management.[5] The focus of these types of applications is mainly the finalization of the price and delivery date for supply requirements. Simply put, the process generally starts with a requisition and ends with receiving the goods on the purchase order.

Many software vendors with procurement-related applications have attempted to build out a full suite of interoperable solutions, seeking to provide "one-stop shopping" for clients. These software vendors are typically adding to their product lines through partnerships, internal development, and acquisitions. Therefore, the resulting procurement suites have had varying degrees of functionality and completeness in terms of the individual applications.[5]

One of the major challenges for the procurement suites is that many procurement subprocesses involve unstructured tasks/activities that leverage unstructured data (like the RFP subprocess, which varies considerably from project to project in addition to the variations in the documents and information that this subprocess generates). On the other hand, some procurement subprocesses such as e-invoicing are structured in terms of the subprocess steps and the data involved. Therefore, the architecture that is required to support these two types of solutions is different, and most software vendors specialize in one or the other.[5]

It is important for companies who are interested in improving their procurement process to compare procurement suite providers to best-of-breed software vendors on an application-by-application basis, rather than expecting a single suite to address all business needs. It is also crucial to choose the application or suite that meets the firm's functional requirements, as identified through research and references. (For more information on software vendor selection, please refer to Chapter 7.) It is also important to recognize that software suite vendors may abandon modules that do not gain significant traction over time in the market.[5]

According to Gartner, procurement suites (which are also called *SRM suites*) will not adequately, in the short term, address the complete set of procurement processes and will therefore not dominate the enterprise-class market. Sample vendors are Ariba, Global eProcure, Infor, Ketera Technologies, Lawson, Microsoft, Dynamics, Oracle, and SAP.[5]

Contract Management

Enterprise contract management applications provide a central, searchable database repository for all types of agreements. Other primary features include templates for initiating agreements, workflows that can be configured to each agreement type, and exceptions or alerts for pending expirations. The contract management application market has begun maturing and an increasing number of firms are starting to see benefits from this type of application.[7]

More firms will use out-of-box functionality for contract management applications to avoid customization, and strive to achieve rapid ROI from those features that have proved to be useful, including template support, approval workflows, and exceptions (alerts). Establishing contract governance and choosing corporate legal terminology before investing in a contract management application is a must for a successful implementation. Sample vendors are Apttus, Ariba, Contiki, Ecteon, Emptoris, Nextance, Oracle, SAP, and Selectica, SpringCM, Symfact, and Upside Software.[7]

Online Supplier Directories

Online supplier directories are a third-party-owned registry of credible B2B suppliers. It is important to mention that the online directory is not a search engine, but is an organized resource for business buyers, and a channel for suppliers to find and attract new buyers. Typically, the effort required to locate suitable prospects from which to source goods can consume considerable time and resources from the buying organization. Online supplier directories improve the buying organizational efficiency by reducing the time it takes to find suitable suppliers significantly.[7]

These applications/directories also have a meaningful, positive impact on the small suppliers who lack effective sales channels to expand their market. On the other hand, these directories might be appealing for large suppliers with brand recognition and an established customer base. Sample software vendors are Ariba, B2BChinaSources.com, eBay, MFG.com, Quadrem, and ShiftWise.[7]

Supplier Portals

The majority of procurement-related ERP applications and best-of-breed procurement suites offer some sort of portal extension that enables suppliers to view records, update files (like supplier item descriptions) and/or submit bids via a secure login on an Internet website. Supplier portals are very specific to a buyer, often configured to the buyer's specific requirements, and branded with the buyer's logo.[7]

Supplier portals deliver value to buyers and suppliers by reducing the amount of manual work (phone calls, fax, and exchanging paper by mail) and speed up the information exchange. One thing companies need to avoid is enabling multiple, limited-use portals tied to specific applications like what occurred in the 2000s. Although suppliers support this type of application, they are challenged by having the information provided to them in a single format, requiring the supplier to download and manipulate the data if it wishes to upload the information directly into its own systems. This challenge becomes bigger if a supplier is dealing with a number of customers with unique portals. Therefore, it is recommended to use supplier portal technology to communicate with smaller or less technically experienced suppliers, while providing system-to-system integration for strategic suppliers. Sample vendors are Emptoris, i2, Infor, Lawson, Oracle, SAP, SciQuest, and Verian Technologies.[7]

A supplier portal can be extended to provide a single repository (database) containing supplier profiles, capabilities, catalogs, contracts, insurance certifications, diversity, sustainability, payment terms, inventory requirements, performance data, quality information, pricing, etc. Supply management executives may find as much as a sevenfold improvement in efficiency and cost reduction to manage suppliers by leveraging best practice processes and extended supplier portals.[10]

A great example is the implementation of Aravo Supplier Information Management (SIM) at General Electric (GE), which illustrates how reliable supplier portal technologies can achieve better supplier visibility, information consolidation, and significant cost savings. In current global rollout, GE has centralized information for its 500,000 global suppliers into the Aravo SIM system.[10]

Purchase Order Management

Purchase order management (POM) applications support purchase order acknowledgment, generate exception if the acknowledgment is different than the purchase order, monitor raw material arrival at the supplier, display the supplier's production plans, monitor production in-process events, track quality control results, create or receive advance shipment notice and compare it with the purchase order, track carrier pickup for goods, provide visibility into in-transit shipment status and events, track custom clearance events, receive and display proof of delivery, track warehousing events, and manage invoice and settlement events.[11]

We recommend the book *Purchase Order Management Best Practices: Process, Technology, and Change Management* for the reader who wants to know more about POM applications.[4]

Transportation Management System

Transportation management system (TMS) software is a technology enabler for the scheduling and execution of the external physical movements (transportation) of products across the value chain. It includes load consolidation, routing, mode selection, carrier selection, execution (such as tendering loads to carriers and freight audit and payment), and shipment visibility (global visibility, event management, business activity monitoring, track and trace, and analytics). TMS applications are not new, but market penetration compared with other SCM applications is estimated to be modest.[12]

A number of forces are impacting the TMS market and shaping its future:

- Globalization in terms of international TMS deployment and multileg, multimode international shipment. An increased focus on global transportation management is a significant driver of new software application investment.
- Major technology trends driving the SCM market (including TMS), including the impact of SOAs, the emergence of BPPs, and more global transportation technology capabilities (leading TMS vendors are investing in this area heavily).
- Striving for lean and agile value chains is increasing the demand for applications that enable related best-practice processes and adapt fast to the changing needs of the business without extraordinary costs (the solution should be affordable, yet scalable).
- Although basic scheduling has traditionally been the focal point of TMS evaluations, there is a growing interest from buyers in areas such as freight audit and payment, and collaboration.

SaaS TMS solutions might become the emerging notion of trading partner networks. These networks are composed of many carriers and are expanding to include suppliers and buyers. As SaaS TMS vendors add trading partners to their platforms, the partners become immediately available, at little to no added cost, to current and future clients. New capabilities are enabled through the notion of the network, such as carrier portals that enable shippers and carriers to collaborate starting from freight sourcing through settlement.[12]

A reality check for cost of ownership for an SaaS TMS application is crucial. There is a significantly lower up-front cost in terms of the software subscription compared with a traditional on-premise (on-site) TMS license, and a reduction in implementation cost principally in the areas of installation and carrier on-boarding. However, the longer-term cost differential between on-premise versus SaaS TMS is less favorable to SaaS; beyond five years it can favor on-premise TMS.[12]

SaaS is making inroads within TMS, and is expected to account for 13 percent of TMS revenue by 2012, and be the prevailing choice of delivery model for small- to mid-size businesses.[12]

In general, transportation costs amount to a significant percentage of a company's total spend. There is huge room to leverage cost savings in this process. Enabling best-practice process supported by TMS should minimize transportation costs, improve communication with carriers and partners, reduce shipment delays, reduce paperwork and related errors, and provide real-time visibility and early problem detection, and more.

E-Procurement

E-Procurement applications provide internal users with self-service mechanisms for drafting purchase requisitions, accessing catalog content, obtaining management approval, and sending the resulting purchase orders to suppliers. It is typically a catalog-based mechanism and is used to manage indirect material. Some key capabilities are support for approval workflows, support for multiple and partitioned catalogs, support order aggregation and splitting, and providing external content access on supplier portals or at an e-marketplace. E-Procurement applications effectively automate approximately 20 to 25 percent of a typical enterprise's overall indirect spending. In particular, utilities, complex categories (e.g., hiring of contingent labor), and non-invoiced spending are best left outside of e-procurement.[7]

Best-of-breed e-procurement applications are highly recommended for companies with a large budget for indirect material. For midmarket and smaller organizations with revenue less than $1 billion, it is recommended to leverage the e-procurement functionality provided by ERP in their suites. Sample vendors are Ariba, Basware, CGI, Compusearch, Coupa Software, Ketera Technologies, Microsoft, Oracle, Perfect Commerce, Proactis Group, PurchasingNet, Puridiom, SAP, and Verian Technologies.[7]

SCM-ENABLED SOFTWARE APPLICATIONS

SCM applications have been in the market longer than SRM and CRM applications. Therefore, they are more mature and robust. In this section, we will focus on key applications to give the reader a good idea about the new generation of innovative applications.

Supply Chain Network Design-Enabled Software Applications

Strategic Network Design

Strategic network design (SND) applications are run periodically (perhaps quarterly or annually) to simulate network changes and determine strategic structural changes. The business objective is to minimize total supply chain network costs. These applications use sophisticated mathematical solvers like linear programming and mixed integer programming to optimize network designs, given specified constraints.

Strategic planners use SND to decide how to allocate capital, where to source materials and services, where to store inventory of finished products, from which location to satisfy customers' orders, etc., based on current network, costs, management priorities, and other factors.

Historically, these solutions were used strategically (for 1-5 years) to determine the optimal overall physical network and material flow. SND applications have been enhanced to consider other objectives in addition to cost. For example, they look at responsiveness and flexibility, and provide support for tactical planning scenarios (of less than a year) by adding the time dimension and other modifications.

There are several vendors for SND applications: i2, Optiant, Insight, Oracle, Barloworld/CAST, Infor, JDA, and LogicTools.[5]

The authors expect that these applications will be extended to consider the total landed cost when optimizing a supply network. Also, average lead time and variability will be supported for seasonal or fashion goods.

Sales and Operations Planning-Enabled Software Applications

Sales and Operations Planning

Sales and operations planning (S&OP) applications enable the S&OP process, which is a cross-functional business process that aligns business strategies and operational plans across sales, marketing, manufacturing, distribution, product development, and finance. Key capabilities for these applications are as follows: performance management tools (e.g., dashboards and scorecards), "what-if" functionality, event management for exception-driven workflow, data aggregation, ease of navigation, drill down and roll up, and financial impact analysis.

Specific S&OP applications are maturing, although not as fast as user requirements. However, there are several very capable independent S&OP applications starting to enter the market. Sample vendors are i2, JDA Software, Logility, Oracle, SAP, and Steelwedge.[5]

Supply Chain Planning Suites

Supply chain planning (SCP) suites refer to applications that optimize the delivery of goods and services, balance supply and demand, and integrate with transaction systems to provide informed planning and real-time analysis of "what-if" scenarios. SCP suites typically include SND, demand planning, inventory planning, supply planning, scheduling, and collaboration applications.

SCP suites provide comprehensive supply chain plans that incorporate strategic (long-term) planning, tactical (medium-term) planning, and operational (short-term) planning and scheduling.

The suite products are now more scalable and easier/faster to implement, and are seeing a healthy growth. They enable firms not only to balance supply and demand but also to optimize it, which brings in more cost saving and efficiency.

It is important to mention that SCP suites do not make decisions, but they give managers and users tools to make informed and intelligent decisions. Therefore, they also called *decision-support systems.*

SCP suites are based on advanced planning and scheduling (APS) logic, which is a major breakthrough after manufacturing resource planning (MRPII) logic. APS is a constraint-based planning logic that emerged in the early 1990s. APS complements ERP systems by adding a layer of smart planning (forward-looking) over ERP transactional (backward-looking) capabilities. Therefore, sometimes SCP suites are called *APS applications.*

SCP takes transactional data from ERP systems, performs planning, and then writes back the optimized schedule to ERP (as a system of records for transactional and finance data) and to execution systems (e.g., manufacturing execution system).

Migrating SCP suites to be web-based applications and leveraging web services for integrations introduced the new generation of SCP suites.

Demand Planning

Demand planning applications create demand plans that consider many factors such as historical trends, promotions, pricing, and seasonality. They capture forecasts by product, region, customer channel, and time. There are several forecasting techniques available in the demand planning applications from which to choose.

Forecasting techniques can broadly be classified as qualitative and quantitative. Qualitative techniques are subjective projections based on judgment, intuition, and so forth. Quantitative techniques can broadly be classified into extrinsic (causal methods) like multiple regression, and intrinsic (time series).

During tough economic times, firms will increasingly need to factor in macroeconomic data into the forecasting techniques because the state of the economy affects consumer behavior and pricing among other things.

Inventory Planning

Inventory is the lifeblood of SCM, especially in recessionary times. Inventory optimization was one of the top three application investment areas for supply chain executives used to meet their main supply chain objective.[3]

The goal of inventory planning applications is to decide the best locations to keep safety stocks, and then compute how much of a safety stock should be carried in the selected locations for planning purposes. They determine the most optimized inventory levels. These applications are different than the inventory management applications that are responsible for transactional management of inventory.

Supply Planning

Supply planning applications support the master planning process by providing blueprints for production, distribution, and purchasing.

One of the limitations of the MRPII logic (used to enable the master planning process) is the sequential planning of material and capacity constraints. The best-practice approach is the ability to do "real-time concurrent planning" taking into consideration material, time, and capacity constraints. This is possible using the supply planning applications, which have trimmed the planning time from a few days down to a few hours.

Demand Fulfillment-Enabled Software Applications

Supply Chain Inventory Visibility

Supply chain inventory visibility (SCIV) provides a network-wide view of inventory at a multi-enterprise level to enable more flexible management of inventory at the network level. This reduces inventory costs and improves responsiveness, which will lead to an improvement in customer service levels. SCIV holds a single view of inventory balances at different locations for planning purposes. It integrates tightly with ERP and warehouse management system (WMS) systems since the most common place to manage inventory is at the enterprise level in ERP, or at the facility level in WMS. This network inventory view can form the foundation of SCM applications.[5]

The emerging set of applications, in addition to providing a network inventory view, tie this network view of the inventory to business processes, enable SCM applications, and leverage service-oriented order management capabilities. Sample vendors are E2open, i2, Manhattan Associates, and Sterling Commerce.[5]

Mobile (Wireless) SCM

Mobile (wireless) supply chains represent the integration of several infrastructure technologies such as frequency identification, Wi-Fi, GPS, and vehicle connectivity, to improve the effectiveness of SCM processes by automating data capture, communication, and user activities.

These applications have the capability to integrate the processing of activities by mobile workers with enterprise applications, as well as monitor and track mobile assets, such as trucks. For example, mobile users can access and share information such as deliveries and delivery confirmations. Another example is using GPS tracking to monitor the location of a vehicle in order to send an automated message to the receiving facility when it is within a specified distance and schedule an appointment accordingly.[5]

Maximizing the impact of this type of application requires high levels of standardization and redesigning of business processes based on the business requirements and technology capabilities, such as real-time data capture, input, and distribution. Simply applying mobile technology (such as RFID) to existing processes without redesign will have a minimal benefit and is not likely to yield much ROI.[5]

Mobile technologies that pull data from onboard computers on trucks and distribute that information using satellite communications are mature, but historically expensive. Newer technologies like cellular phones are less expensive, which would increase the market for mobile applications.[5]

Capable-to-Promise

Capable-to-promise (CTP) applications enable firms to promise a delivery date for a customer order or a quote based on available resource capacity and inventory. It is important to note that CTP applications are more sophisticated than ATP applications, which consider mainly inventory as a constraint. CTP applications require greater integration and more data.

CTP applications consider resource (equipment, people, and materials) availability/capacities, constraints, work in progress, and various rules to calculate accurate promises. Newer applications also factor nonproduction-related constraints such as transportation into promise dates.[5]

Although CTP technology has been around for several years, adoption has been slow due to data availability, information latency, and cultural change, which has translated into less demand for CTP applications. Many firms have settled to less-sophisticated ATP applications even though visionaries already are talking about concepts beyond CTP such as profitable-to-promise applications (PTP). PTP combines CTP with a profitability analysis to determine how profitable a certain customer order would be after considering all costs.

CTP applications play a big role in enabling postponement, make-to-order, and assemble-to-order strategies to better use a firm's assets and improve customer satisfaction by providing more intelligent promise dates. Sample vendors are Adexa, i2, Infor, JDA Software, Logility, Oracle, and SAP.[5]

Supply Chain Analytics

Supply chain analytics applications are used to monitor and manage the performance of a supply chain. They provide portals, dashboards, and business activity monitoring capabilities. They also provide a set of KPIs and industry templates for reuse and leverage. Supply chain analytics applications give firms with a proactive and intelligent performance measurement system that allow it to monitor progress and adjust direction if the expected behavior is not achieved. The big challenge to these types of applications is the dependency on developing the measurement strategies and then deploying the necessary processes and integrated systems.

Therefore, firms should look first at the supply chain analytic applications that are seamlessly integrated with their core SCM applications. Sample vendors are i2 Technologies, IBM Cognos, Informatica, JDA Software Group (Manugistics), Manhattan Associates, Oracle EPM, SAP (Business Objects), SAS Institute, and Teradata.[5]

CRM-ENABLED SOFTWARE APPLICATIONS

CRM innovative technologies support customer segmentation, customer analytics, customer collaboration, innovative strategies such as make-to-order or mass customization, market knowledge and analysis, and service/call center automation and scheduling. The objective of CRM applications is to determine customers' needs and deliver the products and services in a way that can achieve a positive customer experience. In the next section, we will focus on key applications in the three CRM processes: marketing management, selling management, and customer service management.

Marketing Management-Enabled Software Applications

Marketing Analysis

Marketing analysis applications enable the marketing management process to identify customers' needs, determine which customer segmentation to serve, and assist in deciding the product mix for every customer segment (channel).

They also help to evaluate campaign and pricing strategy and monitor customer satisfaction.

These applications leverage business intelligence functionality to support analytical analysis, provide reporting capabilities, and conduct data mining. Data mining is a method to study data in order to search for previously unknown correlation, patterns, and preferences.

These applications can provide marketing with online access to a knowledge management repository. This repository has access to sources of information that are stored in each department that are difficult to automate. This information includes marketing presentation material, historical sales and marketing reports, industry and competitor analysis, contract templates, and so forth.

MDM for Product Data—Sell Side

MDM for product data applications is used to achieve a "single version of the truth" for product data across the enterprise by cleansing, identifying, linking, harmonizing, and publishing common product information. It manages a database-based system of record (central product master) to provide a single product view across channels, systems, and business units. This would strengthen the firm's ability to cross-sell, cross-market, provide consistent and appropriate customer experience, and achieve operational excellence objectives. It is a big enabler for the marketing process. An MDM for product data application (sell side) typically encompasses customer, product, supplier, employee, location, asset, and financial master data.[5]

Although MDM for product data application is made up of complex requirements, its market is maturing and growing quickly. MDM for product data—sell side (formerly known as *product information management*) is more mature than MDM for product data—buy side, and there are differences in awareness and adoption depending on the industry. It is expected that, through 2012, the MDM market will continue to see major changes, acquisitions, and new entrants.[5]

These applications have the potential to fully address the challenge of inconsistency and the spreading of product data across many systems. This problem makes it very difficult for firms to streamline business processes and develop lean and agile business processes. For example, without a single view of a product, firms cannot effectively up-sell, cross-sell, and leverage operational benefits from merger and acquisition activity. It is important to note that successful implementation of this application requires architectural vision and business commitment.[5]

Selling Management-Enabled Software Applications

Campaign Management

Campaign management applications use Internet technology to capture, extract, and analyze campaign information. They support managing promotions online, and cross-selling and up-selling offerings.

These applications provide a good user interface experience for customers when they view promotions, offers, and new products online. They also provide an effective way to measure the success of a certain campaign.

Configuration and Pricing

Configuration and pricing applications assist in the development of quotations and entry of complex orders that require sophisticated product configuration and pricing rules. The i2 Pricer and Configurator for laptops in the computer industry are good examples of these applications.

These applications should be tightly integrated with customer service applications that are responsible for order processing. Thanks to SOA and web services, this integration will be a no brainer in the next few years.

Direct-Point-of-Sale Analytics

The direct-point-of-sale (POS) analytics application enables a seller to automate, manage, and ensure inventory-based customer service levels at customer locations by guiding the replenishment subprocess. These applications store POS and other demand-type data from many sources and in many formats, including RFID and scanning data.[5]

Direct-POS analytics applications for vendor-managed inventory are increasing rapidly. Their main focus is to ensure accuracy of the inventory data and demand trigger at the store level. Direct-POS analytics applications for vendor-managed inventory help firms to align supply (inventory and purchase orders) and demand data (direct-POS, RFID triggers, and sales orders) and business plans (sales, forecasts, promotions, and replenishment) between retailers and their sellers. This would improve in-stock rate availability at retailer locations, even in intensive periods with excessive seasonality or promotions, thus increasing sales and profitability.[5]

Multitier Supply Chain Collaboration

Multitier supply chain collaboration supports the unique set of requirements that come from multiple stakeholders who share a common objective (forecast, promotion, business plan, product launch or development). Such types of collaboration are structured and can use industry standards, such as collaborative planning, forecasting, and replenishment. These applications will evolve rapidly leveraging the newer infrastructure technologies like MDM and SOA/web services.

Sample vendors include Agentrics, E2open, Eqos, i2, JDA, Logility, and Oracle (Syncra).[5]

Customer Service Management-Enabled Software Applications

Customer Service Applications

Customer service applications support providing information on products and services to customers online, and allowing them to visit catalogs, configure orders, review prices, enter orders, receive order status, enter return orders, file complaints, and have access to frequently asked questions and answers.

Service Parts Planning

Service parts planning (SPP) applications enable firms to optimize the forecasting, stock locating, and replenishment planning of service parts, and balance customer service and inventory carrying costs. These applications support specific SPP process requirements like modeling of returns, forecasting erratic and irregular demand, and multi-echelon inventory optimization. These applications improve parts availability while reducing inventory carrying costs by having the right parts available when needed. But more importantly, they improve service reliability and increase customer satisfaction. In addition, they provide firms with an opportunity to gain a competitive advantage by excelling in the aftermarket.[5]

There are a growing number of vendors targeting SPP including specialized SPP-only vendors, SCP vendors, and some ERP vendors. ERP vendors have extended their SPP offerings so competition in this market segment is high. Sample vendors are Baxter Planning, Click Commerce (Xelus), Logility, MCA Solutions, Oracle, SAP, SAS, Servigistics, Syncron, and Tools Group.[5]

REFERENCES

1. Manufacturing Insights. August, 2008. Global and North American supply Chains 2008 Top 10 predictions: An Interim Report Card. 1–7. Framingham: Manufacturing Insights.
2. Forrester. September, 2008. US IT market outlook: Q3 2008: The U.S. recession and tech slowdown will hit in late 2008. 1–24. Cambridge, MA: Forrester.
3. Aberdeen Group. October 2008. Supply Chain Innovator's Footprint for Closed Loop Inventory Management. Research Brief, 1–8. Boston: Aberdeen Group.
4. Sabri, E., A. Gupta, and M. Beitler. 2006. *Purchase Order Management Best Practices: Process, Technology, and Change Management*. Fort Lauderdale, FL: J. Ross Publishing.
5. Gartner. August, 2008. Hype Cycle for Supply Chain Management. Report, 1–52. Boston: Gartner.

6. Manufacturing Insights. July, 2008). Profitable Proximity: Product Sourcing Decisions in the Modern Supply Chain. *Manufacturing Insights*, July, 1–17. Framingham: Manufacturing Insights.

7. Gartner. August, 2008. Hype Cycle for Procurement Applications. Report, 1–43. Boston: Gartner.

8. AMR Research. November, 2009. The Supply Management Market Sizing Report, 2007-2012. 1–28. Boston: AMR Research.

9. Gartner. April, 2008. Magic Quadrant for Sourcing Application Suites. 1–24. Boston: Gartner.

10. AMR Research. May, 2009. GE Lights Up Supplier Management with Aravo. Boston: AMR Research.

11. Aberdeen Group. October 2008. Facing the New Challenges of Today's Global Supply Chain: The Growing Role of Visibility. Research Brief, 1–7. Boston: Aberdeen Group.

12. Gartner. October, 2008. Market Trends: Transportation Management Systems, Worldwide, 2007–2012. Report, 1–20. Boston: Gartner.

Part III: Project and People Management with Lean and Agile Value Chain Transformation

Chapter 7: Transformation Program Cycle

Chapter 8: Change Management Supported Processes

Chapter 9: Lean and Agile Value Chain Transformation Case Study: Office Systems

Chapter 10: Lean and Agile Value Chain Success Stories and Lessons Learned

7

TRANSFORMATION PROGRAM CYCLE

INTRODUCTION

Many organizations redesign processes and find it impossible to implement them. In other situations, a new process is introduced, but within weeks or months everyone is back to the old way of doing business. When this happens, people tend to play the blame game. Chapters 7–10 in this book provide the recipe for success for any transformation program.

Many firms are struggling with implementing process improvement programs related to value chain or supply chain and achieving the promised value or *return on investment (ROI)*. In addition, currently, there are doubts and questions on the best practices in integrating new Internet technologies into supply chain operations because companies encounter many challenges such as the inability to master change management, a need for new skills to support processes that span across suppliers and partners, sustaining continuous upper management support, the lack of comprehensive metrics and continuous monitoring, and the criteria to select the software-providing partner if a new technology is needed.

Also, many firms fail to recognize that improving one process in isolation rather than considering the big picture of the value chain is a recipe for disaster. A value chain is like a system with several moving parts, and a change to one moving part without considering the impact on the overall system or the other moving parts might lead to catastrophic implications.

Therefore, companies are looking at framework and guidelines for successful program transformation. Chapter 7 provides a detailed set of instructions, a step-by-step description of how to proceed with the value chain transformation program. The

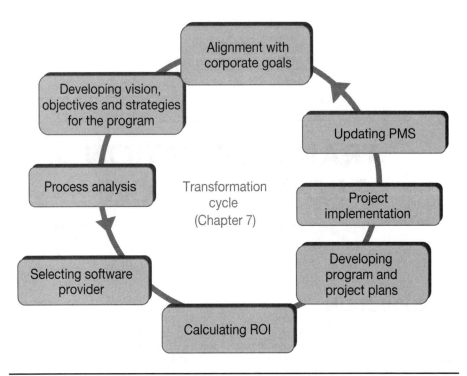

Figure 7.1 Transformation program implementation framework

following framework (Figure 7.1) is proposed to address the previous challenges and provide best-practice guidelines for program transformation.

Also, Table 7.1 provides a sample for a transformation program checklist that includes timeline, responsibility (resources), key deliverables, source (input), and comments for every step in the value chain transformation program. This checklist can be used as a baseline to create the program and project plans.

ALIGNING THE TRANSFORMATION PROGRAM WITH CORPORATE GOALS

Understanding the corporate goals fully is the first step in any transformation program. It enables the value chain transformation program and related changes to be aligned successfully with the corporate goals.

This step is crucial to secure the buy-in from upper management, who typically ask for an explanation of how the change helps in implementing the organization's

Table 7.1 Sample for transformation program checklist

Transformation program cycle steps	Timeline	Responsibility	Deliverables	Source (Input)	Comments
1. Aligning with corporate goals					
Understand corporate goals		Sponsor			
Establish a need for transformation (improvement change)		Sponsor			
Establish the linkage between transformation program and corporate goals		Sponsor			
Communicate the need for transformation to upper management		Sponsor	Point of view presentation		
Obtain the go ahead to proceed to the next step		Sponsor			
Select the transformation program team to establish the vision of the program		Sponsor and program manager	Staffing plan		See Chapter 8 for details
2. Developing vision, objectives, and strategies of the program					
Develop the vision of the program		Transformation team			
Conduct benchmarking analysis		Process consultant	Competitive analysis		
Develop the objectives of the program		Transformation team			
Develop the strategies of the program		Transformation team			
Communicate the vision, objectives, and strategies of the program to the stakeholders		Program manager	Communication plan		See Chapter 8 for details
3. Process analysis					
Conduct a high-level as-is assessment, conduct maturity assessment (using CMM), and identify pain points		Process consultant			
Create high-level future end state		Process consultant	Program blueprint		

Table 7.1 Sample for transformation program checklist (continued)

Transformation program cycle steps	Timeline	Responsibility	Deliverables	Source (input)	Comments
Identify KPIs for the program		Process consultant			
Identify the list of business requirements		Process consultant			
4. Selecting a software provider					
Identify the list of functional requirements		Architect (functional consultant)			
Gauge software capabilities		Selection committee			
Select a software provider		Selection committee	Contract with the software provider		
Communicate the decision to stakeholders		Program manager		Communication plan	See Chapter 8 for details
5. Calculating ROI					
Identify operational benefits		Program manager			
Identify financial benefits		Program manager			
Create cost estimates		Program manager			
Conduct ROI analysis		Program manager	ROI analysis		
Communicate the ROI to sponsor and upper management		Program manager		Communication plan	See Chapter 8 for detai
6. Developing program and projects plans					
Define high-level program and project plans, with assumptions		Program manager	Program road map, program plan, and project plans		
Define risks and mitigation plans		Program manager		Tracking and controlling	See Chapter 8 for details
Finalize scope		Sponsor and program manager	Program charter definition		
Conduct program review		Program manager		Communication plan	See Chapter 8 for details

7. Project implementation

Task	Role	Deliverable		Notes
Identify and document as-is process and pain points	Process consultant and subject matter experts (SMEs)	As-is process document		
Design to-be process	SMEs, process consultant, architect, and change agent	To-be design document		
Keep all stakeholders informed and engaged during this step	Program manager and change agent		Communication plan	See Chapter 8 for details
Configure hardware and software (if a new technology is implemented)	Modeling and integration consultant	Test plans		
Deploy the solution (combination between to-be process and supported technology)	SMEs, modeling and integration consultant (technical architect)	Solution acceptance criteria and training material		
Anchor the new process	Change agent and sponsor	User manual	Education plan and cultural support	See Chapter 8 for details
Conduct ongoing maintenance (if a new technology is implemented)	IT support representative	IT operational manual		
8. Updating the Performance Management System (PMS)				
Update PMS with new performance measures or adjust targets and owners for existing measures	Project manager, program manager, or sponsor	Updated key performance indicators (KPIs) list		
Monitor performance	Project manager			
Perform trend analysis and root-cause analysis	Project manager			

strategic plan and achieving corporate goals, before committing organizational resources (time, energy, and money) to the transformation program.

It is necessary to develop a communication plan that expresses the importance, urgency, and strategic link of the change or program. Communication management, which is one of the change management supported processes, is discussed in detail in Chapter 8. After considering the strategic relevance of the program, it is then necessary to identify the team who would lead the transformation. Chapter 8 also provides detailed guidelines to select and develop the team.

DEVELOPING VISION, OBJECTIVES, AND STRATEGIES OF THE PROGRAM

A clear vision of the program is the second step for a successful transformation. Executives need to understand the big picture, the interactions between all the processes and value chain applications to help them in creating this vision.

It is crucial to "begin with the end in mind" by first visualizing what the end picture looks like and then actively striving to reach that image. Defining where the company wants to be after the transformation program is creating the vision. The vision statement should be short, clear, concise, and simple, like an *elevator speech*, of where we want to be in the future. Next, detailed planning and discussion should be done to arrive at objectives that would transform the vision into reality, and strategies that provide the "how" to achieve the objectives. A few examples of vision statements for a transformation program for the demand fulfillment process include:

- Becoming the industry leader in providing reliable and quick delivery to customers
- Gaining competitive advantage and market share by promising what we can deliver and delivering on every promise

Coming up with vision or elevator speech should be a group activity and not an individual (sponsor) activity so as to establish ownership and avoid resistance during the implementation phase. This is why we have recommended selecting the transformation team in the previous step. The individuals or departments most impacted by the program should participate in vision development to strengthen their commitment and buy-in to the program.

A formal group process, possibly facilitated by an independent consultant, is one way of coming up with the vision, objectives, and strategies. Then, these items must be communicated to every stakeholder inside and outside of the organization.

Defining the program objectives should be done based on customer requirements and best practices of industry leaders. Benchmarking is a great method to help in coming up with objectives.

Benchmarking

Benchmarking is the process of assessing and evaluating a firm against a standard or another firm in the industry. It helps in identifying areas of improvement and determining the goal of the transformation program. Benchmarking can be done against companies in the same industry (competitors) or any best-in-class company across industries.

Benchmarking can also be used to validate a potential benefit or gain in performance measures for lean and agile value chain (LAVC) processes. Benchmarking can help answer questions such as "How is the company doing compared to their competitors or industry average and how much do we want to improve in certain performance measures?"

The supply chain operations reference (SCOR) model metrics provide another standard for assessing the current performance and determining realistic goals for improvements. The Supply Chain Council (SCC), owner of the SCOR model, conducts regular benchmarking surveys for its members, which are used as a standard for the industry. These help other firms to judge their own performance against firms that are using the SCOR metrics.

Benchmarking can be divided into three broad approaches that provide an effective way to assess the existing process or processes and choose realistic, yet inspiring objectives:

1. Internal benchmarking: Benchmarking across different business units within a firm is one example. It's natural to have more faith and trust in your business unit's ability to reach an improvement target if colleagues in your company have achieved that target successfully in their business units.
2. Competitive benchmarking: Comparing performance, strategy, and processes with competitors within an industry. Observing another company in your own industry exceeding your performance in a core competency process or implementing a best-practice strategy for a certain process offers perception and motivation for possible improvements.
3. Best-in-class (generic) benchmarking: Comparing performance, strategy, and processes with the best in any industry. This type of benchmarking gives an opportunity for a firm to learn about best practices and their impact on performance in other industries.

PROCESS ANALYSIS

In this step, the transformation team should identify and analyze core business processes. The team, for example, might suggest outsourcing noncore processes to improve efficiency and focus on the value-added processes. In addition, the team should design the new processes such that it achieves program objectives and further gains a competitive advantage.

Processes need to be designed to maximize their ultimate contribution to results (key performance indicators [KPIs]), and support the program objectives that were defined in the previous step. Every core process within the business must be reexamined to maximize its contribution to top-level goals.

KPIs data are crucial for this step. Without capturing KPI data (operational and financial), an accurate assessment of the contribution that the transformation program would have toward improving the bottom line and achieving LAVCs cannot be made. Also, there is no insurance that redesigned processes can meet targeted improvements or even win executive support.

Finally, if the new organizational structure doesn't support the new processes, restructuring should be part of the recommendation and deliverables.

The main purpose of process analysis (also called *design and requirements*) is to use modeling methods like process mapping to analyze *as-is* business processes, identify the existing challenges (pain points) in the current processes, and validate the *to-be* process improvements against the best practice benchmarks.

During process analysis, we take a hard look at the firm's value chains in order to identify processes that would need improvement. Analysis of specific processes involves breaking them down into subprocesses and then into activities. Once the current process or processes are mapped, redesigning can take place by improving the process by removing, combining, or adding activities.

Process analysis also determines the extent of process and technology changes possible in the current or existing systems, and identifies additional software capabilities (if any) required to support the to-be processes. These capabilities or functional requirements would be the input for the next step.

The reader should note that the process analysis at this step is conducted at a high level since it's typically done across several processes in the value chain. Once the potential benefits are justified for improving a certain process, a detailed process analysis should be conducted next (this will be explained in a later step).

LAVC principles and enablers (explained in Chapter 1), and continuous improvement methodologies (explained in Chapter 2) should be used in the process analysis step. The most successful transformation programs rely on more than one improvement method due to the nature and maturity of the process, characteristics of the business or value chain, and degree of market competition.

SELECTING A SOFTWARE PROVIDER

Selecting a software provider for technology capabilities is required only if the functional requirements that were determined in the previous step are not supported by the existing systems. Selecting a software vendor that provides LAVC applications is a hard undertaking, almost as difficult as selecting an enterprise resource planning vendor. As a best practice, firms need to identify the best-of-breed solution that is most suitable for the required functionality of their business, taking into consideration software technology maturity and sustainability. Supporting leading industry standards for e-business technology like web services is crucial during the selection process.

Some guidelines for selecting a software application provider as well as deploying these applications include:

- Identify, based on the objectives of the transformation program, the *must have* and *good to have* functional requirements or features for the desired solution. The must have functional requirements should be satisfied by any software vendor under consideration, while good to have can be used as a deciding factor in case of a tie between the competing software vendors. It is also very important to set realistic expectations and ensure that the end goal is achievable from a requirement, budget, and time perspective. Often programs have failed due to unrealistic expectations.
- Gauge software vendor capabilities. The organization must determine the capability of potential software vendors. Special attention must be given in areas where the organization needs the most help from a capability standpoint. Also, if the solution is a global one, internalization capability of the solution will play a key role in its success.
- Achieve alignment and buy-in. Before getting deep into the software provider selection, it is crucial to get a buy-in from all stakeholders and ensure alignment.
- Stay focused on the end goal. Software vendors might try to shift focus from the end goal to the latest features and new technology in their products to position themselves better and have an edge on their competitors. Define a set of rules to ensure a fair and objective selection process and stick to these rules. They must be defined and disseminated among vendors early in the selection process.
- Ensure that the selection team has the decision-making authority. Software vendors commonly bypass the selection team and try to sell directly to the top management within the organization. If vendors are successful with this tactic, it may result in a suboptimal solution. Top management must ensure that any information sharing with vendors is directed to the selection team.
- Insist on a demo and have it on your own terms. The agenda for the demo needs to be developed and controlled by the selection team. A script that reflects "a day in the life of an internal user" and/or an external user (supplier or customer) to the process under consideration should be developed. Be sure to pay special attention to usability and efficiency since the end users will be spending a lot of time with these applications (systems). Items that may appear as minor inconveniences to the selection team may be unacceptable to the end users. This script should be shared with the competing software vendors and they should be forced to adhere to it.

An external facilitator can be a valuable resource in managing demo sessions. When vendors do not have certain functionality in their products they tend to resort to using PowerPoint-ware in an attempt to sell a solution that is not available. The selection team should focus on functionality available during the demo and defer anything else.

- Negotiate the terms and conditions. Negotiation should be on the solution instead of just software licenses. During negotiation, make sure to consider the total cost of ownership and include licenses for all third-party software and components without which the solution will not work. Often, organizations negotiate on licenses for the core software product and not components, which lead to cost overruns. Also include maintenance and training in negotiations.
- Make a decision and communicate it to stakeholders. In order to ensure that key stakeholders are kept up-to-date with the selection process, communicate decisions at predefined milestones, on success, or in the event of an issue. Once a decision is made, it is important to communicate the decision and the reason behind selecting a specific vendor to the stakeholders.
- Select a service provider. A software application is a crucial step in achieving the end goal, but it is only one part of the solution. Complementing this selection with the selection of a service provider to assist in the implementation is needed. Implementation contributes a large portion to the program cost and time. If execution is flawed, the result would be a solution that may not work as expected or may have significant cost and time overruns. Select a service provider who has implemented similar solutions and has a good knowledge of the business and industry.
- Communicate the decision with explanations to all software vendors who are not selected.
- Minimize, if not eliminate, application customizations (customized coding). Everything that is a candidate for customization needs to be challenged. Efforts should be made to configure out-of-the-box software functionality instead of customization whenever possible.[1]

CALCULATING ROI

Calculating ROI is the process that compares the potential benefits to the costs associated with implementing a transformation process.

Calculating ROI is crucial for securing the buy-in from upper management to implement a certain transformation program. A strong ROI means continuous support and commitment from senior executives.

Using only ROI traditional models (cost-benefit analysis, net present value, ROI financial, internal rate of return, and others) in LAVC transformation programs could face many challenges, such as the inability to consider soft (operational) benefits that cannot be easily converted into financial ones. Also, there is a need for an effective ROI model that can help in selecting the best initiative (low-hanging fruit) from several competing process improvement initiatives. In addition, an effective ROI model should help to identify the real factors that have impacted the company's recent performance and how much they have attributed to the transformation program.

Ehap Sabri, and colleague Aamer Rehman developed[2] an ROI model that addresses the above challenges. They recommend a bottom-up approach. It starts by capturing all operational benefits that are usually generated by addressing the current pain points in a process or processes. For example, an operational benefit could be improvement of on-time delivery. The operational benefits and their equivalent metrics (e.g., on-time delivery percentage) need to be monitored at least on a monthly basis. Then, these operational benefits are converted into financial ones, if possible. A financial benefit in the above case is the reduction in transportation cost. The financial benefits and their equivalent metrics (e.g., transportation cost percentage) need to be monitored at least quarterly.

In many situations, it is not possible to convert certain operational benefits into financial ones, but that does not mean that they should not be captured and monitored just because they cannot be used in the traditional ROI models.

There are two main reasons why these operational benefits need to be captured: First, these operational benefits can be converted in the future into financial benefits once the data is available. For example, an increase in customer satisfaction is an operational benefit that is difficult to quantify in financial terms, but with time and more available data, it might become clear that more business/revenue is generated from existing customers because of the specific process change in the transformation program. Then the operational benefit can be translated into a financial one. Second, operational benefits will help to justify the investment if no financial benefits are generated at a certain time, or to compare between two competing initiatives with similar financial benefits.

All cost elements such as the consulting cost for process mapping and change management, hardware, software license (if a new application is acquired) and upgrades, internal resources, integration cost, ongoing maintenance and support, and training need to be captured and monitored closely. There are two types of costs, the initial cost (which is needed at the beginning of the implementation) and ongoing cost (which is needed to sustain the new process and solution).

Finally, all financial benefits and costs should be considered in the ROI financial calculation. The operational benefits that are not quantifiable in financial terms should also be captured and communicated. A detailed breakdown of benefits and cost needs to be shown to indicate the magnitude of the program. Guidelines for computing ROI are as follows:[2]

- No overlap is allowed in financial benefits or metrics (a metric is the measure of the benefit). For example, if premium freight cost is considered to be a financial metric, logistic cost should not be considered as another

financial metric because premium freight is a subset of logistics, otherwise benefits are double-counted.
- A comprehensive set of metrics should be considered. Sometimes improvement in one area is achieved at the expense of another. For example, an increase of the fill rate might happen at the expense of reduction in inventory turnover.
- The ROI model should be sustained by the existing skill sets in the organization.
- The simpler the ROI model, the easier for it to be maintained.
- Optimize the level at which metrics data need to be captured because sometimes the effort and the time of capturing data exceed the benefits.
- Automate the capturing of performance data.
- Computing the ROI should not be a one-time exercise that is done only at the beginning of the transformation program to justify it. It should be an ongoing exercise to maintain momentum and buy-in.

DEVELOPING PROGRAM AND PROJECT PLANS

Adopting a value-driven approach to conduct LAVC transformation programs is very crucial. An effective transformation program typically takes 2 to 5 years, with several intermediate projects (go-lives) that can pay for the rest of the program. So, the transformation program is built on the idea of incremental value delivery.

It is crucial to have a long-term (program) plan for success, but one should not ignore the importance of providing some short-term wins (projects). Organizational stakeholders look for short-term results, and managers are under pressure to present short-term wins.

These short-term wins do not necessarily need to be tremendous. But they need to be big enough and visible to keep momentum going and to silence resisting forces. Short-term wins build the credibility of the overall program and justify tackling even more or bigger projects as part of the program. Short-term wins should be woven into the timetable of the program. We recommend approximately six months as being a good timeline for a short-term win. Each project delivers a set of capabilities that have a positive impact on process, metrics, and people, addresses a distinct business need, and contributes to the bottom line.

When transformation or change seems to be too difficult, it is crucial to consider dividing the change into several projects because there are major obstacles and resistance to be faced if the change is perceived to be disruptive to the business.

During large transformation programs, multiple projects may be taking place at the same time and others in sequence. It is necessary to schedule these improvement projects in a way that can maximize the use of resources (time, energy, and money). The stakeholders should agree on the projects' timelines.

The program plan should include developing realistic schedules for the overall program and for every project, distribution of delivered solution capabilities into several projects, identifying needed resources, assigning responsibilities and roles, and securing a budget and a buy-in from senior management and stakeholders. It also includes defining a risk management plan.

For every project plan, milestones, tasks, budget, and resources are identified. In addition, deadlines for the project, a project manager, and a target for every KPI or performance measure are determined.

The program manager and sponsor must continue to diligently monitor the progress of every ongoing project. This step requires senior management's best efforts not only to maintain but also to build momentum for the change. This prevents the resisting forces, who are waiting for an opportunity to make a comeback, from slowing the project down. Whenever senior management lets up before the job is done, critical momentum can be lost and the change effort can stall.

The program plan should be marching toward targeted benchmarks (performance measures). Since the implementation strategy is to accomplish it in incremental steps, these projects need to be tracked and checked off one at a time as the program approaches the benchmark. Chapter 8 discusses monitoring and tracking of the program and related projects in more detail.

It is acceptable for the program manager and sponsor, while tracking the progress toward the end state and targeted benchmarks, to rethink the goal and even adjust the target either because of encountering roadblocks or because of some emerging opportunities that didn't exist previously.

PROJECT IMPLEMENTATION

Implementing one project as part of the overall transformation program should go through four phases: (1) describing where we are (as-is), (2) deciding where we want to go (to-be) and planning on how we are going to get there, (3) taking the journey of change (deploying the new process or solution), and finally (4) anchor the change in the culture of the organization (stabilizing the new process). Phase 1 and Phase 2 are considered to be the planning portion, Phase 3 is the deployment portion, and phase 4 is the sustaining portion of the project.

All projects in the program would go through the same four phases. But the program manager may find it useful to conduct a single phase across several projects. Conducting the as-is phase for Project 1 and Project 2 together is one example. The program manager may also decide to do multiple steps in parallel rather than sequentially to meet the organization's particular timeline.

There is no one best method or one-size-fits-all solution to achieving successful implementation. Organizations are best served when implementation methodology is tailored to meet its unique needs of the organization.

There are several industry-wide implementation methodologies available in the market such as Six Sigma. Some firms study these methodologies and come up with their own version of implementation methodology that can fit their needs. Regardless of which methodology is selected, firms need to make sure it has the following characteristics to be effective in LAVC projects:

- Scalable methodology, which means it has a well-defined work breakdown structure with a clear description of the high-level phases, milestones, activities, and deliverables required by all projects
- Providing templates and best-practice examples for the required deliverables
- Adopting a value-driven and quick delivery approach for implementation
- Providing a template for capturing ROI and monitoring metrics and KPIs
- Training and education on the methodology should be available
- Predefined check points along the duration of the project for compliance
- Simple and easy to use
- Built around the idea of continuous improvement
- Managing people change management, scope, and quality of work effectively
- Ability to support implementing new technology activities, deliverables, and milestones if the transformation program requires a technology upgrade

Phase 1: As-is Process and Pain Points

This phase is to analyze where the organization stands today in terms of processes under project consideration; often referred to as the starting point.

From our experience, organizations are more willing to spend time and resources on where they want to be, rather than explore where they are today. However, without a complete understanding of where they are, it is unlikely that they will be able to get to where they want to be.

The people doing the job and subject matter experts who developed the existing process know best how it is being done. Their involvement in describing the current reality (as-is) is essential. The following questions can help in identifying the as-is process and determine the challenges (pain points):

- What are all the steps in the process today?
- What is important?
- What is measured?
- What skills are required to run the process effectively?
- Who are the key players?
- What is the reward system?

- What are the major pain points?
- What are the areas of improvement?

Process mapping is the most popular and successful technique used in developing a detailed description of the process. A process map is a workflow diagram to bring forth a clearer understanding of a process and illustrate each step in the process. It can also include duration of every step, boundaries, required resources, and cost elements.

Mapping the process helps the transformation team to identify aspects or sources of inefficiency and areas of improvement in the process.

Phase 2: Root-Cause Analysis, To-Be Process, and Gap Analysis

This phase is to determine where we want to be. We should begin with finding the root causes of the pain points that were identified in the previous phase. This will help in developing a to-be process, which should address these pain points and streamline the process.

Root-cause analysis helps uncover the real reasons for the problem that might lie underneath pain points and complaints. From our experiences, asking "why?" at least three times will provide a good chance of finding the root cause.

The gap analysis provides the foundation for the list of solution requirements. It is necessary to realistically assess the gap between where the organization wants to be and where the organization is currently. This analysis must consider all of the following critical elements for a successful transformation program: (1) strategic alignment, (2) structural support, (3) cultural support, (4) resources support, and (5) technology support.

Establishing a set of KPIs and capturing the baselines need to be done before implementing the solution and should be based on expected improvements. For example, if the objective of this project is to improve on-time delivery, related KPIs to on-time delivery should be captured and tracked.

The set of KPIs should measure the effect on customers and the bottom line, so that it is easy to link it back to the ROI model at the program level that we covered before. Every KPI should have a baseline and a target.

LAVC principles and enablers (explained in chapter 1), and continuous improvement methodologies (explained in chapter 2) should be used in this step also.

Phase 3: Deploying the Solution

Once the transformation project team has analyzed a process, identified the improvement to be made, and selected a target to the performance measure or KPI, they are ready to deploy the solution.

If a new technology is going to be implemented, a close consideration is needed to what existing functionality can be configured and leveraged versus customized. Customization (writing a special code to fulfill a certain functional requirement) is expensive and a nightmare for ongoing maintenance. The authors recommend the following two rules of thumb to address this issue:

- The new software application that is selected should cover a majority (more than 70 percent) of the functional requirements. Technology is following the process in this context. Few exceptions can apply here—like a process so unique that there is no software application that can support it without a major customization.
- The rest of the functional requirements (less than 30 percent) should be questioned whether they actually support a core competency subprocess or activity. If not, an out-of-the-box functionality alternative might be good enough to satisfy it without customization. Process is following the technology in this context. This rationalization should be done in a structured manner with a good representation from the stakeholders and senior management. The last thing a sponsor wants to see is for the program to run over budget because a senior manager was not present to make the hard decision on customization.

One significant challenge for transformation projects that span across different organizations is the willingness of partners to share information and use the new process. Conducting a small-scale pilot can help in addressing the challenge by demonstrating the value of the project and building trust toward the process involved in the improvement initiative.

Partners and stakeholders, during the pilot phase, can see how to make the project work to their advantage, so the project becomes a win-win situation. Conducting a pilot, if done correctly, inspires confidence and makes full implementation easier and smoother.

Phase 4: Anchoring the New or Improved Process in the Culture (Sustaining Phase)

Although the sustaining phase is the most difficult phase in any project transformation, there is relatively little research concerning sustaining change in organizations. While planning and implementing a change (new process) can occur relatively quickly, sustaining change involves a long period of time. Maintaining a sense of urgency and a significant level of interest is difficult over time. This phase can take months or years.

Once positive change occurs and a successful process improvement project (short-term win) is accomplished, management must work to make it part of the organizational culture. The new process must be reinforced by the policies for recruiting, selecting, promoting, compensating, evaluating, and training. The importance of organizational culture support for change efforts cannot be emphasized enough.

Acknowledging and rewarding stakeholders for new behaviors is essential to stabilize the new process and anchor the new culture, because using new skills involves risk (of failure), and acknowledging and rewarding those who use the new skills encourages others to do the same.

Senior management typically underestimates the amount of resources required for the "sustain" phase. The authors suggest a separate budget for this phase to bring attention to it.

System Maintenance

Although companies acknowledge the importance of ongoing operational management and support, few of them think ahead of time and allocate the right resources for it. Once the new processes and systems are in place, companies find themselves with an urgent need to manage the ongoing maintenance. Ongoing monitoring and maintenance is necessary, for example, to ensure 100 percent uptime and compliance. The lack of a defined and clear plan for maintenance might negatively impact the entire transformation program.

The ongoing maintenance process should include adding new value chain organizations and removing existing ones as necessary. It includes ongoing training programs and process compliance by monitoring related metrics. It also includes the identification of all user groups and the processes of adding new users, changing user authorization levels, profile maintenance, and user deletion. In addition, contingency plans should be reviewed periodically to make sure of its readiness. Contingency plans represent predefined courses of action to be followed in case of the occurrence of a drastic event, for example, when the sources for inbound information go down.

UPDATING THE PERFORMANCE MANAGEMENT SYSTEM

Establishing a performance management system (PMS), which supports a consistent metrics tracking and publishing process, is a prerequisite to this step. It should also be completed before implementing the transformation program (Chapter 8 discusses establishing a PMS in detail).

This step is responsible for updating the PMS to reflect the new performance baselines, and anchor the new culture after executing a certain transformation program by coming up with new performance measures, modifying existing ones, or establishing owners to the performance measures. Measuring the benefits and ROI should begin during and after the implementation of the transformation program.

Since the PMS depends mainly on monitoring the metrics, it is critical to spend enough time on defining these metrics. The PMS should manage and coordinate the development of the metrics. In their article on the topic of performance measurements in the *Journal of Operations Management*, Melnyk, Stewart, and Swink[3] highlighted that metrics provide the following three basic functions:

- Control: Metrics enable managers to evaluate and control the performance of the processes
- Communication: Metrics communicate performance to internal and external stakeholders
- Improvement: Metrics identify gaps (between actual performance and expectation) that ideally point the way for intervention and improvement

Establishing the appropriate performance metrics and incentives/compensation are critical to reflect the vision and objectives of the transformation program, and to reward the behaviors that help in anchoring the new culture of improvement.

For example, improving forecast accuracy that is mainly entered by the salespeople in a certain organization can be achieved by adding this performance measure (forecast accuracy) as one of the parameters in a sales bonus. This would align sales goals with program targets because sales will be motivated to provide an accurate forecast to meet their bonus target, which means the old behaviors of overestimating to make sure enough inventory exists when sales occur or underestimating to lower the bar of their quota will disappear.

REFERENCES

1. Sabri, E., A. Gupta, and M. Beitler. 2006. *Purchase Order Management Best Practices: Process, Technology, and Change Management*. Fort Lauderdale, FL: J. Ross Publishing.
2. Sabri, E., and A. Rehman. 2004. "ROI model for procurement order management process, 1–24. "In Proceedings of Lean Management Solutions Conference." Los Angeles, CA: Institute of Industrial Engineers.
3. Melnyk, S. A., D. M. Stewart, and M. Swink. 2004. "Metrics and Performance Measurement in Operations Management: Dealing with the Metrics Maze." *Journal of Operations Management*, 22:209–221.

8

CHANGE MANAGEMENT SUPPORTED PROCESSES

INTRODUCTION

People-related change management supported processes are the foundation for any transformation program. When we speak about change processes here, don't confuse these *people* processes with the *operational* processes that we discussed in Parts I and II of this book. The majority of transformation initiatives fail because the human aspects are poorly addressed or altogether neglected.

Several transformation projects have failed at the beginning because of lack of preparation and familiarity of the life cycle of transformation. Other projects or programs started perfectly by conducting process analysis, identifying waste, developing a clear and concise plan for implementation, but failed later because of the resistance of the people which was beyond the control of the program manager or sponsor.

Typically, the failure does not happen suddenly, but you can feel it coming if you are an expert in this field. There are some indications that the project is not going anywhere, for example, the sponsor is struggling to find out what has gone wrong, the project loses steam, team members get assigned to different tasks that are supposedly more urgent, or the project suffers a serious halt, disappears from executives' radar and is eventually forgotten.

This chapter provides the foundation for effective people change management to avoid putting a transformation project in jeopardy (Figure 8.1).

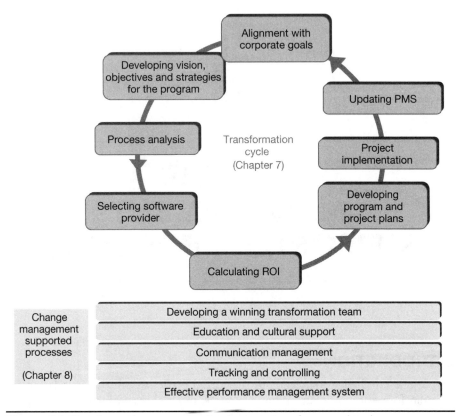

Figure 8.1 Transformation program implementation framework—change management supported processes

DEVELOPING A WINNING TRANSFORMATION TEAM

Overview

We believe that building the right transformation team is the most important change management support process in any program or project. In the process of building the team, the senior management must be sensitive to the unique needs of the program/project environment. Also, both the nature and number of team members change as the program/project moves through its life cycle.

The structure of the organization also plays a big role in selecting and building the transformation team. For example, if the organization follows a matrix organizational structure, there will be two managers for a team member: a project manager who supervises the day-to-day work of the team member and provides feedback to others, and a people manager who takes care of the people development aspects of the team member such as promotion, salary review, and career needs/interest. In this environment, the performance evaluation and incentive plan should be tailored to support this structure.

Building the most effective team optimizes the efforts of the team and increases the chances of having a successful program or project. On the other hand, a weak team structure would undercut the efforts of hard working team members, reduce morale, and impede a project's success.

This process is done by senior management including the sponsor who is responsible for the program. The project manager, after being selected, should have a say in selecting the rest of the team members and ensure that the team structure meets the requirements of the project.

The challenge of creating and developing a winning team in today's business environment is that every transformation program has its own nature and staffing requirements. For example, in a global transformation program, the characteristics of the program will include a significantly large project team size, very specialized skills, differing organizational goals and program cultures, wide experience requirements, and members scattered across the globe. Although there is no single recipe for success in selecting the transformation team, this section will provide the reader with guidelines and a framework to develop a winning team.

The first step of this process is to document the required skills for every role (functional consultant, process consultant, developer, architect, program manager, project manager, etc.) based on the program/project charter document. This also includes determining the number of resources needed for every role.

The second step is to match people to roles and the following factors should be considered:

- When the resources/roles are needed and for how long.
- Any special skills required over and above those roles (e.g., a proficiency in a certain language in a global project).
- Training requirements (e.g., on a new technology).
- Costing information and assumptions. For example, it might be possible to select or hire fewer but more experienced and more expensive resources and keep the cost the same. One good practice is to select a mix of experienced and fresh team members to balance the cost of the project and provide a good environment for knowledge transfer.
- Experienced resources with critical roles (e.g., architect or process consultant) might be shared across projects or programs. Involving these resources should be based on the need and the stage of the implementation (life cycle). For example, a process consultant is needed heavily at the beginning of the project during the process analysis or root-cause analysis phases.

Establishing a process to evaluate the performance of resources and define an incentive plan to keep them motivated is the last (third) step in selecting and building a winning transformation team. It includes team-building activities when appropriate. Some examples for team-building exercises include a kickoff meeting, site meetings, extended off-site meetings, team-behavior exercises, recognition events, and so forth. The three steps to building a successful team will be explained in greater detail in the following sections.

Defining Team Structure and Required Skills

It is necessary to have a team structure so that all the team members of the project, including the program/project manager, understand their roles and responsibilities. The team structure also includes the relationships of the resources managing and working on the transformation project.

The following considerations are important in defining the team structure: (1) the objective of the project, (2) the nature of work required, (3) the project charter, and (4) roles that are known to be expensive and/or in short supply.

The output of this step is a list of required roles for the project transformation. This list includes a description for every role highlighting typical activities and responsibilities; number of resources needed per role, and required skills for each role. For example, some of the required skills for a project manager are as follows: strong motivator, self-discipline, coaching experience, excellent communication skills, conflict resolution skills, experience in diversified culture (critical for global programs), delegation, team development skills, ability to establish measurable goals and metrics, ability to synchronize project activities, foster ownership of tasks effectively, lead by example, collaborate effectively with other program/ project managers or organizations, and ability to review the current distribution of work and use of resources and consideration of alternatives.

The list of roles needed for the project is typically used by recruiters and resource managers to obtain resources from appropriate sourcing organizations. Table 8.1 is an actual example of a transformation team structure that was responsible for streamlining a procurement process by implementing a new software application.

Finding and Matching Resources to Roles (Staffing Plan)

This step focuses on finding and selecting the right resources, either internal or external to the firm, who have the required skills to perform the needed roles. The objective of this step is to identify the right resources with the required skills that are available for the needed duration within the allocated budget.

The recruitment manager, project manager, and/or sponsor review each candidate's resume and compare it with the required skills for the role (determining candidates' skill levels based on their resumes and performing gap analysis). Constraints (e.g., if an internal employee only should be considered for a project manager role) should be considered at this time. Previous experience, soft skills, personal style and characteristics, availability, and cost should also be considered. Once the candidates are shortlisted and an experienced interview team is formed, an interview is then conducted. If the candidate is selected, planning for hiring and training should be done for the newly selected resource.

Establishing an Incentive and Motivation Program

This step consists of setting the performance expectations for the team, putting a process in place to assess the performance of the project manager and team members, and providing a framework to enhance the performance to keep the team motivated.

Setting performance expectations and individual objectives should be based on project or program objectives. Individual objectives should be measurable and can include a milestone on-time achievement, quality of work, teamwork, and project manager or sponsor satisfaction.

Assessing the performance of team members is the responsibility of the project manager based on achieving the individual objectives leveraging the individual status report and personal observation. Assessing the performance of the project manager is the responsibility of the program manager. Also, the sponsor would assess the performance of the program manager based on meeting the program objectives, leveraging the program status report, and personal observation.

Other factors that could be considered in this assessment are: (1) innovative ideas, (2) ability to work as part of a team, (3) gaining respect of the team and sponsor, (4) amount of supervision (hand-holding) needed, and (5) ability to ramp up quickly.

Based on the authors' experiences, the program manager and sponsor need to leverage a framework to enhance performance and keep momentum going. This framework consists of the following:

- Communicate clearly the program and individual objectives and expectations in addition to roles, responsibilities, and accountabilities.
- Communicate the value that the customer would gain from the program/ project. This strengthens the sense of purpose and provides motivation to the team.
- Encourage the following team characteristics: trust and mutual respect, creative thinking, a free flow of information, ability to rally around the purpose and vision of the project or program, flexibility to help every team member reach their potential, and adaptability so that the team members can see change as an opportunity to learn and improve. This will help the team to move forward as one unit in harmony.

Table 8.1 Key roles, descriptions, and tasks for a transformation team

	Key responsibilities	Key tasks and deliverables
Sponsor	• Providing executive-level support when needed • Providing oversight and governance to the project • Ensuring obstacles and issues are addressed in a timely manner	• Review the project charter/definition • Review actual costs versus budget estimate • Review the project deliverables and recommendations • Attend monthly status meetings • Approve the program plan (a set of several project plans related to each other)
Project manager	• Understanding customer priorities and managing project scope, budget, and timeline • Project planning • Coordination of resources and activities • Resolution of technical or personal issues	• Review and refine all deliverables • Lead project plan meetings • Facilitate status meetings with sponsor or stakeholders • Provide project status report on a regular basis • Project resource and cost estimates • Understand team roles and responsibilities
Process consultant	• Understanding value opportunities • Ensuring optimal value of implementing the new process	• Identify business processes and metrics to be improved • Document as-is process and define to-be process • Get detailed business requirements and develop functional requirements
Overall architect	• Responsible for the overall design and quality of the solution	• Get functional requirements and identify solution scope and objectives • Manage all activities relating to the definition, development, and implementation of the future state of solutions (a solution is a combination of a new/improved process and a software application) • Solution design document
Change agent	• Managing all activities relating to aligning organization, policies, and metrics to new business processes	• Develop and execute education plan • Tailor the communication plan • Assess organizational change readiness • Facilitate solution training • Facilitate software application transition to IT support organization • Develop the user manual

Subject matter experts	• Providing insights for major challenges in the as-is process and the best way to address these challenges	• Assist in defining process requirements, and participate in validating the usability of solution
Modeling consultants	• Helping in the activities relating to development and implementation of the future technology architecture	• Participate in requirements gathering, creating the software application models, developing demo scripts, and delivering demos • Configure solution per agreed upon functional requirements • Develop functional test plans • Test the solution using the test plans
Integration consultants	• Helping in the activities relating to integration and data requirements	• Develop integration adapters • Develop integration test plans • Test the integration adapters using the test plans
IT support representative	• Responsible for defining IT policies and standards, system and database administration guidelines, application maintenance procedures, system usage, and contingency plans	• Provide systems and data support as necessary

- Encourage two-way communication and listen to project or personal issues in addition to informal communications, and invest to improve team cohesiveness.
- Design a process for reviewing and responding to ideas, suggestions, concerns, questions, and perceptions from all team members.
- Create an identity (name) of the team based on the purpose of the program, work environment, and situation, or the nature of the transformation team. For example, if the timeline is aggressive but achievable, since most of the team members are experts in their field, this would be the identity or the spirit of the team. *Team of excellence* or *achievers* could be the identity or the name of the team.
- Strengthen the sense of team identity for all team members by creating a team name and leveraging off-site meetings, team reward events, and other team events.
- Establish leadership for the team. It's recommended for the sponsor to establish authority and support leadership. The project manager on the other hand needs to establish problem-solving, conflict resolution, and leadership coordination. Someone from the transformation team should establish thought or guidance leadership. This person can be internal or external to the organization. Typical roles for this type of leadership are architect, process consultant, or change agent.
- Design and implement performance review processes and provide means of self-monitoring for individual performance. For example, providing the team member on a regular basis with a subjective evaluation of his/her performance, and how the team member is progressing toward the measurable individual objectives. This will take time from the project manager or sponsor but it's worth it because "what gets measured gets improved."
- Design incentive compensation to recognize good performance, and decide on the incentives (to increase job satisfaction) for the team, such as a team trip to Las Vegas if they go-live on time, or taking the team to dinner or having a party. Also, individual incentives should be planned and tailored based on the individual and role, for example, a promotion, bonus, flat-panel TV, and so forth.

EDUCATION AND CULTURE SUPPORT

Overview

Any program transformation requires organizational culture support. Organizational culture by its very nature refuses to accept change, but over time and with education and upper management enforcement, organizational culture does change.

For example, an organizational culture that formerly supported low cost and mass production will, at the beginning, resist the move to a mass customization environment which requires drastic changes for activities, layout, and structure for the business that is involved in this shift.

Structural changes can come in different forms, but will invariably affect organizational culture. Changes in decision-making authority are typically resisted by cultures that reward the old behaviors and punish the new ones.[1]

Therefore, the education plan should address this issue and the reward/incentive system should be reviewed to ensure that the desired new behaviors are reinforced. Also, structural changes between individuals and teams have psychological and social affects that must be considered. Failure to diagnose and plan for resistance to these changes will lead to problems when trying to implement the transformation program.

The authors have seen several programs or projects that were driven by a date instead of a value achieved. In an attempt to meet the date (often unrealistic) target, training, documentation, and change management are often neglected, resulting in something that has a short life span or that does not deliver the full benefit. Other projects have gone live but have not been well accepted or embraced by end users.

The education and cultural support processes should address all human process interventions, which include:

1. Team building
   • Team building exercises should be considered for new and existing teams.
2. Conflict management
   • Conflict must be managed if the transformation program is to be effectively implemented and sustained.
   • Conflict management interventions should be used whenever conflict is being inappropriately handled. We don't want to eliminate conflict. Different viewpoints and different ways of doing things (diversity) are what give effective teams their strength.[1]
3. Leadership development
   • Leadership development is essential if some of the individuals who will be responsible for the program have little or no leadership experience. The education program should be tailored to help the individuals acquire these skills.
4. Training and skills acquisition
   • Value chain transformation programs require training, new skills, and attitudes for the users of the new or improved processes, as well as for the leaders of the transformation program. The proper allocation and commitment of resources (time, energy, and money) to conduct training and help employees in their skills acquisition is critical to the success of changes.

Learning Methods

Learning can come through a variety of means such as instructor-led classroom training, instructor-led web-based training, self-directed learning, and one-on-one coaching.

The instructor-led training is appropriate and highly efficient and effective when there are large numbers of trainees, a need for declarative knowledge, traveling is not a big issue, and a small amount of training time is available. This training is conducted by simply getting the stakeholders (employees, suppliers, and customers) in a room and providing the instructor with all the resources necessary to facilitate learning.

When getting stakeholders in one room becomes an issue because of cost or the global nature of the program, instructor-led web-based training should be considered. Special material and resources will be needed to support this type of learning.

When instructor-led training (room or web-based) is impractical or inappropriate, other methods of learning should be considered, such as self-directed learning or one-on-one coaching.

Self-directed learning facilitates the learning for a wide variety of stakeholders with different levels of knowledge and different learning speeds. This method typically involves providing stakeholders with books, manuals, workbooks, CDs, and/or videos, and it can include technology to facilitate information sharing.

One-on-one coaching is typically appropriate after an official training in which basic knowledge is acquired. Coaching can be provided on the job by a supervisor, peer, or consultant. This method is useful and needed if traditional training does not transfer well to the real-world job.

Knowledge Management

Every organization must be able to acquire, capture, and transfer knowledge. The "learning organization" concept has become more important than ever because of the 21st century emphasis on knowledge-driven organizations. Learning organization facilitates the learning of all its members and continually improves itself. The characteristics of a learning organization are:

1. Developing collective and individual learning plans
2. Leveraging lessons learned from previous experiences to produce better results
3. Engaging actively with external organizations, especially universities, research consulting firms, and industry
4. Adopting continuous improvement as a way of life

Knowledge management includes a range of practices, insights, lessons learned, and experiences that comprise knowledge.

Knowledge management can help individuals and groups to share valuable insights, reduce redundant work (avoid reinventing the wheel by starting from scratch), reduce training time for new employees, and adapt quickly to a changing and dynamic business.

Many large firms and nonprofit organizations have resources dedicated to establishing an internal knowledge management system to store and transfer knowledge across all departments and functions.

Hidden knowledge, that is "stored" in the minds of a highly experienced practitioner, is difficult to capture. One effective method to document hidden knowledge is arranging knowledge sessions for a group of practitioners who meet to discuss their experiences. The members share problems, challenges, frustrations, new ideas, encouragement, and support. Upper management should encourage and nurture these sessions.

How to Handle Downsizing?

One of the issues that this process should handle is educating employees on the impact of the transformation program related to restructuring and downsizing. It is necessary to look at the structural support for the change or program. If the foundation structure is deemed to be inadequate, restructuring becomes necessary. Restructuring interventions range in degree from minor adjustments to large-scale organization-wide changes that affect virtually every member of the organization.

Questioning the basic assumptions about how the firm does business can be deeply disturbing to an individual's sense of security. Managers, project leaders, and consultants must become familiar with the psychosocial aspects of change. Anytime a program involves downsizing (which is not always the case), it is especially disturbing for all workers. Downsizing involves early retirements, attrition, redeployment, and/or layoffs. The ultimate result of fewer people is typically upsetting to both terminated employees and those that survive.

Motivating remaining employees in the post-downsized organization should be part of an upper management task list and education plan. Surviving employees of downsizing will question the necessity of the downsizing, the criteria used for termination, and caretaking.[1]

Change Leaders Versus Change Agents

The education (change management) plan should allow a project manager to get help when needed. Often, during implementation, the transformation team runs into barriers. Typically, they do not recognize that the barrier is something that they cannot overcome. This results in wasted time and money. The plan needs to identify risks and develop mitigating steps. Also included in the plans must be well-defined criteria as to when to seek additional help upon encountering a barrier.

An effective education plan should also consider gaining and keeping strong executive sponsorship. Without executives' buy-in and support, a transformation program will be much closer to failure than success. It should also involve all value chain partners in the program, and establish benefit sharing and an incentive mechanism.

Leading the way is ultimately the responsibility of the senior upper management. These executives, which includes the sponsor, should be effective change leaders in addition to being managers. The involvement of organizational leaders cannot be overemphasized. Leaders must be visible during the planning, implementing, and sustaining the transformation program. If the leaders are not visible, organizational members assume the change is not important. And once the change effort stalls, it's difficult to get it moving forward again. Therefore, leaders must be visible.

While the planning phase of the project is critical, typically the implementing and sustaining portions are considerably more difficult. Stakeholders (internal employees, suppliers, and customers) are sometimes calm and rational during the planning portion. But they might experience strong negative emotions during the implementing and sustaining portions of the project. Therefore, senior management and sponsor must be change leaders and familiar with the psychological, sociological, cultural, educational, and political issues involved in implementing and sustaining change. Lack of knowledge of these issues can be very costly to the organization. Independent change agents can help in this area. A change agent is a catalyst who can enable and facilitate change.

Leading change is best accomplished by using a path-goal leadership approach. Path-goal leadership starts with a highly collaborative change planning process involving leaders and the transformation team. The "path" becomes the focus after a collaboratively developed change plan is completed. The job of the leaders during the implementation phase is to clear the *path* so that the transformation team can accomplish the *goal*.[1]

Leaders, in addition to being visible, should also establish a sense of urgency. To get the attention and commitment of the organizational managers, the leaders (senior upper management) and sponsor must convince the managers of the importance—the urgency—for the change.

Raising the urgency level involves senior management responding, with the guidance of an independent change agent if needed, to each of the sources of anxiety. They must also immediately confront rumors and provide inspiration for their teams.

Change agents help the sponsor overcome resistance while facilitating transformation program activities and sustaining gains. Successful change agents find ways to communicate the need for change, instill the sense of urgency, and clarify the value of changing versus not changing.

Change agents, by training or natural ability, are able to see the big picture from an outsider's perspective and identify opportunities and benefits of change. They can also sell it to business owners to get their commitments to implement changes that can achieve agreed-upon objectives.

Art of Handling the Life Cycle of Change

Individuals experience change differently. Each individual experiences different intellectual and emotional responses. There may be withdrawal, denial, and a feeling of helplessness that will take time for individuals to work through. There is, of course, a lot of room for individual variation when it comes to change.

Change response can be divided into three phases: (1) resistance, (2) acceptance, and (3) breakthrough. It is important to mention that not all individuals/organizations go through each phase; the phases may be different, and the length of time for each phase will vary since people accept change at different speeds.

Phase 1: Resistance

The initial response to change is varying degrees of resistance and denial. We often see the resistance in various types of negative behaviors like becoming defensive, angry, confused, or disoriented. Typically, resistance is followed by denial. Some individuals start to act defensively almost immediately, avoiding all aspects of the change. Productivity declines as individuals waste energy and time discussing the impending change, which distracts them from their work.

The root cause of resistance can be due to: (1) not understanding the change (resistance occurs when people don't get the change); (2) fear (fear of losing one's job, power, or control); and (3) lack of trust in the transformation team or sponsoring organization.

Therefore, the sponsor and program manager should not ignore the feeling of fear from stakeholders that may be the root cause of the resistance, because only if they understand the cause and acknowledge it will they be able to respond to it.

During this phase, the sponsor and program manager must provide opportunities for impacted individuals to feel more in control of what is happening. This is the time to get them involved in planning—as stakeholders. Because change that is imposed is often resisted, implanting a sense of ownership is essential to overcome obstacles. Change should be embraced rather than enforced.

Also, senior management must start communicating to the stakeholders how they will be affected by the change and why the change is necessary by communicating the benefits of it to the organization. An informed stakeholder has a greater sense of control and a greater sense of control leads to less resistance to the change.

Five types of fear of loss must be understood because this could give upper management and the sponsor valuable insight into why individuals and groups are resisting during the implementation:[1]

1. Security: Loss of security in the form of possible job loss will be fought against with every possible tactic.
2. Competency: It is the very essence of professional satisfaction. Anytime we ask an individual to exchange their current set of skills for a new one, we are asking that individual to endure a period of incompetence. Therefore, providing training and support to make that period as short as possible is essential.
3. Relationships: Human beings are social creatures. Thus, the possibility of losing a valuable relationship will be met with resistance.
4. Sense of purpose: It is another reason for professional satisfaction. For example, for an individual, being the go-to expert in a certain field is a reason for job satisfaction. If the reason for being for an individual in the organization is threatened, resistance to the proposed change will be the output.
5. Territory: Threats to the territory that one owns will be met with resistance. Parking spaces, offices with good views, and workspace are fiercely defended.

Phase 2: Acceptance

In this phase, stakeholders begin to accept (not necessarily like) the change. During this phase, they will be involved in performing the new process or using the new system. Before things get better, they get worse, in terms of productivity and job satisfaction.

The downturn in productivity will continue until users master the new process. It's crucial in this phase to plan for several training sessions for the users to achieve a faster learning curve and increase job satisfaction. During Phase 2, senior management must also reward early adopters (pioneers) and provide learning opportunities in as many forms as possible.

Some stakeholders, who were skeptics about the change and put up obstacles in the previous phase, can become your biggest champions.

Phase 3: Breakthrough

This is the phase of breakthrough performance growth. Breakthrough is only achieved after the users have obtained significant levels of confidence, security, and new skills.

During Phase 3, senior management and the sponsor must remain visible, measure improvement with appropriate metrics, and reward new behaviors.

Focus on the Pioneers

Change leaders and agents must anticipate resistance and be prepared to deal with various change adoption rates. From a change management perspective, it is important to focus on pioneers and early adopters first. These individuals who are a subset of the stakeholders' group are the most open to change; they are the first to embrace something new. Therefore, it is recommended to get these people onboard as quickly as possible.

It is not necessary to have 100 percent buy-in initially from all stakeholders. The 80–20 concept applies here where if you get buy-in from 20 percent of the stakeholders (initially), change becomes unstoppable, and the majority (80 percent) will soon follow. This percentage is based on who adopts first. For example, if senior managers and subject matter experts adopt first, lower numbers are sufficient and vice versa.

It is important to note here that the most serious resistance to change comes from senior management. Some senior managers might agree to the need to change and improve, but they might debate on how to do it. And when senior managers don't like or agree on a certain transformation program, everything stops until someone does something that can change their mindset and get them onboard.

To summarize, the people factor is the most important pillar for a successful transformation program. Experts might debate if the process should follow the technology, or the technology needs to follow the process, but no one can debate that the people (end users) should follow the new process and use the new technology that enables the process. Therefore, the sponsor and program manager should pay attention to the people because it is the individual who will make or break a transformation program. People should be excited, committed, and believe in the vision of the program.

The importance of social information—information that is gained from others through conversations, observations, and interactions—cannot be underestimated, since an employee might value views of a fellow coworker more than the views of top management. Hence, in conjunction with top-down official information, management should also stress bottom-up social information by communicating the importance of the change at the grass roots, especially to the employees who have the credibility and authority.

This will ensure that the change is adopted and not just imposed. Also, it is important to get the key players onboard who not only have the authority but also who their fellow colleagues find credible. The use of training, incentives, and rewards go a long way in reinforcing and sustaining the change.

COMMUNICATION MANAGEMENT

Overview

This section covers the generation and execution of the communication plan related to the transformation program participants and program stakeholders. A transformation program, typically, consists of several projects or initiatives.

Effective communication within the transformation team and between the team and other program stakeholders is essential for smooth and successful implementation. The journey (How did we get there? Was it a smooth ride?) is as important as the results (we got there) because it gives motivation and keeps the momentum going for another transformation program or process improvement (continuous improvement).

Effective communication provides a clear understanding of what is taking place, motivates the team members, avoids any miscommunication between team members, keeps upper management engaged and involved, reduces the risk of conflicts, and more importantly, keeps everyone informed, at a different degree, about the cost, schedule, and timeline of the program.

It's a common misconception that if people are talking to each other it means they are communicating. Communication needs to have a framework and format to be effective. Another common pitfall of communication is that people think if they send a message, the message should be received and acted upon, which is not true in most cases. The last common pitfall is that one communication plan template fits all programs or projects. While all program or projects share the need for a communication plan, they differ in the type of information needed, frequency, and methods of communication.

In the work entitled *Leading Change*, Kotter[2] offers the following suggestions for effectively communicating organizational change:

1. Simplicity
2. Metaphor, analogy, or example
3. Multiple forums
4. Repetition
5. Leadership by example
6. Explanation of seeming inconsistencies
7. Give-and-take

The responsibility for developing the communication plan and then monitoring its execution and effectiveness falls on the program or project manager's shoulders. Typically, most of the project manager's time is spent on communication and coordination within his/her team or externally with stakeholders and other organizations. The project manager should make sure that the communicated message is clear, concise, meaningful, targeted, and consistent.

Therefore, project managers should have the right skills when it comes to generating the correct communication plan that fits the special needs of a project or a program. They need to be effective communicators, selecting the right method (media) and format of communication in normal or urgent situations, and ensuring two-way communication to improve effectiveness. Successful communication requires trust and understanding of everyone's communication needs.

Also, conducting and orchestrating an effective meeting is another essential leadership skill for the project manager since meetings are the most used method of communication. Writing style, presentation techniques, conflict resolution, and time management are other soft communication skills that are highly recommended for a project manager to have.

In a global transformation program, program managers should be able to build and execute a communication plan across geographic, organizational, and cultural boundaries. With today's reality, having a single location (co-located) for all team members is not an option anymore. Teams are set in different locations, time, and organizational boundaries. Therefore, a physical meeting is not a practical method of communication anymore for a global program, and leveraging technology for remote meetings is a must.

An important fact that program managers should recognize is that as the number of stakeholders increases, the complexity of communication increases exponentially.

Developing the Program Communication Plan

The communication plan identifies meetings, reporting, methods, and format of communications that will occur with the core team, program sponsor, stakeholders, partners, IT, and internal and external organizations. In this book, we will consider all of the above individuals or departments as the stakeholders of the program or project. The plan should be comprehensive enough to satisfy the information needs of all of the stakeholders. It typically provides a description of what piece of information is needed, who needs it, why it is needed, when it is needed, how it is communicated, and by whom.

A program communication plan should incorporate all related project communication plans and maintain the link to and impact on each other to leverage information consolidation if possible. For example, one update on the program as a whole needs to be seamlessly communicated to the sponsor or vice president instead of several updates or meetings for every project. This provides efficiency and standardization.

That said, tactical objectives might vary per project based on the specific information need. For instance, a program might have five improvement projects with four of them internal while one is external. The external project is required to keep partners like suppliers informed about the progress of the project. This would require the project manager to set up an external web meeting to share a presentation or a demo, while this setup is not needed for the internal projects either because a physical meeting or an internal web meeting is already available. Therefore project communication may need to be tailored based on the needs and characteristics of the project. Table 8.2 provides a sample template for the communication plan.

The first step in the process of coming up with the communication plan is preparation. The program or project manager should review memos from the sponsor, the charter document which includes the scope and timeline, and other documents that talk about the information needs of the stakeholder constituencies involved in the project and communication frequency.

The second step is to determine the communication objectives for each stakeholder, based on the documentation review and interviews. This also needs to be documented. For example, one of the typical communication objectives of the project manager with his/her project team (core team) is to be proactive, and understand the concerns or issues the team members have related to the project or at the personal level by inviting them to a team-building exercise meeting. Another objective is to give the team an update about upper management support and recognition. These two objectives explain why, in some situations, communication should be two-way.

Reiterating the strategic project value to the stakeholders, and getting informed on the major issues that need the sponsor's attention and involvement to resolve are good examples for the objectives of program-sponsor two-way communication.

The third step is to determine the information that should be provided to achieve the communication objectives of every stakeholder. This should help the project manager to categorize (segment) stakeholders into several groups.

The fourth step determines the sources for the information. It's important to maintain a list of all of the sources and establish a mechanism to gather the data.

In the fifth step, the method and format of communication for every stakeholder group should be determined after considering and analyzing the different available communication methods.

The system used in information retrieval and archiving is determined in the sixth step. Some examples for retrieval and archiving systems would be manual filing systems or databases.

The seventh step (last step) is to document the communications plan based on the above information and send it for approval by the sponsor and management. This document should also adhere to the documentation control procedures published by the company.

It is recommended to review the communication plan (after approval) on a regular basis throughout the program or project to find out if there is room for improvement based on feedback from the stakeholders. If there is a need to

Table 8.2 Sample template for the communication plan

Audience (target)	Key objectives	Format	Method	Frequency	Facilitator (owner)
Steering committee/ upper management	1. Maintain executive support 2. Provide next steps	Presentation	Face-to-face (physical) meeting	Monthly and at milestone completion	Sponsor/program manager
Sponsor	3. Maintain sponsor support 4. Resolve major issues 5. Monitor progress versus plan	Program progress status report	Face-to-face (physical) meeting	Bi-weekly, at milestone completion, and as needed	Program manager
Transformation team (including core stakeholders)	1. Gather update on tasks 2. Monitor progress versus plan	Program plan document	Face-to-face meeting and conference call for remote resources	Weekly	Program manager
Core project team	1. Monitor progress versus plan 2. Resolve technical or project issues	Project plan document	Conference call	Bi-daily	Project manager
All stakeholders	1. Provide update on accomplishments 2. Keep stakeholders engaged	Stakeholders progress update report	Internal website, e-mail, and newsletter	Quarterly	Program manager

change the plan, a reapproval will be required, and publishing the changes to all stakeholders is a must.

Communication Methods

There are several communication methods that the project manager can choose from based on the information requirements that need to be delivered. Thanks to technology, the number of methods has exploded exponentially. Some examples are:

- Physical meeting
- Mail
- Phone conversation
- E-mail
- Conference call (audio conference)
- Video conference
- Internal website
- Secured and shared electronic folder for all electronic documents (project related)
- Online meetings (web meetings)

The format of communication can vary significantly from a quick meeting, to extended meetings, to a five-day workshop. The format, in some situations, is dictated or limited by the selected communication method. For example, if phone conversation is selected, format will be limited to word of mouth and no document can be shared unless phone is combined with e-mail as a complementary communication method by sending the document ahead of time.

There are various factors that may influence selection of communication methods and formats:

- How immediate is the information needed?
- Is a face-to-face meeting needed?
- Is two-way communication needed (is interaction needed)?
- Is two-way, real-time communications needed?
  - If yes, internal website, mail, and e-mail will be out of consideration.
- Is there is a need to share a document?
- The reason for communication. (Is the communication needed to facilitate decision making or just update?) There are four typical reasons for communication or meetings:

1. Informational
2. Problem solving
3. Decision making
4. Hands-on (e.g., come up with a project plan, define the scope and deliverables for the program, etc.)

- Location of the stakeholders.
- Frequency of communication.
  - For example, if there is a need for a weekly meeting with stakeholders for a global transformation program that has players around the world, a physical meeting will be out of consideration. They can probably meet physically at the beginning of the program or once a quarter but definitely not every week.
- Familiarity of the project participants or stakeholders to communication methods.
  - If people in a company are familiar with the IBM Lotus Sametime tool for an online meeting, introducing a new tool for them might require some training or the need to download software to their computer.

Types of Communication

There are several types of communication: formal, informal, and as-needed basis (emergency). Formal communication is a well-structured type of communication that keeps everyone informed at a predefined frequency.

Informal communication provides insights or intelligence about the program that might otherwise go unnoticed. It typically uses face-to-face conversation as the method of communication, and the format can vary from hallway or kitchen conversations to an open-door policy where employees can stop by at a certain time.

Emergency communication is needed when unplanned events occur. For example, late software release delivery, a major issue that can threaten the timeline or continuation of the program/project, a new program sponsor, loss of a key program player, or bad news that cannot wait for the next planned communication cycle. It is true that no one, including stakeholders, like to receive "bad news," but often people hate it when they are not informed. Lack of timely information can lead to mistrust and rumors.

Face-to-face is the best communication method for emergency communication since questions can be answered immediately and misunderstandings can be avoided. But if face-to-face is not an option due to a geographic obstacle, a phone conversation is the second best method.

These three types of communication should be mentioned in the communications plan. In addition, the timing/frequency and mechanism of formal communication should be stated clearly in the plan. Some informal communication can also be mentioned.

Although the exact reason, method, and timing of an emergency communication cannot be mentioned ahead of time in the communication plan, a framework on how to handle this type of situation should be inserted.

Guidelines for Key Communications

This section contains general guidelines regarding successful communications and how to conduct effective meetings.

Communications with Project Team and Sponsor

Communications with the project team should focus on being on the same page by keeping the team informed and encouraging a continuous flow of communications within the program/project team, especially if the project team members are located in different places.

The program/project manager needs to communicate with the project team formally (face-to-face, over the phone, or online) on a regular basis (daily, weekly, every other week) to get an update on the project progress and status of every task in the project plan. In addition, other subjects can be discussed such as overall status of the program or project, specific problems, achieved milestones, and any changes to the team members or stakeholders.

The project manager can leave some time (5 or 10 minutes) at the end of the formal meeting to encourage two-way informal communication to discuss non project-related subjects that are of interest to the team. The authors found this time would help in strengthening the relationship between the team members and project manager, and inculcate a feeling of the "one team spirit."

Other methods to encourage informal communication can be off-site lunches or dinners, and team-building exercises where titles are not part of the picture. It would be a great idea to invite the sponsor to this type of activity to give the team members some face-to-face time and encourage an open and honest dialogue. This event should include all team members—internal employees and external consultants (contractors).

The program manager should focus on his/her communications with the sponsor on managing expectations and ensuring sponsor satisfaction with the progress. Regular communications should address any miscommunication or unstated and unrealistic expectations. This can be achieved through formal and informal communications. Also, remember perception is different than reality, and ongoing communication closes the gap between them.

Whenever miscommunication or dissatisfaction is detected, an emergency meeting should be scheduled and an open discussion should take place to calibrate and even reset expectations, if necessary.

Keeping the sponsor informed is crucial to the success of any project. Regular e-mail about project activities might be of interest to the sponsor. A weekly progress report and short meeting are other ways of keeping the sponsor engaged. What a project manager shares (level of details and type of issues) might vary significantly, based on the personality and preference of the sponsor and nature of the program transformation.

Most of the sponsors prefer formal communication with the project manager to be informed, or a progress report that includes a summary of accomplishments for the reporting period and planned accomplishments for the next period at the milestone and deliverables level, in addition to any major issues that introduce risks on the milestones.

The cost, effort, and schedule information also needs to be reported to the sponsor on the progress report. After sending the progress report to the sponsor, it is recommended for the project manager to schedule a meeting with the sponsor to go over the report. The frequency of the report and meeting should be captured in the communications project plan.

Emergency Communications Due to Major Problems

The project manager needs to first evaluate the need for an emergency communication based on the severity of the problem and the urgency surrounding it. The problem should not be underestimated or overestimated. Also, when it's communicated, it should not be overstated or understated. While communicating the problem, an open and honest discussion should be encouraged. The project manager should follow these best practices before communicating the problem to the team, sponsor, or stakeholders:

- Determine the full impact of the problem and consequences.
- Determine who should receive the communication (primary audience).
- Determine who should be copied on the communication (secondary audience).
- Determine the best person/people to communicate the problem to. The project manager could delegate the delivery to someone else if necessary, but he/she needs to be present to provide an explanation.
- Determine the best method of communication.

Meetings

Meetings are the project manager's major method for communicating with the team members, sponsor, and stakeholders, and consume the majority of his/her time. Therefore, we will focus in this subsection on the best way to conduct a meeting. There are four major reasons for a meeting based on the reason for communication: (1) informational meetings, (2) problem-solving meetings, (3) decision-making meetings, and (4) hands-on meetings.

Informational (update) meetings are conducted to keep everyone informed and on the same page. A weekly project plan update meeting is an example of an informational meeting. The kickoff meeting is another example where it is held at the beginning of the program or project for all team members and key stakeholders to share a clear understanding of the project.

The main objective of problem-solving meetings is to explore solutions and/or alternatives to problems facing the program or project. Decision-making meetings are conducted to come up with a decision on a certain issue, design, strategy, budget, or direction.

The hands-on meetings are used with a project deliverable that needs a lot of discussion and debate and requires the attention and attendance of several players. Examples of when a hands-on meeting might be necessary include coming up with business requirements, an as-is process, a to-be process, developing a detailed project plan, use cases, and so forth.

To conduct an efficient and effective meeting, several guidelines must be followed:

1. Decide on the purpose and audience of the meeting after reviewing the communications plan to determine the meeting intent and participation.
2. If disputes are expected between certain executive stakeholders, it's safer for the project manager to hold multiple meetings.
3. Send out the agenda, related material, and the purpose of the meeting to the audience who should attend the meeting ahead of time.
4. Carefully consider the size of the meeting room if it's a physical meeting.
5. Introduce all of the participants if they don't know each other.
6. Establish the meeting rules and logistics.
7. Assign a facilitator, scribe, and decision makers.
8. State the purpose of the meeting from the beginning and all related information. Obtain an agreement on the agenda from the audience to secure their involvement and commitment.
9. Summarize after finishing one agenda item.
10. During the meeting, follow the agenda, and allow enough time to go over the action items from the previous meeting.
11. Encourage participation, but when time is running out on a certain topic, ask participant permission to put it on the parking lot (issues log) and move to the next agenda item. Keeping the conversation relevant is crucial for finishing on time.
12. Document the minutes, action items, parking lot issues, and decisions that have been taken in the meeting, if any.
13. Before closing, review decisions, actions, and issues raised during the meeting, and assign an owner for every action or issue raised with a completion or follow-up date.
14. Finally, publish it in the same day if possible.

Program and Project Status Reports

Program and project status reports are two key communications reporting forms. A program status report is aggregated data from individual status reports from the projects that belong to one program. A program status report extracts the milestones and deliverables of each project and maintains dependency. Program and project status reports are typically scheduled to be provided on a predefined, periodic basis, such as weekly, biweekly or monthly based on the communications plan. Most of the content of these reports is generic; however, additional content might be needed for specific stakeholders or a special program or project. The following main content items are typical of a one-page management summary (see Figure 8.2 for a sample):

- Achievements since the last reporting period.
- Expected accomplishments for the next reporting period.
- Achievements planned but not completed during the reporting period. Include an explanation of why the work unit or milestone was not completed and the impact to the subproject and/or project.
- Financial status that includes budgeted and actual cost to date.
- Overall position against schedule and its impact on the forecasted completion date. Use effort and schedule variances and trend analysis to project the completion date for the project.
- Issue status, recommended resolutions, risks, and risk mitigation plans.
- List of change requests and their statuses.
- Overall project status. The overall program status rating is done by summarizing the overall status of related projects. Typically, the overall status is given one of the three colors:
  - Green, if the program or project is under control.
  - Yellow, if the project needs some changes in the plans to bring cost, resources, and/or the schedule back on track and under control.
  - Red, if the project has serious problems and drastic changes are unavoidable.
- Individual cost, resources, and schedule statuses are tracked and reported by some project managers.
- The following should not be part of the report:
  - Technical issues for which the project team is responsible and can solve.
  - Reporting something that sponsor or upper management might not be interested in reading, for example, reporting at a very detailed level instead of reporting at the level of milestones and major deliverables.
  - Reporting issues without corrective or resolution plans.

Project Status Report (sample)

A. General information

Project title: _____

Prepared by: _____

Reporting period   *From:*   *To:*

B. Current period activity status

-

C. Significant accomplishments for current period

-

D. Planned activities for next period

-

E. Non-technical project issues

Resources:
- None

Project goals or scope:
-

Project schedule
-

Project cost:
-

Figure 8.2 Sample of a project status report

F. Technical project issues

G. Action items

    1.

H. Risk status

Schedule:
Resource:
Cost:

I. Overall project status

GREEN
YELLOW
RED

J. Status meeting notes

Schedule:
Resource:
Cost:

Figure 8.2 Sample of a project status report (*continued*)

TRACKING AND CONTROLLING

Overview

The tracking and controlling process is crucial for a successful transformation program. It is the process of collecting and validating the schedule, resources effort, and cost of the project or program, analyzing if it is progressing according to the plan, and resolving issues to get implementation back on track or adjusting the project plan if needed to reflect the actual progress. It compares actual to estimates for schedule, effort, and cost (calculate variances), examines their impact on the total project, in terms of total effort, duration, and costs, and decides on needed actions. This process is an input to the progress status report that gets communicated to the sponsor and stakeholders.

Program or Project Tracking

This subprocess includes collecting resources effort, schedule progress, and costs data, examining their completeness and accuracy, comparing them to plan (estimates), and analyzing them. For project tracking, every task on the project can be monitored using the percentage complete. On the other hand, a milestone approach is better to be used for program tracking where only project milestones are tracked and dependency is maintained. Therefore, the schedule expected end date and total effort to complete cannot be determined unless progress is consistently tracked for all projects under the program. The tracking subprocess should be performed at frequent intervals, normally weekly.

To collect effort data, all time spent on tasks should be reported as part of the individual program report or part of the project plan meeting. If a team member has spent time on a task that was not in the project plan, like helping other team members, this task should be identified and added to the project plan. It is also necessary to encourage team members to improve the accuracy of their estimates.

Schedule progress can be tracked by collecting the percent complete or start/finish dates. To collect schedule progress data accurately (for tasks in progress), it is important to understand what work has been performed and what still has to be done.

Collecting costs data can be done by capturing purchase orders, invoices, and expense sheets. Cost-related data include costs for provided resources, travel and living expenses, supplier (software vendor or process consulting services) payments, hardware costs, software (license) costs, maintenance costs, training costs, and office space expenses. Costs data can be incurred one-time or an ongoing basis.

An examination step is important, especially for the program since tracking several projects under one program is not an easy job and sometimes tricky as data need to be analyzed in different ways, and dependencies need to be examined frequently to decide if there is a problem. Also, start and finish dates, or percent complete for all tasks should be examined for validity and consistency with the tracking period. Examining cost-related data is performed when a purchase order, invoice, or expense sheet is received, or periodically during the given period. Incorrect data can be attributed to incomplete data, incorrect allocation, wrong assumptions, or covering different reporting periods or cutoff dates. Data should be reconciliated and corrected if necessary. One traditional example: consulting costs are considered by the project manager when an invoice is received from the supplier (consulting company), while the accounts payable system records the cost when the payment is made to the supplier.

When comparing actual to estimates, it is important to validate with team members and provide a heads up to individuals or the team about actual and estimates to complete.

The purpose of the assessment is to compare the actual schedule, effort, and cost progress for the tasks with the amount that was planned in order to determine deviations. These deviations can be considered in terms of milestones, effort and duration, and related costs. So, tasks that are overrunning budget, effort, and duration along with missed milestones and dependencies can be highlighted. It's important to mention that a task or a project can be overrunning from an effort standpoint, but it's still on budget because cheaper resources are leveraged to do the tasks.

Analyzing variances (difference between actual and estimate) and finding the root causes are important to improve the accuracy of estimates, even if it has no impact on the schedule. For example, a task may have used more time (effort) than estimated because of a learning curve; but the task may still complete on time because the team member would have worked overtime. It is recommended in this step to utilize the following best practices:

- Analyze the trends and their impact on the overall project and project forecasts on a frequent basis and understand situational factors
- Analyze the causes for key variances first and then analyze the rest if time permits
- Focus on variances for tasks of the critical path and variances that have increased from the previous tracking period
- Determine if the root causes for variances are permanent or temporary and which ones can be mitigated and how

Program or Project Controlling

The purpose of this subprocess is to keep the program or project on track, in good financial health, and under control, in spite of variances, by performing continuous adjustments as the program or project moves forward. This includes resolving problems that are impeding progress, redistributing project tasks among the team members to rebalance the workload, and reassigning work. Also, obtain commitments to rework or finish as close to the original plan as possible. At the same time, ensure that the estimates to complete remain realistic and dependencies are not impacted. If impacts cannot be avoided, adjustments are needed.

This subprocess starts after the last step (analysis of plan deviations) in the tracking subprocess in which the root causes for deviations are identified, based on a good understanding of effort, schedule, and cost variances.

The controlling subprocess identifies responses to residual variances to get the project back on track, when needed, and to ensure that the plans remain realistic. It focuses on adjusting program or project plans in better preparation for the next period and implementing corrective actions. There exists a delicate balance between corrective actions, schedule, and costs since the corrective actions to improve the schedule may have a negative impact on costs, while corrective actions to reduce cost may extend the schedule. So it's important for the project manager to evaluate the trade-off before selecting the corrective action to put the project back on track. Some examples of the corrective actions to address cost deviations are:

- Reduce scope (business requirements)
- Reduce labor rates and/or hours
- Eliminate unnecessary tasks
- Reassign work to lower-cost staff

Some examples for corrective actions to address schedule-corrective actions are:

- Authorize overtime
- Add additional shifts
- Add more resources
- Resources development (improve skills of resources)
- Overlap tasks
- Outsource some of the work

EFFECTIVE PERFORMANCE MANAGEMENT SYSTEM
Performance Measurement Challenges

One of the most important foundation elements for effective change management is ongoing and effective performance measurement. Although measuring supply chain performance is not a new practice by any means, it remains a major challenge for most firms today for many reasons:

- The difficulty in identifying what to measure that will yield the most information and benefit for the least investment of time and resources can be due to the overwhelming number of choices.

- There is a need to measure the effectiveness of implementing new enablers like flexibility, in addition to traditional metrics performance measures that focus solely on operational metrics like throughput and utilization.
- There is a need to understand the trade-off and interrelation between metrics to come up with a comprehensive list. For example, an increase in the order fulfillment rate can be at the expense of inventory levels and cash cycle time.
- There is need for a structured process to conduct corrective action. Many firms have metrics in place that they measure, but no one takes any action based on the results. In this case, measurement can become a source of waste.
- Lack of a win-win principle between the firm and its partners when defining the metrics, which results in lack of confidence, ownership, and trust in the results.

Throughout our experiences over different industries, we haven't come across a single firm that believed that they have mastered performance measurement across all of their processes and levels—where managers are measuring, monitoring, and improving the right metrics and helping the company improve its performance and achieve its strategic goals.

The widespread feeling among managers is that they either measure too much or too little, or the wrong metrics. In an article on the topic, Michael Hammer[3] mentioned seven deadly sins (mistakes) of performance measurement:

1. Vanity is to use metrics that will inevitably make the organizations and its managers look good and get their bonuses. For example, firms often measure against what is called latest promise date (the final promise date to the customer), after several changes may have been made to the delivery schedule. Achieving good results on this metric does not lead to customer satisfaction since the customer is typically measuring actual performance with respect to the customer request date.

2. Provincialism is allowing organizations or departments to be measured only based on what they own or fully control, which results in suboptimization and conflict. For example, if the transportation group in a firm was measured mainly in terms of freight costs, this would lead the group to search out the best deals in shipping, even if this means that deliveries to the distribution center would sometimes be early and sometimes late.

3. Narcissism is defining metrics based on one's own point of view, rather than from the customer's perspective. For example, several companies measure on-time shipping in terms of individual components; if it shipped say, 9 of 10 components of a kit on time, it would give itself a 90 percent score. On the other hand, the customer would give the same shipment a score of 0 percent since the system cannot operate without having all 10 components together.

4. Laziness is defining metrics without giving it adequate thought or effort. Firms often jump to conclusions and measure what is easy to measure, or measure what they have always measured, rather than go through the effort of ascertaining what is important to measure.

5. Pettiness is defining a partial list of metrics that leads to measuring a small component of what matters. For example, a telecommunication firm rejected a proposal to allow customers to perform their own repairs because that would require placing spare parts at the customer sites, which would increase inventory levels/costs for service parts—a key metric for the firm. It lost sight of the fact that the total cost of maintenance will go down significantly with the new proposal, since the customer is doing the labor work which would offset the increase in the inventory costs.

6. Inanity is defining metrics without giving any thought to the implications of these metrics on employees' behavior and company performance. For example, the common practice of measuring warehouse inventory at the end of the month encourages warehouse managers to clear goods out (which would reduce or eliminate safety stocks) at the end of the month, and then quickly replace them at the beginning of the month, which would increase operation costs and create chaos.

7. Frivolity is not being serious about measurement in the first place. It is the most serious sin of all. You can recognize this sin when managers argue about metrics, find excuses for poor performance instead of tracking root causes, and blame others rather than combining the efforts to improve performance. This one is a sin of character and corporate culture, while the other sins are intellect shortcomings.

Lean and Agile Performance Management System

The performance management system (PMS) has evolved in the last two decades with the increase of software reporting applications and a huge volume of captured data. A new field of business analytics has been created that has replaced excel spreadsheet reporting with new analysis tools that slice and dice the data. But the challenge for executives is to interpret the data and be able to link them to the corporate strategy.

It is very seldom that you find a firm that doesn't have a tool or a process to capture the financial performance metrics of the firm at the corporate level, but you rarely find firms that capture key business metrics like customer satisfaction effectively.

PMS is the heart of any project and people change management. As the old saying goes, "what gets measured gets improved." PMS should be properly designed and implemented in order to facilitate transformation programs successfully. In the past, firms focused wrongly on performance appraisals rather than performance management. Two performance models shaped the PMS in the last decade: supply chain operations reference (SCOR), and balanced scorecard (BSC).

The SCOR model is the product of the Supply Chain Council (SCC). The SCC was established as a nonprofit consortium in 1996. SCOR talks about three levels of process detail (top level, configuration level, and process element level). The first level has five top-level process types: source, make, deliver, return, and plan. Although SCOR may not cover all the management functions (especially at the strategic level), it does a good job of defining process goals and metrics.

The BSC model was developed at Harvard in 1996 by Kaplan and Norton. Key performance indicators (KPIs) or metrics in this model are divided into four categories: (1) financial (revenue growth, cash flow, profitability, etc.); (2) customers (on-time delivery, customer satisfaction, reliability, etc.); (3) internal business processes (productivity, flexibility, waste reduction, etc.); and (4) innovation and learning (formal training, etc).

These metrics should be aligned with each other. For example, if the marketing strategy is to penetrate a new high-end market, a more rapid, new product introduction cycle from the internal business process perspective might be developed and linked to metrics of the innovation and learning category. Also, a profitability metric in the financial area would be tracked to measure the effectiveness of the marketing strategy. In addition, an order cycle metric from the customer perspective (which would help gain an edge on the other competitors) should be tracked and linked.

Recently, nonprofit organizations like schools also started to adopt the BSC model to improve the performance of their employees and volunteers, as shown in the Charter School success story in Chapter 10.

In this section, we will introduce a framework to establish PMS in the context of lean and agile transformation programs that can measure the progress of firms achieving lean and agile value chains (LAVCs), and address the challenges in the traditional PMS. Lean and agile performance management system (LAPMS) framework offers a structured way for firms to identify and address performance issues at various levels of the business, as well as across the value chain. It enables executives to effectively analyze the impact of improving individual processes on the overall performance of the value chain. It also enables corporate objectives and metrics to be propagated down to the operational level, and allows executives to determine their success, and how well strategic goals are aligned with tactical and operational goals.

LAPMS contains the right level of the right metrics and provides a structured approach to efficient performance measurement and continuous improvement. It highlights the most effective corrective action to take.

LAPMS framework is developed on the concept of measuring and tracking performance at every level of the business, using standards such as the SCOR model and BSC, and based on lean and agile principles. To ensure alignment, metrics are first applied at the strategic level of the business, and then propagated down through the tactical and operational levels.

After defining and tracking the performance measures and metrics at every level, more extensive and in-depth benchmarking and root-cause analysis should be undertaken. Traditionally, benchmarking has been done at the top level, but for LAPMS to work and for executives to create an ambitious, but achievable, transformation program, benchmarking should be conducted at every level.

Once specific process improvements that will support corporate objectives are defined as part of the transformation program, related metrics are tracked using dashboards and scorecards to ensure a continuous cycle of improvement. This will help in building the return on investment (ROI) (business case) for future transformation programs and anchoring the culture of measurement.

In the next sections, we will explain the major elements of LAPMS in more detail: (1) identifying and defining the metrics, (2) performance tracking and monitoring, and (3) triggering root-cause analysis, and (4) anchoring the culture of measurement.

Identifying and Defining the Metrics

Since it is not feasible to measure every activity, identifying a reasonable number of metrics or KPIs that have a direct linkage to the strategic objectives is the first thing that should be done.

Having hundreds of metrics in performance models such as SCOR can overwhelm executives and it may not apply to their own business situation. In LAPMS, we recommend firms to focus on the metrics that are directly related to achieving LAVCs in their business. We recommend managers focus on the handful of measures that are most critical.

Conducting this step requires people with the right combination of skills and expertise. These specialists, whom we like to call *strategists*, should be capable of understanding the situation of the business within its industry, the products and processes of chief competitors, and the key trends impacting the competitive landscape. They should be supply chain domain experts who are able to align specific operations initiatives to the company's overall goals.

These strategists must have in-depth process knowledge and a good understanding of best practices of others in the industry. Finally, they should be able to work with technology experts to bring improvements to life through enabling best-practice processes using technology. This section is a valuable resource for everyone who is in charge of defining these metrics. It is also a good resource for sponsors on what to expect from strategists.

If a company doesn't have full-time employees with the right strategist skills and doesn't have the luxury to train them, we recommend looking for consultants who bring specialized experience and expertise to the table. Because of what's at stake, having ineffective metrics is a recipe for failure for any program transformation.

In the process of identifying the correct metrics, a significant focus should be on end-to-end business processes rather than functions in addition to activities that create value to the customer consistent with LAVC principle 1 (focus on customer success). This helps in creating alignment and a common focus across disparate business units or functions. Also, ensuring that the right metrics are selected and aligned with the corporate goals and strategies is another key factor in the success of this process.

A metric must be well defined, so that there is no dispute about it. Otherwise, managers tend to interpret it in ways that work well for them, which might lead to conflict. For example, an on-time metric can be interpreted by the supplier to be an on-time ship date while the customer might interpret the same metric as an on-time receiving date.

In addition, a comprehensive set of metrics should be considered. Sometimes improvement in one area is achieved at the expense of another. For example, an increase of the fill rate might happen at the expense of reduction in inventory turnover.

Also, metrics should stress results instead of activities. For example, getting more detailed information about the status of a shop order in a factory is good, but unless this is translated to quantifiable financial or operational benefits like customer satisfaction or inventory reduction, this data might be a waste.

Finally, every metrics should have a target performance level based on benchmarking with other companies or based on the company's own goals.

Performance Tracking and Monitoring

Identifying what needs to be measured is just the first step; finding the right way to measure it and then tracking it is the next step. Measuring at regular intervals (e.g., weekly, monthly, quarterly, or annually) is useful to baseline the performance prior to a major transformation program (e.g., implementation of a new process or system) to get a clear picture of the impact of the change on performance.

Firms should think about sustaining the metrics tracking before selecting the method of measurement and consider the existing skill sets in the organization. Organizations need to avoid a complex mechanism for calculating a metric when a simpler one would be sufficient. Also, it's important to start simple so that everyone from the clerk to the CEO should be able to understand the logic.

Every metric must have one or more owners who are personally responsible and accountable for it; these owners, during tracking, must ensure that their metrics achieve the target levels that have been set for them. Strategic or top-level metrics need to be owned by a senior manager with overall authority for related processes, as well as with managers of the various functions involved in the processes.

Triggering Root-Cause Analysis

If the target levels of performance are not met, root-cause analysis is triggered. This will be the starting point to drive performance improvements to achieve the target performance level for each metric. Root causes can be grouped into two categories: (1) process design issues and (2) policy (process enforcement) issues.

In the case of process design issues, the design of the operating process or system simply does not allow it to operate at the target level. Therefore, an LAVC process innovation enabler might be the solution to reach the target. In this case, a holistic redesign of the process is needed.

On the other hand, policy issues like poorly trained or unmotivated workers can be resolved with effective change management. It is important to mention that process redesign will not help in this type of issue and will be a waste of time and money.

In this step, the value of measurement is apparent since tracking metrics or measurement is not the goal; the goal is to enable improvement.

To summarize, any metric or performance measure should have six parameters:

1. The category and scope of the measure that is being addressed (like customer satisfaction for the demand fulfillment process).
2. Performance targets that represent an external focus (e.g., developed by benchmarking) and an internal focus (e.g., developed during internal strategic planning sessions) to achieve certain corporate goals, and these targets need to be reviewed and adjusted regularly.
3. Actual performance value that requires a system to capture it and save it. This should include the time period of the value.
4. Owner of the performance measure who is accountable for success or failure of the measure.
5. Frequency of capturing and communicating with the cost of capturing the data should not outweigh its value.
6. Set of action plans when target is not achieved.

As an example of parameter 6, during the typical life cycle for a trendy new product, there will be a time when point-of-sale data indicate a drop-off in cash register sales—often in anticipation of a new, competitive product that is about to be launched. Instead of holding a series of urgent meetings, and making an ill-informed decision, a set of predefined actions should be laid down ahead of time for business managers to select from, such as expediting the launch of the new product that will replace the current one, or squeezing the margin on an existing product by offering discounts so that the firm can sustain or boost market share.

Anchoring the Culture of Measurement

It is crucial to establish a culture of measurement to sustain the PMS. The first step in this direction is upper management commitment for PMS followed by a public demonstration of executive commitment, and using every opportunity to emphasize the importance of measurement to the health of the company.

It is crucial to be aware of senior managers or executives who built their reputation on using guts to make decisions, since they might not be big fans of the PMS. They might even not like rewarding a measurement-oriented analytic manager who is rigorous about establishing the facts.

The incentive system should reward managers for using the right metrics and not reward managers who lack the discipline to use them, even if they achieve desirable results.

Another method that would help in anchoring the culture of measurement is for the upper management to insist on reviewing the quantitative business case (ROI) to approve the budget to any improvement project or program. This will force middle managers to use metrics to come up with the business case.

How Metrics Help in Developing LAVC Objectives

Objectives and strategies are developed first at the upper management levels and propagate down through the levels of management. At every level, managers are responsible for synchronizing objectives in their departments or functions with the value chain and corporate strategies. Objectives should be SMART (S: specific, M: measurable, A: attainable, R: relevant, and T: time-bound) at any level.

Based on the corporate objectives (where we need to be), certain strategies (how to get there) are adopted to achieve the objectives. Metrics is the main source of intelligence to come up with these strategies.

Sometimes strategies need to be changed if they're not proven effective in achieving the objectives, or the target levels of the objectives are changed due to a market shift or other reasons.

Now, the strategies that get developed at the corporate level would be an input to a second layer of management who should come up, in collaboration with upper management, with their own objectives to realize the strategies set by upper management. This is how managers can synchronize their activities and focus on corporate and value chain strategies.

The next step for the second layer of management is to come up with strategies to achieve their own objectives, and so on, until you reach individual employees.

LAVC Metrics

To evaluate the health of a company or a value chain, and based on the framework that we explained in the previous section, seven top-tier metrics should be considered, as shown in Figure 8.3:

1.   Perfect order
2.   Order cycle time

3. Time to recovery
4. Demand forecast accuracy
5. Value chain management cost
6. Cash-to-cash cycle time
7. Value chain management profit

This comprehensive list of metrics should give executives a feeling about the health of the firm and the progress toward achieving an LAVC. The first four metrics have agility attributes while the last three have lean attributes. Figure 8.3 maps these metrics attributes to SCOR and BSC models. The agility attribute combines reliability + responsiveness + flexibility in the context of this book. Also, the lean performance attribute combines value chain cost reduction + asset (like inventory) reductions + operational excellence performance attributes.

Table 8.3 shows the second level of LAVC metrics along with their definitions, and how they are linked to the top-tier metrics. The top-tier level would focus on common corporate objectives (goals), while the second focuses on understanding, at a detailed level, why certain metrics are low today—and what specific operational changes and initiatives can lead to significant improvements. For example, the cash-to-cash metric is below the target (set based on previous benchmarking). The second level can help in identifying the areas of poor performance to conduct further analysis. So, for example, if at the second level, the only metric below the target is inventory days, an analysis of the inventory planning process would be the next step.

Also, in the last column of the table, some examples for process of diagnostic metrics are mentioned. These metrics, such as forecast accuracy, look deeper than results-oriented metrics, such as cash-to-cash cycle, to find the root cause of poor performance or immediate opportunities for improvement. These metrics are fluid and can change based on the nature of the business and defined strategies.

For example, when you look into a high SCM costs metric, it is recommended to review if capacity utilization (diagnostic metric) is low, and that might be the reason for higher SCM costs. Then, the second question might be if a low capacity utilization is an acceptable outcome due to the slow economy (nature of the market), or acceptable due to a new strategy of building upside flexibility for competitive advantage. If the answer is no, improving capacity utilization might be the goal of the next improvement project.

As another classic example, a firm may define an overall corporate goal of maximizing cash flow. Every process within the company must be aligned with this top-level goal in order to achieve it. However, close examination may reveal sales compensation may be based only on bookings, and that can be an obstacle in achieving the corporate objectives since salespeople should also be measured on achieving cash-collection objectives that will improve days sales outstanding.

LAVC metrics (top/corporate level)	LAVC metric attribute	SCOR metric attribute	BSC metric attribute	Metric definition
Perfect order	Agility	Supply chain reliability	Customer perspective	The order is perfect if the value chain delivers the correct product, to the correct place, on-time, in the perfect condition and packaging, in the correct quantity, with the correct documentation, to the correct customer
Order cycle time	Agility	Supply chain responsiveness	Innovation and learning perspective	Average order cycle time starts from the order receipt and ends with customer acceptance of the order (procurement cycle time + fulfillment cycle time)
Time to recovery	Agility	Supply chain agility	Customer perspective	Number of days needed to recover from un-planned events. The event to be tracked is determined based on the risk management study for a firm
Demand forecast accuracy	Agility	Not determined	Internal business perspective	The difference between final/consensus forecast and actual demand
Value chain management (VCM) cost	Lean	Supply chain costs	Financial perspective	The cost associated with operating the value chain which includes the following: • Direct purchasing operating cost (if any), transportation cost, manufacturing operating cost, WMS/DC operating cost, customer service operating cost
Cash-to-cash cycle time	Lean	Supply chain asset management	Financial perspective	The cycle time b/n when a firm spends cash to buy raw materials to the time that customers pay for the finished products (inventory days + days sales outstanding – days payable outstanding)
VCM profit	Lean	Not determined	Financial perspective	VCM profit = VC sales – VCM cost

Figure 8.3   Mapping LAVC metrics to SCOR and Balanced Scorecard at the top level

Table 8.3: Level 2 of LAVC metrics

Top Level	Level 2 metrics	Definition	Related super-processes	Diagnosis/process metrics examples
Perfect order	Complete order performance	Percentage of orders in which all of the items on the order are received, and received quantity is equal to committed quantity (within mutually agreed tolerances)	SCM	Percentage of orders changed within company's lead time
	Delivery performance	Percentage of orders that are fulfilled on the agreed and committed date (within mutually agreed tolerances)	SCM	• Forecast accuracy • In-transit delays • Customer satisfaction
	Quality performance	Percentage of orders delivered in an undamaged state that meet specification set by the customer	SCM	Percentage of trained people in the process
	Documentation performance	Percentage of orders with accurate documentation supporting the order (shipment, invoice, and any compliance documentation)	SCM	
Order cycle time	Procurement time	The average time associated with the procurement process	SRM	• Supplier cycle time • Carrier cycle time • New product development time
	Fulfillment time	The average time associated with the fulfillment process	SCM	• Idle time • Type of replenishment (engineer to order, build to order, assemble to order, build to stock)
Time to recovery	Upside fulfill flexibility	The number of days required to achieve an unplanned sustainable increase in quantity (e.g., 25 percent) delivered with the assumption of no other constraints	SCM/CRM	
	Downside procure flexibility	The number of days required as a notice prior to delivery to achieve an unplanned reduction (e.g., 25 percent) in raw material with no inventory or cost penalties	SRM	Supplier flexibility performance

Demand forecast accuracy	System forecast accuracy	The difference between actual demand and system forecast	SCM	
	Marketing forecast accuracy	The difference between actual demand and marketing forecast	CRM	Sales/marketing compensation system
	Product manager forecast accuracy	The difference between actual demand and product manager forecast	SCM	
	Customer forecast accuracy	The difference between actual demand and customer forecast	CRM	
Value chain management cost	SRM costs	The costs associated with operating the SRM super-process, which include direct purchasing operating cost, raw material cost, inbound transportation cost, and supplier strategy, selection, and negotiation costs	SRM	• SRM risk mitigation cost • Supplier delivery performance • Total landed cost for raw materials
	SCM costs	The costs associated with operating the SCM super-process, which include manufacturing operating cost (if any), outbound transportation cost, warehouse/distribution center operating cost, inventory holding cost	SCM	• SCM risk mitigation cost • Capacity utilization
	CRM costs	The costs associated with operating the CRM super-process, which include product marketing, sales management, and customer service operating costs	CRM	CRM risk mitigation cost
Cash-to-cash cycle time	Inventory days	Average days of inventory (stocks) on hand	SCM	
	Days sales outstanding (order-to-cash)	Average number of days from invoicing (sale is made) to cash receipt	CRM	
	Days payable outstanding (procure-to-pay)	Average number of days from receipt of raw materials to payment made to suppliers	SRM	
Value chain management profit	Value chain sales	Total sales made by the value chain	CRM	Sales growth percentage
	Value chain management costs	The costs associated with operating the value chain	CRM/SCM/SRM	

The same framework can be used to come up with a third level to provide more breakdowns to metrics and help in root-cause analysis. This breakdown can be done to some of the metrics based on the need. This would require breaking down processes into subprocesses. The subprocesses can vary significantly between one firm and another and across industries.

One last comment on Table 8.3 is that the level 2 metrics for "time to recovery" are just examples, and based on the risk management plan/study. These metrics should be identified for every firm and should be changed whenever new risk areas are found. The balance between the risk and investment in increasing flexibility should be investigated and maintained. Examples of flexibility investment would be supplier contingency planning, multi-mode fulfillment capability, and so forth. Time to recovery is increasingly included on the executive scorecard.

CLOSING REMARKS

Many firms completely overlook change management when they aim to improve their value chains, which result in catastrophic implications. Change management supported processes are crucial for the success of any transformation program. Because no matter how sophisticated and powerful the software applications and how effective best-practices processes, in the end, it is the stakeholders (people) who play the most significant role in success or failure of the program. Value chain stakeholders represent different organizations and different roles (operators, managers, planners, suppliers, customers, warehouse receivers, carriers, etc.).

Senior management and the sponsor need to motivate stakeholders to change by offering the right incentives, keeping them informed and engaged, and not assuming that they are already motivated to change "for the greater good." They need to make sure that people, processes, and technology are all aligned to achieve high-level results.

Once the top-level vision and objectives are defined, all stakeholders should be aligned around it by having the right metrics, incentive programs, education plan, culture support, transformation team, and communications plan. A monitoring and controlling process is essential to sustain the alignment and apply corrective actions to keep the alignment and program on track.

Monitoring and enforcing progress toward program goals in an aligned environment of shared benefits and responsibilities are imperative for the success of the program. Alignment is not a one-time exercise, but an ongoing commitment in which the sponsor and program manager must engage.

Best-practices processes and technologies that were covered in the previous chapters of this book range from simple to sophisticated, but they cannot be fully leveraged until the level of the people who deploy them rise as well.

Chapter 9 will present a case study of a successful transformation program where the concepts in this chapter and the previous one are illustrated.

REFERENCES

1. Sabri, E., A. Gupta, and M. Beitler. 2006. *Purchase Order Management Best Practices: Process, Technology, and Change Management.* Fort Lauderdale, FL: J. Ross Publishing.
2. Kotter, J. P. 1996. *Leading Change.* Boston: Harvard Business School Press.
3. Hammer, M. 2007. "The 7 Deadly Sins of Performance Measurement and How to Avoid Them."*MIT Sloan Management Review,* 48 (3): 19–28.

9

LAVC TRANSFORMATION CASE STUDY: OFFICE SYSTEMS

INTRODUCTION

The idea of this hypothetical case study came from Paul Harmon's book, *Business Process Change* of 2003. We did not want to describe problems associated with any specific client or industry. At the same time, we wanted a case that can cover the full range of concepts and techniques that we have discussed in this book. This case study blends the problems faced by several firms that we have dealt with in order to make it as realistic as possible. In this case, we will follow the generic transformation program cycle that we have explained in Chapter 7.

OFFICE SYSTEMS, INC.

Office Systems, Inc. is a midsize company with sales of approximately $800 million in 2008. The company started in 1998 by producing office chairs for executives who spend a huge chunk of their time interacting with computers. Its chairs are comfortable, ergonomic, impressive, and have proved very popular during the 2000s. In 2003, Office Systems started a new business line by selling modular office units that could be assembled into work areas with features specially designed for employees who use computers. They thus changed their vision to focus on providing complete office environments and not just chairs. It also, in the same period, shifted its organizational structure to be process-oriented.

Office Systems has a matrix organization in which business line managers are responsible for processes, while functional managers are responsible for activities (smallest subprocesses) performed by employees in their departments. Figure 9.1 shows how Office Systems is organized. Office Systems has two value chains, office chairs and office modules, each divided into several business processes.

The company's overall strategy is not to become a dominant producer in this area, but to remain a specialized, high-quality producer that can maintain a high profit margin.

When direct selling, or business to consumer (B2C), through the Internet started to emerge strongly in late 2006 in the industry, customers started to ask for Internet capabilities, and the competitors of Office Systems adopted them as part of their strategy. Key distributors began to ask for an ability to buy and obtain information online. In addition, surveys suggested that the company's image was being undermined by its lack of a website. In lieu of these environmental changes, the CEO invited the strategy and technology subcommittees to meet together to analyze the situation and provide recommendations.

ALIGNING THE TRANSFORMATION PROGRAM WITH CORPORATE GOALS

The committee reviewed the existing corporate objectives (Figure 9.2), and concluded that none needed to be altered. Incorporating the Internet technologies (strategy) into their operations would put them in a better position to achieve or even exceed the existing objectives, by providing better service to customers, improving the coordination of the internal processes, and developing a more efficient relationship with suppliers.

By selling online, the margins and growth could be improved. The subcommittees mentioned in their business case study that growth could be increased from the current target of 3 to 4 percent. At the same time, they suggested that sales order cycle time could be reduced by an average of three days. All of these assumptions were based on the root assumption that they would be selling 25 percent of their chairs via the Internet by the end of the year.

The focus of this study was only on the *office chair* value chain, from which most of the revenue was coming. Future study needed to be planned to address the *office modules* value chain since the characteristics of the business differed from the *office chairs* line of business.

The report talked about recent bankruptcies of several of their competitors, a potential to increase market share, and the urgent need to be more efficient to stay afloat during the recession.

This study was completed in the last quarter of 2008, during which the banking meltdown and credit shortage was shaping the future of the economy. An amendment to this report was done later to add another objective, which was

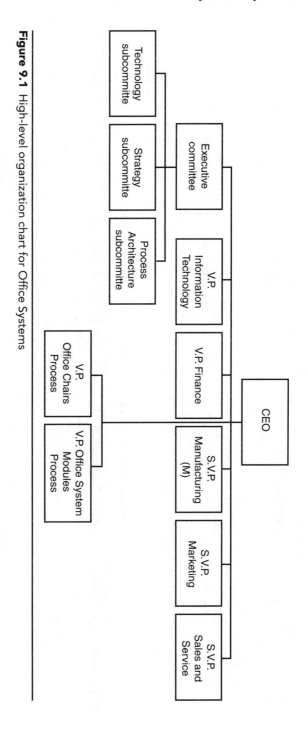

Figure 9.1 High-level organization chart for Office Systems

Objectives and Measures Worksheet for the Firm as a Whole

Organization objectives	Measures	Desired performance	Actual performance (2008)
Selling the best-designed and manufactured office systems for high-tech environments, and commanding best prices	Comparison of sale price of office chair and two closest competitors	At least 5% more than competitive products	Products sold for 5.6% more than competitive products
Maintaining the highest profit margin in the industry	After-tax return on net sales	After-tax return on net sales to exceed 10%	Profit margin 8%
Maintaining modest growth	Growth rate judged by 3rd party	Growth to be 5%	Growth was 4.5%
Reducing assets	Cah-to-cash cycle time	22 days	35 days

Objectives are Assigned to a Specific Value Chain or Processes

Value chain	Organization objectives	Measures	Desired performance	Actual performance (2008)
Office chair	Best-designed chairs	Design reviews	Best design award in design press	Won best design award in business week
	Command best price	Sale price comparisons	Chairs sell for at least 5% more than competetive products	Chairs sold for an average of 6% more than competitive chairs
	Maintain highest margin	Profit margins	Profit margins to exceed 80%	Profit margins were 71%
	Maintain growth goals	Sales growth	Growth will be 3%	Growth was 2.7%
	Reduce assets	Cash-to-cash cycle time	27 days	42 days
Office modules				

Figure 9.2 Organization objectives and measures worksheet

reducing the cash-to-cash cycle time to free up some much-needed assets. Office Systems used to pay its suppliers in 33 days on average, but its customers took an average of 45 days to pay Office Systems. This metric highlights some immediate opportunities. Streamlining the fulfillment process would reduce the time to close the order and would reduce days sales outstanding (DSO).

In addition, it was noticed that inventory days was 30, which was significantly higher than the industry average of 20 days. Typically, if you have excess inventory, the probability of stockout is less, but not in the case of Office Systems (the perfect order rating was low and below the industry). This could have been due to wrong inventory mixes and a high level of inventory of raw material due to lack of visibility, which results in increasing safety stocks.

Based on all of the above factors, they set an aggressive target of reducing cash-to-cash cycle time by 15 days. The current performance then was 42 days (45 + 30 − 33).

When the transformation team got selected and sat down to discuss objectives alignment, they sorted out the office chair value chain objectives (Figure 9.2) as follows:

1. This objective, best-designed chairs, was mainly for the new product development process (product design). Last year's performance was above the desired performance (green).
2. The objective, command best price, was used to set the price after comparing Office's price with competitor's. Previous year's performance was above the desired performance (green).
3. The objective, maintain highest margin, could be achieved by cutting value chain cost directly applied to the demand fulfillment process by making this process as lean as possible. Previous year's performance was worse than desired (red flag).
4. The objective, maintain growth goals, applied to Office's sales manager and his team and was delegated directly to the respective sales groups. The previous year's performance was worse than desired (red flag).
5. The objective, reduce assets, was related to both the demand fulfillment process and selling management. Previous year's performance was worse than the desired performance (red flag). The objective for sales was to reduce DSO by 5 days, while the objective of the demand fulfillment process was to reduce inventory days by 10. So, the total reduction in cash-to-cash cycle time was expected to be 15 days.

Two additional objectives were formalized based on the value chain management principles to reflect the transformation program:

6. Assure that customers are happy with the office chairs.

7. Assure that customers and suppliers who use the web portal are happy with the user interface experience.

Both of these objectives were going to be measured by surveys that Office Systems planned to undertake periodically.

DEVELOPING VISION, OBJECTIVES, AND STRATEGIES OF THE PROGRAM

This transformation program was established to address objectives 3 through 7. They concluded that they wouldn't try to change the company overnight, but they would prepare to implement four strategies:

1. Create a portal that would allow customers and prospects to collaborate and contact the company via the web. The portal would provide information about the firm, a product catalog for office chairs, and the ability to order either wholesale or retail.
2. Improve the promising and delivery subprocesses in the demand fulfillment process of the office chair value chain to handle Internet orders.
3. Create a portal to communicate with the suppliers at the execution level (procurement order management subprocess).
4. Establish a dashboard for metrics to allow measuring of program progress, identify areas of improvement, and use it as a baseline for incentive plans.

Given the key role of the *office chairs* value chain, the executive committee decided to focus on it for this initiative. John Kaplan, the vice president of office chairs value chain, was designated sponsor of the redesign (transformation) effort. The CEO appointed several members of the executive committee to serve on a steering team to oversee and evaluate the proposed strategies.

The day after the appointment, Mr. Kaplan phoned Dr. Bill Clark, who was an expert in process change, and asked him to facilitate this program transformation. Dr. Clark agreed and arrived with his associate, Mr. Taylor, to Office Systems three weeks later to attend the kickoff meeting arranged by Mr. Kaplan.

The process sponsor and the facilitator reviewed the organization chart, value chain diagram, and organization objectives and measures worksheet.

The steering team was asked to identify individuals who could serve on the program transformation team and assure that they would have time to work on the program. One of the key decisions that Kaplan and Clark made was to use lean and agile value chain management (LAVCM) principles and enablers in the redesign effort and creating the portal.

They developed a plan that reviewed the objectives of the program and established a schedule that would result in a redesigned process in just three months.

As part of the communication plan, they presented their plan to the steering team, received approval, and proceeded to the next step.

PROCESS ANALYSIS

The key to the analysis of the as-is processes was to develop a good understanding of how the existing process currently worked. Clark and his assistant interviewed each of the transformation program team members to see how they would describe the process and what kinds of problems/pain points they would identify. Clark also talked to the stakeholders to gain a broader understanding of the process and any problems that it might have.

When all the interviews were complete, Clark came up with a high level diagram for the as-is processes related to the transformation program (Figure 9.3). Clark requested a meeting to present this to the whole transformation program team. That meeting was also an opportunity to provide everyone with a way of understanding how to document (format) the processes.

This high-level diagram (Figure 9.3) was the focus of the transformation program. The transformation program had an impact on four processes: sales management, customer service management, procurement, and demand fulfillment. These processes manage the operational/execution part of the value chain. The demand fulfillment process has several subprocesses, but the focus of the program is on three subprocesses displayed on the diagram: production, delivery, and invoicing. The focus of the program in the procurement process is on the purchase order management subprocess. The call center subprocess under the customer service management process was another focus area for the program.

Figure 9.3 suggests that three departments would be directly involved in the program: sales, finance, and manufacturing. Functional groups within each department were identified to make it clear which managers, supervisors, and employees would be responsible for the subprocesses and activities shown on the diagram. Thus, for example, three functions within the manufacturing department were identified: production, purchasing, and shipping.

The as-is processes interact with two application systems that had been developed in the past and had been in use for several years. One was a financial application that maintained records of customers, undertook credit checks, and prepared invoices. This application was acquired from PeopleSoft (an enterprise resource planning software vendor). The other application had been built in-house by the information technology (IT) department. It controlled the inventory and shop floor (production) subprocess. A separate instance of this system was located at various manufacturing sites.

The sequence of events for an order was as follows: (1) once an order was entered into the system, a record was created in the database; (2) when the order was approved by finance, the order was scheduled for production if no finished product

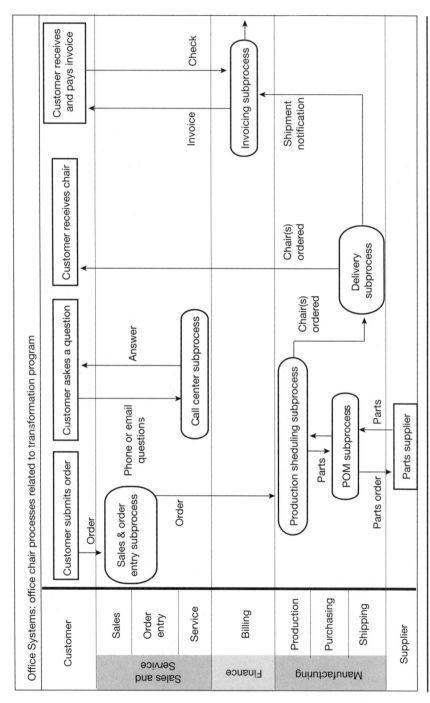

Figure 9.3 High-level as is processes

was available; (3) when the schedule was created, inventory was checked to see if raw materials (parts) would be needed for the specific order; (4) if parts were needed, that information would show up on a shortage report; (5) the individual responsible for monitoring inventory would prepare and mail purchase orders to the appropriate parts suppliers; (6) once the production was done and finished goods for the sales order were ready, a signal was sent to Office Systems trucks for pickup; and (7) at the same time, the shipping group would transmit the customer receipt to finance and would initiate billing and handle the payment.

After agreeing on the high-level diagram, the team began to drilldown and refine some of the details of how an order would flow through the various processes. By the end of the first week, the team arrived at the first version of the as-is diagram. This new diagram contains more details than the first one.

At this point different project teams were set up to examine the as-is subprocesses in more detail and recommend a high-level to-be process. One team from the manufacturing-production function wanted to analyze the production scheduling subprocess in more detail, while another team from sales chose to examine the sales and order entry process in more detail. Also, a third team, made up of a material planner, purchasing representative, and supervisor, focused on the procurement-purchase order management subprocess. Another team focused on the rest of the subprocesses, which are the call center, invoicing, and delivery subprocesses. A final project team, made up mainly of managers, focused on the performance management system (PMS) and describing the metrics currently used by managers to evaluate the existing process.

Dr. Clark conducted a workshop for the project teams on the methodology to come up with the to-be process and how to leverage LAVCM enablers to eliminate or alleviate the pain points and achieve the objectives.

Production Scheduling Subprocess Project Team Analysis

The production scheduling subprocess project team identified that the existing process was not fully adequate to support B2C, where small batch runs would be needed and near real-time visibility into the status of the order under manufacturing would be a must. Therefore, the team recommended to start supporting a new replenishment type, which is *build-to-order* for B2C (online end customers), and continue to support *build-to-stock* for B2B (business-to-business for distributors). The team also recommended complementing the team with an expert in build-to-order replenishment to help the team in deciding on the needed changes to the process and leverage best practices (strategy innovation enabler) in this area. Based on the recommendation, a new external member was added to the team who had extensive experience in this area and in the office furniture industry.

After a series of discussions, the team came to the conclusion that this move would require production to revise their procedures so that they could insert single or small orders within their schedule (build-to-order environment). The production members of the team mentioned that they had already been moving in this direction since they executed lean initiatives in the past that made the move to build-to-order achievable.

Sales and Order Entry Subprocess Project Team Analysis

The sales and order entry subprocess project team identified three major problems with this subprocess. Salespeople were sometimes late in submitting new orders, causing delayed delivery. Order entry clerks sometimes incorrectly entered orders, causing problems and delays for re-entry. The team suggested a process to incorporate a portal into the sales and order entry subprocess to streamline it (enabler 3: technology). The team also recommended equipping salespeople with laptop computers and letting them enter orders directly. It would eliminate the entry clerk's job, avoid transcription problems, and allow salespeople to submit all orders on the day they received them, which would reduce cycle time significantly (enabler 6: process innovation).

The team also wanted the new portal to have product configuration capabilities that allowed the customer to configure the office chair the way he or she wanted. This would attract new customers that would buy online. The team documented their findings on a process analysis and improvement worksheet.

Purchase Order Management Subprocess Project Team Analysis

The purchase order management subprocess team noticed the supplier on-time rating was 6 percent lower than the average in the industry, which might result in building more safety stocks and might be the reason for high Inventory Days which had a negative impact on cash-to-cash cycle time. The team also noticed that the company was paying their suppliers relatively quickly, which had more negative impact on cash-to-cash cycle time, but was not receiving the service levels it required from its suppliers. By looking into the "direct material costs" metric, the team noticed that it was slightly on the high side, which meant that the company was not leveraging its suppliers well. They also noticed that the transportation cost was high due to freight expediting costs because of a lack of visibility for in-coming shipments. Higher costs resulted in a reduction in profit margin.

The team talked to a group of suppliers to find out the root cause and solution for poor on-time performance, and came to the conclusion that electronic connections (enabler 3) to speed up the communication of purchase orders with suppliers, and providing quick visibility to purchase order changes by the company would fix the problem and improve performance. This would also allow the company to reduce safety stock levels.

In addition, to reduce the expediting occurrences, the team asked the suppliers to start sending advanced shipment notices from the new portal to provide visibility of inbound shipments (enabler 1: visibility). The purchasing representative on the team promised the suppliers to maintain paying them quickly and fully if the on-time performance was improved significantly. They started achieving their targets under the new process and followed the new process of sending advanced shipment notices.

In building their business case, the team mentioned that implementing the above to-be process for purchase order management would help in achieving objectives 3 (growth in profit margin), 5 (cash to-cash cycle time reduction), and 7 (making suppliers happy).

Call Center, Invoicing, and Delivery Subprocesses Project Team Analysis

The fourth project team who was responsible for the call center, invoicing, and delivery subprocesses faced the challenge of supporting a build-to-order environment since the delivery subprocess was not designed to handle individual deliveries. Therefore, the team recommended outsourcing the delivery subprocess for B2C deliverables to a third-party logistics (3PL) provider, since it wouldn't be cost effective to use their own trucks to make individual or even small deliveries outside the area of their existing warehouses. Also, delivery (transportation) is not a core competency process, which meant outsourcing it was a good decision.

They also recommended that the purchasing department should negotiate with the 3PL provider to link their production's scheduling system with the logistics provider's tracking system so that online customers could determine when their orders would arrive and track their progress and delivery from the website. Later, purchasing initiated the request for quote process, and FedEx was selected. As part of the contract agreement, FedEx agreed to provide end-to-end tracking for online customers.

Since the new portal would allow customers to buy online, everyone on the team agreed to extend the existing customer credit and invoicing system to allow invoicing customers through the portal that might improve the DSO metric.

After talking to FedEx technical consultants, they found that they would not need to make an entry into the order system to generate invoices (functional requirement) because FedEx provides automatic electronic notification when chairs are delivered, and that information is now automatically input into the order system.

In the to-be process, the call center representatives would be using the new portal to enter the sales orders. The portal would include error checking and logic validation to make sure that only accurate sales orders are entered in the system.

PMS Project Team Analysis

A project team made up of a group of managers improved and formalized the performance management system of the organization, including the incentive system. Like most firms, Office Systems had always claimed it aligned its corporate goals to process and departmental goals, but it had always been an informal process with several holes. As part of the transformation program, management made a commitment to create a more formal and effective PMS.

The PMS project team came to know, based on interviews, that some of the existing metrics were out of line with stated company objectives, and that managers' metrics should be reassessed to assure that they were measuring the right things.

They also recommended Kaplan to interview leading customers to determine what they wanted in the portal. Kaplan would turn the customers' requests into a survey that would be used in the future to measure customer satisfaction with the site.

The team recommended that the incentive system needed to be revisited to compensate salespeople who lost sales to the website. They also recommended that management consider working out an arrangement with distributors to point their customers to the website. One practice they mentioned from the high-tech and automotive industries is to share income with the distributor from sales made through the company website from referrals from the distributor's website.

As part of the propagation of the objectives down to the lowest level, Kaplan had to sit down with various senior managers involved in the transformation program and allocate sub-goals and agree with the managers on metrics. Figure 9.4 shows how metrics (including performance targets) that the management team had developed were ultimately assigned to specific subprocesses within the overall process.

Best in class organizations develop role/responsibility worksheets that align each manager's goals to the processes' goals. Figure 9.5 was what Kaplan and the sales manager had prepared for a meeting with the subordinates to establish their objectives. In the end there was a set of 30 role/responsibility worksheets defining every manager's and employee's goals for the *office chair* transformation program.

The PMS project team and Kaplan wanted a placeholder for metrics and an easy way to track it; otherwise, their effort in formalizing PMS would be a waste. They decided to come up with the functional requirements list for a metrics reporting application. High on the list were the following requirements: powerful scorecards, dashboards, and analytical reports that could highlight discrepancies

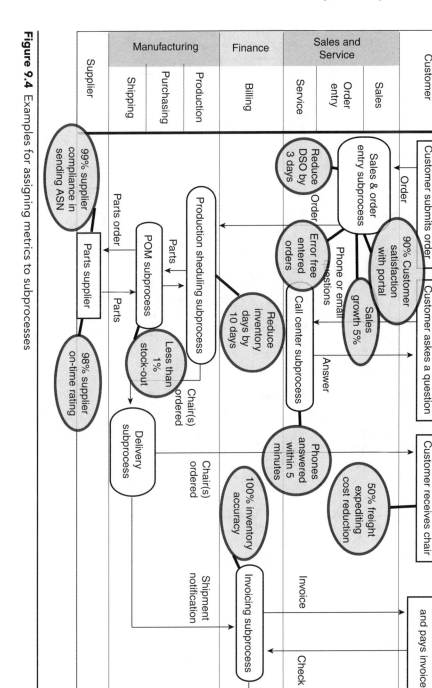

Figure 9.4 Examples for assigning metrics to subprocesses

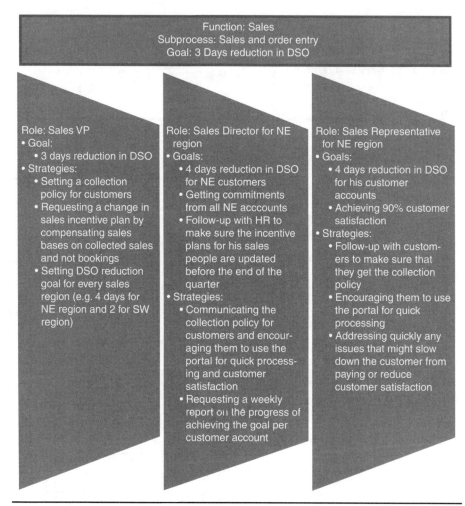

Figure 9.5 Goal assignment worksheet

between expected and actual performance in a quick way and could point out where to look for root causes.

In addition to listing high-priority functional requirements, they listed *nice to have* requirements such as the ability to test multiple *what-if* scenarios and predict the impact of their decisions. For instance, a business with a fill rate of 85 percent might be considering a new objective of 93 percent. The application, in this case, should enable managers to assess the actual operations cost of reaching this objective, while still supporting the company's top-level objectives.

The IT group suggested using their expertise in building reports to build this application addressing only the *must do* requirements. Office Systems had a corporate license for Hyperion (a business intelligence tool) from Oracle, which could be configured by the IT group to address the requirements.

Creating Functional Requirements

Every project team, during the benchmarking and process analysis phase, worked with the help of IT representatives to determine the additional software application capabilities that were required to support the to-be processes and that could not be supported by the existing systems.

At the end of the benchmarking and process analysis phase, the transformation team met to prioritize the functional requirements (application capabilities) into two categories, based on the value they added to the to-be process in relation to the degree of alignment with the corporate objectives, degree of implementation difficulty, and user feedback: (1) must do and (2) nice to do. Only necessary changes (must do) would be considered initially. The team decided that they wanted to finish implementation in six months. Thus, if a requirement could not be implemented, in the opinion of IT, within the next six months, the team decided to place it on a list of things to be considered for a subsequent transformation program. The team agreed that the Office Systems portal should include these major (groups of) functional requirements:

1. A catalog of Office Systems products. It included a web page to communicate announcements about part changes and answer frequently asked questions about office chairs.
2. A configuration and pricing workflow that would allow prospects to specify chair configurations and then buy office chairs online.
3. A supplier portal to allow communication and collaboration with the supplier online.

These capabilities or functional requirements would be the input for the next step (phase).

SELECTING A SOFTWARE APPLICATION PROVIDER

The IT group decided to buy a customer relationship management package to manage online sales and support—the first two major functional requirements. It also provided the salespeople with the ability to enter orders directly into the customer system via the Internet.

In addition, the IT group decided to buy an order management package to manage the execution phase of the order with the suppliers, and support the third major functional requirement.

A selection committee was formed. This committee adopted four guidelines in selecting the technology provider:

1. Select a software vendor that provides a solution which is most suitable for the required functionality for the business. Look for off-the-shelf software for much of the IT aspects of this effort.
2. Take into consideration software technology maturity and sustainability.
3. Usability and efficiency of the software application is a key.
4. Leading industry standards for e-business technology, such as web services, must be supported.

The best three software providers were invited to conduct a demo that reflected the requirements. A script that reflected *a day in the life of a sales representative* was developed to be covered by the demo. After selecting the software provider based on the guidelines and demo results, several consultants from the software provider company were asked to join the transformation team as external consultants. The costs of licenses and implementation were inputs for the next step.

RETURN ON INVESTMENT

After compiling the recommendations of the entire transformation team, the sponsor and Dr. Clark started on building the business case and expected benefits of the program.

All cost elements were captured including consulting cost, change management, hardware, software licenses and upgrades, internal resources, integration cost, ongoing maintenance and support, and training.

The benefits of this transformation program were summarized under the following: (1) order cycle time, (2) value chain management costs, (3) cash-to-cash cycle time, (4) profit margin, and (5) customer satisfaction.

The recommendations of the entire transformation team and the ROI were submitted to the steering committee. Once approved, the team was asked to prepare detailed program and project plans.

DEVELOPING PROGRAM AND PROJECT PLANS

The sponsor of the transformation program understood that adopting a value-driven approach to conduct LAVC transformation programs was very crucial. Therefore, they selected Six Sigma as the project methodology for the implementation. Office System's executives understood that an effective transformation program typically takes two to five years, with several intermediate projects (go lives) to achieve the value needed to pay for the rest of the program.

But with the worst financial recession since the depression, they secured a budget only for eight months (two months in 2008, and six months in the first half of 2009). Therefore, the timeline for the transformation program was eight months, and a second phase was scheduled to start after it pending budget availability. The assumption was that implementing the first transformation program successfully would save money that could justify the second transformation program. The scope of the second transformation program was not finalized.

The approved transformation program consisted of five projects going in parallel since they didn't have the luxury of time to go in sequence. It was a very aggressive plan. The executives of Office Systems understood the risk, and decided to go ahead with the program after forming a strong risk mitigation plan. The five projects were decided as part of the process analysis phase previously:

1. Production scheduling subprocess
2. Sales and order entry
3. Purchase order management
4. Call center, invoicing, and delivery
5. PMS

PROJECT IMPLEMENTATION

The first two months of the program were spent in process analysis for all projects. The last six months were allocated for project implementation. The program manager had a difficult job in resource management since several subject matter experts were needed on more than one project, but he managed to pull it through with the help of the sponsor.

Detailed Design and Development

IT had representatives on the transformation team extend the *as-is* and *to-be* process documents developed during process analysis to provide the requirements and use-case documents that IT and the software consultants needed before they could begin their work. During this phase, more detailed discussion took place among the transformation team and the user community on the use cases.

Dr. Clark mentioned that most firms who spent a significant amount of time and money defining the to-be process and use cases, would usually spend much less and produce a better quality system.

Clark then conducted a workshop for the entire transformation team to meet again, review the detailed requirements, and sign off on them and the use cases. This phase was relatively short since the transformation team did an excellent job previously during the process analysis phase in documenting the as-is and to-be process, and the gaps at a detailed level.

Kaplan assigned a group of senior managers from various departments the responsibility of meeting with distributors, parts suppliers, and FedEx to work out contracts for the new relationship that Office Systems wanted to enter into with them. Kaplan also assigned the sales head the responsibility of communicating with customers about the new portal and the collection policy.

A group of users from distributors and parts suppliers were selected to participate in the user acceptance testing for the portal.

The human resources department was assigned the task of modifying the existing compensation and incentive plans to accomplish some of the specific changes required by the new design. They linked 50 percent of managerial bonuses to meet the new objectives.

Although several tasks were conducted in parallel, the bottleneck for the five projects was the IT configuration and integration, which was scheduled to last five months including testing.

Deployment and Rollout

The program manager and sponsor for the transformation did a great job in keeping the program under control and following the recipe of success for transformation programs. This resulted in a relatively smooth deployment, considering the aggressive timeline. For example, the program and every project had a clear statement of scope. They secured and then maintained the support from the steering committee and upper management throughout the life cycle of the program. They managed to get sign-off on the design reviews on time, and applied the pressure required to get their users to implement the resulting to-be process. They also obtained the commitment of employees early on.

The new portal was ready on time, and the new process was implemented eight months from the day the transformation program began, just as management requested. They went live just after the 4th of July holiday. There were some problems in the first four weeks as expected after the go-live, but by the end of the second month, everything was running smoothly and the new objectives were being met. Management was extremely happy with the results and began to think of the scope for a second transformation program.

Anchoring the New or Improved Process in the Culture

Kaplan and his team started after the first two months from launching the portal to e-mail the survey to all of their customers and suppliers who were a part of the rollout to determine if they were meeting their objectives. The initial feedback from customers was that they were pleased when they got the chairs they ordered quickly and exactly as ordered, and with a correct bill. The survey results also showed that customers and suppliers were happy with portal use and they confirmed that the portal was user friendly. This significant success (win) was enough to anchor the new process in the culture. Also, the managers were being judged based on the new metrics and not the old criteria.

The transformation team continued its work until were able to compare actual 2009 performance against the planned performance and evaluate the results.

CASE STUDY QUESTIONS

- Identify which decision/strategy/objective was based on a customer-driven LAVCM principle.
- Identify which decision/strategy/objective was based on establishing a win-win supplier relationship.
- Identify the major consideration an organization needs to pay attention to when moving to a build-to-order environment and B2C market.
- What was the recipe of success for Office Systems transformation program? What can other companies learn from Office Systems?
- Mention the LAVCM principles and enablers used in this case study.

10

LEAN AND AGILE VALUE CHAIN SUCCESS STORIES AND LESSONS LEARNED

SUPPLIER RELATIONSHIP MANAGEMENT-DRIVEN SUCCESS STORIES

Success Story 1: Supplier Relationship Management Best Practices at Emerson

Emerson (www.emerson.com) has over 60 divisions with more than 270 manufacturing facilities around the world. Raw materials are approximately 40 percent of our sales procurement processes are therefore important to our overall performance.

At the corporate level, we handle the sourcing for any materials or components that have leverage opportunities across business divisions, and that turns out to be about 60 percent of our direct materials. Procurement is the only function that is center-led. Corporate commodity teams are organized in a business/commodity matrix, leaving the business divisions to manage commodities that are non-leverageable at the corporate level.

To measure our performance and to drive improvements, we look at one overarching metric, and that's return on total capital (ROTC), which we then break down into its components—cost of goods sold and working trade capital.

On the cost side, we monitor net material inflation, which we manage to reduce the cost of goods sold. We've developed a proprietary tool to track certain events that influence our material costs. If, for example, we see changes coming in the cost of steel or copper, we get early warnings on that and we take action to deal with it.

We measure inventory monthly and net material inflation at least quarterly. Based on that data, there are a number of ways we can respond. We can look for alternative materials or sources. We are very fond of online and electronic negotiations—including reverse auctions, Dutch auctions, and multivariate events—all of which are well-known methods that help us reduce component costs.

In those processes, however, we are always very careful to only invite suppliers that we are very comfortable with. We will never invite an unqualified supplier to bid just to drive down costs, as sometimes happens in this business. You introduce a lot of supply chain risk into your operations if you are not careful in that way. When you cut corners, you jeopardize market integrity, and that's something we won't do.

We also find it very important to get in front of the product development process by inserting the procurement function into new product design, so that our engineers are working with a design-for-sourcing mentality. This is important because once a bill of materials is fixed for a product, a good purchasing person can only take about 10 to 20 percent of the material cost out of that product by using the best sourcing practices available. When you get engineering and purchasing working together in the conceptual phase, however, you can often take 35 to 45 percent of the material costs out of the product. So that's where the biggest gains are made.

Return on Total Capital

On the trade, working capital side of the metrics, we look at *raw-material inventory velocity*, which is measured by days-on-hand of inventory. It's a commonly used measure of asset utilization. We also strive to improve days payable outstanding, so we shorten the days in the cash cycle, which is also known as the cash conversion cycle.

We take this approach because we think that when you tie everything back to ROTC, you manage all things relatively well. You end up making more holistic decisions about sourcing by not just focusing on one element.

These days, anyone can go to Asia and get significant cost reductions, but you also have to consider the additional capital costs required for that decision, or the supply chain risks that enter into the equation. The longer the pipeline, the larger the bullwhip effect.

Of course, we are well established in Asia, but we primarily use Asian sources for supporting domestic production. We also use Asian suppliers to support North American production, but we use a sourcing decision support tool to help us analyze price, working capital, and supply chain risk. It's also a multi-function effort—it's not just procurement sitting in a vacuum. Everyone has a seat at the table and that helps us make the best decisions.

Because our business models are so diverse, all functions except procurement are led at the division level. So to share supply chain best practices, we have quarterly meetings, where division and corporate leaders gather to exchange ideas, to inform each other about what their teams are doing, and to set strategy.

At Emerson, we are growing at a healthy clip, and we have to ensure that our supply chain is as solid as it can be to sustain our top-line growth and to mitigate risk. Therefore, carefully monitoring our supply chain and measuring its performance are critical to our ongoing success.

This work was previously published in an article titled "How (and How Often) Do You Measure Supply Chain Results?" in *Supply Chain Leader*, Volume 3, Number 1, written by Michael Cohen, pp. 28–29, copyright 2008, by i2 Technologies, Inc.

Concluding Thoughts

James Geesey, the Director of eSourcing at Emerson, shared his success story in capturing the right performance measures (metrics).

This success story provides several examples for process and strategy innovation enablers (best practices) in the area of the supplier relationship management superprocess, which includes strategic sourcing, product design, and procurement.

Success Story 2: Supplier Portal for GE

The main challenges that GE (www.ge.com) used to face in managing global supplier information were the cost of maintaining accurate data in the global supplier list and the inability to communicate effectively with suppliers.

As a result, the GE transformation team started to look at packaged applications from various vendors. Aravo (a software vendor) stood out because of its out-of-the-box approach and software-as-a-service (SaaS) delivery model which was an opportunity to gain benefits faster.

The first phase of the project started in March 2008, and went live in October 2008. It included the supplier's profile, banking information, and payment terms. The go-live included 500,000 suppliers across all of GE's business units, and six languages. Right now, the solution is being rolled out for all pertinent supplier information with new suppliers coming online daily.

The technology enabled GE to provide supplier information across the enterprise, thereby increasing efficiencies, improving supplier data quality (fewer supplier information loading errors), driving compliance, and reducing costs. Financial benefits included lower hardware and software costs, reduced audit costs, and reduced total cost per supplier.

The above savings have allowed GE to set its sights on the next enhancements to achieve more savings like supplier catalog enablement and insurance certificate review and approvals.

Concluding Thoughts

This success story is based on an article published in May 2009 by Mickey North Rizza in AMR Research under the title of "GE Lights Up Supplier Management with Aravo," describing the success implementation of a single repository for supplier information.

GE is one of the largest installations of SaaS technology to date, with over 500,000 suppliers online. The successful implementation of a portal for supplier information at GE, leveraging the Aravo SaaS delivery model, offers a great example of how reliable SaaS technologies can pave the way to better supplier information visibility and consolidation, and significant cost savings.

SUPPLY CHAIN MANAGEMENT-DRIVEN SUCCESS STORIES

Success Story 3: BLUESALON's Journey with Lean and Agile Value Chain Concepts

BLUESALON (www.bluesalon.com) was established in 1981 in Doha Qatar. Now, it is one of the leading luxury goods retailers in the Middle East with more than 1,400 employees and around 70 stores. BLUE SALON is one of the companies under ABUISSA HOLDING (www.abuissa.com).

The BLUESALON board recognized that instability and a slowdown in business, which they were facing, was a symptom of things to come in the future. They knew that one day only *excellent* companies will survive. Hence, they decided to focus on the future and take necessary actions to be ready for it.

In mid-2007, BLUESALON started a value chain management project based on the recommendation of a newly hired strategy consultant. At the beginning of the project, the major challenges were identified:

*   The need to deliver products to the outlets and customers when and where they need it, exactly the way they want it, with a competitive price and in a cost-effective manner.
*   The need to have real-time data at the right time with the right format.
*   The ongoing alliance and joint ventures between big players in the retail market that enforce more aggressive and flexible pricing and distributing strategies.

- Increasing complexity of supply chains due to increasing number of suppliers and distribution channels.
- Increasing cost of the supply chain due to the dramatic increase in shipping, manpower, and warehousing costs.
- Seasonal demand and unpredictable life cycle for most of the products.
- Expensive and limited amount of retail space.
- The local market had become more demanding, more competitive, and pickier. A lot of the competitors were spoiling the customers with more advertising, more promotions, more gifts, more entertainment, and more luxurious outlets. The need to have a mechanism that would optimize the dramatic vertical and horizontal expansion.
- The need to GET and KEEP the good staff all the time.
- To keep an excellent relationship with the suppliers and to monitor them.
- To maximize customer satisfaction and loyalty.

BLUESALON developed a plan to address the above challenges by forming a complete value chain management transformation program. After six months of proper diagnosis, gap analysis, and development, it was determined to::

- Develop a new organization structure, vision, and mission.
- Identify the major processes, determine the pain points and performance issues, and brainstorm the best way to solve it.
- Adopt several lean and agile value chain (LAVC) principles to overcome these challenges, enhance the business performance, and achieve operational excellence for the BLUESALON processes including:
  - Align company resources.
  - Eliminate nonvalue-added activities, and make sure that every process is adding value to the organization.
  - Close the loop between planning and execution.
  - Leverage the core competency of each organization or process.
  - Implement the LAVC processes in some departments first rather than go for a big-bang approach. The complete implementation and system adjustment was expected to finish in mid-2010.

The LAVC processes footprint was developed across different departments and units: human resources, logistics, purchasing, accounts payable, accounts receivable, treasury, marketing, facility management, merchandising, replenishment planning, channel management, promotion planning, etc. Examples of these processes are highlighted below.

Purchase Order Management

BLUESALON identified the challenges that were facing the purchase order management (POM) subprocess (or procurement process):

- No control of delivery time of the purchase orders. More than 60 percent of the shipments are delayed due to various reasons such as:
  - Shipments from logistics firms cannot be cleared through customs due to short documentation or lack of basic requirements to Customs authority.
  - Logistics, sometimes, do not know who has placed a certain order because some brand managers can place orders while traveling and might forget to add them to the system.
- Processing purchase orders takes three weeks on average.
- Lack of accuracy in orders. Fifteen percent of the orders are received incomplete or with wrong items.
- No visibility into purchase orders. Some brand managers have to wait two to three days to get an answer about the status of an order.
- High logistics cost—almost 13 percent of the invoice value. Based on the industry standards it should be between seven and nine percent.
- Confusing relationship with suppliers due to delays in payment or double payments because of poor coordination between purchasing and payables.

Based on value chain management principles, major changes to the process were performed. Sellable goods requisitions were standardized and automated through the enterprise resource planning (ERP) system. Now requisitions are sent to a centralized purchasing unit after passing the budget check that is linked to the finance part of the ERP. Buyers check the quality of the requisition; make sure that they have complete information like payment terms, INCO terms, and delivery time. Buyers send to the suppliers a system-generated order with full information. As per the new process, the logistics people are informed immediately from the system that an order had been generated using the shipping order format; they start acting and nominating the best forwarder to pick up the shipment when ready. At the same time, the system is giving a signal to the payables to prepare the requested payment.

All communications during the order lead time are stored in the master log book and all parties have access to it so that they can take necessary actions if needed. Brand managers can access the master log book and get the status of their orders so thy can prepare the distribution plan. The process was designed in a way that the information is available to everyone who needs it from the time the order is placed to the time the order is fulfilled. Also, the process is flexible enough to adapt to any turbulence in the supply chain. The framework for the POM subprocess can be summarized in the following diagram (Figure 10.1). The benefits that

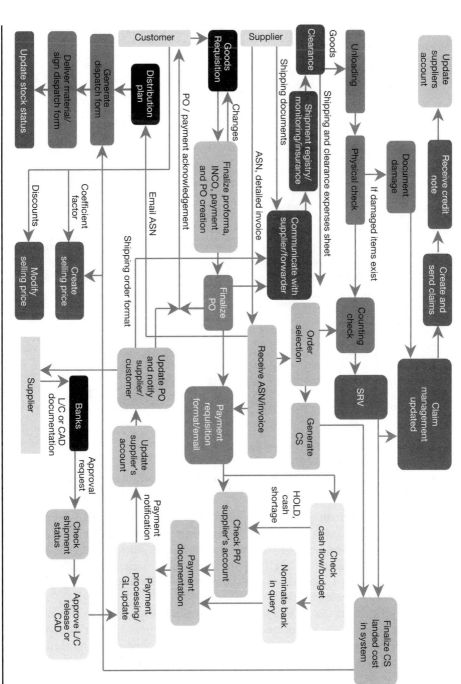

Figure 10.1 The modified POM process for BLUESALON

have been achieved so far from implementing these operational changes and addressing the pain points include:

- On-time delivery
  - Before: The on-time delivery was only 50 percent
  - After: The on-time delivery is 84 percent
- Processing purchase orders lead time
  - Before: Three weeks
  - After: Four working days
- Lack of accuracy in orders
  - Before: 15 percent of the orders were received incomplete or with wrong items
  - After: Two percent
- No visibility of the purchase orders
  - Before: Brand managers used to spend 2 to 3 days to get an answer about the status of an order
  - After: Brand managers can access the master log book and get information on the spot
- High logistics cost
  - Before: 13 percent of the invoice value
  - After: Nine percent

Stores and Merchandise Planning

The challenges in the store management process were identified as follows:

- High stock aging
- High level of stockouts
- Delay in marketing and promotion plans
- Very high level of damaged items; stock write-off rate was 5 percent
- High level of stock shrinkage in the outlets, around 1.5 percent

The major change management success was to convince all brand managers to prepare budgets for each single brand. Net profit and stock aging for each brand was decided to be the key performance indicators for each brand manager. The buying plans were added to the system so once the purchase requests exceeded the limits, the system would stop the order issuance. Revision of the budget by a higher authority was a must in the new process.

A new unit called the retail support unit was added to manage the marketing events and measure the performance of each store or brand. Monthly reports can now be issued consistently to take necessary actions when negative performance trends occur. Basically, the management was transformed from a reactive mode to a proactive mode.

The value chain processes and their interactions (the big picture) are shown in Figure 10.2. The benefits achieved so far from improving value chain processes and implementing the above strategic changes include:

- Stock level: The average stock level was for 12 months of sales. Now, the average stock level is 6 months of sales. Based on the trend, it is expected to reach four months at the end of 2009. Almost half of the stock investments were saved and utilized in other expansion projects such as opening more outlets and acquiring more brands.
- Marketing and promotion plans: The average increase in sales during promotion was 10 percent. Now, with proper planning and execution, the average increase per event is 25 percent.
- Sales increase compared to the previous year: Sales increased by 23 percent for the retail stores.
- Brand performance: Average net profit per brand increased dramatically.

Concluding Thoughts

It is clear how LAVC principles and enablers can have a major impact on a midsize company in the retail industry. The improvements and results that BLUESALON has achieved in a short time is amazing and good news for every company that decides to implement LAVC principles.

Special thanks to Mr. Eyas Sabri who shared this success story. Eyas started with ABU ISSA HOLDING two years ago as a strategy consultant, and his journey of developing strategies and improving the performance of the group started with BLUESALON company. He was able to take it to the next level of LAVC maturity. I'd also like to recognize Mr. Ashraf Abu Issa, Chairman of ABU ISSA HOLDING, for his leadership and vision. The support and understanding of upper management is a must in this type of transformation program. Another lesson from this success story is that once you implement an LAVC transformation program successfully in one company, it's easier to replicate the success for other companies under the group, even if they are in different lines of business since the LAVC concepts and knowhow can be transferred to other companies or business units.

Success Story 4: Cooper Tire Rolls Out New System for Better Demand Fulfillment

The Cooper Tire and Rubber Company (www.coopertire.com) has provided the world's motorists with a full line of tires and rubber products for more than nine decades. The company has maintained a simple distribution goal: positioning the right product in the right place, at the right time, at the lowest possible cost. But achieving that goal wasn't so simple, given that Cooper's 25-year-old legacy

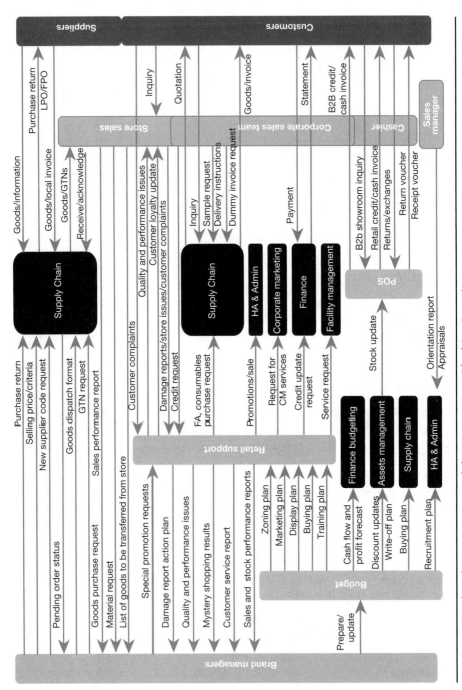

Figure 10.2 Value chain processes and their interactions (the big picture)

replenishment mainframe system ran just once a week. Every Monday morning, inventory planners would receive a new report that reflected customer orders and available inventory.

"You could see that there was a problem with generating reports only on a weekly basis," says Bob Sager, Cooper's manager of supply chain research and design. "If we received a customer order on Monday, and the customer service representative did not come over to the replenishment area to inform our planners of the order, they were unaware of it until the next week."

In addition, Cooper faced increasing complexity in its product offering. The company was constantly adding more SKUs, and warehousing more SKUs in additional locations. As that complexity grew, many believed that to provide the same level of customer service, higher levels of inventory would be required. It was evident that new processes and tools were needed to remedy the situation.

Distribution and Replenishment Planning

With several i2 solutions already implemented, including those that addressed transportation management and advanced planning and scheduling, Cooper Tire was confident that i2 had both the solution and the resources necessary to help the company achieve its goals for distribution and replenishment planning.

"The world that we were moving into was one that I dreamed of, but had never experienced," says Tim Rupright, Cooper's inventory planning administrator. "The i2 consultants really had the ability to understand our business, to communicate what we needed to do, and to train us on what the system was capable of doing."

Today, i2 Distribution and Replenishment Planner (DRP) serves as Cooper's daily execution system, performing replanning functions every night. The solution is used to plan the movement of inventory across the company's entire North American distribution network.

After using this system for approximately six months, the Cooper/i2 team took a hard look at what was and wasn't working. The team began a continuous improvement project aimed at fine-tuning the system, evaluating the utilization of existing tools and processes, identifying 15 areas of improvement, and developing an action plan for those improvements, all of which focused on improving fill rates and inventory turns. Cooper has realized a sizable reduction in finished-goods inventory and outside storage costs with the system.

"The management at Cooper views DRP as a competitive weapon," Sager says. "The whole idea around the daily rebalance of supply to demand makes us more competitive because we can handle complexity and be more responsive to customer demand. In the past, if something happened yesterday, we weren't able to respond to it today. We can now."

Master Data Management

Shortly after deciding to implement DRP, Cooper also realized it needed a better mechanism for maintaining its legacy mainframe information, as well as the new information that was required for the new i2 planning systems.

"We had a choice to build our own infrastructure, or to go with i2 Master Data Management (MDM), and we chose i2 MDM," Sager says. "We use i2 MDM to store, maintain, and clean the data that we send out to our planning systems."

In the past, making adjustments to the replenishment system data required users to go to many sources, and changes were often manual and done by the information technology department. i2 MDM serves as a single source across multiple systems, where changes can be made at any scale by the user. It enables Cooper's planners to manipulate criteria to change behavior in DRP based on business needs. "I have difficulty envisioning DRP functioning without MDM," says Rupright. "We can use MDM to make adjustments to the replenishment system, and the results are visible the next day. It's an iterative process that is pretty amazing."

Distributed Inventory Management

In addition to having redundant versions of its master data, Cooper also maintained five versions of inventory on its mainframe (which corresponded to the systems that used inventory). As a result, the company faced challenges in achieving one accurate picture of inventory. This situation was exacerbated by the fact that inventory was also valued in differing units of measure—by the pound or by the unit.

"The mainframe lost its transaction detail after two weeks, and this made it very difficult to go back and determine why an issue happened without having detailed data," says Craig Durliat, Cooper's manager of operation accounting. "In addition, the system was very North American-focused, and, as we started growing, we needed a more global footprint of the inventory."

To tackle these challenges, Cooper Tire implemented i2 Distributed Inventory Management (IMx) to help get its inventory system off the 30-year-old legacy inventory mainframe and assimilate into IMx all of its ties to order management, finance, and the other integrated supply chain processes. IBM served as Cooper's systems integrator on this project.

"The IBM team came onboard and really helped manage the inventory management project—not just the implementation of the IMx software. All inventory processes were looked at and either redesigned or redeveloped," Durliat says. "And that part of the IBM partnership, plus the experience of i2's resources on the supply chain side, were critical to the success of the project."

Cooper Tire uses IMx to post inventory, sales, and production activity every day. The system enables the company not just to look at units, but also to validate the dollar value of those units.

"That ability helps us determine whether we have good control over our inventory, from a unit standpoint and a trend standpoint, as well as from a financial perspective, which is very important in this world of Sarbanes-Oxley," Durliat says.

End-to-End Visibility

Through its IMx implementation, Cooper not only has a single, real-time, accurate view of actual inventory today, but also a projected inventory view—positioning the company to support demand fulfillment. Increased visibility into inventory enables Cooper to quickly determine the cause of inventory problems and to implement processes that can prevent the same problems from occurring again.

By integrating all instances of inventory onto the IMx system, Cooper has removed approximately 400 programs and 100 jobs from its mainframe, and it has reduced the number of inventory reports from 140 to 50.

"As users, we are much more self-sufficient with inventory transactions through IMx," Durliat says. "It's easy to access the data, the detailed transactions are there and analysis is simplified."

Having an integrated and flexible supply chain has allowed Cooper to improve its response to demand—ultimately better serving the end consumer and improving the company's bottom line. "The initial implementations got us part way there, but it was the continuous-improvement activities and increased planner experience that produced the biggest returns and allowed us to achieve our stated goals," Sager says.

This work was previously published under the same title in *Supply Chain Leader*, Volume 2, Number 2, written by Lauren Bossers, pp. 22–23, copyright 2007, by i2 Technologies, Inc.

Concluding Thoughts

This success story highlights how Cooper used several LAVC enablers to improve the demand fulfillment process. The enablers that were used: (1) visibility, (2) technology, and (3) process innovation.

Cooper followed several LAVC principles in this process transformation as well, such as to eliminate waste and reduce nonvalue-added activities (principle 3) when they removed approximately 400 programs and 100 jobs from its computer mainframe. It has also reduced the number of inventory reports from 140 to 50. Cooper also institutionalized continuous improvement (principle 4) which helped them to achieve their goals. In addition, it did a great job in selecting the right team for program transformation.

By being more agile, Cooper improved their responsiveness in serving the end customer, which resulted in improving the company's bottom line.

Success Story 5: ADTRAN's Solution for its Global Value Chain

For the past few years we've been doing a lot of work on our sales and operations planning processes to help us better understand demand and react appropriately. That will continue to be a top priority. In particular, I want to be able to get better information from our customers, and quickly interpret that information in ways that are relevant to our business—not only from an operations perspective, but also from a revenue and margin perspective. I believe the supply chain is really a demand chain. Customer demand drives it all, so if we can do better with forecasting and understanding the demand up front, then that's three-quarters of the battle. Of course, dealing with demand is difficult, forecasting accuracy is always tough, and getting the information that we need, when we need it, to make the right business decisions can be a challenge.

What we need to do now is to get more point-of-sale data, and more point-of-usage data about our products, from our customers. Sales data sharing happens in the retail sector all the time, so if it works for them, then I say why can't it work for us? Of course, it can be more challenging for us to get the data, particularly for our enterprise clients, which we serve through distributors. But we're now establishing some pilot projects for that market to see if we can improve our performance.

Today, many of our distributors have different stocking strategies, some with monthly reporting, others with quarterly reporting. As a result, on any given day it can be very hard for us to know what's really going on with our distributors' inventories, what they have on hand, what their sales to end users look like, and so on.

On top of that, the inventory information we do have now can hide, or at least disguise, the real consumption numbers. We don't necessarily know if a demand fluctuation is real, or if someone is stuffing the channel for some reason. We can easily get burned by someone going on vacation.

For example, during the course of regular operations we'll see that an ordering trend has a different curve and we won't know what's behind that change. So we'll assume it's real demand, and we will build new stock to deal with that increase, but sometimes it will turn out to be a false demand signal. What may have happened was someone had gone on vacation and ordered more stock to cover for a week or two. That sort of thing happens all the time, given the current state of our information and processes.

Greater Visibility and Vendor-Managed Inventory

To try and get access to better customer sales data, we're working on pilot projects to develop weekly reports from two of our key distributors, and at the same time to increase our visibility into their inventories and their pipelines. We expect this effort will provide us with a better understanding of real consumption, and we can adjust our production accordingly.

Another priority for ADTRAN (www.adtran.com) is establishing more vendor-managed inventory programs with our key suppliers. Better use of vendor-managed inventory can help us ensure that a lot of our standard items are readily available, while removing inventory from our books.

We do have a global supply chain. More than half of our products are manu-factured in Asia by our electronics manufacturing-services partners, and we have very good relationships and strong collaborations with them. We have a quick-turn chain; we can change our production schedule in the current week, even though we're manufacturing most of our products halfway around the world. So our focus now is primarily on the customer and demand side of things, because that's where I think we can make the greatest improvements.

Finally, one area that I believe supply chain leaders must never lose sight of is what we call CIPs—continuous improvement programs. At ADTRAN, we're well along the road toward building a culture of continuous improvement into the DNA of how we operate.

This work was previously published in an article titled "What are the Priorities in the Supply Chain Management for your Business?" in *Supply Chain Leader*, Volume 2, Number 2, written by Michael Cohen, p. 34, copyright 2007, by i2 Technologies, Inc.

Concluding Thoughts

Thomas L. Dadmun, the vice president for Supply Chain and Program Man-agement at ADTRAN, had shared the above thoughts with us indicating how ADTRAN is handling globalization and outsourcing. ADTRAN develops and manufactures networking and telecommunications solutions to carry voice, data, video, and Internet communications across copper, fiber, and wireless network infrastructures.

Visibility, cross-organizational collaboration, and process innovation (vendor-managed inventory solution) were the main enablers for ADTRAN to achieve success and manage its global value chain. ADTRAN also didn't lose sight of building a culture of continuous improvement (LAVC principle 4) along the road.

Success Story 6: Managing Sprint's Value Chain

Supply chain efficiencies remain a focus at this wireless operator, as it applies the most advanced technologies to solving the riddle of getting the right product to the right customer at the right time.

Michael Hahn is the vice president of Product Operations at Sprint (www.sprint.com), the third largest wireless operator in the United States (revenue,

$41 billion). Hahn is responsible for inventory management, demand planning, procurement, transportation, and warehouse logistics for all products purchased and sold in Sprint's distribution channels. Before joining Sprint in 2004, he had a similar role with AT&T Wireless for nine years, where he was vice president of Consumer Equipment, responsible for logistics, inventory management, supplier management, and product portfolio. Prior to entering the telecommunications industry, Hahn had experience working for major U.S. retailers, such as Circuit City and Macy's.

In this interview, conducted by *Supply Chain Leader* editor Victoria Cooper at Sprint's headquarters in Overland Park, Kansas, in late January 2008, Hahn discussed the results of a wide-ranging supply chain initiative at the company.

What is the scope of the products your team supports at Sprint?

The products include our core wireless devices, including our standard handsets, and our data devices, such as PDAs (personal digital assistants), wireless modem cards, smart phones, and the accessories to support all of these devices. The distribution channels include the independent dealer/agents, our national retail partners—such as Best Buy and RadioShack—and more than 1300 Sprint-owned retail locations. In addition, Sprint has an extensive direct fulfillment effort utilizing the web (Sprint.com), telesales, and the Sprint Business Direct sales team, across small, medium, and large businesses, plus public sector accounts.

Are there any other supply chain organizations within the company?

Yes. There is a corporate supply chain organization, with responsibility for the supply chain activities with our network equipment, capital purchases, contract management, and cost negotiations. My team has an outstanding working relationship with this organization, which also provides us with our performance metrics and handles supplier disputes.

Product operations is the customer-focused organization, and serves as the last line of defense before the products leave our warehouse and reach the customers' hands or the distribution channel.

How closely do you work with Marketing?

My team reports into the product development organization, and we are closely aligned with both the sales and marketing organizations. We're an integral component of the planning cycle for understanding what our product needs are for the future. Sprint has always been known for creating unique and innovative products—for instance, Sprint offered the first GPS-enabled phone in 2001, and we are leaders in navigation and location-based services for mobile phones. We work closely with the marketing and sales organization to understand the demand for our products and then work with our suppliers to ensure that we have adequate supply available at the right time and location throughout all of our distribution channels.

How have customer demands changed over the past few years, and what has this change meant at Sprint?

Simply put, customers have become more demanding, calling for greater diversity in the types of devices offered. Quarter after quarter, we have seen that our customers enjoy doing more with data services on their phones, such as e-mail, web surfing and access to entertainment. They want "smart" phones, whether they're on a Windows, BlackBerry, or Palm operating device, with full access to their e-mail and the Internet.

Currently, Sprint has some of the hottest products on the market, ranging from devices that allow you to text message easier via a cell phone with a slide-out qwerty keyboard to many of the most innovative data devices in the marketplace. The devices are getting more cutting-edge, offering a wide variety of different applications. To meet the growing needs of our consumer and business customers, we must be able to offer a diverse collection of feature-rich devices.

The traditional use for a basic wireless phone—making calls back and forth—is still a substantial share of the business. But, that said, the number of customers utilizing data capabilities over the Sprint network continues to grow, quarter over quarter. And Sprint's new "Simply Everything" unlimited voice and data pricing plan for $99.99 opens the door for even more customers to fully explore data services on their wireless phones and truly appreciate what wireless mobile data services can offer.

Is the product mix going to get greater?

Yes, and fortunately, Sprint has a long history of being ahead of the curve when it comes to products. The needs of the customer are forever changing, and there is more of a need for segmentation in our channels. We have a great deal of diversity in our customer base, from the small business owner to the *Fortune* 100 corporate customer, from the individual consumer to the government client. We have to make sure that we have the diversity in our product assortment to meet their needs, whether it's a desire for data, music, video, text messaging or Direct Connect (push-to-talk), or a combination of such features. And yes, we still offer voice products.

What is your product volume?

Across all of our products in our distribution network, Sprint "touches" more than 4 million units a month, from a forward and reverse perspective. But the types of orders that Sprint fulfills range from tens of thousands of units shipped in bulk to a national retailer to a single phone with customized software shipped to a satellite business location. So the range of "where and who" we ship to is quite diverse.

What is the nature of the competitive environment?

The global telecom market is forecasted to manufacture over 1 billion devices in 2008. It's a very competitive environment, with more than 80 percent saturation in the United States. The companies who succeed will be the ones who plan, forecast, and procure accurately and in a timely manner with their suppliers.

What was your first challenge when you came to Sprint almost four years ago?

When I joined Sprint, we needed to improve in our inventory forecasting and distribution. We experienced challenges with supply during product launches as well as with forecasts for procurement and replenishment. In addition, we faced long vendor lead times and delivery inconsistencies.

When we merged with Nextel, our distribution network became even more complex, with legacy systems that did not "speak" to each other and were mostly manual rather than automated fulfillment processes. We determined that to achieve world-class demand and supply management we would need to change our organizational structure, our processes, and our systems technology.

What role did i2 (a software technology provider) play in your initiative?

When I arrived at Sprint, the company had just inked an agreement with i2. I guess you could say I inherited it, but I then became its champion. We liked i2's history and background working with similar-sized corporations that manage inventory across multiple distribution channels. We chose i2 for its ability to help us manage the flow in inventory through our points of distribution and, in turn, monitor the demand that we have planned with our suppliers to ensure that they manufacture and deliver the goods when we need them. What we needed was more accuracy and more agility in our demand and supply modeling.

What we didn't want was to have our suppliers manufacturing the wrong quantities—too few or too many. We didn't want them manufacturing the wrong models or the wrong colors, having too much of one model or too little of another. We need for them to focus on building to what our true demand needs are. With the i2 forecasting and replenishment tools and capabilities, we were able to create the solution.

The applications and systems that we worked with i2 to develop have allowed us to better forecast our inventory needs, more accurately distribute our products to the right places across our distribution channels, and better replenish our warehouses and locations.

Sprint had the vision years ago to recognize that the portfolio was going to expand, to get more diverse, with a fashion component. We realized we would not be able to enlarge our inventory, but rather would have to manage it in a more disciplined way across multiple models. We could not do this on our own, without some of the advanced technology offered by a company like i2.

Did you need to change your organizational structure?

By automating many of our processes and achieving more accurate demand planning and replenishment management, we have been able to structure our organization more efficiently. Instead of having people structured by channel, working at very detailed levels for lack of automated tools, we have now organized our management processes across the following competencies: warehouse logistics, demand planning and procurement, and replenishment and distribution. And I've instituted a fourth function: program management across these three groups.

What about your warehouse logistics network?

To further simplify our business we went from 19 warehouses (after the merger) to 2 central warehouse facilities. Our main point of distribution is centralized in one of the largest distribution hubs in North America: Louisville, Kentucky. We have a great partnership with UPS, whom we work with on our transportation and warehouse needs. UPS provides the brick and mortar as our outsourced, third-party logistics partner, but Sprint manages the processes and requirements. The partnership between UPS and Sprint is excellent and involves executives at the most senior level of each company's management team.

Sprint also uses Brightpoint in Indianapolis to support the logistics management in our dealer/agent distribution network. Brightpoint is the most capable supply chain provider focused in the wireless space, and has a long history of partnership with Sprint.

By consolidating and centralizing our logistics needs, we can leverage tremendous savings and maximize efficiencies. And we are now next day to anywhere in the country, regardless of order size.

What are some of the improvements you've realized?

In addition to cost savings, we've reduced inventory levels across all of our distribution channels. We've improved our in-stock levels, despite the fact that our product portfolio is more diverse than ever. This is a substantial improvement for any industry, not just the wireless space.

We've seen significant improvements in forecast accuracy. The purchase forecast accuracy (3 months out) has doubled to around 70 percent, while the replenishment forecast accuracy (1 week out) has improved by 60 percent. We've automated more than 90 percent of our replenishment orders.

Doesn't Sprint have a large retail presence?

Yes. Often what we don't get credit for—and I think this applies to all telecom operators—is that we are a large retailer, in addition to our other distribution channels. We have more than 1300 retail locations. How many retailers have that many locations? So retail is very important to us.

What is your next challenge?

How can we reduce the inventory levels even further? How do we reduce the timeframe between when an item is manufactured in Asia to when it is delivered to the Sprint warehouse?

What I'd like to see is a true just-in-time scenario. This will require collaboration with all of our partners, involving third-party logistics operators, our IT partners, transportation providers, and our device suppliers.

Clearly, the device suppliers are our partners in this endeavor. We cannot insist on something that is a surprise to them, so we have to engage them in our processes from the earliest moment. They have to understand what we're working on, and what our customers demand. We work continuously with them to make improvements in quality, availability, and efficiency.

Our role in the food chain works like this: We work with the manufacturer on the requirements and capabilities needed to support the customer and their needs. All of our potential devices are then tested thoroughly on our network, before they are launched and approved for sale on the Sprint network.

We are working on the development of a device from 12 to 24 months before it's launched. It's up to Sprint to understand what the content should be, what the software needs are, and what services the customer requires access to. We do not manufacture the devices, although we need to forecast and plan the quantities correctly so our supplier partners can meet our inventory needs.

We're developing devices today that will ship in the second half of 2009. The ironic part is that because the life cycles of our devices are as short as they are, it's even more important than ever to "buy and plan it right, from the start," and our partnership with i2 has helped Sprint make this happen.

This work was previously published in an article titled "Buying it Right at Sprint" in *Supply Chain Leader*, Volume 3, Number 1, written by Victoria Cooper, pp. 16–19, copyright 2008, by i2 Technologies, Inc.

Concluding Thoughts

This success story is a great example for the challenges in the telecommunication industry and the degree of competition in today's market. It highlights several strategy innovation examples like consolidating and centralizing logistics needs, and organization restructuring to become process-oriented instead of channel-oriented when it comes to replenishment to enable best-practice processes.

The next challenge is to achieve the fourth level of maturity in a value chain by achieving process collaboration with all of their partners, involving third-party logistics operators, IT partners, transportation providers, and device suppliers.

Success Story 7: Global Supply Chain Management System at Fairchild

The global supply chain management systems team at Fairchild develops and manages the global supply chain systems and related business processes that drive our supply chain success. Our CEO, Mark Thompson, highly values and understands the leverage that an efficient supply chain can give the company, and has given us the resources to be successful. Our supply chain organization consists of several hundred people in locations around the globe, and forecasting and measurement are key components of our success. Our focus on supply chain measurement and process improvement during the last five years has delivered great results.

Every week our team measures key supply chain performance metrics and reports the results to our senior executives. The report includes our top-tier metrics, such as inventory turns, shipment-to-commit and delivery-to request performance, and the revenue outlook—measuring our backlog and our position relative to revenue realization. We also take it to the next level and look at areas like new product delivery performance, customer delivery performance, and lead times.

While geared toward C-level management, these weekly metrics reports are also distributed to the supply chain team. This broad distribution offers visibility into our metrics achievement throughout the supply chain, allowing team members to quickly review the performance of their product group or manufacturing site and, if necessary, to do a root-cause analysis and remediate issues. Speed is another key component to our success. There is significant complexity in our supply chain, and sudden changes in demand, supply, or costs require us to be fast, flexible, and able to react based on real-time information.

Our longer-term view of the supply chain is managed through a monthly sales and operations planning process (S&OP). The comprehensive metrics package we publish plays an important role in that process. We start with a consensus forecast roll-up, and then managers from each functional area of the business meet to determine our capability to respond to that forecast—and what that means in terms of revenue and expense for the company. Visibility and accessibility of supply chain performance data are critical to the S&OP process because they empower us to better respond to requests for internal or subcontractor capacity, analyze progress on major initiatives such as new product introductions, or capitalize on excess capacity for increased revenue-generating opportunities.

Annually, we conduct a supply chain metrics review to assess our total supply chain management costs and asset utilization. We engage a consulting firm to conduct a comprehensive SCOR® (supply chain operations reference model) assessment for us, and also to benchmark Fairchild against others in our industry. We use this annual review process to identify performance gaps and solutions to close those gaps, as well as to prioritize improvement initiatives and investments.

One of the areas of significant improvement realized through the metrics and benchmark analysis process is delivery performance to commit date. Fairchild targeted 10-plus percentage points of improvement to increase our competitive advantage in service. We used detailed root-cause analysis and regular metric reviews, and also developed some new functionality to monitor performance through the factories to proactively manage late work in process instead of waiting until the time of shipment. Timely availability of results allows the planning teams and factories to rapidly respond if things are off track.

Our root-cause analyses also revealed that our order promising system was not adequately accounting for a number of secondary constraints. Despite some products being nearly interchangeable in our system from a capacity perspective, we were not fully allowing for these when promising orders. Consequently, we factored more detail for significant secondary constraints into our process models, and the problem was resolved.

Another important area of improvement for Fairchild involved taking better control of our channel inventory. An extensive review of our channel inventory processes has enabled us to substantially improve our inventory controls and sell-in, helping us to mitigate the bullwhip effect. Our weekly measurement and monitoring have led to significant improvements in stability of weeks-on-hand and buffer stock.

I am fortunate to work for a company with an executive team that realizes and appreciates the strategic value that a well-managed supply chain brings to the overall business. Our focus on results and commitment to weekly, monthly, and yearly monitoring and evaluation have made us a more efficient, productive company—and made supply chain management a competitive differentiator for Fairchild Semiconductor.

This work was previously published in an article titled "How (and How Often) Do You Measure Supply Chain Results?" in *Supply Chain Leader*, Volume 3, Number 1, written by Michael Cohen, pp. 27–28, copyright 2008, by i2 Technologies, Inc.

Concluding Thoughts

Mary Wilson, the director for Global Supply Chain Management, Planning Systems at Fairchild Semiconductor, shared the above study with us highlighting the importance of the performance measurement system in closing the loop between plan and actual (LAVC principle 5) and driving the supply chain success.

It highlights the importance of the role of SCOR®, benchmarking, and root-cause analysis in identifying performance gaps and solutions to close those gaps.

Success Story 8: Performance Measurement Best Practices for Supply Chain Management at Timken

The steel group at Timken (www.timken.com) has approximately 2500 employees, and in 2007, we had more than $1.5 billion in revenue. We have a complex business, performing 100 different operations, with more than 300 different steel types, and about 9,000 customer specifications in our system.

It is important that the supply chain group shares a significant portion of the economic responsibility for the overall business, because what we do drives much of the financials for all of Timken Steel. In a similarly correlated relationship, the accuracy of our planning assures better customer service through on-time delivery to our promises and more precise determination of lead times.

We must excel at a number of key factors to leverage our supply chain performance; having, and meeting, the right performance metrics at all levels of the business is critical to our success. At the highest level, you need to bring together the key metrics that interact with each other. We call it a balanced metrics approach, because you can't just look at any one metric in isolation.

On our top-level scorecard, we balance throughput, inventory, on-time delivery, lead times, and cost. They are all connected, and you have to consider them all to understand the whole supply chain picture. I view our metrics like a pyramid, with each element getting segmented and more detailed as you move down each level on the pyramid.

Our top-level management group focuses on the top of the pyramid—the metrics that look at process path constraints and other key areas for our business. For example, melting steel, or "heats," as we call it, is a critical process. Every day we see the number of heats from our melt shops, and as long as we're achieving the planned heats per day and the planned output from a handful of other key processes downstream, then we're not sweating the metrics at the next level down on the pyramid—those metrics will be for others to monitor.

If we don't see the right output at key process points, then we know we're not going to be able to finish and ship the right amount of product this period, and we need to start asking questions. Each time you take a step down on the pyramid the amount of data explodes, so we stay focused at the top. You can't look at everything or you'll be overwhelmed.

Of course, we have people on the sales, manufacturing, and supply chain teams that are looking at the data at each step down the pyramid. At any given level in the pyramid, we can measure data in months, weeks, days, hours, or minutes. We'll get down to the level of one work center or machine. We'll measure the inventory in front of that machine, and the sequencers will monitor and schedule that machine on a shift-by-shift basis. We're looking at lead times every week, comparing working capital to sales on a monthly basis, and reviewing operating expenses on a daily, weekly, and monthly basis. When we see deviations at any level, the people responsible for that area will start asking questions, performing analysis, and taking actions as required.

A Balancing Act

None of this happens in a vacuum. These metrics are used in our S&OP (sales and operations planning) process, which my group leads. Every Wednesday afternoon we bring the business representatives to the table to review the metrics, our plan, and where we stand. And, unless it's Christmas Day, we seldom cancel that meeting. It's not unusual for Timken Steel's president to stop by and participate in that meeting—and it is huge for us to have that kind of support. It shows that he views the supply chain as important to the success of the business.

In that weekly meeting we balance the needs of the sales team with those of the manufacturing team. These needs are inherently at odds with each other in any organization. Sales folks want every product available in any quantity, at all times, to satisfy customers anywhere in the world. Manufacturing folks want to make batch sizes and sequences of similar items to get production efficiencies. My group is responsible for bringing these teams together and achieving a mutual goal of delivering both customer and shareholder value.

We're constantly adjusting capacity in response to demand, taking into account the whole picture from raw materials to customer delivery. Our system of checks and balances forces us to think through the overall ramifications of various supply chain decisions. This includes playing the hand you've been dealt as best you can, as well as influencing future scenarios. To me, it's just common sense, although some would argue that common sense is not all that common.

This work was previously published in an article titled "How (and How Often) Do You Measure Supply Chain Results?" in *Supply Chain Leader*, Volume 3, Number 1, written by Michael Cohen, pp. 29—30, copyright 2008, by i2 Technologies, Inc.

Concluding Thoughts

That was William Bryan, the director of Supply Chain and Supply Chain Economics at Timken Steel Group, on how strategic metrics should be linked to tactical and operational metrics to allow a pyramid view of the business.

This approach helps in understanding the big picture and figuring out the root cause for poor performance.

Success Story 9: Continental Tire Speeds Planning Cycles and Inventory Turns

Continental Corporation is the fifth-largest automotive supplier in the world, with extensive know-how in tire and brake technology, vehicle dynamics control, and electronic sensor systems. With targeted annual sales of more than €26.4 billion in 2008, Continental employs approximately 150,000 people in 36 countries, at nearly 200 plants, test tracks, and research and development centers. As a leading technology partner to the automotive industry, Continental develops and manufactures a broad product range that includes tires, brakes, chassis, air bags, power trains, and advanced electronics components that enable S&OPhisticated features such as electronic stability control and adaptive cruise control.

Tire Division Planning and Inventory Challenges

Continental supports two tire divisions: Passenger and Light Truck Tires, and Commercial Vehicle Tires. Like many manufacturers, the tire divisions face two major supply chain management challenges: driving economies of scale in production while maximizing inventory efficiency in the distribution network. For Continental's tire divisions this is no easy task: With 14 major worldwide production sites, over 80 warehouses, and more than 6000 products, S&OPhisticated software tools are necessary to cope with the huge data volumes processed by optimized production and replenishment plans.

Continental has two major tire business areas—OEM and Replacement—each with very different supply chain management requirements. On the OEM side, the order volumes are relatively high, and every order needs to be fulfilled on time. In the Replacement business, however, the situation is very different— demand and product variability are high, order volumes are lower, and profits differ widely depending upon the product and sales channels. Because brand loyalty on the customer side is a continuous challenge, ensuring that product is available at point of sale is critical to profitability.

"In supply chain management you have to balance these conflicting requirements, always trying to achieve the global optimum," says Dirk Petermann, head of the Competence Center of Supply Chain Management for the Continental Corporation's tire unit.

Continental recognized the complicated customer demand/inventory efficiency conundrum as a major opportunity to improve its supply chain management. Company executives concluded that they needed significant changes in business processes, organizational structure, and planning methodology.

Continental established its as is and to be positions, and identified the providers who could support the company in its transition to the to be state. "We made a short list of three providers, one of which was i2," Petermann says. "At the end of the day, i2 won because they were able to show us significant experience in solving problems like ours, with a very high number of installed solutions. The people from i2 proved that they could provide what we wanted, and from the very beginning they were passionate about helping us drive value with our supply chain management initiative."

To address its supply chain challenges, Continental implemented i2 Supply Chain Planner and i2 Inventory Optimization in a phased approach. First, i2 Supply Chain Planner was implemented for European master planning. The planning system prioritizes incoming orders and forecasts demand in "demand layers." Next, it creates a production and replenishment plan, accounting for supply chain and business rules unique to Continental. A new replenishment plan is created midweek to respond to changes in the demand pattern. A major increase in inventory turns resulted, and consequently Continental extended the new demand planning system globally to include all cross-regional (Americas, Europe, and Asia) suppliers.

With demand planning in place, Continental continued to see potential for improving inventory turns further, in tandem with improving the service level for its most valuable customers and most profitable products. The company turned to i2 Inventory Optimization, developed to optimize the relationship between inventory management, customer service, and product line profitability.

"Inventory optimization helps us to define different service levels based on the product and sales channel," Petermann says. "This means we are now able to focus our investments in inventory exactly on the products where Sales wants to have a high service level. Overall inventory efficiency does not take a hit, and on the other side, we can reduce inventory levels for products with a lower service." As a result, the tire divisions' distribution network is now extremely responsive and inventory is deployed according to the rules defined by the sales organization.

"After dramatically increasing speed in the distribution network we learned that production cannot keep up without taking a hit on production efficiency," Petermann says. "Consequently we started looking for possibilities to increase the agility of production without influencing productivity negatively."

On-the-Floor Responsiveness

Creating a detailed production plan before the i2 implementation required entering in all demand, supply, and production constraints. It took several days to create these production "campaigns," and to support stable production, the production plan was frozen over a period of weeks. Consequently, demand changes within this frozen period had no impact on production.

Now, however, Continental's campaign planning functionality via i2 Supply Chain Planner creates an optimized production plan within hours, cutting the shop-floor stability freeze by half with the potential to reduce it further. Demand shifts can now be quickly accommodated on the shop floor, thereby eliminating excess materials, labor, and inventory costs as well as maintaining valuable customer loyalty with superior service.

"i2's business expertise is highly welcome at Continental Corporation," Petermann says. "We always engage i2 in our discussions of business processes, identifying weaknesses and areas for improvements, the business processes that should be implemented, and the tools to support those business processes. We really appreciate the experience that i2 brings to those discussions."

Continental's Results

Continental has succeeded in making its supply chain significantly more responsive, agile, and reliable. Prior to implementing i2 solutions, planning was done on a monthly basis and as a result, plans were outdated by the time they went into effect.

"Since we implemented Supply Chain Planner, planning is done weekly and replenishment planning is done twice a week. Planning time was reduced by more than 90 percent, and the planning horizon was multiplied by 10. Inventory turns increased substantially," Petermann says.

Through its use of Inventory Optimization, Continental is achieving significantly improved service levels, which has contributed to an increase in profit margins. "After the Inventory Optimization implementation with i2, we recognized that we often shipped tires much too early into the regional distribution centers," he adds. "We learned that to increase overall service levels, we have to hold them much longer in the plant warehouses and ship them later. By keeping inventory upstream, we can respond to demand changes with much more agility."

A mutual, long-term dedication to achieving results has made the relationship between Continental and i2 a successful one. "Looking back through the years, i2 was really a valuable partner, helping us to permanently improve our supply chain," says Petermann. "The next improvement steps are already under discussion and the journey will continue."

This work was previously published in an article titled "Continental Tire Speeds Planning Cycles and Inventory Turns" in *Supply Chain Leader*, Volume 3, Number 2, written by Lauren Bossers, pp. 22–34, copyright 2008, by i2 Technologies, Inc.

Concluding Thoughts

This success story shows how lean and agile demand planning and inventory optimization subprocesses can maximize service and cut costs by addressing the following challenges:

- The need to respond more quickly to changes in demand
- Balancing customer service level and inventory
- The need to continuously increase inventory efficiency

The solution to address the above challenges was a combination of best-practice processes and enabled technology using an incremental implementation approach. The benefits from the transformation program can be summarized as follows:

- Nearly doubled inventory turns
- Significantly increased product availability
- Increased velocity of the planning process
- Improved flexibility and responsiveness of production and distribution
- Improved ability to determine target inventory levels to achieve desired service levels
- The ability to provide differentiated service level by product and sales channel

Success Story 10: Increasing Profits and Service Levels at Cementos Argos

With more than 50 percent of the cement market in Colombia, Cementos Argos was well positioned as a local industry leader. The company sought to expand its position regionally and internationally, but its complex network and disjointed supply chain processes and systems made this goal daunting—despite its presence in ten countries.

From 2005 to 2006, Argos combined eight Columbian cement companies to maximize synergies and economies of scale, and acquired another to expand its international reach. However, the acquisitions left the cement manufacturer essentially functioning as nine separate companies, all of which operated in silos.

Supply Chain Management to Expand Global Reach

As a result, designing a new network posed a significant challenge to the company's management, whose goal was to understand its customers in the United States as well as its customers in Central and South America.

"We wanted to ensure we were attending to our customers in terms of time to delivery and quantities. In the cement industry, meeting the delivery time you provide is the key driver to achieving customer satisfaction," says Luis Cappeletti, supply chain planning manager for Cementos Argos.

To improve customer satisfaction and increase value for its shareholders, Argos needed to create a new organizational structure and supply chain processes. "Supply chain is more than demand and production planning, raw material procurement, and transportation and logistics," says Cappeletti. "We're trying to get as close as possible to supply chain best practices. That requires not just technology solutions, but also a culture, procedures, and processes that support excellence in supply chain management. Argos is taking a holistic approach to supply chain management."

Partnership for Supply Chain Excellence

With these goals in mind, Argos began looking for a company that could provide both superior supply chain management technology and the long-term service relationship to help support a culture of supply chain excellence.

"We wanted to get away from the enterprise resource planning solution we had used in the past, but we had to make sure that we were recommending a supply chain solutions provider that would inspire confidence from our board of directors," says Juanita Quintana, logistics optimization director for Cementos Argos. "We needed supply chain knowledge and experience to help us change culture, mindsets, processes, and procedures. i2 represented all of that. Companies like Oracle or SAP are not just focused on supply chain. i2 was a supply chain specialist, and we were impressed with i2's history. i2 demonstrated its commitment to jointly developing an ongoing relationship focused on supply chain concepts, as well as on the tools."

Argos uses i2 Demand Manager to understand its product movement and its market, as well as to plan demand for up to 10 years. Demand Manager is used on a monthly and weekly basis, enabling the company to alter its demand projections according to new information it receives through the solution.

"Because we are trying to understand our global business for the next 5–10 years, we need to understand what all of our locations are doing," says Quintana. "With Demand Manager, we now have all of our information in one place, which means we can better understand our market." Demand Manager enables Argos to create product strategies that incorporate special events, external variables, historic patterns, prices, and the variability inherent in international orders.

i2 Transportation Modeler and i2 Supply Chain Strategist work in tandem on Argos' network design planning. Supply Chain Strategist operates as the calculator of all of the production and the distribution plans. Together, the two solutions determine long-term network options, stock policies, and node locations, as well as transportation, warehousing, and production costs and capacities. Argos also uses Transportation Modeler and Supply Chain Strategist to create bills of material for grinding and packing.

"Demand Manager, Transportation Modeler and Supply Chain Strategist enable us to have as much information as possible to provide useful recommendations to our production systems," says Cappeletti. "We are operating internationally, and those operations—including our 12 plants and 32 distribution locations—have to be absolutely synchronized every day. Using i2 solutions enables us to understand the full international picture."

Improving Profitability, Synchronicity, and Customer Satisfaction

By establishing an organization-wide supply chain model, coordinating weekly with its sales and operations planning team, and conducting daily adherence tracking between the plan and reality, Argos has now integrated and optimized its strategic planning processes. The company can define service standards, sales forecasting, production plans, distribution, and supply in the long, medium and short terms. i2 solutions enable Argos to closely supervise and monitor production plans, and to make quick corrective actions to adjust those plans when necessary. All of these process improvements help Argos to define, ensure, and improve its contribution margins and to better fulfill service offers.

Synchronizing production plans with demand has enabled Argos to reduce its distribution costs. "We continue to discover lots of new ways to do things more efficiently in production and distribution planning, and our savings continue to go up as a result," says Quintana. "In the first 10 months of our implementation, we reduced transportation costs by 7 percent and increased our delivery service level significantly. We are pleased about the return we have received on our investment with i2. Most important, we have the partnership that enables us to establish the supply chain processes, technology, people, and structure we need to succeed as a company."

The Future: Looking for Increased Savings and Service Levels

Cementos Argos is also implementing i2 Transportation Manager to increase control over shipments of finished products and raw materials to positively affect production for internal customers and delivery service capabilities for external customers.

"This is really a culture transformation process," says Cappeletti. "It's not just about IT. It's about the way we are reaching our financial goals, because our sales and operations planning team can make more informed, transformative decisions by leveraging new technologies and new people skills."

This work was previously published in an article titled "Increasing Profits and Service Levels at Cementos Argos" in *Supply Chain Leader*, Volume 3, Number 2, written by Lauren Bossers, pp. 40–41, copyright 2008, by i2 Technologies, Inc.

Concluding Thoughts

The major challenge facing Cementos Argos was the international expansion initiative, which was significantly hampered by a fragmented and inefficient supply chain. By leveraging best-practice processes, new technologies, and new people skills, Cementos Argos was able to improve the supply chain management superprocess and achieve significant benefits like improved product margins and customer service.

Success Story 11: Green Value Chain versus Lean and Agile Value Chain

Instead of asking if a green supply chain can be an efficient supply chain, I really believe that the question should be "where doesn't green fit into a corporation's overall strategy?" When I was managing Dell's green supply chain strategy, I didn't view green initiatives separately from the corporation. The corporation as a whole had an impact on the environment in one form or fashion; hence the corporation needed to be green.

With regard to the supply chain, a green consciousness plays an integral role in companies' strategies. Companies would be well served to source as much product locally as possible and eliminate long, costly cross-country transport runs to deliver products. Obviously, purchasing locally significantly reduces transportation costs and carbon emissions. Additionally, it allows for a more rapid response to replenishment and time to market, making the business cycle more efficient.

Companies can find efficiencies combined with environmental friendliness in a number of areas, starting with transportation. In my articles and in speeches given at logistics conferences, I always state that one of the best investments a company can make is to have its entire supply chain analyzed to identify the optimal transportation network. Optimal transportation networks identify opportunities to consolidate parcel shipments into less than truckload (LTL), and LTL shipments into truckload shipments, and to convert air shipments to more efficient ground shipments where feasible.

Many companies are achieving significant reductions in logistics-related costs by ensuring that they have a network in place that eliminates unnecessary transportation and uses the optimal mode of transportation for all shipping. With Dell, and with my current employer, supply chain analysis and transportation management software has made reduced logistics costs a reality. This analysis not only ensures cost savings and efficiencies for companies, but also renders their supply chain greener.

Green Product Packaging

Another area in which a company can go green is in product packaging. At Dell and at the companies I work for in my current role, packaging is one of the primary areas addressed. My recommendations include:

- Collaborating with suppliers and customers to identify the optimal packaging configurations to eliminate unnecessary materials
- Utilizing logistics beams and air bags in trailers to double-stack pallets safely to eliminate damage in transit
- Identifying opportunities to collaborate with customers on recycling
- Utilizing multi-pack shipping boxes to eliminate the number of individual boxes needed to fill an order
- Creating a "design for sustainability" mindset whereby all packaging is designed to be as green as possible

Green Product Design

At Dell we spent a tremendous amount of time and effort to design and sell the most green and energy-efficient products on the markets. We also designed products configured specifically to require less packaging—thereby saving money for Dell. Companies also need to be aware of what happens to their products at end of life. This is an area that makes a tremendous impact on the environment. If you can design products with end-of-life considerations inherent in their design, you will recognize tremendous savings when it comes to handling waste, and at the same time be environmentally conscious.

It is clear that supporting an efficient supply chain goes hand-in-hand with green concerns, and green fits everywhere in business. Unfortunately, far too many companies have jumped on the green bandwagon merely for the sake of public relations. At Dell, however, we understood that all of the efforts we put into product design, supply chain analysis and management, packaging, supplier collaboration, and so on, all increased Dell's competitive advantage.

Measurable savings from green initiatives come in the form of reduced transportation, packaging and component costs. In addition, when suppliers and customers recognize the value of collaboration, relationships strengthen and sales grow—making a green supply chain a smart supply chain.

This work was previously published in an article titled "Can a Green Supply Chain Be an Efficient Supply Chain?" in *Supply Chain Leader*, Volume 3, Number 2, written by Guy Courtin, pp. 35-36, copyright 2008, by i2 Technologies, Inc.

Concluding Thoughts

Brittain Ladd, formerly of Dell and currently the Director of Logistics and Manufacturing at Cognizant Technology Solutions, shared with us his view on green supply chain initiatives such as optimizing transportation, packaging, and increasing collaboration between suppliers and customers during the design phase.

It's clear from this success story that LAVC enablers and principles will help firms achieve a green supply chain.

CUSTOMER RELATIONSHIP MANAGEMENT-DRIVEN SUCCESS STORIES

Success Story 12: Customer-Centric Approach Drives Global Growth for Tata Steel

The steel manufacturing industry has never been known for being particularly responsive to market needs. In fact, until recently, the industry has been plagued by extremely long lead times, poor customer service, and high levels of manufacturing inefficiencies. But there's a quiet revolution going on, serving up more change in the last decade than in the 150 years preceding it. The use of leading-edge technology has driven business efficiencies, and continued globalization has created further economies of scale, with both fueling rapid industry consolidation.

Tata Steel, the flagship of India's $22 billion Tata Group, is Asia's first and India's largest private-sector steel company. One of the lowest cost producers of steel in the world, it was ranked fifth in the *Asian Business Week* 50 performers in 2005, and has twice topped the "World-Class Steelmakers" list issued by World Steel Dynamics, a leading steel information service. Tata recently purchased Thailand's Millennium Steel and Singapore's NatSteel Asia, and in January 2007, announced the acquisition of Anglo-Dutch Corus Group in a $12 billion transaction.

"Before we started looking at supply chain optimization, we suffered from all of the typical problems manufacturers face: non-optimized asset utilization, long cycle times, disparate IT systems, and lack of visibility into demand, orders and shipments," says Anand Sen, vice president of Tata's Flat Product Division. "We knew that we simply couldn't meet our strategic objectives by maintaining the status quo."

Customer Satisfaction

Customer satisfaction was a real issue at Tata Steel. When orders were placed, customers were promised a due date that was not based on hard data, plant capacity, or raw material availability. Orders were delivered when promised only about 50 percent of the time. To make matters worse, customers would generally not receive advance notice if their order would not be ready as promised, and this lack of communication burdened customer resources down the line, in the finishing and distribution channels.

The plant would often scramble to address the needs of high-priority customers, further alienating customers whose orders may have been just as important but less urgent. Without any method to analyze forecast versus actual performance, it was impossible to design improvements in the overall delivery system.

Realizing that its industry-leading position was hanging in the balance, Tata started the improvement process by articulating its strategic drivers: improved customer satisfaction and higher asset utilization. To address customer needs, the company conducted an exhaustive survey to establish detailed customer requirements. The survey yielded three imperatives. First, provide an accurate promise as to when the order would be delivered. Second, in the event that the order due date would be missed, notify the customer early in the process—not at the point of the missed delivery. And third, accurately project a revised delivery date so that the customer could modify its schedules accordingly.

Business Process Reengineering

After mapping the entire supply chain process in great detail, Tata engaged in an extensive business process reengineering effort. The objectives were to evaluate the gaps in current supply chain processes with respect to industry demands, to redesign the processes to achieve a dominant service position, and to identify the IT enablers that could make this happen. "We saw the relationship with i2 as a critical partnership," says Biswajit Roychowdhury, chief of planning for Tata's Flat Steel Division. "Our final decision to go with i2 Sales and Operations Planning, i2 Factory Planner, and i2 Material Allocator was the culmination of a long process of due diligence and included all members of executive management."

The business issues Tata wanted its process reengineering and IT implementation to address included:

- Optimizing inventory investment, including raw materials, work in process, and finished inventories
- Maximizing the value of supplier relationships
- Improving the accuracy of price and volume forecasts
- Determining the best product mix
- Making reliable customer delivery promises
- Utilizing key assets optimally
- Prioritizing orders for key customers
- Improving quality and product yields through better scheduling decisions
- Improving transportation efficiency

Tata Steel completed its technology implementation earlier this year and has seen significant improvements already in critical areas. Most importantly, 85 percent of orders are promised within the desired delivery week and do not require any manual intervention or adjustment—up from 50 percent. "Sometimes it's even as high as 92 percent," asserts Roychowdhury. "Now, when we understand that an order is in jeopardy, we have the tools in place to troubleshoot the order and can often take corrective action to fix the problem before we even have to notify the customer." In addition, late orders running in the production line have been reduced to less than 10 percent, and order-booking efficiency has risen to above 80 percent.

Forecasting Capability

Tata's forecasting ability has also improved dramatically. Prior to implementing supply chain software, the company had no systematic insight into how to evaluate the accuracy of its forecasts for demand as well as for raw materials. Now, it has the tools to analyze its forecast predictions against actual results, enabling root-cause analysis capabilities to identify what has caused the differences. "Improving our ability to forecast allows us to use due-date-based planning, which helps us to meet demand with higher utilization of assets," says Roychowdhury. "Also, instead of manually balancing resources as before, we can now automatically identify bottlenecks deep in our processes, and take corrective action to increase our overall production efficiency, thus realizing the benefits of continuous improvement. In support of our strategic objectives, our supply chain data are fully integrated with the rest of Tata Steel's business infrastructure, so we're able to scale effectively as we grow."

The new-generation software from i2 has given Tata planners several capabilities they lacked prior to implementation. Planners can now project business over a year's time and monitor performance against those projections. They can also make product mix decisions based on profit optimization goals and take orders as late as possible with postponement strategies. Tata's planners can also refresh the expected time of arrival with up-to-the-minute information.

Prognosis

The rapid pace of change in the steel industry—and, for that matter, in heavy industrial manufacturing in general—is not expected to slow down. Stoked by these results, Tata executives are optimistic. "We're shifting from being order-takers in a relatively controlled pricing environment 20 years ago to being S&OPhisticated marketers adroitly negotiating the profitable space between supply and demand across multiple markets on an almost daily basis," says Sen. "Someday, we'll be able to predict not just the delivery date, but the actual hour that our truck will be pulling up to a customer's warehouse. It opens up a whole world of possibilities."

This work was previously published under the same title in *Supply Chain Leader*, Volume 2, Number 2, written by Elizabeth Greer, pp. 30–31, copyright 2007, by i2 Technologies, Inc.

Concluding Thoughts

This success story highlighted how Tata Steel was able to improve their supply chain management superprocess and the selling management process under the customer relationship management superprocess, which resulted in significant benefits in several areas. Tata Steel faced several challenges in the areas of delivery, forecasting, order promising, supply allocation/product mix based on profitability and customer priority, and balancing supply and demand—similar to other companies in the market. But Tata Steel was able to address them by leveraging process reengineering and enabled technology effectively and in a comprehensive way.

Tata steel was driven by a customer-centric focus (LAVC principle 1), proactive identification and elimination of problems' root causes (principle 4), and closing the loop between planning and execution by leveraging optimization ideas (principle 5).

Success Story 13: Lenovo's Superior Online Buying Experience Leads to Competitive Advantage

As vice president and general manager of Lenovo Global eCommerce and Direct Sales, Ajit Sivadasan is responsible for all global eCommerce functions including direct sales (online and phone) operations in Australia, Japan, Canada, and the United States. This territory may soon expand, as Lenovo is exploring similar options for its customers in other mature markets, such as the United Kingdom.

In addition to sales responsibilities, he also leads several other eCommerce functions including capabilities development, site production and merchandising, usability, and design—with each element aligned to ensure an optimal online customer experience. Within a year of joining Lenovo—having spent a five-year stint with Gateway as executive producer and senior director of eCommerce—Sivadasan moved Lenovo from a traditional customer-to-fulfillment supply chain to an online configure-to-order (CTO) model to enhance the customer experience.

Partnering with i2, Lenovo redesigned its eCommerce user interface, linking all CTO processes and choices to back-end order execution, thereby optimizing the end-to-end experience for customers. Synchronizing the eCommerce strategy with supply chain execution resulted in triple-digit growth in online revenues and profits. Currently, Lenovo's annual sales exceed US$16 billion, and the company employs more than 23,000 people worldwide. Lenovo made its first appearance on the Global Fortune 500 list this year.

What was your most pressing challenge upon arriving at Lenovo?

Our user experience online had several gaps from a customer's standpoint [after the Lenovo Group acquisition of the IBM Personal Computing Division in 2005]. The single biggest challenge was enabling customization and the ability for users to get access to products in an intuitive and logical manner. Our capabilities relative to competition were significantly lower.

Once we clarified our priorities, the next challenge was to figure out how to redesign the experience within the framework of the legacy constraints. We met with the i2 team and developed a blueprint that looked to dramatically improve the experience end to end, all the way from the research (configuring and ordering) phase through the manufacturing and fulfillment phase. We crafted a solution built on the i2 agile Business Process Platform that allowed for such an experience from a customer standpoint and that is scalable and manageable from Lenovo's standpoint.

What was behind the decision to change Lenovo's direct sales strategy to a configure-to-order approach?

The premise of configure to order (CTO) is not new—it's been done by several others in the industry, but it is quite complicated and requires great diligence to execute well. The value proposition behind selling online is providing a much greater level of flexibility and convenience to users. In other words, the online channel has the ability to offer an almost infinite number of options to customers without traditional constraints of physical space faced by brick and mortar stores. The fact that we've seen such huge growth in online commerce signifies that customers want merchants to show them what they want to buy in a way that makes sense to the buyers. In our specific case, the switch to the new model allowed our customers to pick and choose what they wanted with minimal confusion.

At the end of the day, this is what most online merchants are trying to do—sell more by simplifying the online experience. This seemingly simple notion was missing in our online sales experience. This in no way was revolutionary—neither was this a new discovery—but it allowed us to catch up to our competitors in a big way on the customer-facing front end and make improvements in our planning processes on the back end.

How do you identify and segment your customer base?

We service a broad spectrum of customers online, from individual consumers who buy one or two items from the website for their homes and home offices, to small and midsize business owners who buy for their businesses. Business customers also buy online but typically buy from customized business-to-business sites, where they can have access to their negotiated bids, volume discounts, and specific models that fit their needs. Business customers fall into several segments ranging from midmarket—500 to 5,000 employees—to large enterprise customers with numbers from 5,000 and up. We also serve education customers—higher education and K-12 institutions that buy in bulk—as well as public service entities such as various government agencies in the federal and state ranks that purchase large volumes for their constituents.

In the case of business customers, we build custom sites that are password protected, have unique product sets, and occasionally highly customized workflows that enable flexibility and business efficiency for the company. In many cases, the procurement department uses these sites to place purchase orders with us directly on behalf of their user groups. The whole process also has an account management structure around it to ensure that customers have the ability to voice their concerns directly to Lenovo. Most of our business customers are looking for efficiencies, and ordering online is the most efficient way they can execute procurement. Billions and billions of dollars in sales happen through such B2B sites globally— it's pretty significant, both for Lenovo and others in the industry.

How do B2B channel revenues compare with revenues generated from the consumer/home business site?

Sales on the business side far exceed the consumer sales for Lenovo, especially outside of China, because until very recently the majority of the products we sold were for the small-to-medium business, public sector, and enterprise audience. The ThinkPad's reliability—it continues to be among the best-designed and engineered products in the marketplace—has earned it a niche in the business community. However, Lenovo recently announced its Ideapad line of products, aimed at the consumer segment. These products have a colorful and stylish design and upscale features such as facial recognition for security and advanced Dolby sound capabilities.

Lenovo looks to distinguish itself on the high end—as a company, our aspiration is to delight our customers through an unequaled ownership experience, whether they buy our products for their homes or their offices.

What was i2's role in the website redesign and CTO shift?

i2 helped us conceptualize and develop a solution that worked end to end: from a customer's initial research through to back-end supply chain processes. The partnership has worked very well for us, in part because i2 is very focused on the customer. They go out of their way to make sure that the solution delivers value. In custom development it's all about how you optimize the code. At the end of the day every bit of code that you write should improve the overall user experience, while addressing flexibility and scalability. There are pluses and minuses with out-of-the box configurable solutions versus custom development, but with custom development you can control how you develop the application front to back.

Working collaboratively, we had to think about all the nuances on the eCommerce end to figure out how to execute each decision to do the things we needed to do on the back end—to drive sales conversion and all aspects that are important to the customer. We worked very closely with i2 on this project for the initial six months on what was a pretty significant amount of custom development work. All of the new processes have gone as planned, with only minor hiccups here and there. I would say that the relationship we have built, the team that we have today, and the quality of the people we work with—all of these things seem to click well for us and are not very typical of similar project teams I have seen in the past.

In the last 18 months, we've been through six or seven releases of custom-developed capabilities, and I'm very pleased that we have continually added value to the customer's purchase experience. We feel that there are things we can continue to do to gain a bigger share of the market, so we continue to focus on improving capabilities and focusing on user experience. The competitive landscape is tough—Apple, Dell, and HP are worthy competitors, all trying to improve the user experience. I am confident that with our intense and unwavering focus on our customers, we will continue to raise the bar in customer experience.

How does this system now position you to handle future challenges more effectively?

The one thing I can tell you with some confidence is that, as Internet penetration continues, and people spend more time online researching products and figuring out what they want to buy, the purchasing decision is more and more influenced by the online experience. As an example, if you go on a website trying to buy a computer, or for that matter anything, and if your experience on the site is bad in spite of the product being good, and all other things being equal, it can absolutely impact the buying decision. We know that 70 to 80 percent of customers who go online to buy don't follow through for one reason or another.

For me it is very simple. You have to really focus on things that help customers make that decision properly. Everything in the online experience matters from a user standpoint. For example, consider flexible credit options. We recently integrated PayPal because it's an easy way of transacting without having to worry about fraud from giving out credit card numbers. We've added chat capabilities where customers can interact online with our agents without having to call. We've added customer reviews—so customers can provide feedback and look at feedback from other customers to firm up their decisions. In these seven releases we've added 300-400 features that all look to help our customers make the right decisions quickly and conveniently.

How does this new system position Lenovo to contend with current economic fluctuations?

Market conditions will fluctuate from time to time. When the economy turns downward, customers may migrate to the lower end and some may defer. But the surprising thing from a technology standpoint is that PCs have become so central to people's lives, it is almost impossible for most people to operate without them. In most cases, newer versions of products introduce significant improvements in capabilities, whether it is a new version of a graphic card, increased computing power owing to a new chipset, wireless bandwidth, or some other capability. You really can't go on too long without upgrading if you want to take advantage of the advances in technology. PC sales continue to be strong. The current economic outlook may see some shifts in how customers buy, but at the end of the day, growth in this sector will continue to be strong.

This work was previously published in an article titled "Lenovo's Superior Online Buying Experience Leads to Competitive Advantage" in *Supply Chain Leader*, Volume 3, Number 2, written by Deborah Navas, pp. 29–31, copyright 2008, by i2 Technologies, Inc.

Concluding Thoughts

Lenovo success story is a great example on how configure-to-order strategy and synchronizing the customer relationship management superprocess with the supply chain management superprocess (back end) can help a company achieve a competitive advantage and increase market share.

For Lenovo, the key to growing online market share is an intuitive user interface portal backed by a highly synchronized supply chain. Lenovo used LAVC enablers like process innovation, strategy innovation, and technology, and leveraged the first principle of LAVC (focus on customer success).

Success Story 14: Whirlpool Transformation Program

Whirlpool makes a diverse line of products (value chains) like washers, dryers, refrigerators, dishwashers, and ovens, with manufacturing facilities in 13 countries. This success story is a real-life example of a firm that adopted many of the best-practice guidelines that were highlighted in previous chapters in implementing their transformation program.

Whirlpool needed a strategy that can minimize supply chain cost and achieve competitive advantage. Their strategy was to focus on customer requirements first and proceed backward. Therefore, Whirlpool studied consumers' desires with regard to appliance delivery. They found that consumers were asking mainly for accurate promises "Give a date, hit a date,"

Whirlpool leveraged AMR Research, Gartner, and Forrester Research to benchmark themselves against competitors and obtain cross-industry information and competitive intelligence. Then they mapped out what was considered best-practice performance along 27 different supply chain capability dimensions. This exercise helped them identify areas of improvements.

Before moving forward, the program transformation team had to build a compelling business case to get the buy-in from upper management. They had to justify their program wholly on expense reductions and working capital improvements.

Effective transformation plans were developed for implementation, performance management system, change management, and rollout.

Whirlpool started with improving the S&OP process to get the most benefit. The current process was inadequate with Excel spreadsheet feeds. After the transformation program, Whirlpool was able to generate synchronized long and short plans that can consider marketing, sales, finance, and manufacturing constraints or requirements.

The second project involved launching a collaborative planning, forecasting, and replenishment (CPFR) pilot, to share their forecasts using a web-based application and to collaborate on the exceptions, which enabled them to cut forecast accuracy error in half within 30 days of launch. Then, Whirlpool implemented a suite of advanced planning and scheduling software products to help in reducing inventories while sustaining a high service level. A blind Internet survey showed Whirlpool, as a result of the transformation program, to be "most improved," "easiest to do business with," and "most progressive" in the eyes of their trading partners.

Whirlpool segmented their products and followed a different strategy for each product line. For high volume SKU like dishwashers, refrigerators, and washing machines, they used the build-to-stock replenishment technique with their customers. For smallest-volume SKUs, Whirlpool followed the pull replenishment technique with the more flexible build-to-order process. The inventory savings on the small volume SKUs would balance out the costs of stocking up on the high-volume SKUs. They started also to move away from having a "one-size-fits-all" approach—one service level across all products to recognizing that some products are more important or more profitable than others and should have a higher service level.

Several things were absolutely critical to keep the transformation program on schedule and on track; a highly disciplined and "Winning" transformation program office and upper management support. The implementation strategy "think big but focus relentlessly on near-term projects" was the reason for a smooth success. Whirlpool organized the change effort into 30-day chunks, with three new capabilities or business releases rolling out monthly, some on the supply side and some on the demand side. The main job of the program transformation office, which adopted Six Sigma methodology, was to ensure the completion of projects on time, on budget, and on benefit.

The transformation program office contracted Michigan State University and the American Production and Inventory Control Society (APICS) to develop a competency model that can outline the skills and roles required in a top-tier organization. Whirlpool also revisited the compensation system to allow employees to be rewarded for increasing their expertise even if they are not being promoted into supervisory roles. They also put a huge emphasis on developing employees' management skills, and used a model developed by the Project Management Institute, as a standard for evaluating and enhancing the organization's project management capabilities. Finally, Whirlpool assembled a supply chain advisory board to provide guidance and assess the transformation program results and direction.

Concluding Thoughts

This success story is based on an article published in October 2004, by Reuben Slone in *Harvard Business Review* under the title of "Leading Supply Chain Turnaround," talking about the Whirlpool transformation program over a four-year period.

Whirlpool adopted several LAVC principles (like being customer-oriented), and leveraged LAVC enablers (process innovation, technology, and strategy innovation) to redesign their processes, and followed best practices in its program transformation efforts. In return, Whirlpool achieved more than 95 percent in product availability service level, and the inventory of finished goods dropped from 32.8 to 26 days. In one year, the working capital was reduced by almost $100 million and supply chain costs by $20 million with a return on investment of two years.

Success Story 15: The Dell Story—From Mass Customization to Mass Hybrid

In 1984, Michael Dell founded the company as PCs Limited with capital of $1,000 selling computers from his University of Texas at Austin off-campus dorm room. The company changed its name to "Dell Computer Corporation" in 1988. In 1996, Dell established its website and began selling computers through it. This completely revolutionized the PC selling business. The direct build-to-order model had tremendous advantages:

1. Less inventory cost because Dell built computers only after the customer placed the order by requesting materials from suppliers as needed.
2. Less cost of obsolescence because PCs had very short product life cycles and everyone wanted the latest, greatest, and fastest computer available in the market as the software available (e.g.. Microsoft Office) required high processing power.
3. Directly dealing with customers provided Dell with valuable customer information (customer preferences, tastes). Dell used this information to get critical insights into the customers' buying behaviors and was the basis for Dell's mass customization.

4.   Dell also developed strong collaborative relationship with a few suppliers and was able to get great deals from them because of the long-term contracts.

Dell had a negative 40 days cash-to-cash cycle. Thanks to their build-to-order model, Dell collected money from the customers first and paid the supplier 40 days later. On the other hand, a typical PC maker paid for parts before the computers were sold. Dell was basically living on customer and supplier financing.[1]

Dell was able to pass the savings (inventory costs, less cost of obsolescence, economies of scale) to the customers, and the customers were more than happy to oblige by giving Dell more business.

Dell started to capture market share and in 1999, Dell overtook Compaq to become the largest seller of PCs in the United States with $25 billion in revenue reported in January 2000. The period from 1996 to 2002 were some of the best days Dell had ever seen. The $1,000 idea had turned into a $56 billion dollar business. Dell had the lowest cost structure in the industry, which allowed it to win market share because of economies of scale driving down costs. Dell's dominance increased its worldwide market share from 5 to 15 percent and U.S. market share from 10 to 25 percent.[2]

However, toward the end of 2005 things started to change. Though Dell had become the darling of Main Street and Wall Street with stellar earnings, Dell had also become complacent. Rather than invest in research and development, customer service, global expansion, and innovation, Dell was only focused on keeping its costs low. HP on the other hand had appointed Todd Bradley as their new CEO. Todd realized that PC growth was moving from corporate desktops (which Dell had a 70 percent market share) into personal laptops, which consumers typically like to try out in person, "kick the tires before you buy them." Hence, HP targeted Dell with the "Computer is personal again" ad campaign. HP also realized that they were fighting on the wrong battlefield with Dell in the build-to-order model. HP decided to focus on HP's strength in the retail stores, the build-to-stock model where Dell hardly had any presence at all. Amid intense competition with high capacity, low demand, and cutthroat margins, IBM sold their PC business to Lenovo preferring to sell services rather than the hardware. The U.S. PC market growth had started to slow down though the emerging markets in Asia had a strong growth, where people demanded a fixed PC configuration rather than custom configuration. HP sold their products through third parties and Dell did not.[3]

As if this was not bad enough, complaints about Dell more than doubled in part because of poor customer service, problems with faulty capacitors on the motherboards, and the flammable battery fiasco. They were also a subject of a SEC investigation. Dell's worldwide market share decreased from 17 to 14 percent and Dell finally succumbed to complacency and lost its place at the top of the PC market to HP in 2006.

Sunil Chopra[4] suggested in 2006 that Dell should adopt a "hybrid model that embraces both direct and reseller channels." His reasoning was that though the direct online model has lower facility and inventory carrying costs than going through the traditional retail channel, it was not responsive enough for consumers who wanted to go to a store and buy a preconfigured PC. Hence, the key point was that Dell needed to have the flexibility (Direct Configure to Order) and the responsiveness (in-store make-to-stock [MTS]) to meet customer needs. Chopra's general point was that "companies cannot select one channel and expect it to always be successful" forever. For example, the relative value that the consumers derived from the faster and customized computer has diminished considerably, and the consumer of today does not mind buying an off-the-shelf (MTS) PC at the retailer where they can test, try out, touch, and feel the PC before buying it.

Sure enough in 2007, Dell announced that they were going to enter the retail market and offer preconfigured notebooks (mass produced) and Dimension PCs through Wal-Mart and Sam's Club.

REFERENCES

1. Mallon, C. 2004. The $600 Billion Cash Cow. http://www.fool.com/investing/general/2004/09/27/the-600-billion-cash-cow.aspx (accessed April 2009)
2. Marcus, A. A. 2009. *Winning Moves: Cases in Strategic Management*. Lombard, IL: Marsh Publications.
3. Lawton, C. 2007. "How H-P Reclaimed Its PC Lead over Dell." *Wall Street Journal*, June 4.
4. Chopra, S. October 2007. A New Channel Strategy for Dell. http://insight.kellogg.northwestern.edu/index.php/Kellogg/article/a_new_channel_strategy_for_dell. (accessed April 2009)

Concluding Thoughts

Long-term success demands constant reinvention and to get a sustainable competitive advantage companies must align their strategies with product and market characteristics and focus on the customer.

SUCCESS STORY FROM THE SERVICE INDUSTRY

Success Story 16: Manara Academy Charter School Using Balanced Scorecard

Manara Academy Inc. is a nonprofit service organization. In February 2008, it applied to open a charter school in Texas. A charter school is a government-funded school and as such is open to all students and would have NO Tuition. What it does offer is the autonomy and flexibility of a private school but with the accountability of a public school. The application was accepted in November 2008. The school opened in August 2009.

As part of the application, Manara Academy adopted the innovative performance management methodology "Strategy Maps-Balanced Scorecard" to formulate, manage, and plan for executing their strategy. Multiple research efforts show that the most common cause for failure for nonprofit organizations like a charter school is failing to execute their strategy and keeping accounting books in order. The founders of Manara Academy followed the balanced scorecard (BSC) framework to translate the school's vision and mission into specific objectives at various levels of the organization.

The ultimate objective at Manara Academy was to reach its vision by successfully achieving and sustaining the mission. The vision of the school is to be *the pinnacle of* knowledge, character, ethics, and community building. The school has chosen Expeditionary Learning (*www.elschools.org*) as their teaching methodology. The Expeditionary Learning School (ELS) approach promotes a rigorous and engaging curriculum; active, inquiry-based pedagogy; and a school culture that demands and teaches compassion and good citizenship. Manara Academy is the first ELS school in Texas. Another key feature that makes the school different is teaching a foreign language (French or Arabic) in a unique way beginning in Kindergarten.

Manara Academy established the Strategy Map to facilitate achieving its strategy. One of the basic principles behind the BSC framework is to establish specific objectives that will provide the path to reach the vision. These objectives are divided into five different perspectives:

1. Financial health (BSC Financial Perspective): Includes building and administrating accountability systems, developing and managing human capital, and allocating resources in alignment with the strategy.
2. Human resources (BSC Innovation and Learning Perspective): Includes recruiting and re-training teachers, sharing best practices, and using performance data to guide decisions and create accountability.
3. Stakeholder involvement (BSC Customer Perspective): Includes the understanding of how cultures, resources, stakeholders, and environments reinforce each other and support the deployment of strategy in the school. Stakeholders include parents, school board, community, and advocacy groups and policy makers.
4. Administration and education process (BSC Business Process Perspective): In order to improve student achievement, best-practice administration and education processes need to be adopted in increasing teachers' skills and knowledge, engaging students in learning, and making sure that the curriculum challenges students academically.
5. Student achievement (BSC Customer Perspective): Student achievement is the ultimate goal and long-term vision of Manara Academy. Student

achievement includes excelling in three different dimensions: academic, character, and community building.

The student achievement perspectives constitute the ultimate goal at Manara Academy. The other perspectives constitute the path that will support achieving Manara Academy's vision and sustain its mission on a consistent and sustainable basis. Objectives across these perspectives are related through a cause-and-effect relationship. At the foundation level, Manara Academy needs to maintain its financial health, which will enable investing in its human resources. Next, qualified human resources will attract and improve stakeholders' involvement at Manara Academy. With strong financial health, stakeholder involvement, and continuously trained human resources, Manara will excel in its administrative and education processes. Finally, the effective and efficient administrative and education process will facilitate students in achieving excellence in academics, character, and community building.

Executing the strategy and mapping it to each employee's role were the biggest challenges to achieving the organization's mission. The next step would be to translate Manara's Strategy Map into actionable items executed throughout the organization. The step is formulated through establishing a BSC for Manara Academy. The BSC was constructed by identifying specific measures for each objective on the strategy map.

Manara Academy selected strategies to achieve excellence in every dimension. The effectiveness of these strategies is measured as part of the BSC.

For example, Manara Academy adopted the core practice benchmarks of ELS as the main strategy to drive excellence in the "administrative and education process" dimension. The core practice benchmarks of ELS serve several purposes (http://www.elschools.org/aboutus/practices.html). They provide a planning guide for school leaders and teachers, a framework for designing professional development, and a tool for evaluating expeditionary learning implementation. The principal of Manara Academy is targeting the following core practices for the first year:

1. Using effective instructional practices schoolwide
2. Using effective assessment practices
3. Building school culture and fostering character
4. Fostering a safe, respectful, and orderly community
5. Developing a professional community
6. Engaging families in the life of the school

A sample BSC is outlined in Table 10.1. This scorecard is a sample scorecard for Manara Academy that will be established annually. Measurement and targets may vary yearly according to multiple variables. This scorecard will be cascaded down for individual scorecards enabling staff to recognize how and what they need to do to translate the strategy into reality so the school can achieve its vision. The

Table 10.1 BSC sample for Manara Academy

Objective	Measure	Target	Actual
Student Achievement Perspective			
Excellence in reading, math, social studies, and science	Percent success on standardized tests		
	Number of students achieving commended performance level on TAKS		
	Number of students receiving local and national awards		
Character building	Student character rating		
	Number of students involved in character building activities		
Community building	Number of student volunteer hours		
	Number of community service projects		
Administrative and Academic Process Perspective			
World language	Arabic and French language test scores		
Instructional best practices and techniques	Number of ELS core practice benchmarks adopted in school		
Leveraging diverse cultures	Number of cultural events during the year		
Stakeholder Involvement Perspective			
Enriching and safe environment	Number of severe discipline incidents in the school based on public education information management system (PEIMS) annual incident report		
Parental satisfaction and involvement	Number of parent volunteer hours		
	Parent responses on surveys		
Community partnership	Number of local organizations involved with Manara Academy		
Competent and productive staff	Percent of key teachers retained		
Human Resources Perspective			
Improve school effectiveness	Number of effective initiatives taken by teachers		
Leveraging technology innovations	Percent of students accessing multiple information sources on projects and in classroom activities		
Staff satisfaction	Percent of satisfied personnel responses on survey		
Continues staff improvement	Percent of staff completing required training objectives		
Financial Health			
Effective fund-raising	Percent of school revenues from fund-raising		
Comply with financial regulation	Financial audit results		
Sound fiscal management	Percent of school funds spent on education staff		

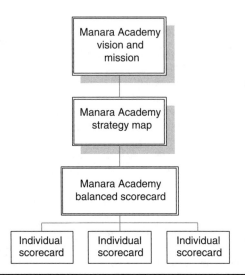

Figure 10.3 Translating Manara Academy vision into actionable individualized objectives

principal will use Manara Academy's Scorecard as her BSC for the year. The principal will in turn work with staff and establish a BSC for each individual.

At this stage, each individual at Manara Academy will have specific objectives and measures. These objectives and measures are linked to Manara's strategy enabling efficient execution of the strategy. In addition, each staff member at Manara Academy would understand his/her role on how to contribute to achieving the vision and sustaining the mission of Manara Academy. Figure 10.3 illustrates how the BSC framework is used to translate Manara Academy's vision and mission into its strategy. Next, the strategy is translated into measurable objectives at the school level. These objectives are cascaded down to each individual according to their role in the organization. The framework not only provides an efficient performance measurement and appraisal framework, it also allows members in the organization to understand how and what they need to do to reach the overall organization's vision.

Concluding Remarks

The BSC framework is being used by multiple nonprofit and educational institutions like Manara Academy Charter School. Thanks to Manara Academy Board members and Principal for sharing their story with us.

Index

A

AATP. *See* Allocated ATP
ABC inventory analysis, 175
Aberdeen Group, 213
Acquisitions. *See* Mergers and acquisitions
Activity-based costing, 42
ADTRAN, 112, 398–399
Advanced planning and scheduling (APS), 22
  concurrent planning and, 183–184
  master planning and, 181
  SCM applications and, 54
Advertising, 250
Agile vs. lean, 7–10
Agility actions, 15
Air transportation, 206
Allocated ATP (AATP), 194, 219
Amano, Yoshikazu, 203
Amazon.com, 236, 251, 252
American Production and Inventory Control
  Society (APICS), 425
AMR Research, 114, 424
Analogous data method, 158
APICS. *See* American Production and
  Inventory Control Society
Applications and trends, 277–300
  CRM-enabled software applications,
    296–299
  LAVC technology infrastructure, 278–282
  SCM-enabled software applications,
    292–296
  SRM-enabled software applications,
    282–291
Approved vendor list (AVL), 25
APS. *See* Advanced planning and scheduling

Asia Pacific, 67
Assemble-to-order strategy, 135, 195
Assembly postponement, 147. *See* Process
  re-sequencing
Assortment management, fashion retail
  industry, 224–225
Atlantic Tool and Die, 102
ATP. *See* Available to promise
ATP, allocated, 194
Auctions
  forward/reverse auctions, 107
  preparation for, 105–107
Automakers. *See* Big Three; Japanese
  automakers; specific automaker
Automated communications, 105
Available to promise (ATP), 218, 258, 263,
  295
AVL. *See* Approved vendor list

B

B2B (business-to-business), 4, 278, 373
B2C (business to consumer), 366, 375
Backup supplier, 90–91
Backward integration, 91
Backward scheduling, 197
Balanced scorecard (BSC), 44, 352, 359–361
  LAVC metrics mapped to, 358
  at Manara Academy Charter School,
    428–433
Baseline forecast: forecasting techniques,
  158–162
  demand patterns, typical, 160
  double exponential smoothing, 161
  extrinsic forecasting, 158–159

for flat demand, 159–161
intrinsic forecasting, 159
qualitative, 158
quantitative, 158–162
for seasonal demand, 162
for trend demand, 161
triple exponential smoothing, 161, 162
BCG. See Boston Consulting Group
Benchmarking, 44, 309
Benetton, 100, 147, 202
Best-in-class benchmarking, 309
Best-of-breed solutions, 279
Best practices, SCM and, 151–153, 163–168
accountability and incentives, 165–166
clean data, 163–164, 181–182
concurrent planning, 183–184
consensus demand planning, 165
demand uncertainty/variability, 145–146,
   167
flexibility and, 184–185, 188
forecasting, 164–165, 182
functional/innovative product strategies,
   143–148
for inventory policies, 173–178
logistics and, 210–215
master planning and, 181–185
North-South/East-West integration, 189
optimization, 152–153, 182–183
order promising and, 194–196
organizational goal, 187–188
performance measurement, 183, 189–190
production scheduling and, 198–203
reverse supply chain strategy, 147–148
risk management, 188
scenario analysis/management, 153, 184
sensitivity analysis, 153
supply chain visibility, 184
supply uncertainty management strategies,
   145–146
talent/training, S&OP workflow and, 189
total organizational profitability, 151–152
training, 165
transportation and, 209–210
Best practices, SRM and, 84–93, 99–103,
   118–124
collaboration, 87–89, 100–101, 118–124
continuous improvement, 103
contract management, 120–121
part rationalization, 86

price minus costing, 102
process re-sequencing, 100
procurement segmentation, 123
push vs. pull, 119–120
returns management, 118
rewarding best-practice behavior, 120
settlement process, 119
simplification, 99
sourcing segmentation, 89–91
standardization, 99–100, 121
supplier base rationalization, 84–86
supplier certification, 86
supplier performance measurement/
   rewarding suppliers, 86–87
technology and, 92–93, 101–102, 121–123
top management support, 93, 103
total cost for contracts, 123–124
total cost visibility, 102–103
total landed cost, supplier selection, 91–92
Biased forecasts, 163
Bid analysis, 107–108
Bid award, 108–109
Big Three, 78–79, 85, 102
Bill of distribution (BOD), 136
Bill of materials (BOM), 136
MRPII and, 50
Birdyback intermodal transport, 207
Blackberrys, 122, 401
Blanket purchase order, bid award and, 108
BLUESALON, success story/lessons learned,
   388–393, 394
benefits achieved, 392
challenges identified, 388–389
plan to address challenges, 389
purchase order management, 390–392
stores/merchandise planning, 392–393
BMC software, 234
BMW, 244, 250
BOD. See Bill of distribution
Boeing, 98
Boston Consulting Group (BCG), 245, 246
Bottom-up forecast, 165
BPH. See Business process hubs
BPP. See Business process platforms
BSC. See Balanced scorecard
Building blocks/evolution, 39–56
business processes, 45–48
information technology, 50–55
LAVC principles/enablers, 39, 40–41

quality & efficiency, 48–50
strategy & management structure, 39–44
summary, building blocks, 55–56
Build/make to order, 34
Build-to-order. *See* Make-to-order (MTO) supply chain
Build-to-stock. *See* Make-to-stock (MTS) environment
Bullwhip effect
  demand planning and, 156–157
  outsourcing and, 92
Bundling. *See* Product bundling
Business processes, 45–48
  building blocks/evolution of LAVC principles/enablers, 46
  business process redesign, 45
  business process reengineering, 45
  human performance improvement methodology, 47
  lean management, 47–48
  simplification, 45, 47
  Theory of constraints, 47
Business processes distribution, superprocesses and, 23
Business process hubs (BPH), 279–280
Business process platforms (BPP), 279
Business process redesign, 45
Business process reengineering (BPR), 45
Business system, 42
Business-to-business. *See* B2B
Business to consumer. *See* B2C
Buyer/supplier, middle points of intersection, 88

C
Canada, 152
Capability maturity model (CMM), 42–43
  five levels of, 43
Capable-to-promise (CTP) logic, 194–195, 263
Capacity requirements planning (CRP)
  MRP and, 179
CAPS Research, 87
Carrier. *See also* Transportation (logistics) carriers
  carrier agreements, 212–213
  definition of, 208
Case study. *See* Office Systems, Inc.
CCO. *See* Chief customer officer
Cellular manufacturing, 199–200, 202

Cementos Argos, 188, 412–415
  future, savings/service levels, 414
  profitability, synchronicity, customer satisfaction, 414
  supply chain excellence partnership, 413
  supply chain management, expanding global reach, 412–413
Centralized return center, 148
Certification. *See* ISO
Change management. *See also* Education/ culture support
  maturity model and, 60
  plan, change leaders and, 331–332
Change management supported processes, 321–363
  communication management, 336–347
  education/culture support, 328–335
  performance management team, 350–362
  team development, 322–328
  tracking/controlling, 348–350
Changeover time reduction, 198–199
Channel, sales mix and, 262–263
Chief customer officer (CCO), 235–236
China-based supplier, 91–92, 151
Chopra, Sunil, 427–428
Chrysler, 114
CITGO, 133
CLM. *See* Council of Logistics Management
Close the loop between planning and execution, 12–14
CLV. *See* Customer lifetime value
CMM. *See* Capability maturity model
Collaboration. *See also* Enabler 2; Supply collaboration
  as best practice, 87–89, 100–101
  cross-organizational, 118
  customer collaboration, order processing and, 196
  internal/external, 101
  intra-company/ cross organizational, 99
  "right information," real-time basis and, 73
Collaborative planning, forecasting, and replenishment (CPFR), 298, 425
Common (public) carriers, 30
Communication. *See also* Key communications, guidelines for
  communications mix, marketing and, 250
  procurement and, 105

Communication management, 336–347
  communication methods, 340–341
  key communications, guidelines for,
      342–347
  organizational change and, 336
  plan development, 317–339
  template for plan, 339
  types of communications, 341
Compaq, 145
Competition
  competitive benchmarking, 309
  as SRM challenge, 95
Complexity
  as SCM challenge, 136
  as SRM challenge, 75
Computer-aided design/manufacturing
  product design and, 27, 94
Concurrent engineering, 98
Configure-to-order (CTO) model, 420
Conflict management, 77, 329
Consensus demand planning, 165
Consignment inventory, 112
Consumer packaged (CPG) industries, 262
Continental Tires, 183–184, 409–412
  benefits of transformation program, 412
  challenges at, 411
  on-the-floor responsiveness, 410–411
  results at, 411
  tire division planning/inventory challenges,
      409–410
Continuous improvement. *See also* Principle 4
  inventory policies and, 177
  top management support of, 103
  TQM and, 48
Continuous production, 142
Contract carriers, 30
Contract management, 105–109
  areas of, 28, 105–107
  best practices and, 120–121
  pyramid for, 106
  service contract management, 269
  software applications for, 288
  as SRM superprocess, 127
  total cost for contracts, 123–124
Controlling. *See* Tracking/controlling
Cooper Tire, 393, 395–397
  distributed inventory management at,
      396–397
  distribution/replenishment planning, 395

end-to-end visibility at, 397
  lack of visibility and, 193
  master data management at, 396
  value chain processes, interactions, 394
Corporate goals, transformation program and,
      304, 308
Corrective action plans, 83
Cost price
  price minus costing, 102
  total cost visibility, 102–103
Council of Logistics Management (CLM),
      203
Council of Supply Chain Management
      Professionals (CSCMP), 203
CPFR. *See* Collaborative planning, forecasting,
      and replenishment
CPG. *See* Consumer packaged industries
Create win-win and trusted environment for all
      stakeholders, 11
Creativity. *See also* Enabler 6
CRM. *See* Customer relationship management
CRM challenges, 231–237
  customer interaction/Internet, 233
  evolution of CRM, 234–236
  future of CRM, 236–237
  globalization, 233
  privacy/security, 232
  top management support, 233 234
CRM-enabled software applications, 296–299
  marketing management-enabled, 296–297
  selling management-enabled, 297–298
CRM processes, 36–38
  customer service management, 37–38
  marketing management, 36–37
  selling management, 37
CRM pyramids, 232
  for customer service management, 264
  for marketing management, 243
  for market research, 255
  for order processing, 266
  for selling management, 257
  for service management, 268
CRM superprocess workflow, 271–274
  customer service management, 273–274
  flowchart for, 272
  marketing management and, 271, 273
  market research and, 271, 273
  market strategy and, 271
  selling management, 273

Cross-docking
    best practices and, 215
    definition of, 209
Cross-functional design, 214
Cross-functional relationships, 243
Cross-organizational collaboration and
    simplification, 15–16
Cross referencing of parts, 90
CRP. *See* Capacity requirements planning
CSCMP. *See* Council of Supply Chain
    Management Professionals
CSRs. *See* Customer service representatives
CTO. *See* Configure-to-order model
CTP. *See* Capable-to-promise logic
Culture. *See also* Education/culture support
    of measurement, anchoring, 356–357
Customer, defining who is, 237–242
    customer lifetime value, 241–242
    customer relationship management,
      239–241
Customer collaboration, 196
Customer experience council, 265
Customer lifetime value (CLV), 241–242
Customer loyalty, word of mouth and, 240,
    241
Customer order profile, 169, 176
Customer relationship management (CRM)
    business process distribution for, 36
    business processes, 23–24
    defining who customer is, 239–241
    definition of, 231
    e-Business applications and, 54
    as value chain superprocess, 21–23
Customer relationship management (CRM)
    superprocess, 231–300
    CRM challenges, 231–237
    marketing management, 242–267
    service management, 268–271
    who customer is, 237–242
    workflow for, 271–274
Customer returns, 147–148
Customers
    expectations of, 244
    "first-come-first-served" basis, 193
Customer satisfaction
    creation of value and, 238
    lack of, 203–204
    at Tata Steel, 417–418
Customer segmentation, 237

Customer service management, 263–266
    communication channels and, 265
    as CRM process, 37–38
    CRM superprocess workflow and, 273–274
    order processing, 273–274
    pyramid for, 264
    service management, 274
Customer service management-enabled
    software applications, 299
    customer service applications, 299
    service parts planning (SPP), 299
Customer service representatives (CSRs), 264
Customer success. *See also* Principle 1
Customer surveys, 158
Customer values, mass customization and, 142
Customized micromarketing, 248

D
D&B. *See* Dun & Bradstreet
Data management
    best practices and, 92–93
    clean data, 163–164, 181–182
    lack of complete/consistent data, 75–76
Data mining
    marketing management and, 244
    privacy/security and, 232
"Dating to marriage"
    customer relationship, 239–241
    supplier relationship, 82–83
Day Sales Outstanding (DSO), 369
Decision-support systems, 293
Deere, 197
Defects. *See* Quality errors
Dell, 97–98, 211, 236, 239, 242, 259, 260,
    265–266, 269, 416
Dell, success story/lessons learned, 426–428
    build-to-order model advantages, 426
    channel selection and, 427–428
Delphi Corporation, 133
Delphi method, 158
Demand, partitioning of, 60
Demand-driven supply system, 140–141. *See
    also* Pull system
Demand forecasting, fashion retail industry,
    222–223
Demand fulfillment, 34–36
    in fashion retail industry, 225–227
    logistics planning/execution, 226–227
    replenishment planning, 225–226

S&OP planning and, 219
S&OP workflow and, 190–191
setup time reductions and, 34–35
technology capabilities and, 35–36
uniform loading and, 35
Demand fulfillment-enabled software
        applications, 294–296
    Capable-to-Promise (CTP), 295–296
    mobile (wireless) SCM, 295
    Supply Chain Analytics, 296
    Supply Chain Inventory Visibility (SCIV),
        294–295
Demand planning. *See also* Flat demand,
        forecasting techniques
    baseline forecast: forecasting techniques,
        158–162
    biased forecasts and, 163
    bullwhip effect and, 156–157
    consensus demand planning, 165
    exception management, 162
    forecast error, calculation of, 162–163
    generic subprocess for, 157–158
    S&OP planning and, 216
    supply chain pyramid for, 156
Demand uncertainty management strategies,
        145–146
Demand variability, 141
    clean data on, 173–174
    minimization of, 167
    reasons for, 173
Deming, W. Edwards, 48
Demographic segmentation, 249
Design collaboration, product design and, 27,
        94
Design for logistics, 97. *See also* Logistics
Design for manufacture and assembly (DFM),
        96–97, 99, 100
Design for reverse logistics, 97–98
Design-for-sourcing mentality, 101
Design for value chain (DVC), 99
DFM. *See* Design for manufacture and
        assembly
Direct mail program, 241
Direct marketing, 251
Disparate systems, as SRM challenge, 76, 96
Distribution requirements planning (DRP),
        MRP and, 179–180
Dow Chemical, 91
Downsizing, 331

Downstream network, 66, 184
DRP. *See* Distribution requirements planning
DRPII. *See* MRPII/DRPII
DSO. *See* Day Sales Outstanding
Dual-sourcing strategies, hot-selling products,
        17, 80–81
Dun & Bradstreet (D&B), 81
Dutch auctions, 107
DVC. *See* Design for value chain
Dynamic order processing, 195
Dynamic routing, 212–213
Dynamic safey stock, 112

E
Early Warning System (EWS), 270
Eastern European suppliers, 91
Eastman Kodak, 215
East-West collaboration. *See* North-South/
        East-West collaboration
e-Business applications, 54, 311
Economic downturn, 262
Economic order quantity (EOQ) formula,
        170–171
EDC report (expedite, deliver, cancel), 111
Education/culture support, 328–335
    change leaders vs. change agents, 331–333
    downsizing and, 331
    human process interventions, 329
    knowledge management, 330–331
    learning methods, 330
    life cycle of change and, 333–334
    pioneers/early adopters, 335
    social information and, 335
80-20 concept, 335
Electronic data interchange (EDI), 29, 105,
        262
Electronic product code (EPC), 55
Elevator speech, 308
Eliminate waste and reduce nonvalue-added
        activities, 11–12
e-marketplaces, 280
Emerson, 85, 92, 101, 107, 386–387
Employee creativity. *See also* Enabler 6
Enablers, 14–21
    Enabler 1, 14–15
    Enabler 2, 15–16
    Enabler 3, 16
    Enabler 4, 17
    Enabler 5, 17–18

Enabler 6, 18–19
Enabler 7, 20–21
future trends and, 61, 66–67
SCM challenges and, 137–139
End-of-life product life cycle, 163
"End-of-quarter push," 162
End on hand (EOH) inventory, 13–14
End-to-end SCM, 67
Engagement. *See* "Dating to marriage"
Engineering, concurrent, 98
Engineering change management/control
    workflows
    product design and, 27, 94
Enterprise resource planning (ERP), 52–53,
    390
    Internet emergence and, 53
    MRP module in, 52
EOH. *See* End on hand inventory
EOQ (economic order quantity) formula,
    170–171
EPC. *See* Electronic product code
e-procurement, 89–90
e-Sourcing, 92, 101, 107
Event management, 281–282
EWS. *See* Early Warning System
Exception notification, 282
Executive management. *See* Top management
    support
Executive supplier council, 88
External collaboration, 101
External customers, 238

F
Fairchild Semiconductor, 405–407
    concurrent order processing at, 195
Fashion retail industry. *See* SCM superprocess
    workflow, fashion retail industry
    assortment management in, 224–225
    demand forecasting in, 222–223
    demand fulfillment and, 225–227
    financial planning, 222
    inventory planning in, 223–224
    S&OP planning, 220, 222–225
    strategic management, 220
Fast-growing regions, 67
Financial impact, supplier base rationalization,
    85
Financial planning, fashion retail industry, 222
"First-come-first-serve," 193, 194

Fishyback intermodal transport, 207
Flat demand, forecasting techniques, 159–161
    linear regression, 160–161
    moving averages, 159–160
    single exponential smoothing, 161
Flexibility
    as Enabler 4, 17
    at every level, 66
    in Master Planning, 184–185
    S&OP workflow and, 188
Flowchart. *See* Workflow
Flow-through cross-docking, 209
Focus on customer success, 10–11
Ford, Henry, 78–80, 141–142, 248
Forecast collaboration, 110
Forecast-driven supply chain, 140–141. *See also*
    Push system
Forecast error, calculation of, 162–163
Forecasting capability, at Tata Steel, 419
Forecasting techniques. *See* Baseline forecast:
    forecasting techniques
Forecast netting, Master Planning and, 182
Form postponement, 34
Forrester Research, 424
Forward auctions, 107
Forward scheduling, 197
4Ps (product, prices promotion/
    communications, and placement/
    channel), 37
Frei, Brent, 234
Freight consolidation, 210–211
Full truckload (FTL), 134. *See also* Less than
    truckloads
    3PL and, 20
    freight consolidation and, 211
    vs. LTLs, 169
Functional/innovative products, 143–145, 148
Functional silos, 100
Future trends, LAVC principles/enablers and,
    61, 66

G
Gap analysis, 317
Gap Inc., 256
Gartner, 424
GATT, 75
GE (General Electric), success story/lessons
    learned, 387–388
Geesey, James, 92, 101, 107

GENCO, 214
General Electric (GE), 234, 269
  Six Sigma methodology at, 48, 50
  Strategic Business Planning Grid, 245, 246,
    247
General Mills, 212
General Motors, 114
Generic demand planning subprocess, 157–158
  baseline forecast, 157
  consensus forecast, 158
  data cleaning, 157
  exception management, 158
Gen Ys, 249
Globalization
  as CRM challenge, 233
  future trends and, 61, 67
  marketing management and, 244
  strategic management and, 31
  total landed cost and, 91
  variability, complexity and, 75
Global optimization, 138–139
"Go-live," businesses and, 67, 137–138, 314
GPS capability, 122, 148
  real-time visibility and, 213
  RFID and, 54
Green products, 97–98
Green Value Chain, 415–416
  freight consolidation and, 211
  green product design, 416
  green product packaging, 415–416
Guiding principles. *See* LAVC guiding
    principles

H
Hahn, Michael, 212
Hammer, Michael, 351
Hard/soft constraints, 184–185
Harry, Mike, 50
"Heijunka," 201, 202, 215
Hewlett-Packard (HP), 98–99, 427
Hierarchical optimization, 152–153
High prototype cost, 95
Hispanic market, 255–256
"Hockey-stick curve," 162
Home Depot, 249, 269
Honda, 74, 78–79, 108
  collaboration and, 101
  number of suppliers for, 85
  root cause of problems and, 87

Honeywell, 238
HP. *See* Hewlett-Packard
Hub, 209
Human performance improvement
    methodology, 47
Human resources. *See also* Transformation team
    development
  resources/roles, matching of, 323
  talent/training, S&OP workflow and, 189

I
i2 solutions
  at Cementos Argos, 413–414
  at Continental Tire, 409–411
  at Cooper Tire, 395–396
  at Lenovo, 420–421, 422
  at Sprint, 404
  at Tata Steel, 418, 419
IBF. *See* Institute for Business Forecasting and
    Planning
IKEA, 97
IMC. *See* Integrated marketing communications
Implementation, transformation program,
    315–319
  LAVC project characteristics, 316
  Phase 1: As is Process/Pain Points, 316–317
  Phase 2: Root-Cause Analysis/To Be
    Process/Gap Analysis, 317
  Phase 3: Deploying the Solution, 317–318
  Phase 4: Sustaining phase, 318–319
  system maintenance, 319
Inbound consolidation, 211–212
Incentive system
  motivation program and, 328
  for suppliers/carriers, 87
Independent shipments, 210
Information sharing. *See also* Collaboration
Information technology (IT). *See also* Technology
  stand-alone, 234
Information technology building block, 50–55.
    See also Technology
  building blocks/evolution of LAVC
    principles/enablers, 51
  e-Business applications, 54
  enterprise resource planning, 52–53
  manufacturing resource planning, 50, 52
  Radio Frequency Identification, 54–55
  supply chain management applications and,
    53–55

Innovation. *See also* Enabler 6; Enabler 7
Innovative/functional products, 143–145
Institute for Business Forecasting and Planning
    (IBF), 168
Integrated lean/agile processes (Level 3), 58–59
Integrated lean processes (Level 2), 57–58
Integrated marketing communications (IMC),
    251
Intelligent visibility, 15
Intermodal transportation, 207
Internal benchmarking, 309
Internal collaboration, 101
Internal customers, 238
Internet. *See also* Online retailing
    customer interaction and, 233
    direct marketing by, 251
    emergence of, 6
    e-procurement, 89–90
    marketing management and, 244
    online surveys, 255
    privacy/security and, 232
Inventory. *See also* Replenishment trigger
        options; Safety stock
    ABC inventory analysis, 175
    end on hand (EOH), 13–14
Inventory planning, 168–178
    in fashion retail industry, 223–224
    goal of, 218
    how much to order, 170–171
    inventory policies and, 172–173
    reasons to hold inventory, 169
    supply chain pyramid for, 168
    when to order, 171–172
    where to hold inventory, 169
Inventory policies, 172–173
    alignment with organizational goal,
        174–175
    analysis of variability, 175
    best practices for, 173–178
    clean data, 173–174
    continuous improvement, 177
    customer ordering pattern, 176–177
    "exchange curves," 176
    glass box, not black box, 177
    physical record integrity, 177–178
    "right sizing of inventory levels," 174
    segmentation strategy, 175–176
Inventory review systems, 171–172
    continuous review, 171

    fixed review period system, 172
    periodic review, 171–172
Investment. *See* Return on investment
ISO (International Standards Organization),
    86
ISO 9000, 48
IT. *See* Information technology

J
Japanese automakers, 102. *See also* specific
        automaker
Japanese *keiretsu* model, 78–79
Java RMI, 278
Johnson Controls, 88–89
Jury of executive opinion, 158
Just-in-time replenishment, 113–114

K
Kaizen, 47–48, 202
Kanbans, 113, 202, 215
Kaplan and Norton, 353
Keiretsu model, 78–79
Key communications, guidelines for,
        342–347. *See also* Communication
    emergency communications, 343
    meetings, 343–344
    program/project status reports,
        345–347
    project team/sponsor, 342–343
Key concepts, SRM superprocess and,
        96–99
Keyes, Jim, 79–80
Key performance indicators (KPIs)
    event management and, 281
    four categories of, 44, 353
    root-cause/gap analysis and, 317
Knowledge management, 330–331
Kodak, 215
KPIs. *See* Key performance indicators

L
Lack of visibility, 96
Ladd, Brittain, 211, 416
LAPMS. *See* Lean and agile performance
        management system
Laterally integrated companies, 74–75
LAVC
    benchmarking of processes for, 309
    benefits of concept, 10

building blocks for principles/enablers, 39, 40–41

competitive advantage and, 4

future trends and, 61, 66

vs. lean value chain, 8, 9

as Level 4, maturity levels, 59–61

measuring progress and, 353

reasons for growth in, 5–6

summary, building blocks and, 55–56

LAVC enablers. *See* Enablers

LAVC guiding principles, 10–14

definitions and, 7–21

principle 1, 10–11

principle 2, 11

principle 3, 11–12

principle 4, 12

principle 5, 12–14

LAVCM. *See* Lean and agile value chain management

LAVC metrics, 357–362

LAVC SRM superprocess, 74

LAVC technology infrastructure, 278–282

business process hubs (BPH), 279–280

business process platforms (BPP), 279

event management, 281–282

master data management (MDM), 280–281

Radio Frequency Identification (RFID), 280

service-oriented architecture, 278–279

LAVC transformation case study. *See* Office Systems, Inc.

Layoffs, 331

Leadership, 328, 329. *See also* Top management support

path-goal leadership approach, 332

Lead time reduction, 167

Lean, 47–48

vs. agile, 7–10

LAVC concept and, 45, 66–67

supply chain and, 5

Lean and agile LAVC maturity levels. *See* Maturity levels

Lean and agile performance management system (LAPMS), 352–357

culture of measurement, anchoring, 356–357

identifying/defining metrics, 354–355

performance tracking/monitoring, 355

root-cause analysis, triggering, 356

Lean and agile value chain. *See* LAVC

Lean and agile value chain management (LAVCM), 370

Lean processes (Level 1), 57

Lean value chain, vs. LAVC, 8, 9

Learning methods, 330

"Learning Organization" concept, 330

Legacy systems, 76, 122

Lenovo, success story/lessons learned, 420–424

challenges at, 420–421

CTO approach at, 420, 421

customer base identification/segmentation, 421–422

economic fluctuations and, 423–424

future challenges and, 423

i2 in website redesign/CTO shift, 422–423

revenue generation channels, 422

Lessons learned. *See* Success stories/lessons learned

Less than truckloads (LTL), 169. *See also* Full truckload

definition of, 208

freight consolidation and, 211

green value chain and, 415

Levels. *See* Maturity model levels

Level scheduling, *takt* in, 35

Leveraging technology, 121–123

Life cycle of change, 333–334

Phase 1: Resistance, 333–334

Phase 2: Acceptance, 334

Phase 3: Breakthrough, 334

Life cycle portfolio matrix, 252, 253

Linear programming (LP), 150–151

Loading/scheduling, uniformity in, 200–201

"Localized assortment," 58–59

"Local" suppliers, 80

Logistics. *See also* Carrier; Design for logistics; Reverse logistics; Transportation carriers

inbound/outbound flows, 204

specialists in, 88

Logistics planning/execution, 203–204

in fashion retail industry, 226–227

pyramid for, 203

"Low-hanging fruit," 44, 146

Low inventory alert, 112

Low value-adding processes, 53

LP. *See* Linear programming

LP optimization, 182–183

LTL. *See* Less than truckloads
Lucent, 134

M

Machine utilization, 199
Make-to-order (MTO) supply chain, 135, 373
  concurrent order processing and, 195
  holding inventory and, 169
Make-to-stock (MTS) environment, 135, 373
  concurrent order processing and, 195
  holding inventory and, 169
  "postponement" in, 33–34
Manara Academy Charter School, 428–432
  BSC frameworks at, 429
  core practices and, 430
  Expeditionary Learning School approach
    at, 429
  sample BSC, 431
  vision/mission at, 430, 432
Manual processes
  procurement and, 105
  RFQ process as, 77
Manufacturing. *See* Production scheduling/
  execution
Manufacturing resource planning. *See* MRPII
Marketing management, 36–37, 242–267
  CRM superprocess workflow and,
    271–274
  market research and, 254–256
  market strategy and, 244–254
  pyramid for, 243
  rapid changes, causes of, 244
  sales mix, 257–263
  selling management, 256–257
Marketing management-enabled software
    applications, 296–297
  Marketing Analysis, 296–297
  MDM for product data - buy side, 297
Marketing plan, 252–254
  executive summary, 252–253
  feedback/controls, 254
  financials, 254
  marketing strategy, 253–254
  situation analysis, 253
Market positioning, 250–251
Market reality, 3–7
Market research, 254–256
  CRM superprocess workflow and, 271, 273
  ethnic groups and, 255–256

  pyramid for, 255
  voice of the customer (VOC), 256
Market segmentation, 248–249
Market strategy, 244–254
  CRM superprocess workflow and, 271
  generic strategies, 247–248
  marketing plan and, 252–254
  product life cycle and, 251–252
  SBU's and, 244–246
  steps in developing, 248–251
  types of, 246–247
Market targeting, 249–250
Marriage. *See* "Dating to marriage"
Mass customization, 59
  customer values and, 142
  to mass hybrid, at Dell, 426–428
  or mass production, 141–143
  product life cycle and, 95
  as SRM challenge, 75
Mass production, or mass customization,
  141–143
Master data management (MDM), 181,
  280–281
  at Cooper Tire, 396
Master data management technology solution,
  92
Master planning, 178–185
  Advanced planning and scheduling (APS),
    181
  best practices and, 181–185
  MRPII/DRPII, traditional approach,
    178–181
  pyramid for, 179
  S&OP planning and, 218
Material requirement planning (MRP), 52,
  137
  module, MRPII and, 179
  as push production process, 200
Maturity model levels, 56–61
  Level 1: lean processes, 57
  Level 2: integrated lean processes, 57–58
  Level 3: integrated lean/agile processes,
    58–59
  Level 4: LAVC, 59–61
  value chain processes, impact on, 62–63,
    64, 65
Mazda, 201
McKesson, 214
MDM. *See* Master data management

Measurement. *See* Metrics; Performance
    measurement system
Meetings, communications and, 343–344
Merge-in-transit cross-docking, 209
Mergers and acquisitions
    backward integration, 91
    retailer acquisition, 247
    as SRM challenge, 75
Metrics. *See also* Performance measurement
    system
    identifying/defining, in LAPMS, 354–355
    LAVC metrics, 357–362
    LAVC objectives and, 357
    six parameters of, 356
    three basic functions, 320
Micromarketing, 248
Middle East, 67
Milk run replenishment, 19, 215
MILP. *See* Mixed integer linear programming
Min-max replenishment policy, 112
Mixed integer linear programming (MILP),
    150–151
Mixed model production, 201
Modular design, 98–99
Motivation. *See* Incentive system
Moving averages, 159–160
MRO items, 89, 123
MRP. *See* Material requirement planning
MRPII (manufacturing resource planning), 50
    APS on ERP and, 54
    limitations, traditional order promising,
        192–194
    major problem with, 52
MRPII/DRPII, 178–181
    limitations of, 180–181
Muda/muri/mua, 200
Multidimensional database, 92–93
Multidisciplinary teams, 98
Multi-enterprise supply chains, 60–61
Multi-objective optimization, 152–153
Multi-sourcing, analysis of variability and, 175
Multi-stop vehicle routing, 210–211
Multivariate events, 107
Muri/mura/muda, 200

N
NAFTA, 75
NDP Group, 255
Net present value (NPV), 241

Niche market segment, 247
Nonvalue-added activities. *See also* Principle 3
    manual work as, 105
North-South/East-West collaboration
    in SRM superprocess, 73–74
North-South/East-West integration, 189
NPV. *See* Net present value
Nucor, 91

O
Objectives, SMART, 357
"Off contract" spending, 115, 120
Office Systems, Inc., 365–383
    alignment, goals/transformation program,
        366, 368–370
    assigning metrics to subprocesses, 377
    call center/invoicing/delivery, 375
    company description, 365–366
    culture, anchoring process in, 382
    deployment/rollout of plan, 382
    event sequence for order, 371, 373
    functional requirements, creation of,
        379
    goal assignment worksheet, 378
    high level as is process, 372
    objectives/measures worksheet, 368
    office chair value chain at, 366
    organizational chart for, 366, 367
    PMS project team analysis, 376–379
    process analysis, 371–373
    production scheduling subprocess,
        373–374
    program/project plan development,
        380–382
    purchase order management, 374–375
    return on investment (ROI), 380
    sales/order entry, 374
    software application provider, 379–380
    value chain objectives, 369–370
    vision/objectives/strategies, 370–371
Ohno, Taiichi, 74, 142
"One-size-fits-all" approach, 104, 142, 169
    customer ordering pattern and, 176
    market segmentation and, 248
    in service contract management, 269
Online retailing, 59. *See also* Internet
Online surveys, 255
Onyx Software, 234
Operational processes, 321

Optimization techniques, 150–151
  Master Planning and, 182–183
  multi-objective optimization, 152–153
Oracle, 52
Order consolidation, wave picking and, 214
Order processing, 266–269
  benefits of effective, 267
  CRM superprocess workflow and, 274
  pyramid for, 266
  steps in, 266–267
Order promising, S&OP workflow and,
    191–194
  best practices and, 194–196
  "first-come-first-serve" basis, 193
  lack of responsiveness and, 193
  lack of visibility and, 193–194
  limitations, traditional order promising,
    192–194
  MRPII order processing logic, 192
  static picture, 192–193
Organizational culture. *See* Education/culture
    support
Organizational DNA, 236
Organizational goal
  alignment with, 174–175
  S&OP workflow and, 187–188
Organizational structure. *See* Strategy &
    management structure
Outbound consolidation, 211–212
Outsourcing
  bullwhip effect and, 92
  outsourcing revolution, start of, 79
  real-time collaboration and, 96
  strategic sourcing and, 25
  variability, complexity and, 75
  visibility, risk and, 91–92
  what to outsource, 78–80
"Over the wall" approach, 95

P

P&G. *See* Proctor & Gamble
"Pacemaker," 202
Packaging, minimization of. *See* Green products
Paint manufacturers, 147
Pareto analysis, 81
Part rationalization, best practices and, 86
Part reuse, 102
PDCA (plan, do, check, and act) methodology,
    48, 136

PDM. *See* Product definition management
People processes, 321
Performance management system (PMS),
    350–362, 373
  LAVC metrics, 357–362
  lean/agile system, 352–357
  metrics, LAVC objectives and, 357
  performance measurement challenges,
    350–352
  top-tier metrics, 357–358
  updating of, 319–320
Performance measurement, seven deadly sins
  of, 351–352
Performance measurement system (PMS), 12–14
  establishment of, 12, 165
  Master Planning and, 183
  rewarding suppliers, 86–87
  for S&OP workflow, 189–190
  seven parameters of, 13
Piggyback intermodal transport, 207
Pipeline transportation, 207
Planned shipment, 112
PMS. *See* Performance management system;
    Performance measurement system
Point of sale (POS) data, 21
POM. *See* Purchase order management
POM subprocess, 111, 112
POM workflow, 114–117
  flowchart for, 116
  SRM pyramid for, 115
Pooling, freight consolidation and, 210, 211
"Pooling effect," 152
Porter's Value Chain, 42
POS. *See* Point of sale data
Positioning strategies, 250–251
Postponement. *See also* Process re-sequencing
  advantages of, 144
  assembly postponement, 147
  in "make to stock" environment, 33–34
  modular design and, 98
  process agility and, 202
Price
  maintaining stable, 167
  price minus costing, 102
  sales mix and, 260–261
Principles, LAVC guiding
  Principle 1, 10–11
  Principle 2, 11
  Principle 3, 11–12

Principle 4, 12
Principle 5, 12–14
Privacy/security, 232
Private carriers, 30
Private marketplace, 279
Process agility, 202
Process analysis, transformation and
   319-320, 309
Processes, people vs. operational, 321
Process excellence, logistics and, 213–214
Process innovation and encouraging employee
   creativity. *See* Enabler 6
Process integration, definition of, 61
Process re-sequencing (assembly
   postponement), 202
   as best practice, 100
Process standardization, 202
Proctor & Gamble (P&G), 112, 156–157, 167,
   255
Procurement
   best practices and, 123
   challenges in, 104–105
   contract management, 105–109, 127
   lean/agile solutions for, 29–32, 124
   purchase order management, 127
   pyramid for, 103
   as SRM process, 28–31, 103–124
   as SRM superprocess, 126–127
   supply collaboration, 127
Procurement design-enabled software
   applications, 286–287
Procurement-enabled software applications,
   287–291
   contract management, 288
   E-Procurement, 291
   online supplier directories, 288–289
   procurement suites, 287–288
   Purchase Order Management (POM), 290
   supplier portals, 289
   Transportation Management System
      (TMS), 290–291
Product and service agreement (PSA), 81
Product bundling, 258–260
Product configuration, 258
Product definition management (PDM)
   product design and, 27, 94, 102
Product design
   challenges in, 95–96
   pyramid for, 94

as SRM process, 27–28
SRM superprocess and, 93–103, 126
technology applications and, 94–95
Product design-enabled software applications,
   286–287
   MDM for product data - buy side, 287
Product flow layouts, 199
Product information management, 297
Production scheduling/execution, 196–197
   best practices and, 198–203
   cellular manufacturing and, 199–200
   changeover times and, 198–199
   constraints, modeling, 198
   frozen plans and, 219
   mixed model production, 201
   process agility and, 202
   process variability and, 198
   production scheduling types, 197
   push vs. pull, 200
   pyramid for, 196
   technology and, 202–203
   uniform loading/scheduling, 200–201
Product life cycle
   decline stage, 252
   growth stage, 251–252
   life cycle portfolio matrix, 252, 253
   market strategies based on, 251–252
   maturity stage, 252
Product portfolio
   monitoring of, 91
   segmentation of, 144
Product standardization, as best practice,
   99–100
Profitability, 151–152
Profitable-to-promise (PTP) applications, 296
Program/project management, product design
   and, 27, 95
Promotion, sales mix and, 261–262
Prototype cost, 95
PSA. *See* Product and service agreement
PTP. *See* Profitable-to-promise applications
Public e-marketplace, 279
Pull-push decoupling point, 20, 141, 200
Pull system
   demand fulfillment and, 35
   for fluctuating/unpredictable demand,
      141
   origin of, 142
   pull signals (kanbans) in, 113, 202

vs. push system, 7, 119–120, 135–136
recommended practices, 20–21
uniform loading/scheduling and, 200
Purchase order management (POM), 114–117
at BLUESALON, 390–392
POM subprocess, 111, 112
POM workflow, 114–117
software applications for, 290
as SRM superprocess, 127
Purchase order/sales order, 108, 267
Push system
compared to pull system, 7
vs. pull system, 119–120, 135–136
vs. push system, 200
Pyramids. *See* CRM pyramids; SCM pyramids;
SRM pyramids

Q
Qualitative forecasting techniques, 158
Quality/efficiency building block, 48–50
building blocks/evolution of LAVC
principles/enablers, 49
ISO 9000, 48
Six Sigma methodology, 48, 50
Total quality management, 48
Quality errors (defects), 12
Quantitative forecasting techniques, 158–162

R
Radio Frequency Identification. *See* RFID
technology
Rail transportation, 206
Rationalization strategies
part rationalization, 86
supplier base rationalization, 84–86
Raw material inventory velocity, 386
RBS. *See* Royal Bank of Scotland
Receiving docks, 213
Recession environment
future trends and, 61
market reality and, 3–4
strategic sourcing and, 25
Redesign, 45
Reliability, trust and, 11
Remote method invocation (RMI), 278
Reorder point (ROP), 171
Replenishment. *See also* Make-to-order (MTO)
supply chain; Make-to-stock (MTS)
environment

frequency of, determining, 26
planning for, 225–226
Replenishment trigger options, 110–114
just-in-time, 113–114
schedule-driven, 110–111
sequence-driven, 114
vendor-managed inventory, 111–113
Request for Proposal. *See* RFP process
Request for Quote. *See* RFQ process
Responsiveness, lack of, 193
Restructuring, 331
Retail aftermarket, 269
Return on investment (ROI), 303, 354
calculation of, 312–314
in case study, 380
culture of measurement and, 357
guidelines for computing, 313–314
RFID technology and, 280
Return on total capital (ROTC), 385, 386–387
Returns management, 118, 270–271. *See also*
Reverse logistics
Reverse auctions, 107
Reverse loading trailers, 19
Reverse logistics, 204. *See also* Returns
management
best practices and, 214
design for, 97–98
Reverse supply chain strategy, 147–148
Rewards, best-practice behavior, 120
RFID technology, 54–55, 280
leveraging of, 122
mobile (wireless) SCM and, 295
RFP process
best and final offer, 106
ISO certification and, 86
as manual process, 77
preparation for, 105–107
standardization and, 121
RFQ process
ISO certification and, 86
as manual process, 77
preparation for, 105–107
standardization and, 121
Risk management
as Enabler 5, 17–18
S&OP workflow and, 188
supply risks, 218
Risk pooling, 165
RMI. *See* Remote method invocation

ROI. *See* Return on investment
Root causes of problems
    identification of, 87
    low forecast accuracy, 33
    root cause analysis, 282, 317
    two categories of, 356
ROP. *See* Reorder point
ROTC. *See* Return on total capital
Royal Bank of Scotland (RBS), 237
Rubbermaid, 97
"Rule-based Forecasting," 164

S
S&OP (sales and operations planning), 22
    definition of, 32
    goals of, 154
    POM and, 127
    root cause of low forecast accuracy, 33
    as SCM process, 32–34
    selling management, 256–257
    strategic sourcing and, 124
S&OP planning-enabled software applications,
    292–294
    Demand Planning, 293–294
    inventory planning, 294
    S&OP planning, 292–293
    Supply Chain Planning (SCP) suite, 293
    supply planning, 294
S&OP planning process, 153–168
    best practices and, 163–168
    demand planning and, 156–168
    evolution of S&OP, 155–156
    in fashion retail industry, 220
    supply chain pyramid for, 154
S&OP workflow, 185–215
    best practices and, 187–190
    demand fulfillment and, 190–191
    five steps in, 185–186
    key players in, 186, 187
    order promising, 191–194
    pyramid for, 185, 191
SaaS SRM applications, 283–284
Safety stock, 91–92. *See also* Inventory
    as buffer, 169
    inventory policies and, 173–174
    "rule of thumb" logic for, 174
    S&OP planning and, 218
    static/dynamic, 112

Sales and operations planning. *See* S&OP
Sales mix, 257–263
    channel and, 262–263
    price, 260–261
    product bundling, 258–260
    product configuration, 258
    promotion and, 261–262
Sales order/purchase order, 267
SAP, 52
Saturn, 146
SBU. *See* Strategic business unit
SCC. *See* Supply Chain Council
Scenario management, 153
    scenario analysis, 184
Schedule-driven replenishment, 110–111
SCIV. *See* Supply Chain Inventory Visibility
SCM. *See* Supply chain management
SCM challenges, 135–137
    push vs. pull, 135–136
    supply demand balance, 136–137
    variability, complexity and, 136
SCM concepts, 138
SCM-enabled software applications, 292–296
    demand fulfillment-enabled, 294–296
    S&OP-enabled, 292–294
    supply chain analytics, 296
    supply chain network design-enabled, 292
SCM evolution, 132–139
    enablers and, 137–139
    goal of SCM and, 134–135
    SCM challenges and, 135–137
SCM processes, 31–36
    demand fulfillment and, 34–36
    strategic management, 31–32
SCM pyramids
    for demand planning, 156
    for inventory planning, 168
    for logistics planning/execution, 203
    for master planning, 179
    for order promising, 191
    for production scheduling/execution, 196
    for S&OP, 154, 185
    for strategic management, 139
    for supply chain network design, 149
    for supply chain strategy, 140
SCM superprocess, 131–227, 216–219
    inventory planning, 168–178
    master planning and, 178–185

S&OP and, 153–168
S&OP workflow, 185–215
SCM evolution, 132–139
strategic management and, 139–153
workflow, fashion retail industry, 219–227
SCM superprocess workflow, 216–219
S&OP planning, 216, 218
strategic management, 217, 218
SCM superprocess workflow, fashion retail industry, 219–217
SCOR. *See* Supply chain operations reference model
Security/privacy, 232
Segmentation
customer segmentation, 237
demographic segmentation, 249
market segmentation, 248–249
of market strategy, 256
procurement and, 123
of product portfolio, 144, 175
of S&OP workflows, 194–195
sourcing and, 89–91
Selling management, 256–257
as CRM process, 37
CRM superprocess workflow and, 273
pyramid for, 257
Selling management-enabled software applications, 297–298
Campaign Management, 297–298
Configuration and Pricing, 298
Direct-Point-of-Sale (POS), 298
Multitier Supply Chain Collaboration, 298
Senior management. *See* Top management support
Sensitivity analysis, 153
Sequence-driven replenishment, 114
SER. *See* Supplier Evaluation Report
Service contract management, 269
Service management, 268–271
challenges of, 268
components of, 268
CRM superprocess workflow and, 274
pyramid for, 268
returns management, 270–271
service contract management, 269
service planning/scheduling, 269–270
Service-oriented architecture (SOA), 122
Enabler 3 and, 16

ERP and, 53
new LAVC technology infrastructure, 278–279
Service parts management, 38
Service parts planning (SPP) applications, 299
Service planning/scheduling, 269–270
Settlement process, 119
Setup time reductions, demand fulfillment and, 34–35
7-Eleven, 79–80, 133
Sherwin Williams, 147
Shewhart, Walter, 48
Shipping docks, 214
Side-loading trucks, 19, 213
Silos, 100
Simplification. *See also* Enabler 2
as best practice, 99
Single Minutes Exchange of Dies (SMED), 198
Single-piece flow, 142
Six Sigma methodology, 50, 425
black belts in, 50
LAVC concept and, 45
TQM and, 50
SKUs (stock keeping units)
proliferation of, 158, 162
variability, complexity and, 136
Slone, Reuben, 426
SMART objectives, 357
SMED. *See* Single Minutes Exchange of Dies
SND. *See* Strategic Network Design applications
SOA. *See* Service-oriented architecture
Soft/hard constraints, 184–185
Software application. *See also* Applications and trends
selection of provider of, 379–380
transformation program and, 318
Software provider, selection of, 310–312
Sony, 249
Playstation consoles, 77, 254
Sourcing. *See also* Dual-sourcing strategies; Outsourcing; Strategic sourcing
to low-cost countries, 66
Sourcing segmentation, best practices and, 89–91
Southwest Airlines, 91
Space planning, assortment management and, 224
Specialized carrier services, 207

Spending analysis software applications, 286
Sponsor, project team and, 342–343
SPP. *See* Service parts planning applications
Sprint, 399–405
    carrier agreements and, 212
    challenges at, 402, 404
    competitive environment, 402
    customer demands, 401
    i2 role in initiative, 402–403
    improvements, 403
    marketing and, 400
    organizational structure, 403
    product mix, 401
    product volume, 401
    retail presence, 404
    scope of products, 400
    supply chain organizations, 400
    warehouse logistics network, 403
SRM. *See* Supplier relationship management
SRM challenges, 74–77
    disparate systems, 76
    lack of complete/consistent data, 75–76
    lack of trust/conflict resolution, 77
    manual processes, 77
    nonstandard supplier performance
        evaluation, 76–77
    variability and complexity, 75
    vertical to lateral integration, 74–75
SRM-enabled software applications, 282–291
    capabilities and, 282
    delivery methods and, 283
    SaaS SRM applications, 283–284
SRM processes, 24–31
    business processes distribution for, 24
    procurement and, 28–31
    product design, 27–28
    strategic sourcing, 25–27
SRM pyramids, 72
    for contract management, 106
    for POM, 115
    for procurement, 103
    for product design, 94
    for strategic sourcing, 79
    for supply collaboration, 109
SRM superprocess, 71–127
    best practices, 84–93, 99–103, 118–124
    North-South/East-West collaboration,
        73–74

procurement and, 103–124
product design and, 93–103
SCM, CRM interaction in, 72
SRM challenges, 74–88
strategic sourcing and, 78–93
workflow for, 124–127
(s,S) replenishment policy, 112
Stable demand/supply, 145–146
Standardization
    best practices and, 121
    continuous improvement and, 12
    product standardization, 99–100
Starbucks, 247
Static safety stock, 112
Stocking areas, 213
Stock out alert, 112
Strategic business unit (SBU), 244–246
Strategic management
    as SCM process, 31–32, 138–153
    supply chain network design, 148–153
    supply chain pyramid for, 139
    supply chain strategy, 140–148
Strategic Network Design (SND) applications,
    292
Strategic sourcing
    contract monitoring/compliance and,
        86–87
    definition of, 25
    pyramid for, 79
    software applications for, 284–285
    as SRM challenge, 78–93
    as SRM process, 25–27, 124–127
    what to outsource, 78–80
Strategic sourcing-enabled software
        applications, 284–286
    spending analysis, 286
    strategic sourcing suites, 284–285
    supplier performance management,
        285–286
Strategy & management structure, 39–44
    balanced scorecard, 44
    building blocks/evolution of LAVC
        principles/enablers, 41
    business system, 42
    capability maturity model, 42–43
    Porter's Value Chain, 42
    supply chain operations reference (SCOR)
        model, 43–44

Strategy innovation, Enabler 7, 20–21
Subassembly (semifinished state), 99
Success, reasons for, 190
Success stories/lessons learned, 385–432
  ADTRAN, 398–399
  BLUESALON, 388–393, 394
  Cementos Argos, 412–415
  Continental Tire, 409–412
  Cooper Tire, 393, 395–397
  CRM-driven success stories, 417–428
  Dell, 426–428
  Emerson, 385–387
  Fairchild Semiconductor, 405–407
  GE (General Electric), 387–388
  Green Value Chain, 415–416
  Lenovo, 420–424
  Manara Academy Charter School, 428–432
  SCM-driven success stories, 388–416
  service industry success story, 428–432
  Sprint, 399–405
  SRM-driven success stories, 385–388
  Tata Steel, 417–420
  Timken Steel Group, 407–408
  Whirlpool, 424–426
"Supermarkets," 35, 200
Supplier base rationalization
  best practices and, 84–86
  financial impact, 85
Supplier/buyer, middle points of intersection, 88
Supplier certification, best practices and 86
Supplier Directories, Online, 288–289
Supplier Evaluation Report (SER), 81
Supplier performance data, procurement and, 104
Supplier performance evaluation, nonstandard process for, 76–77
Supplier performance management software applications, 285–286
Supplier performance measurement/rewarding suppliers, best practices and, 86–87
Supplier Portals, 289
Supplier relationship management (SRM)
  business processes, 23–24
  definition of, 71
  e-Business applications and, 54
  purchase order in, 267
  as SRM challenge, 82–84
  as value chain superprocess, 21–23

Supplier selection. *See also* Executive supplier council
  as SRM challenge, 80–81
"Supplier switching" costs, 71
Supply chain
  simplified, 131, 132
  value chain and, 4
Supply Chain Analytics, 296
Supply Chain Council (SCC), 43, 309, 353
Supply Chain Inventory Visibility (SCIV), 294–295
Supply chain management (SCM). *See also* End-to-end SCM
  APS logic and, 53–54
  business process distribution for, 31
  business processes, 23–24
  as IT building block, 53–55
  Supply Chain Council and, 43
  as value chain superprocess, 21–23
Supply chain network design, 148–153
  pyramid for, 149
Supply chain network design challenges, 150
Supply chain operations reference (SCOR) model, 43–44
  benchmarking and, 44, 309
  at Fairchild Semiconductor, 406
  LAVC metrics mapped to, 358, 359–361
  performance measurement and, 352–353
Supply chain strategy, 140–148
  forecast- or demand-driven, 140–141
  mass production/customization, 141–143
  pyramid for, 140
Supply collaboration, 109–114. *See also* Collaboration
  for long-term horizon, 109
  for medium-term horizon, 110
  pyramid for, 109
  for short-term horizon, 110–114
  as SRM superprocess, 127
Supply risks, 218
Supply uncertainty management strategies, 145–146
Supply variability, 141
  clean data on, 173–174
SWOT (strengths, weaknesses, opportunities, threats), 253
Syndicate service research firm, 255

T

Takt, level scheduling and, demand fulfillment
    and, 35
Targeted marketing, 244
Target markets, 249
Tata Steel, success story/lessons learned,
    417–420
    business process reengineering, 418
    customer satisfaction and, 193, 417–420
    forecasting capability, 419
    prognosis, 419
Taylor, Frederick, 141
Teamwork. *See also* Transformation team
        development
    multidisciplinary teams, 98
    team building, 329
Technology. *See also* Information technology;
        Information technology building block;
        Internet
    applications, 27, 283
    best practices and, 92–93, 101–102
    customization of, 318
    demand fulfillment and, 35–36
    as Enabler 3, 16
    just-in-time replenishment and, 113
    leveraging of, 121–123
    product design process and, 94–95
    visual signals and, 202–203
Telemarketing program, 241, 251
Terminology, transportation/warehousing,
    208–209
Texas Instruments (TI), 74, 253
Theory of constraints (TOC)
    for complex and job shop environments, 47
    LAVC concept and, 45
Third Party Logistics (3PL)
    emergence of, 204
    providers of, 4, 375
3PL. *See* Third Party Logistics
Tier 1/Tier 2 suppliers, 20
Time postponement, 34
Time Warner Inc., 245, 246, 247, 252, 253
Timken Steel Group, 190, 407–408
    balancing act at, 408
    pyramid view at, 408
TMS. *See* Transportation Management System
        software
TOC, 45
Top-down forecast, 165

Top management support
    best practices and, 93, 103
    change management and, 363
    continuous improvement and, 103
    as CRM challenge, 233–234
    jury of executive opinion, 158
    team building and, 323
Total cost visibility, 102–103
    total cost for contracts, 123–124
Total landed cost, supplier selection
    best practices and, 91–92
Total quality management (TQM), 48
    Six Sigma methodology and, 50
Toyota, 74, 78–79, 88–89, 108, 203
    collaboration and, 101
    economies of scale and, 142
    "heijunka" and, 201
    market targeting and, 249–250
    number of suppliers for, 85
    root cause of problems and, 87
Toyota Production System (TPS), 8, 74,
    203
Toys-R-Us, 203–204
TPS. *See* Toyota Production System
TQM. *See* Total quality management
Tracking/controlling, 348–350
    program/project controlling, 349–350
    program/project tracking, 348 349
Trade agreements, 75
Tradeoffs
    contracts and, 123–124
    three conflicting objectives, 91
Traditional sourcing, 81
Training. *See* Education/culture support
Transactional relationship, 83
Transaction systems, disparate systems, 76
Transformation program cycle, 303–320
    alignment with corporate goals, 304,
        308
    benchmarking and, 309
    checklist for, 305–307
    implementation framework, 304
    PMS updates, 319–320
    process analysis, 309–310
    program/project plan development,
        314–319
    ROI, calculation of, 312–314
    software providers and, 310–312
    vision, objectives and strategies, 308–309

Transformation team development, 322–328
  incentive/motivation program, 325, 328
  roles/resources (staffing plan), 324–325,
    326–327
  team structure/skills, 324
Transportation (logistics) carriers
  air, 206
  best practices and, 209–210
  intermodal, 207
  modes of, 204–207
  pipeline, 207
  rail, 206
  terms commonly used, 208–209
  three major types of, 30
  truck, 206
  water, 204, 206
Transportation management
  demand fulfillment and, 36
  transshipment, minimization of, 182
Transportation Management System (TMS)
  software, 290–291
Transportation trade-offs, 30–31
Transshipment, 182
Trans-shipment cross-docking, 209
Travel retailers, online, 248
Trends. *See* Applications and trends
Truck transportation, 206. *See also* Full
  truckload; Less than truckloads
  truckload, defined, 208
Trust
  conflict resolution and, 77
  reliability and, 11
"Turning point" in business, 163

U
UAT. *See* User acceptance testing
Uniform loading, demand fulfillment and,
  35
Unloading trailers, 19
  last in, first out, 213
Upstream companies, 66
  supply chain visibility and, 184
Upstream processes, "pacemaker" and, 202
U.S.-based supplier, 151
User acceptance testing (UAT), 381

V
Value chain, 4, 5. *See also* Design for value
  chain

Value chain superprocesses, 21–23
Value recovery, 147–148
Value stream, defined, 5
Variability
  analysis of, 175
  process variability reduction, 198
  as SCM challenge, 136, 141
  as SRM challenge, 75
Vehicle scheduling, freight consolidation and,
  211
Vendor-managed inventory replenishment,
  111–113, 398–399
Vertical integration, pioneer of, 78–80
Viral marketing, 240, 241
Visibility. *See also* Enabler 1
  dynamic routing and, 212–213
  end-to-end, 397
  lack of, 96, 104, 193–194
  pricing and, 261
  procurement and, 104
  of supply chain, 184
  total cost visibility, 102–103
  vendor-managed inventory and, 398–399
  visual signals, 202–203
Vision, development of, 308–309
VOC. *See* Voice of the customer
Voice of the customer (VOC), 256

W
Wal-Mart, 97, 112, 157, 167, 248, 428
Warehouse management, demand fulfillment
  and, 36
Warehouse management system (WMS),
  294
Warehousing, 207–208
  terms commonly used, 208–209
Waste elimination. *See also* Principle 3
  muri/mura/muda and, 200
Water transportation, 204, 206
Wave picking, 214
Welch, Jack, 48, 50
What-if simulation, 184
Whirlpool, success story/lessons learned,
  424–426
  LAVC principles/enablers and, 426
  SKUs, segmentation and, 425
Win-win environment. *See also* Principle 2
WMS. *See* Warehouse management system
Word of mouth, 240, 241

Workflow
    CRM superprocess workflow, 272
    POM workflow, 116
    SCM superprocess, 218
    SCM superprocess fashion retail, 221
    SRM superprocess, 124–127
Workflow, SRM superprocess, 124–127

X
Xerox, 238

Y
Yamaki, Masaharu, 201
Yazaki Corporation, 87

Z
Zara, 91, 144–145, 202